Sachi's MONSTROUS Appetite

6

Chomoran

Story

Previously, Makie, Izumi, and Tatemochi visited Izumo along with Sachi to find her roots. Despite getting a rough welcome from a local watari, they managed to achieve the objective of their trip without much incident and left on good terms with the watari of Izumo. In the course of their journey, Makie and Sachi also came to understand each other more and deepened their affection for each other, prompting them to re-declare their feelings for each other and officially move forward as lovers. But after returning to Tokyo, their brief sense of calm is quickly disrupted by some surprising news, "Makie's mother is alive."

Chapter 26: One in a Million

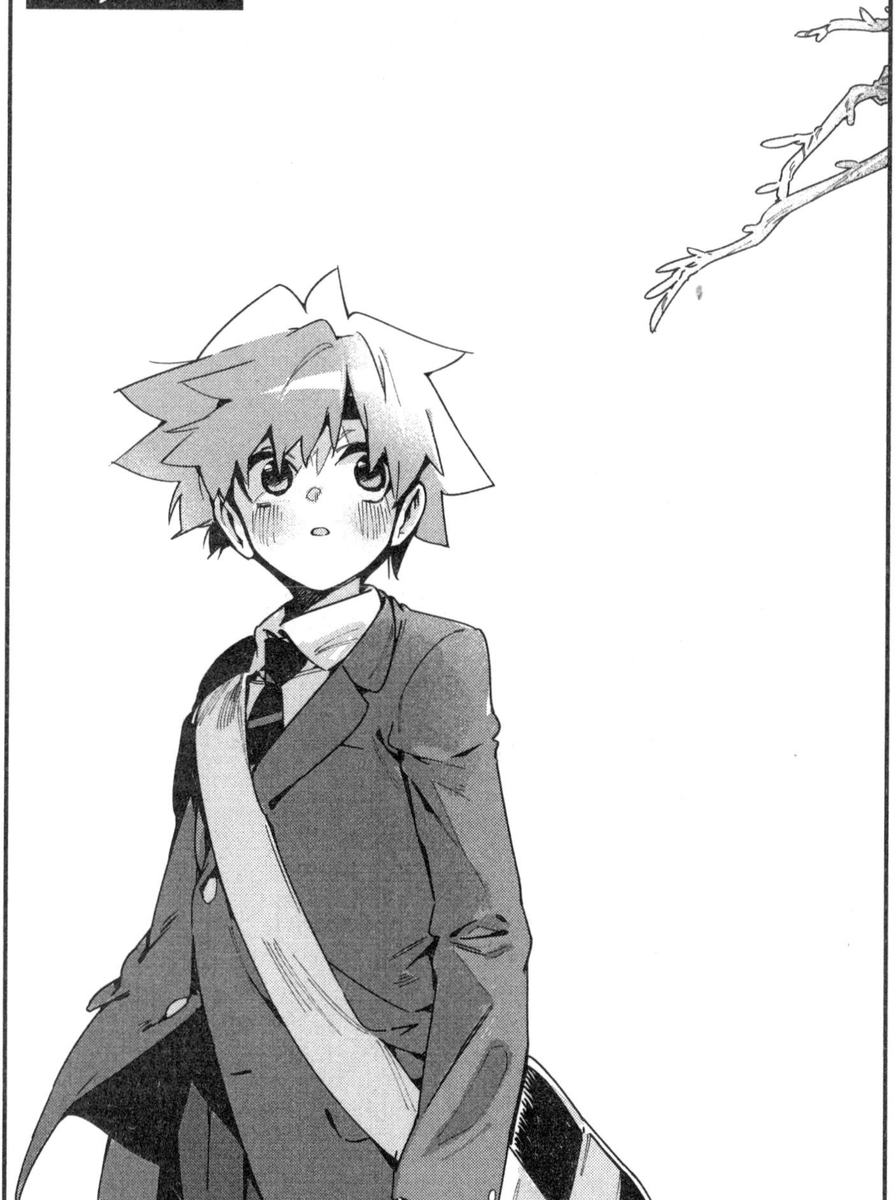

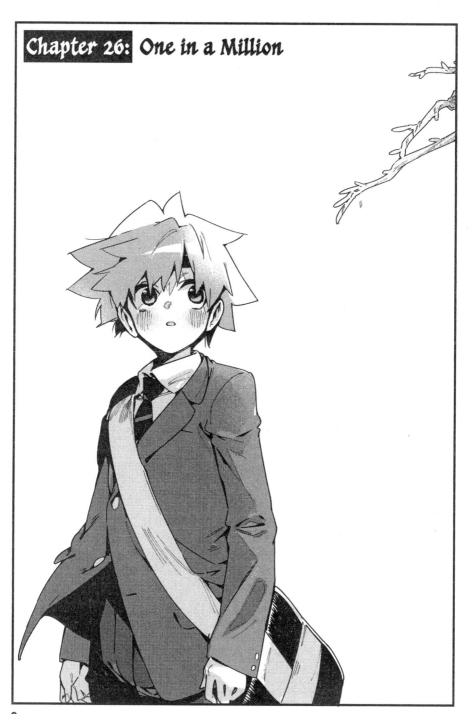

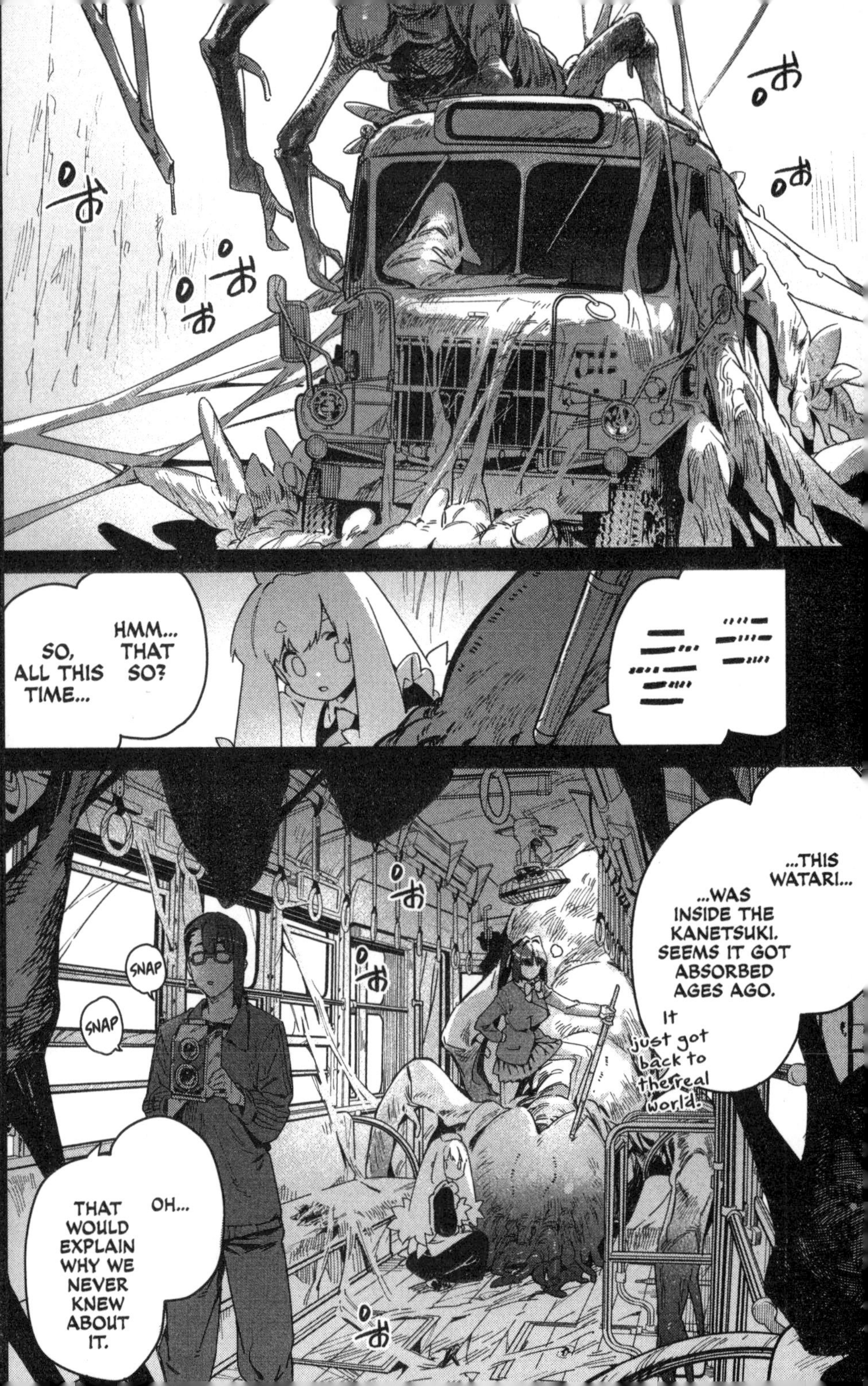
oお
oお
oお
oお
oお
HMM... THAT SO? SO, ALL THIS TIME...
...THIS WATARI... ...WAS INSIDE THE KANETSUKI. SEEMS IT GOT ABSORBED AGES AGO.
It just got back to the real world.
oお
oお
SNAP
SNAP
OH... THAT WOULD EXPLAIN WHY WE NEVER KNEW ABOUT IT.
oお

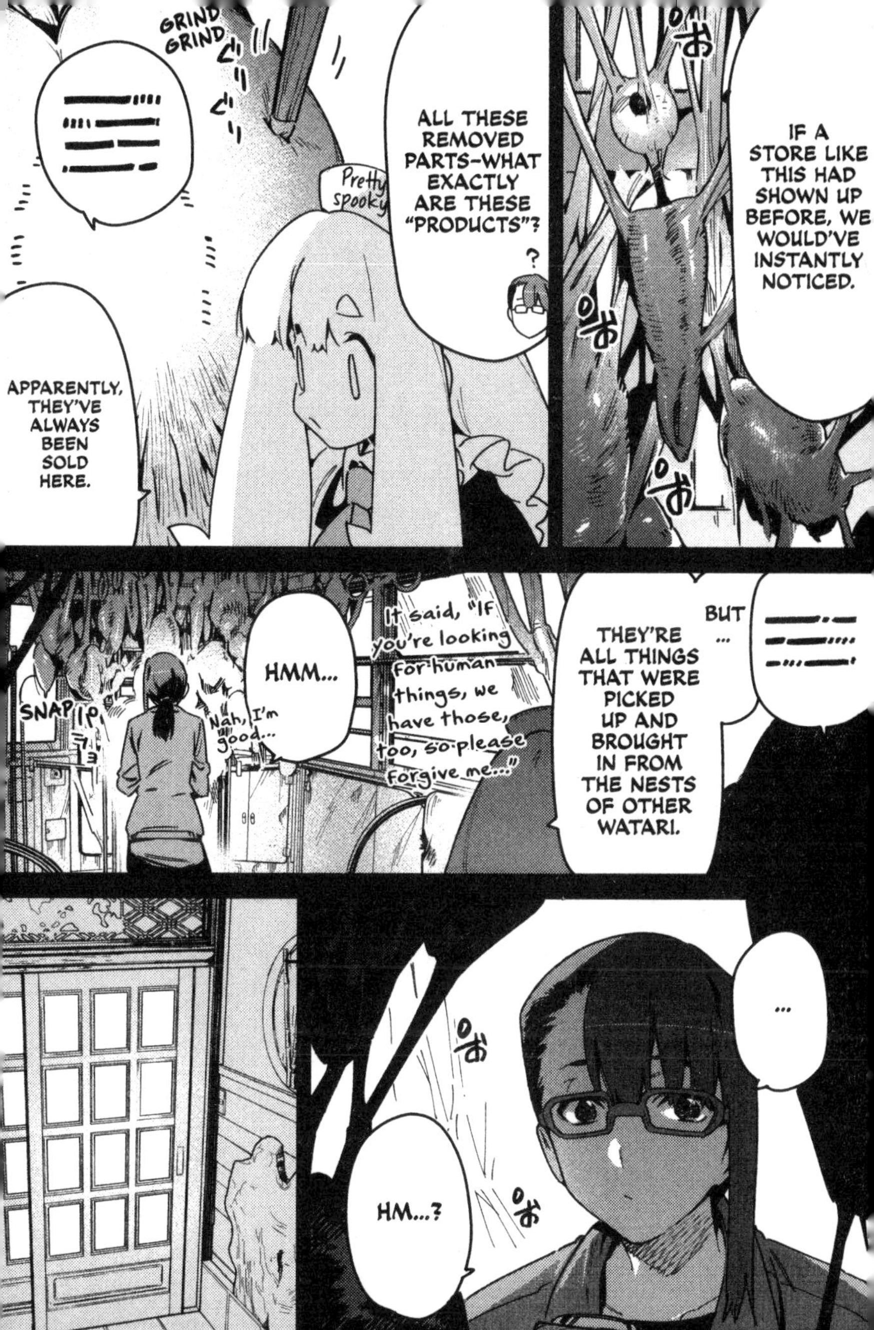

IF A STORE LIKE THIS HAD SHOWN UP BEFORE, WE WOULD'VE INSTANTLY NOTICED.
ALL THESE REMOVED PARTS—WHAT EXACTLY ARE THESE "PRODUCTS"?
Pretty spooky
?
GRIND GRIND
APPARENTLY, THEY'VE ALWAYS BEEN SOLD HERE.
BUT ...
THEY'RE ALL THINGS THAT WERE PICKED UP AND BROUGHT IN FROM THE NESTS OF OTHER WATARI.
HMM...
It said, "If you're looking for human things, we have those, too, so please forgive me..."
Nah, I'm good...
SNAP
...
HM...?

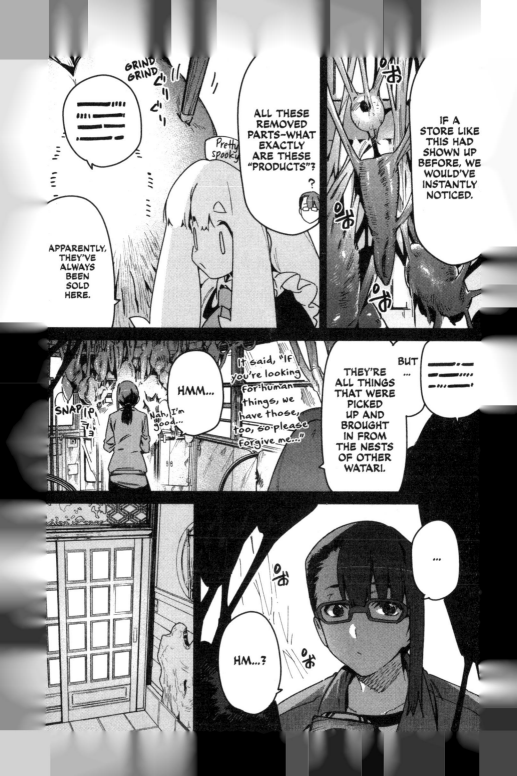

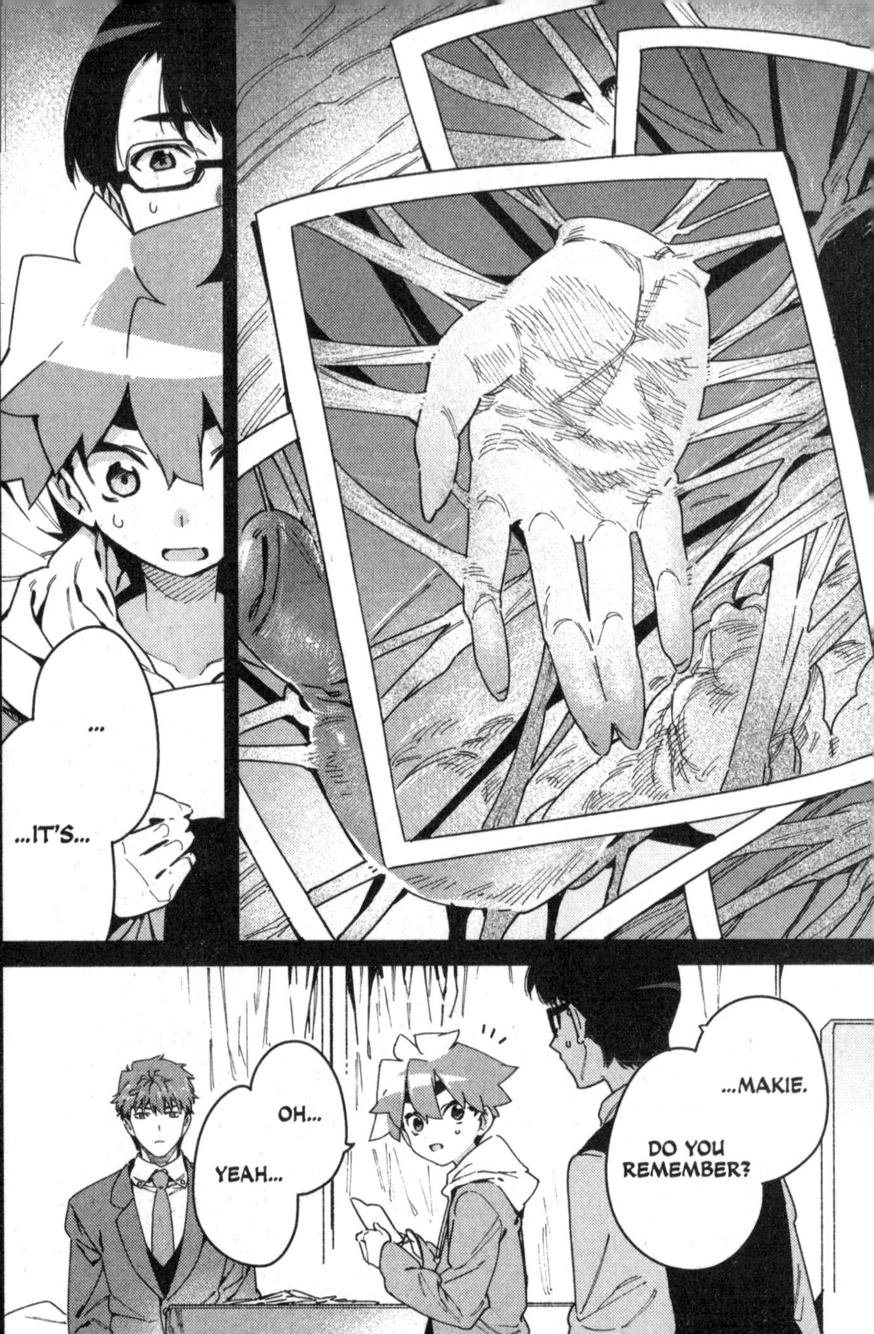
...
...IT'S...
...MAKIE.
DO YOU REMEMBER?
OH...
YEAH...

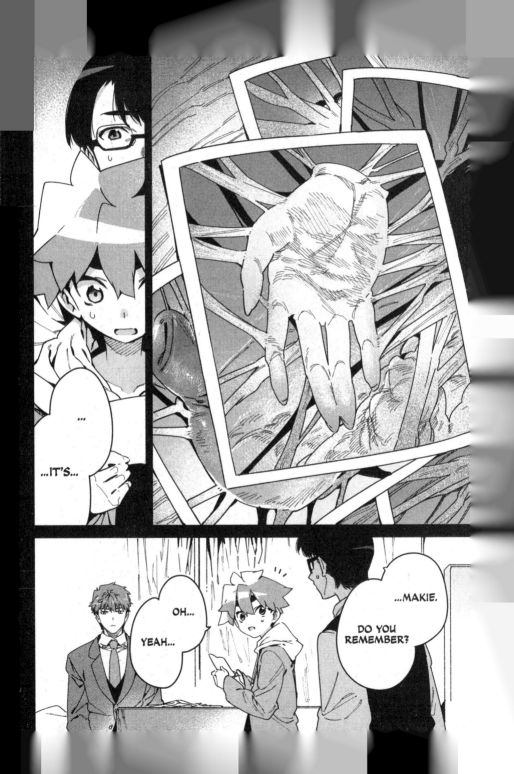

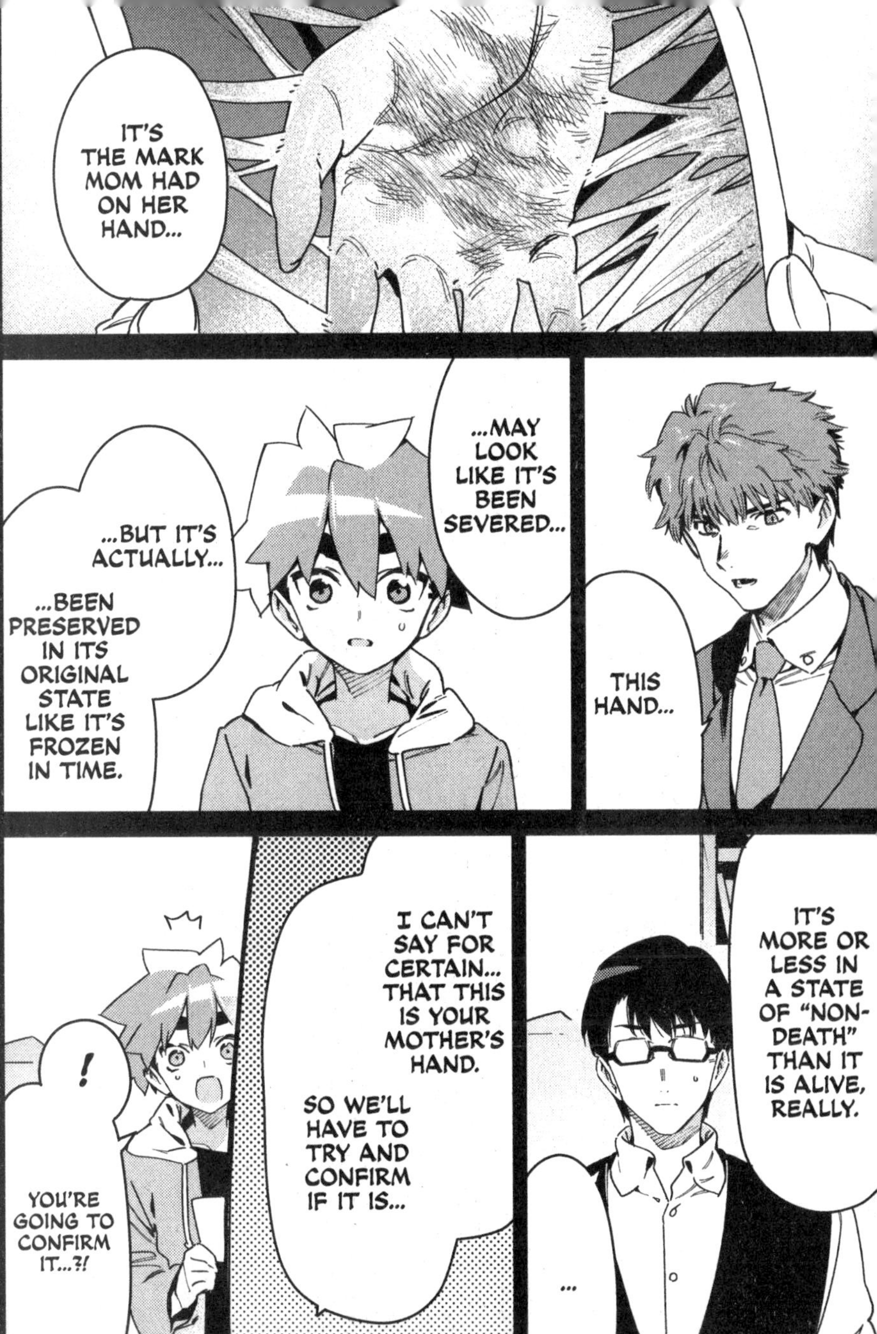
IT'S THE MARK MOM HAD ON HER HAND...
THIS HAND...
...MAY LOOK LIKE IT'S BEEN SEVERED...
...BUT IT'S ACTUALLY...
...BEEN PRESERVED IN ITS ORIGINAL STATE LIKE IT'S FROZEN IN TIME.
IT'S MORE OR LESS IN A STATE OF "NON-DEATH" THAN IT IS ALIVE, REALLY.
...
I CAN'T SAY FOR CERTAIN... THAT THIS IS YOUR MOTHER'S HAND.
SO WE'LL HAVE TO TRY AND CONFIRM IF IT IS...
!
YOU'RE GOING TO CONFIRM IT...?!

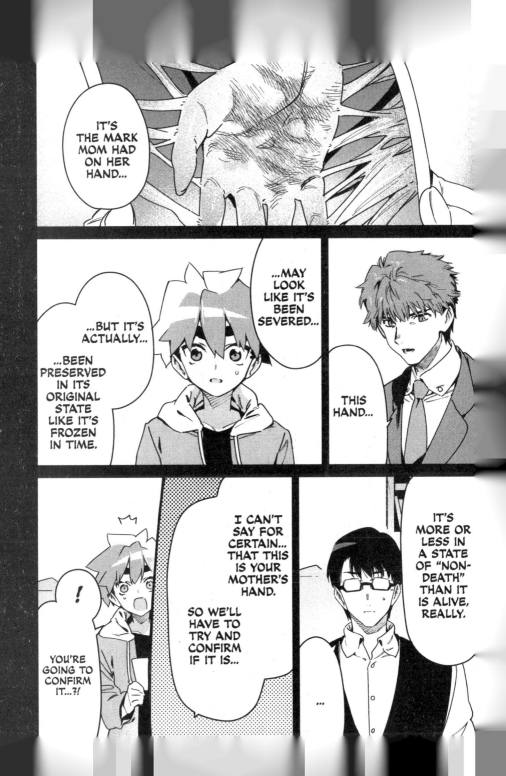

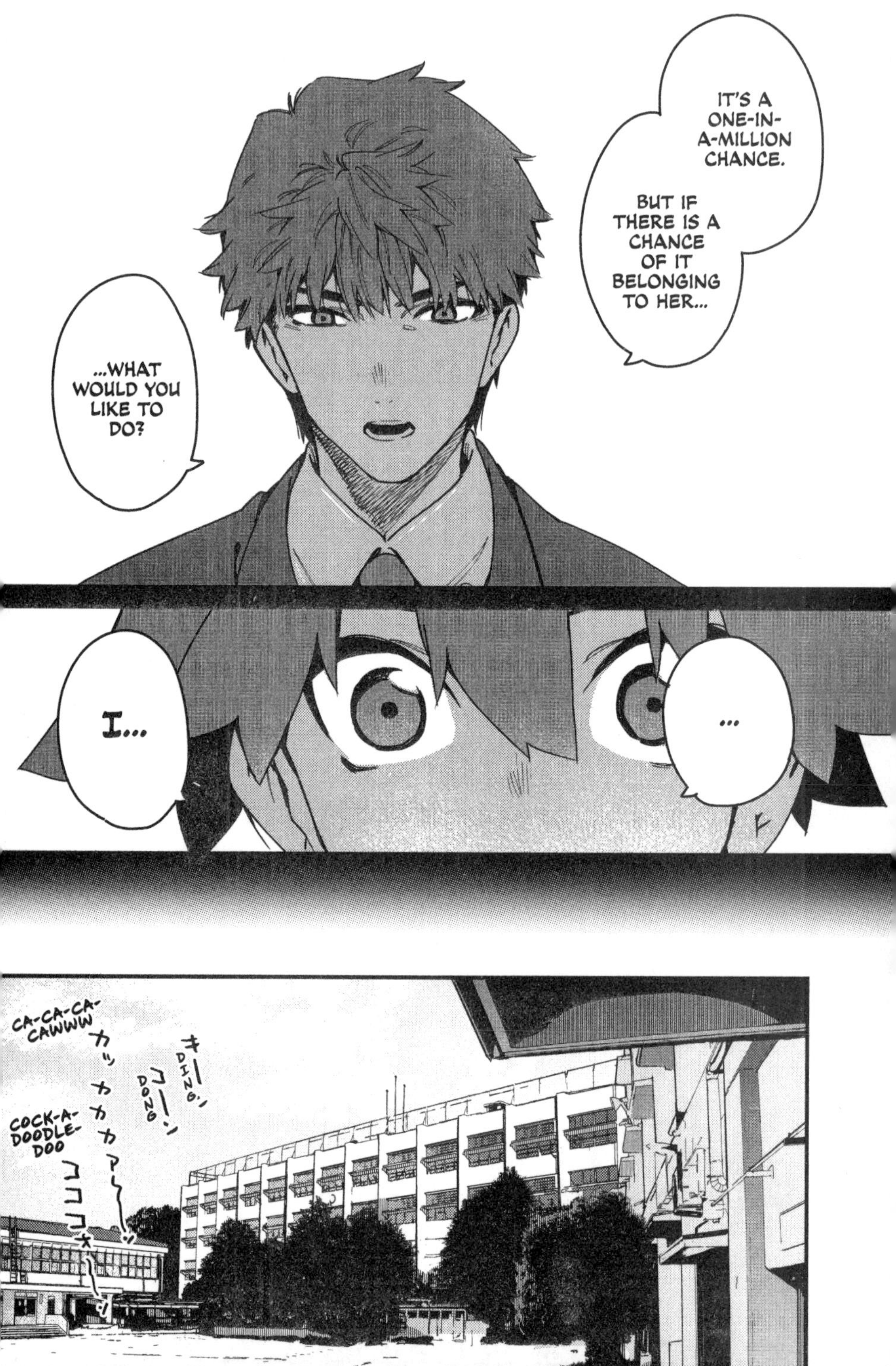
IT'S A ONE-IN-A-MILLION CHANCE.
BUT IF THERE IS A CHANCE OF IT BELONGING TO HER...
...WHAT WOULD YOU LIKE TO DO?
...
I...
DING, DONG
CA-CA-CA-CAWWW
COCK-A-DOODLE-DOO

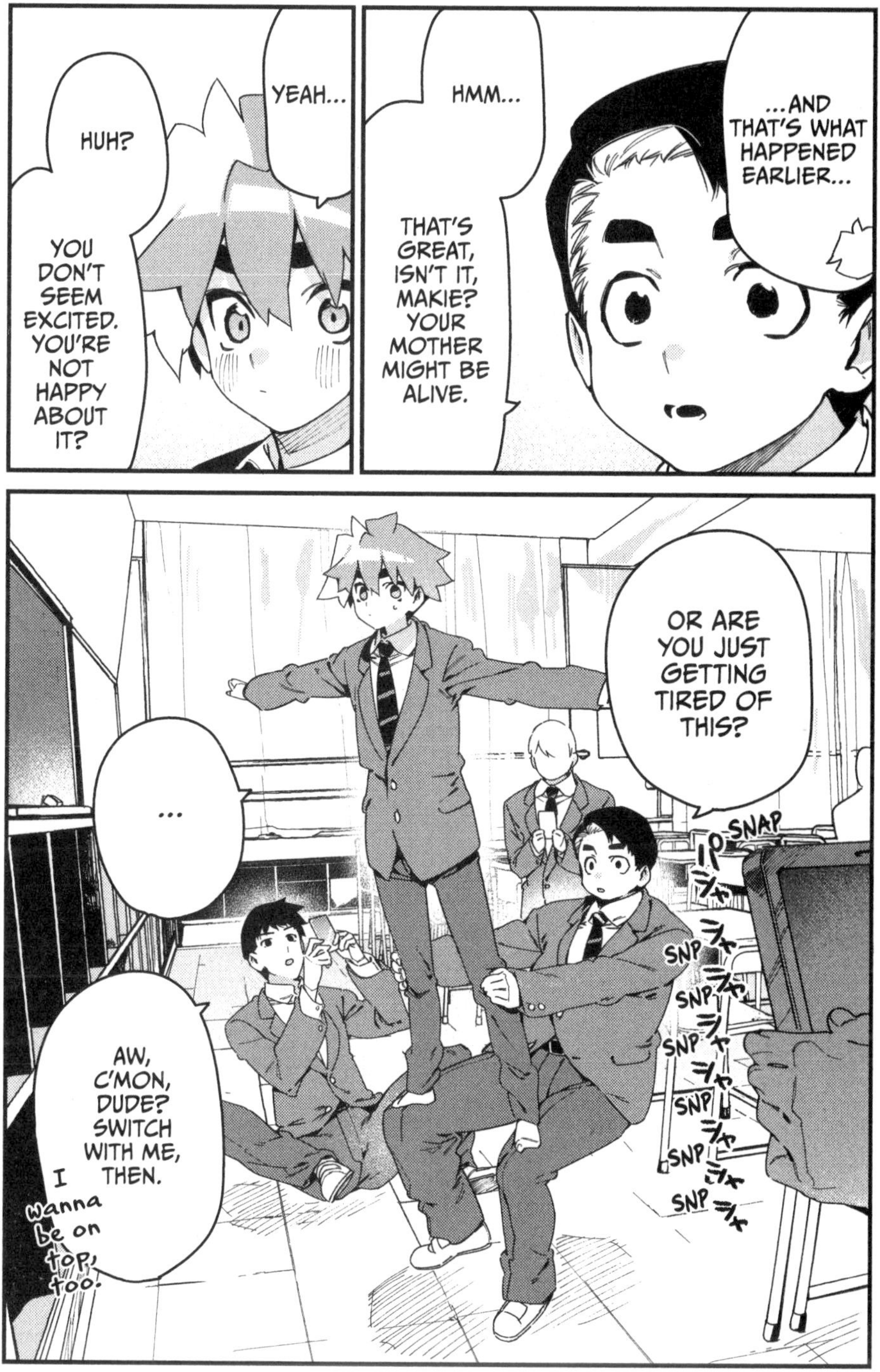
...AND THAT'S WHAT HAPPENED EARLIER...
HMM...
THAT'S GREAT, ISN'T IT, MAKIE? YOUR MOTHER MIGHT BE ALIVE.
YEAH...
HUH?
YOU DON'T SEEM EXCITED. YOU'RE NOT HAPPY ABOUT IT?
OR ARE YOU JUST GETTING TIRED OF THIS?
SNAP
SNP SNP SNP SNP SNP SNP
...
AW, C'MON, DUDE? SWITCH WITH ME, THEN.
I wanna be on top, too.

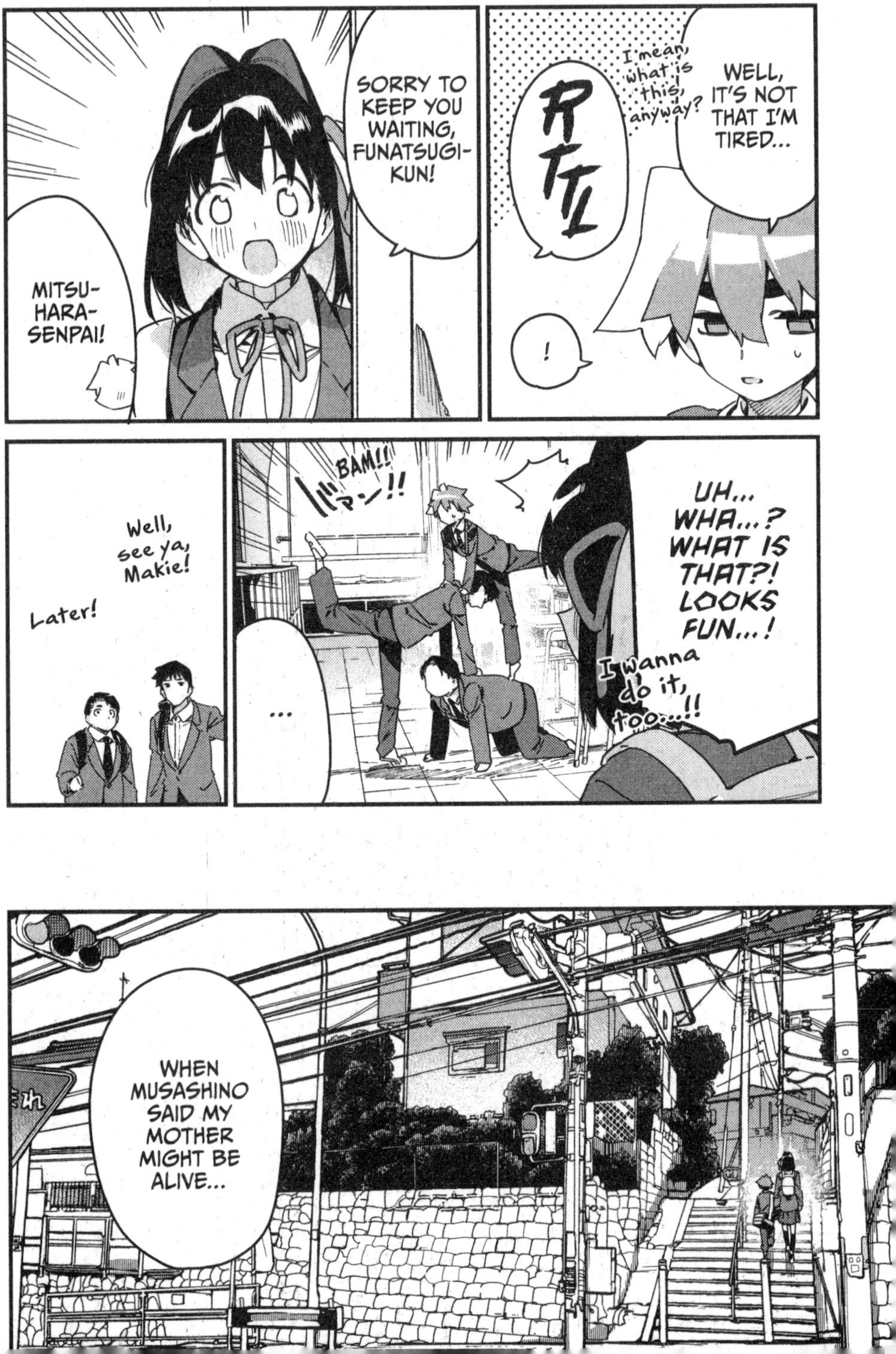
WELL, IT'S NOT THAT I'M TIRED...
I mean, what is this, anyway?
RTTL
!
SORRY TO KEEP YOU WAITING, FUNATSUGI-KUN!
MITSU-HARA-SENPAI!
UH... WHA...? WHAT IS THAT?! LOOKS FUN...!
I wanna do it, too...!!
BAM!!
...
Well, see ya, Makie!
Later!
WHEN MUSASHINO SAID MY MOTHER MIGHT BE ALIVE...

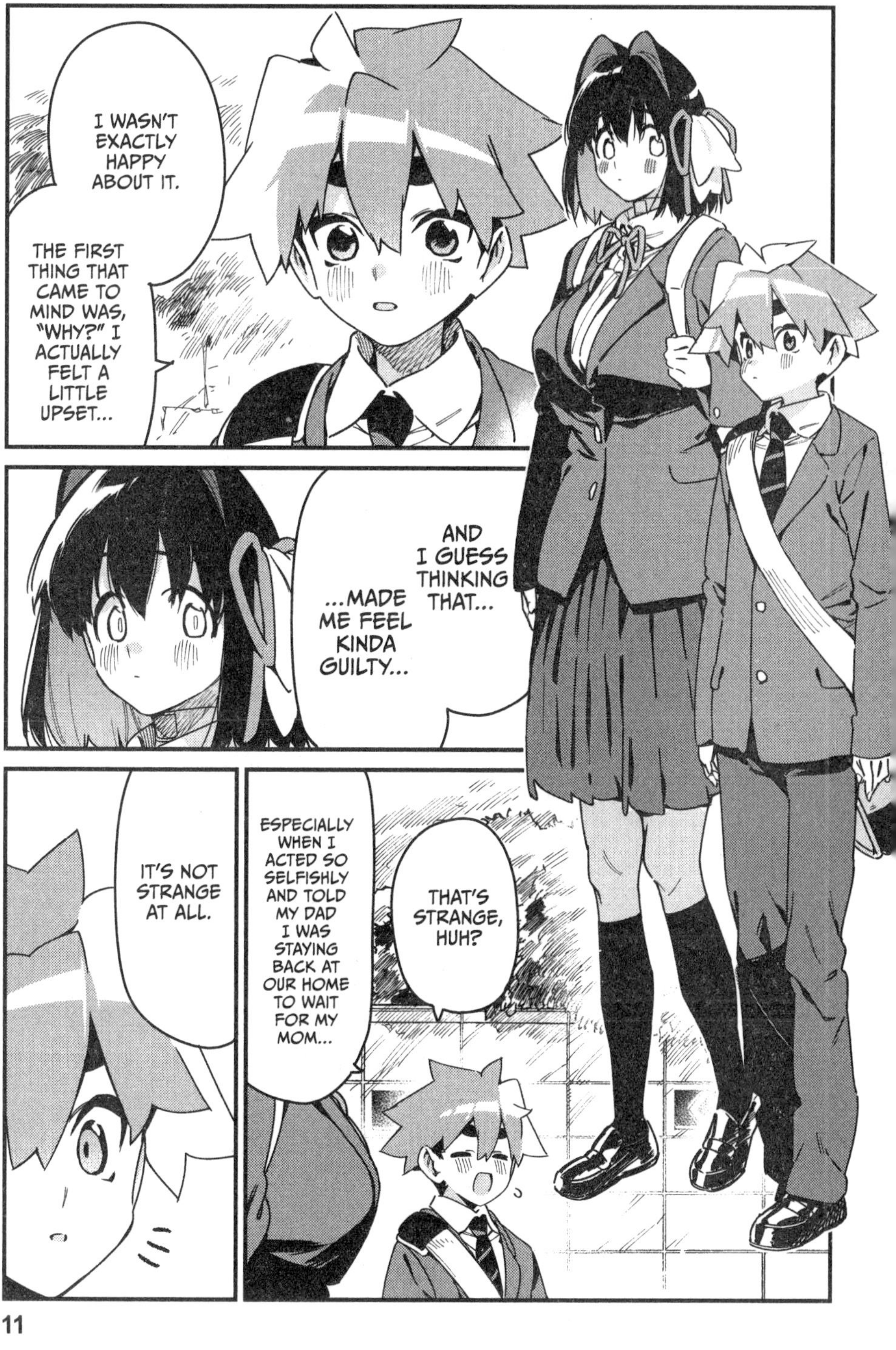
I WASN'T EXACTLY HAPPY ABOUT IT.
THE FIRST THING THAT CAME TO MIND WAS, "WHY?" I ACTUALLY FELT A LITTLE UPSET...
AND I GUESS THINKING THAT...
...MADE ME FEEL KINDA GUILTY...
ESPECIALLY WHEN I ACTED SO SELFISHLY AND TOLD MY DAD I WAS STAYING BACK AT OUR HOME TO WAIT FOR MY MOM...
THAT'S STRANGE, HUH?
IT'S NOT STRANGE AT ALL.

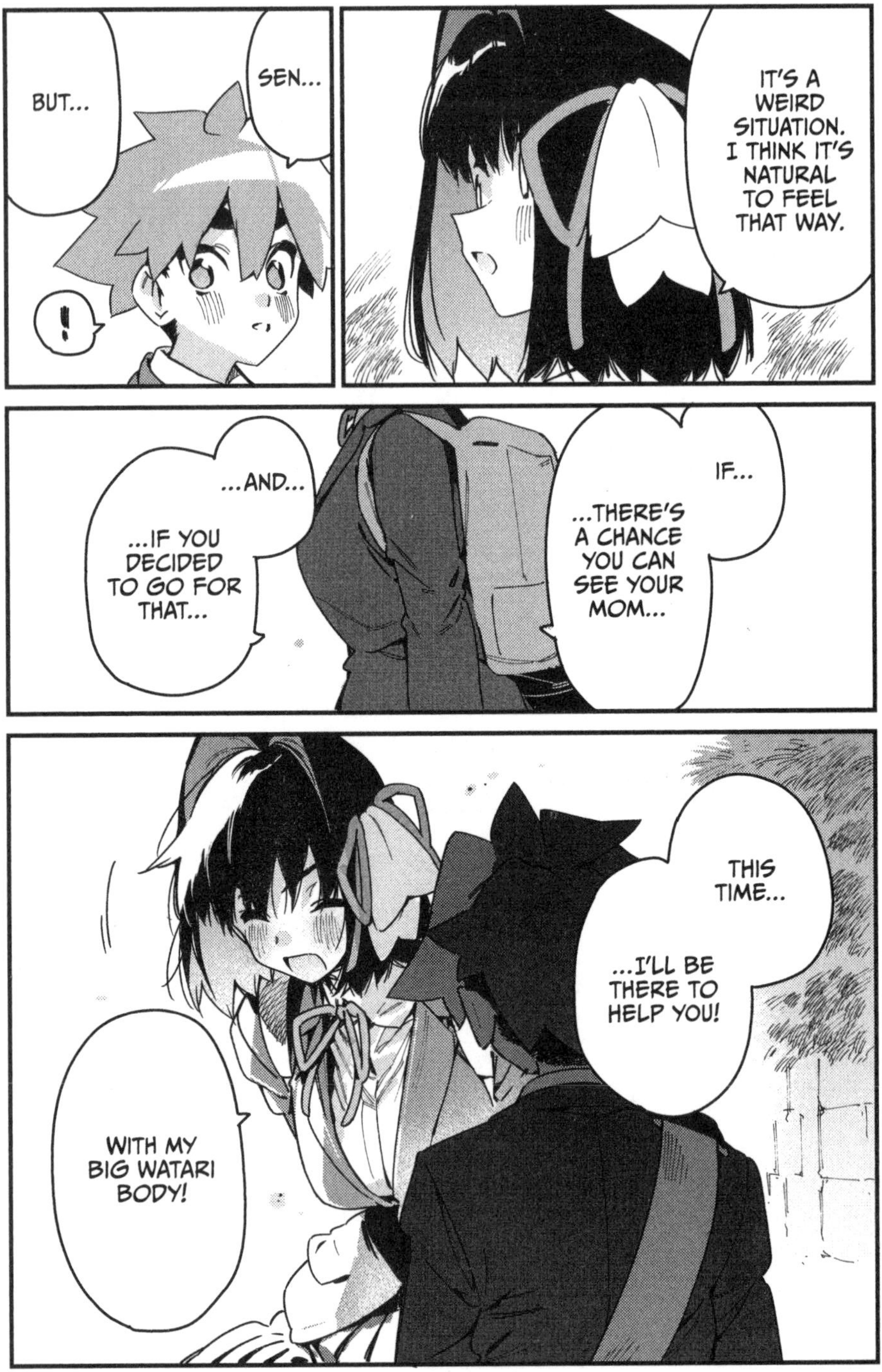
IT'S A WEIRD SITUATION. I THINK IT'S NATURAL TO FEEL THAT WAY.
SEN...
BUT...
!
IF...
...THERE'S A CHANCE YOU CAN SEE YOUR MOM...
...AND...
...IF YOU DECIDED TO GO FOR THAT...
THIS TIME...
...I'LL BE THERE TO HELP YOU!
WITH MY BIG WATARI BODY!

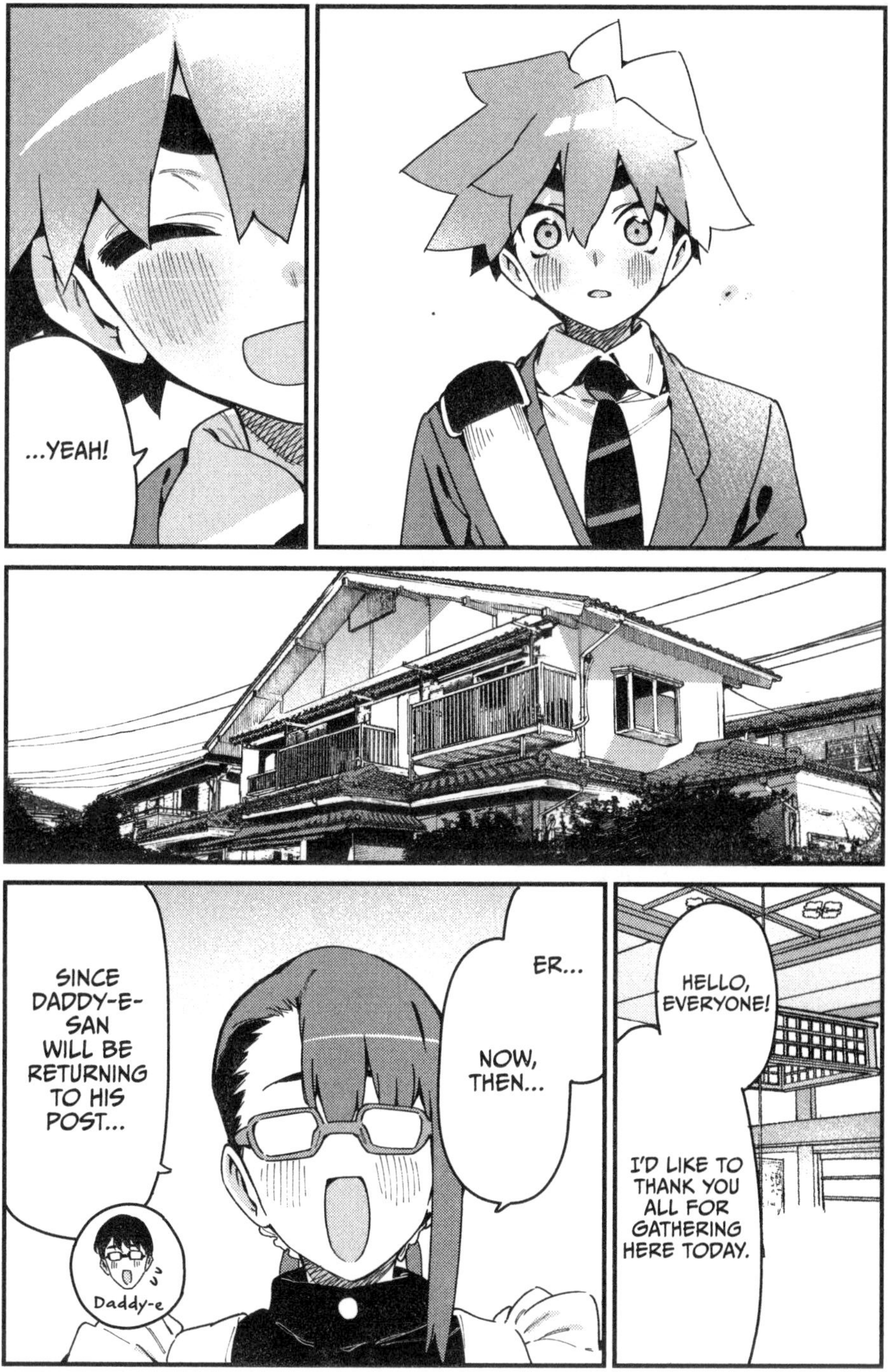
...YEAH!
HELLO, EVERYONE!
I'D LIKE TO THANK YOU ALL FOR GATHERING HERE TODAY.
ER...
NOW, THEN...
SINCE DADDY-E-SAN WILL BE RETURNING TO HIS POST...
Daddy-e

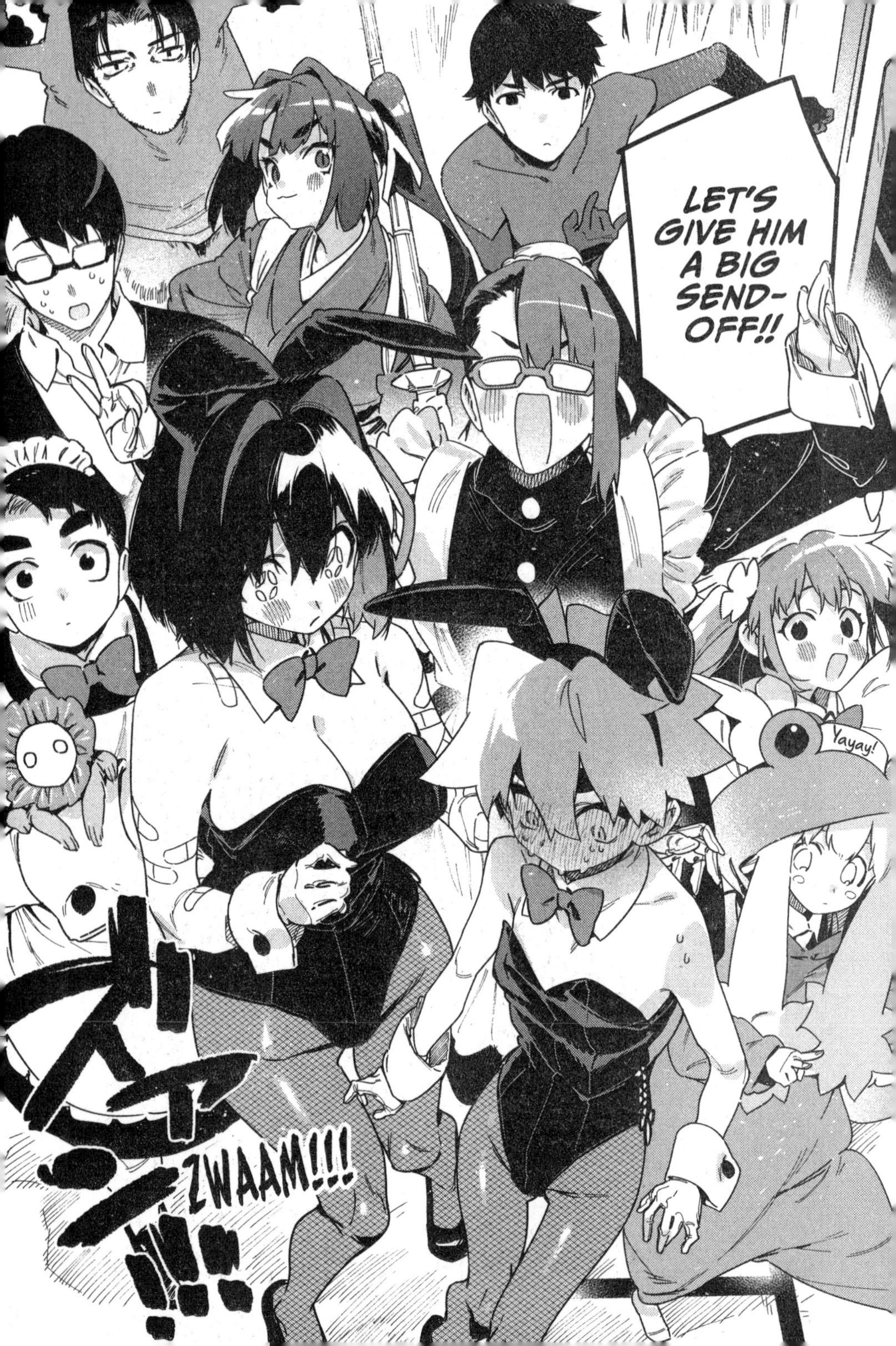
LET'S GIVE HIM A BIG SEND-OFF!!
Yayay!
ZWAAM!!!

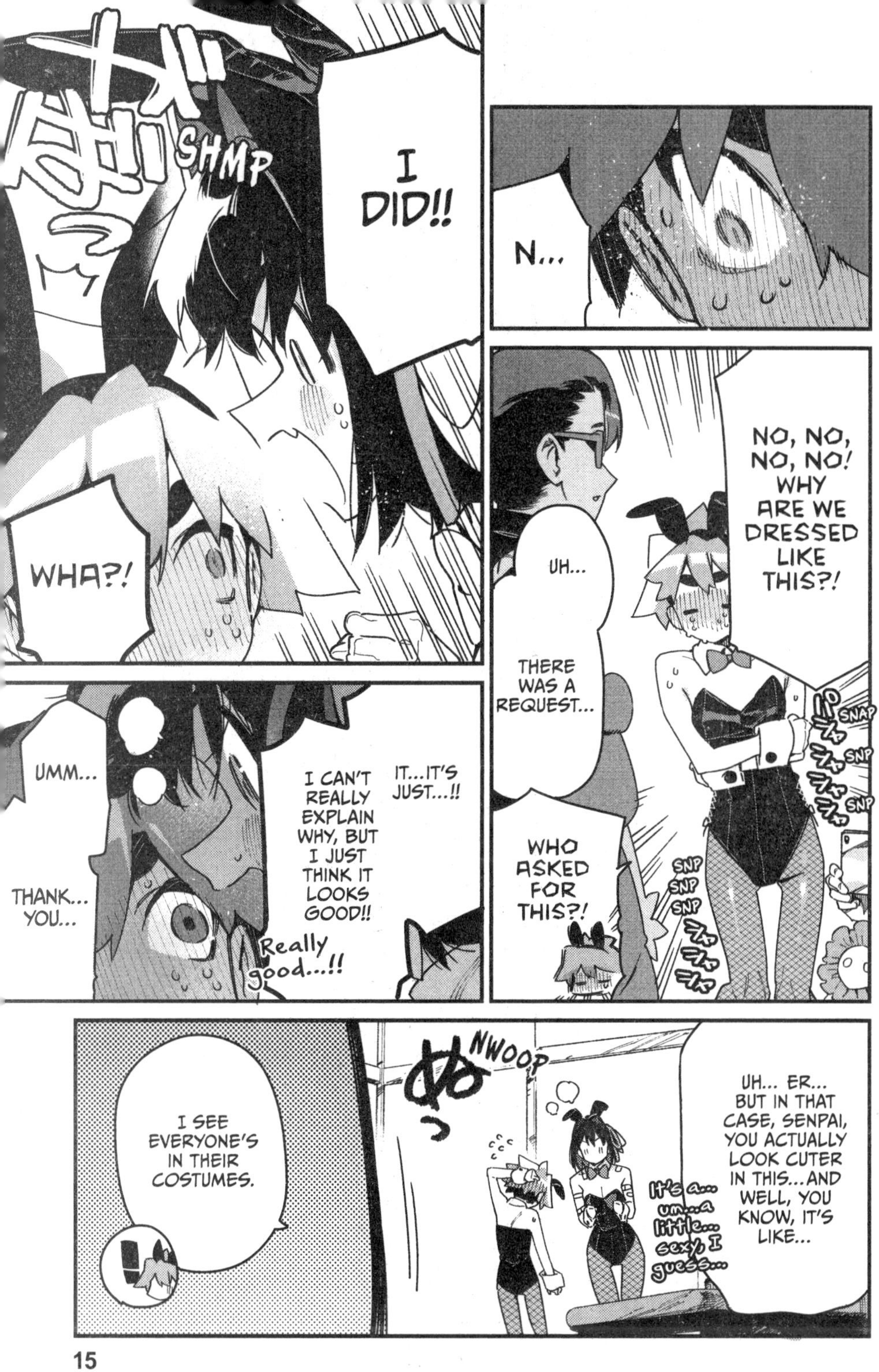
N...
I DID!!
SHMP
WHA?!
NO, NO, NO, NO! WHY ARE WE DRESSED LIKE THIS?!
SNAP
SNP
SNP
UH...
THERE WAS A REQUEST...
WHO ASKED FOR THIS?!
SNP SNP SNP
IT...IT'S JUST...!!
I CAN'T REALLY EXPLAIN WHY, BUT I JUST THINK IT LOOKS GOOD!!
Really good...!!
UMM...
THANK... YOU...
UH... ER... BUT IN THAT CASE, SENPAI, YOU ACTUALLY LOOK CUTER IN THIS...AND WELL, YOU KNOW, IT'S LIKE...
It's a... um...a little... sexy, I guess...
NWOOP
I SEE EVERYONE'S IN THEIR COSTUMES.

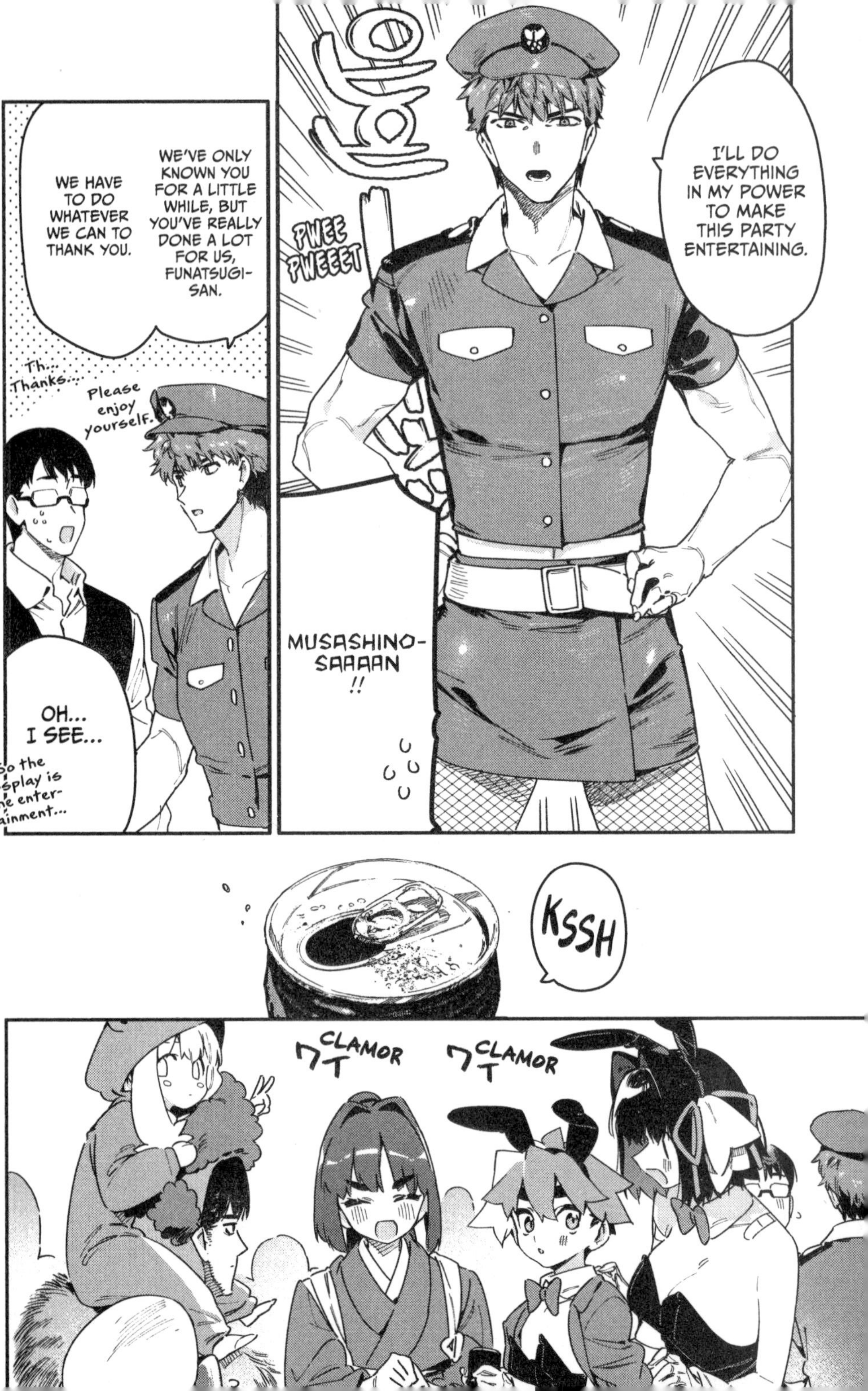
I'LL DO EVERYTHING IN MY POWER TO MAKE THIS PARTY ENTERTAINING.
PWEE PWEEET
MUSASHINO-SAAAAN!!
WE'VE ONLY KNOWN YOU FOR A LITTLE WHILE, BUT YOU'VE REALLY DONE A LOT FOR US, FUNATSUGI-SAN.
WE HAVE TO DO WHATEVER WE CAN TO THANK YOU.
Th... Thanks...
Please enjoy yourself.
OH... I SEE...
So the cosplay is the entertainment...
KSSH
CLAMOR
CLAMOR

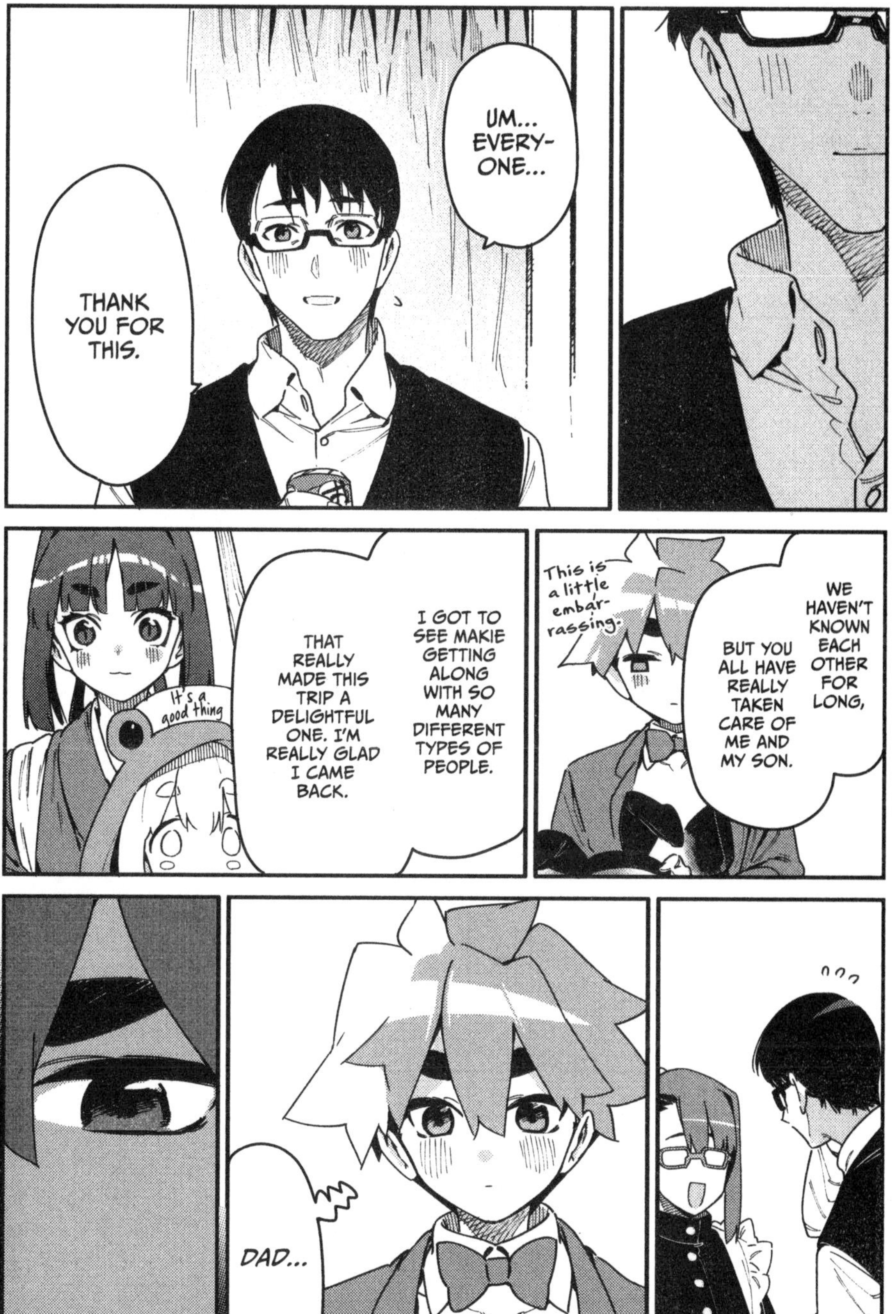
UM... EVERY-ONE...
THANK YOU FOR THIS.
WE HAVEN'T KNOWN EACH OTHER FOR LONG,
BUT YOU ALL HAVE REALLY TAKEN CARE OF ME AND MY SON.
This is a little embar-rassing.
I GOT TO SEE MAKIE GETTING ALONG WITH SO MANY DIFFERENT TYPES OF PEOPLE.
THAT REALLY MADE THIS TRIP A DELIGHTFUL ONE. I'M REALLY GLAD I CAME BACK.
It's a good thing
DAD...

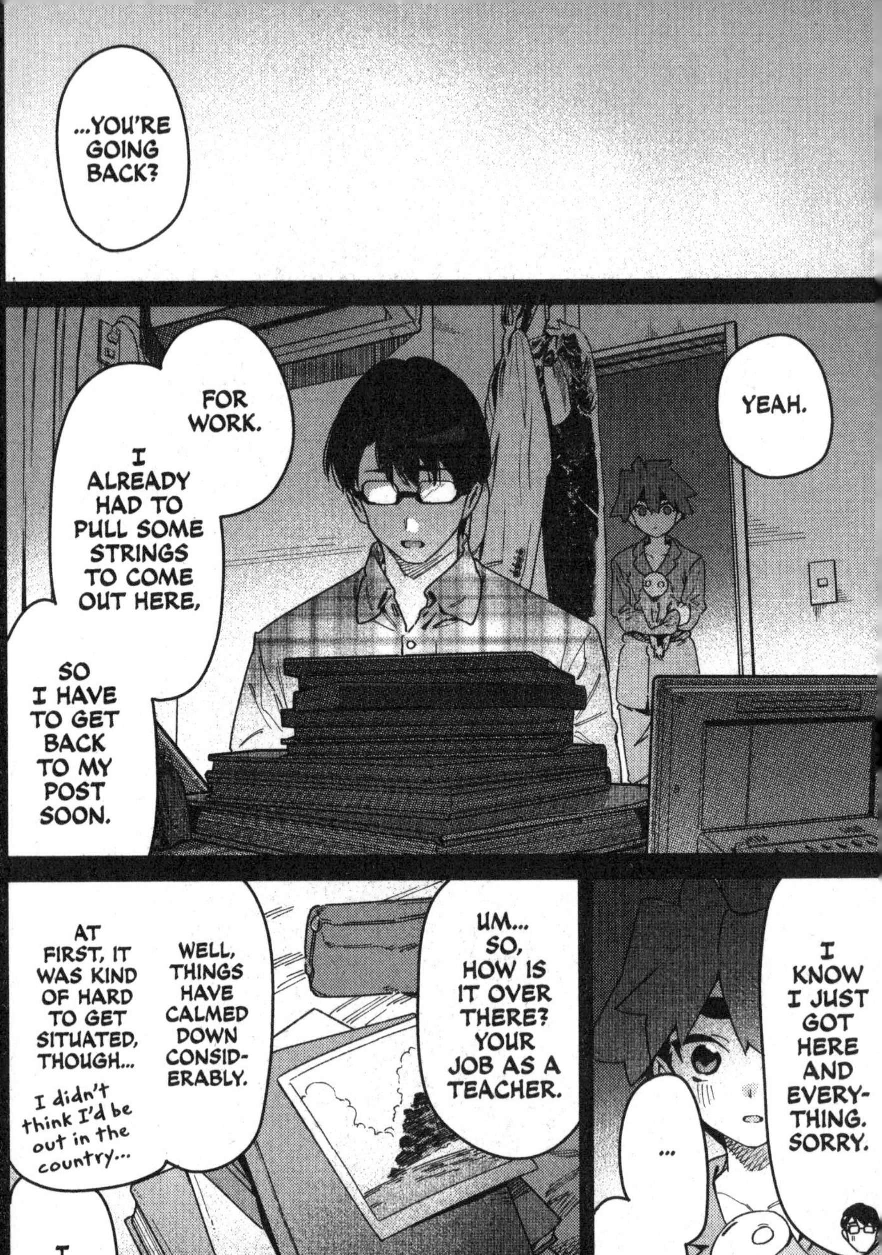
...YOU'RE GOING BACK?
YEAH.
FOR WORK.
I ALREADY HAD TO PULL SOME STRINGS TO COME OUT HERE,
SO I HAVE TO GET BACK TO MY POST SOON.
I KNOW I JUST GOT HERE AND EVERYTHING. SORRY.
...
...NO, IT'S ALL RIGHT...
UM... SO, HOW IS IT OVER THERE? YOUR JOB AS A TEACHER.
WELL, THINGS HAVE CALMED DOWN CONSIDERABLY.
AT FIRST, IT WAS KIND OF HARD TO GET SITUATED, THOUGH...
I didn't think I'd be out in the country...
I SEE...

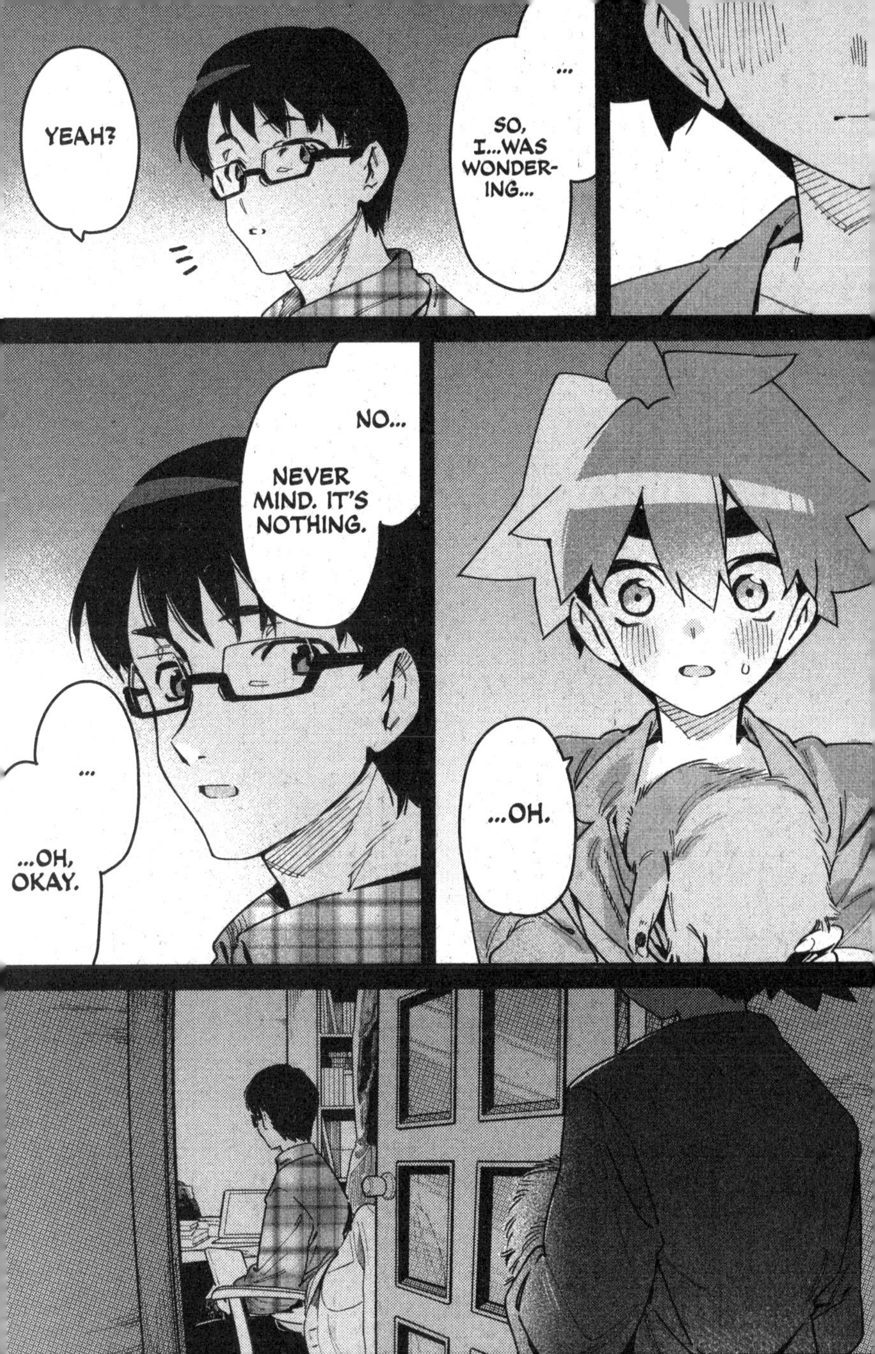
...
SO, I...WAS WONDERING...
YEAH?
...OH.
NO...
NEVER MIND. IT'S NOTHING.
...
...OH, OKAY.

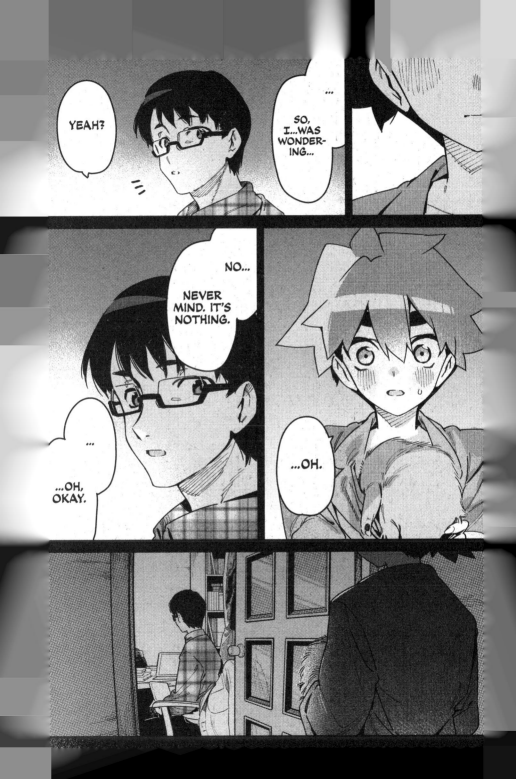

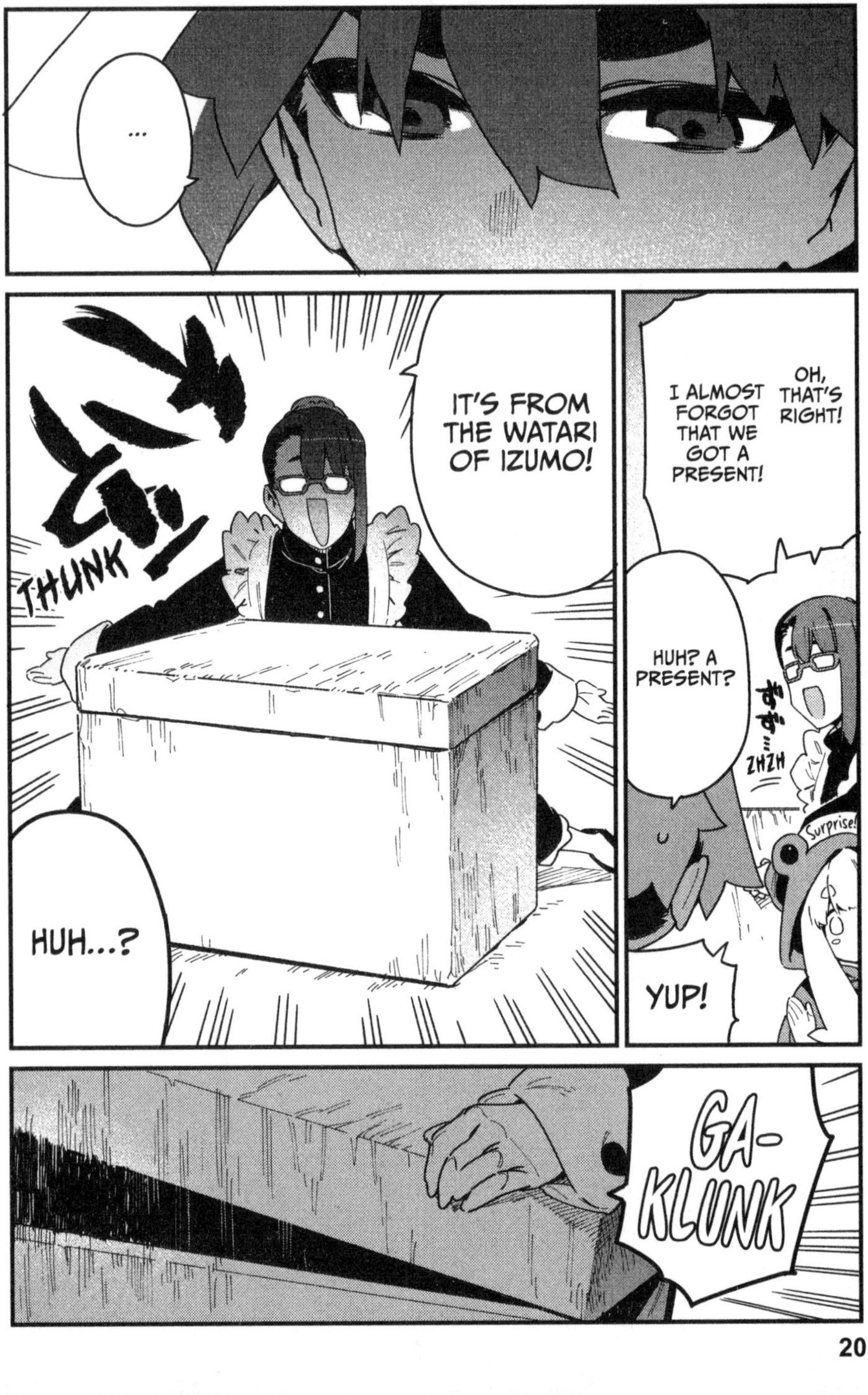
...
OH, THAT'S RIGHT!
I ALMOST FORGOT THAT WE GOT A PRESENT!
HUH? A PRESENT?
ずず…
ZHZH
Surprise!
YUP!
IT'S FROM THE WATARI OF IZUMO!
THUNK
HUH...?
GA-KLUNK

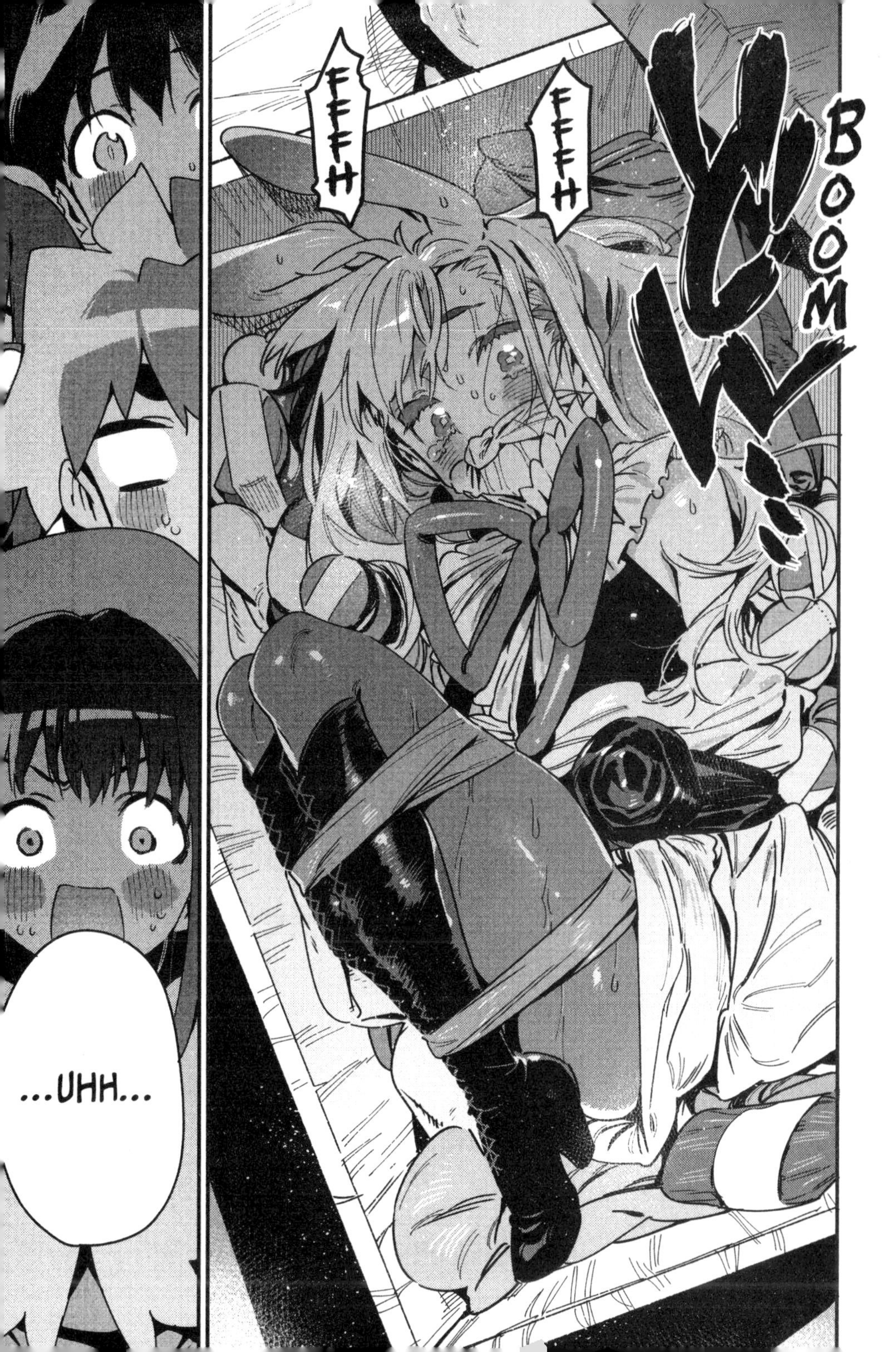
BOOM
FFFH
FFFH
...UHH...

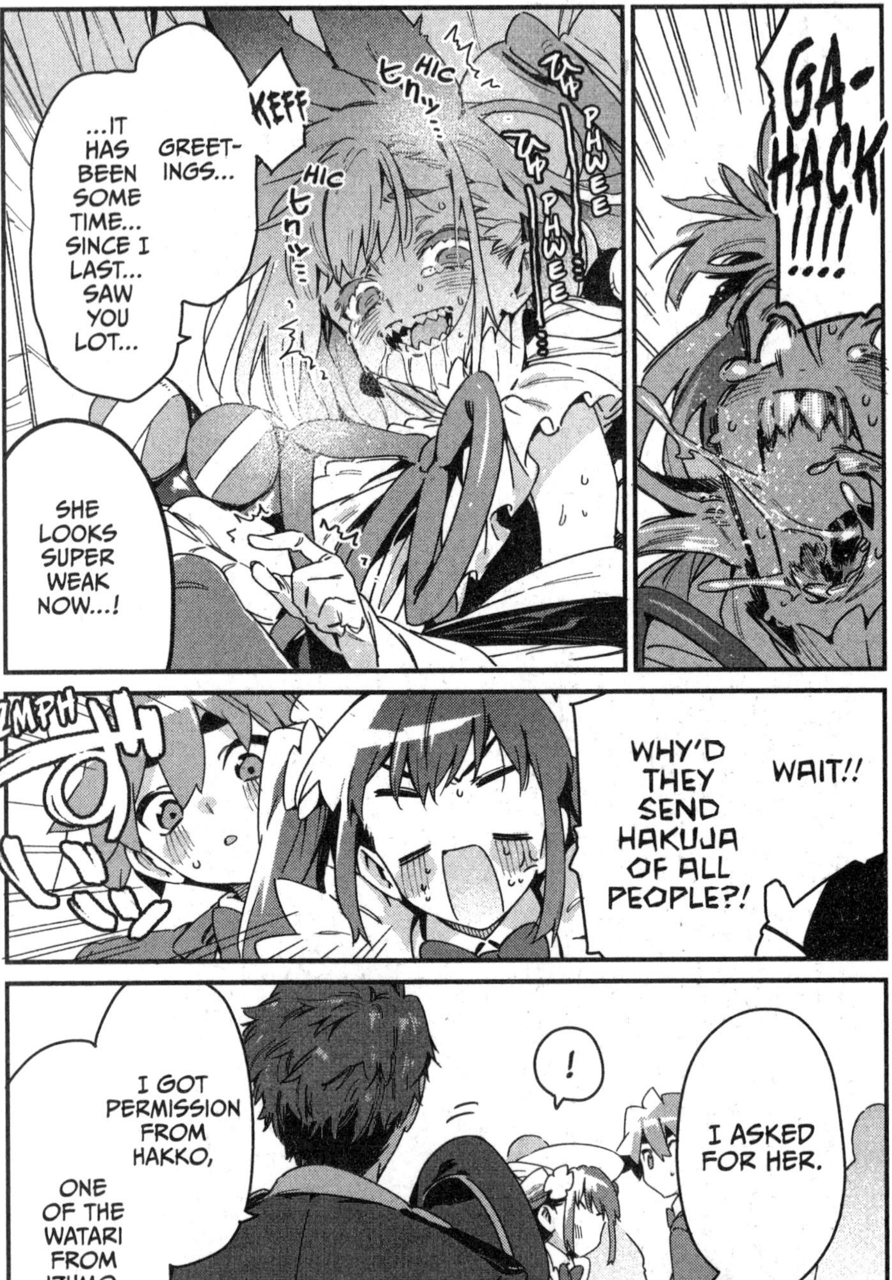
GA-HACK!!!!....
PHWEE
PHWEE
HIC
HIC
KEFF
GREETINGS...
...IT HAS BEEN SOME TIME... SINCE I LAST... SAW YOU LOT...
SHE LOOKS SUPER WEAK NOW...!
WAIT!!
WHY'D THEY SEND HAKUJA OF ALL PEOPLE?!
ZMPH
I ASKED FOR HER.
!
I GOT PERMISSION FROM HAKKO,
ONE OF THE WATARI FROM IZUMO.

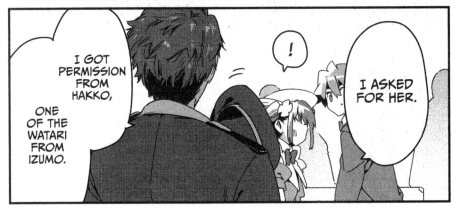

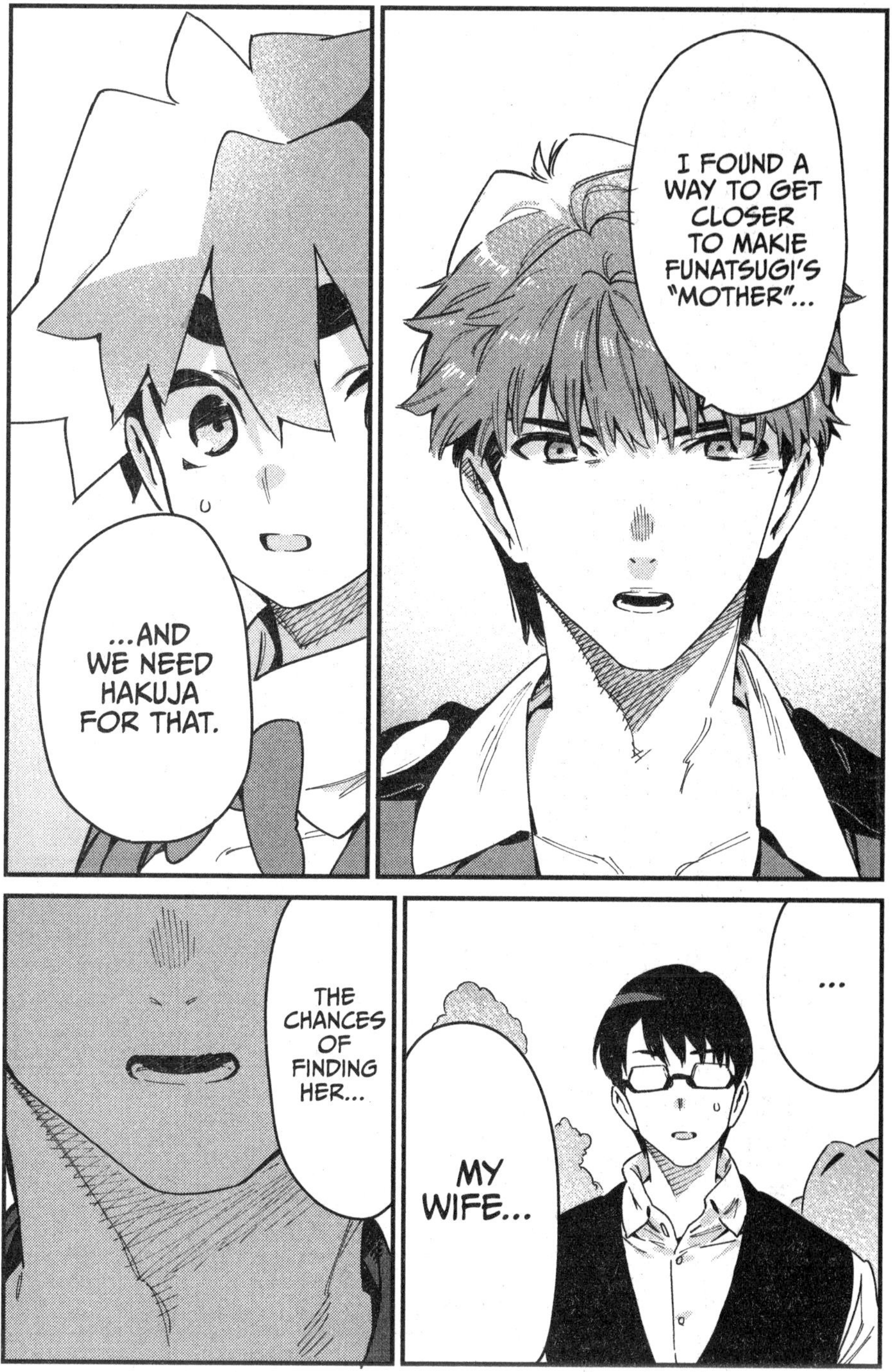
I FOUND A WAY TO GET CLOSER TO MAKIE FUNATSUGI'S "MOTHER"...
...AND WE NEED HAKUJA FOR THAT.
...
MY WIFE...
THE CHANCES OF FINDING HER...

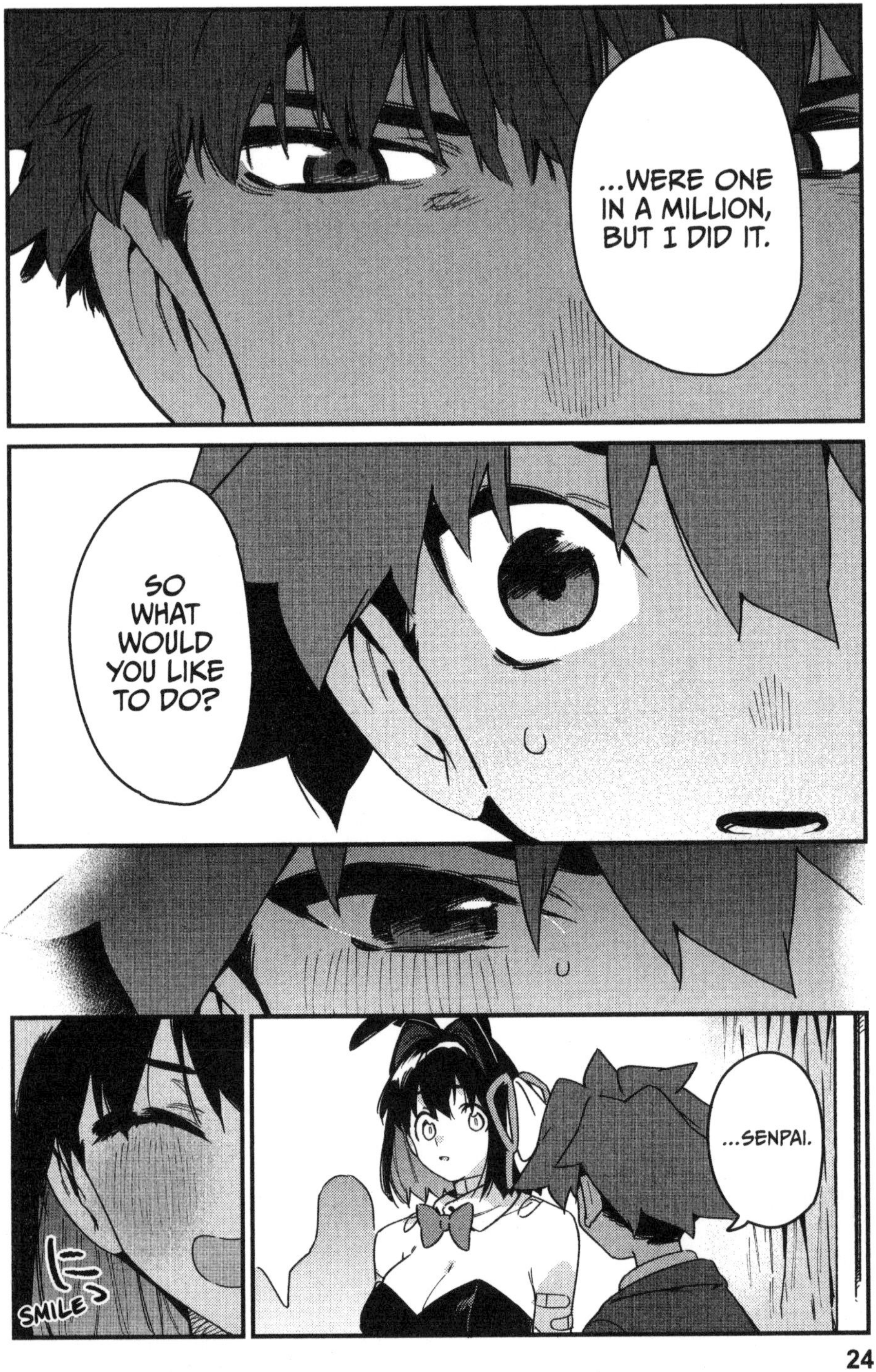
...WERE ONE IN A MILLION, BUT I DID IT.
SO WHAT WOULD YOU LIKE TO DO?
...SENPAI.
SMILE

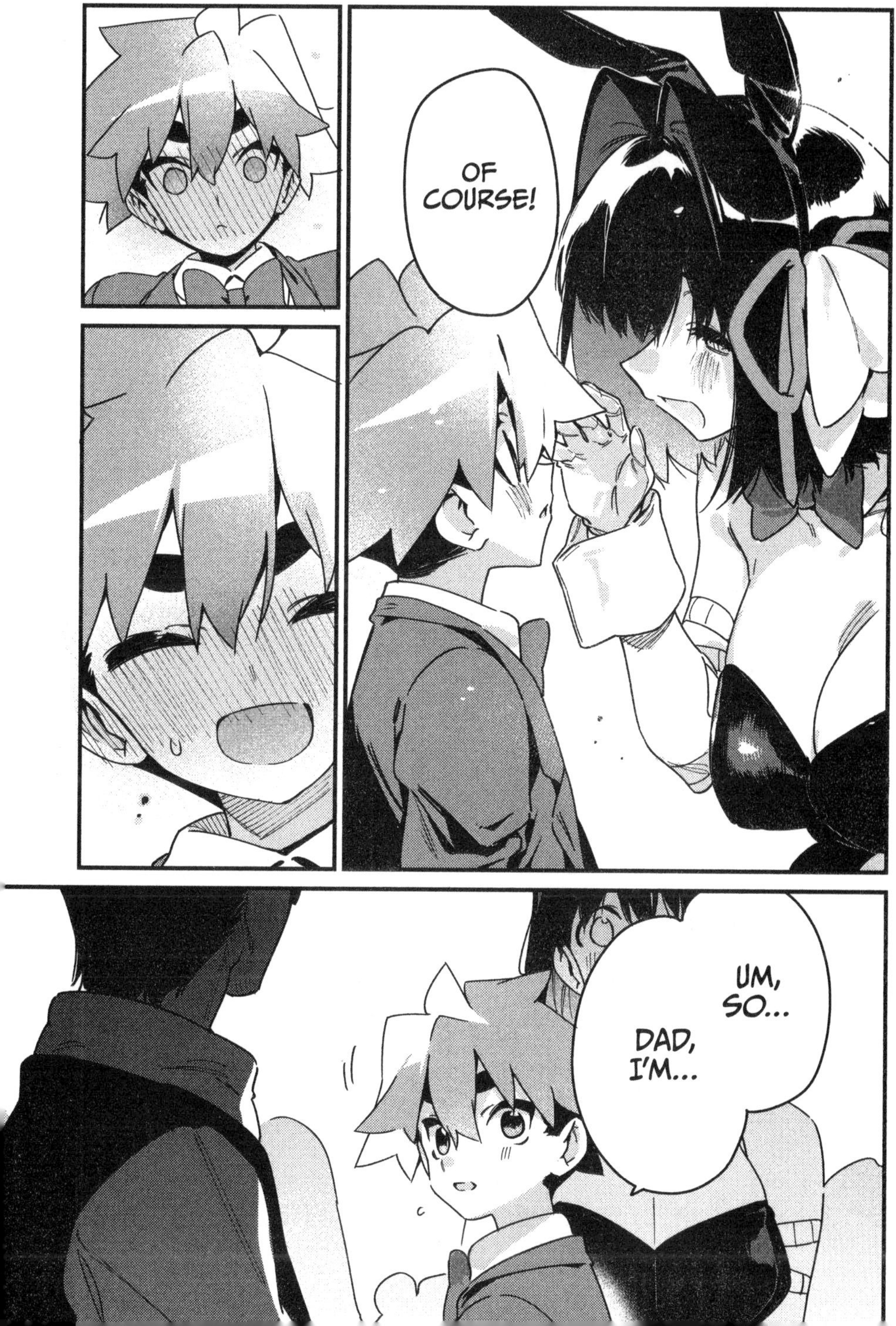
OF COURSE!
UM, SO...
DAD, I'M...

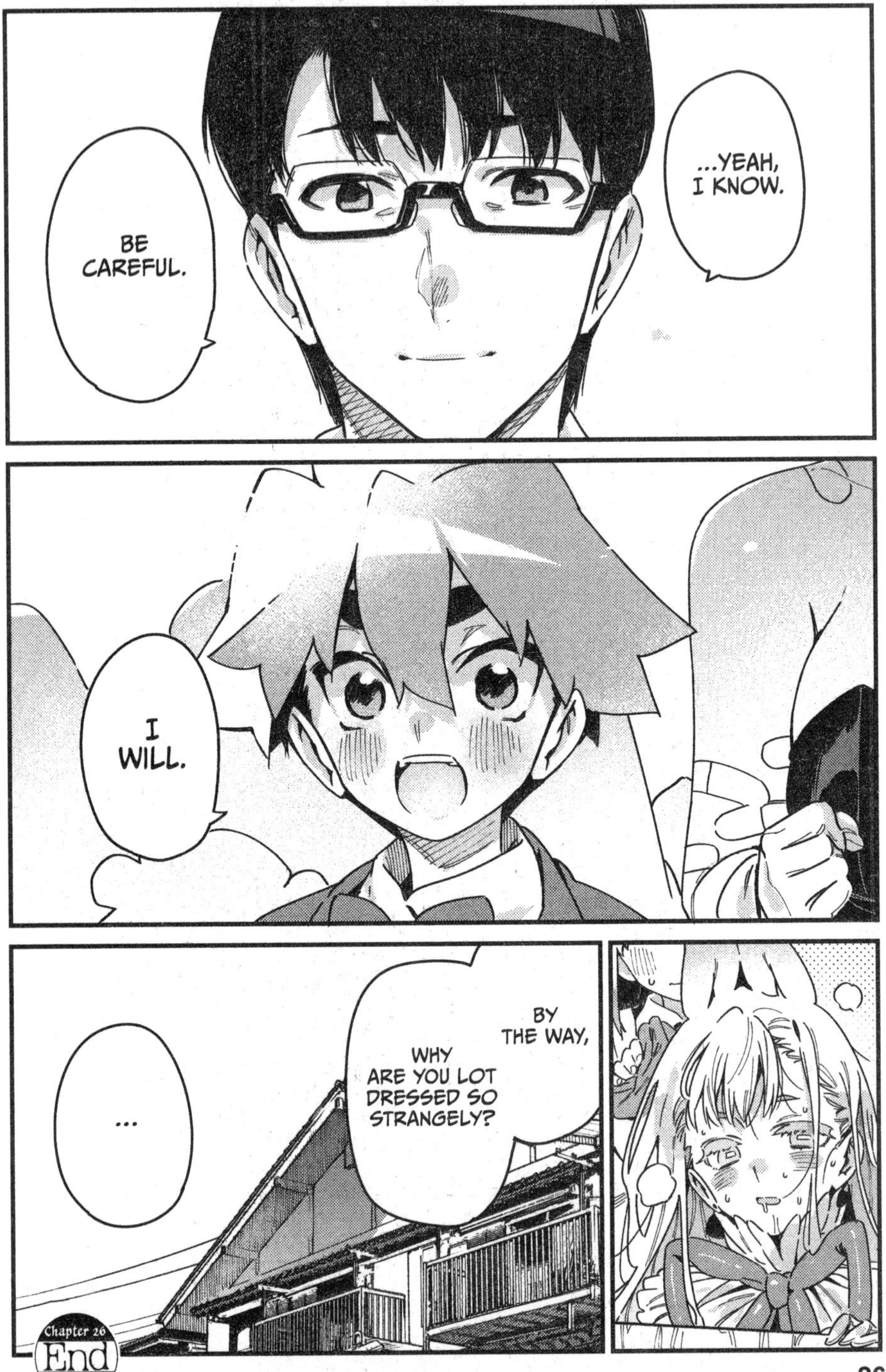
...YEAH, I KNOW.
BE CAREFUL.
I WILL.
BY THE WAY, WHY ARE YOU LOT DRESSED SO STRANGELY?
...
Chapter 26 End

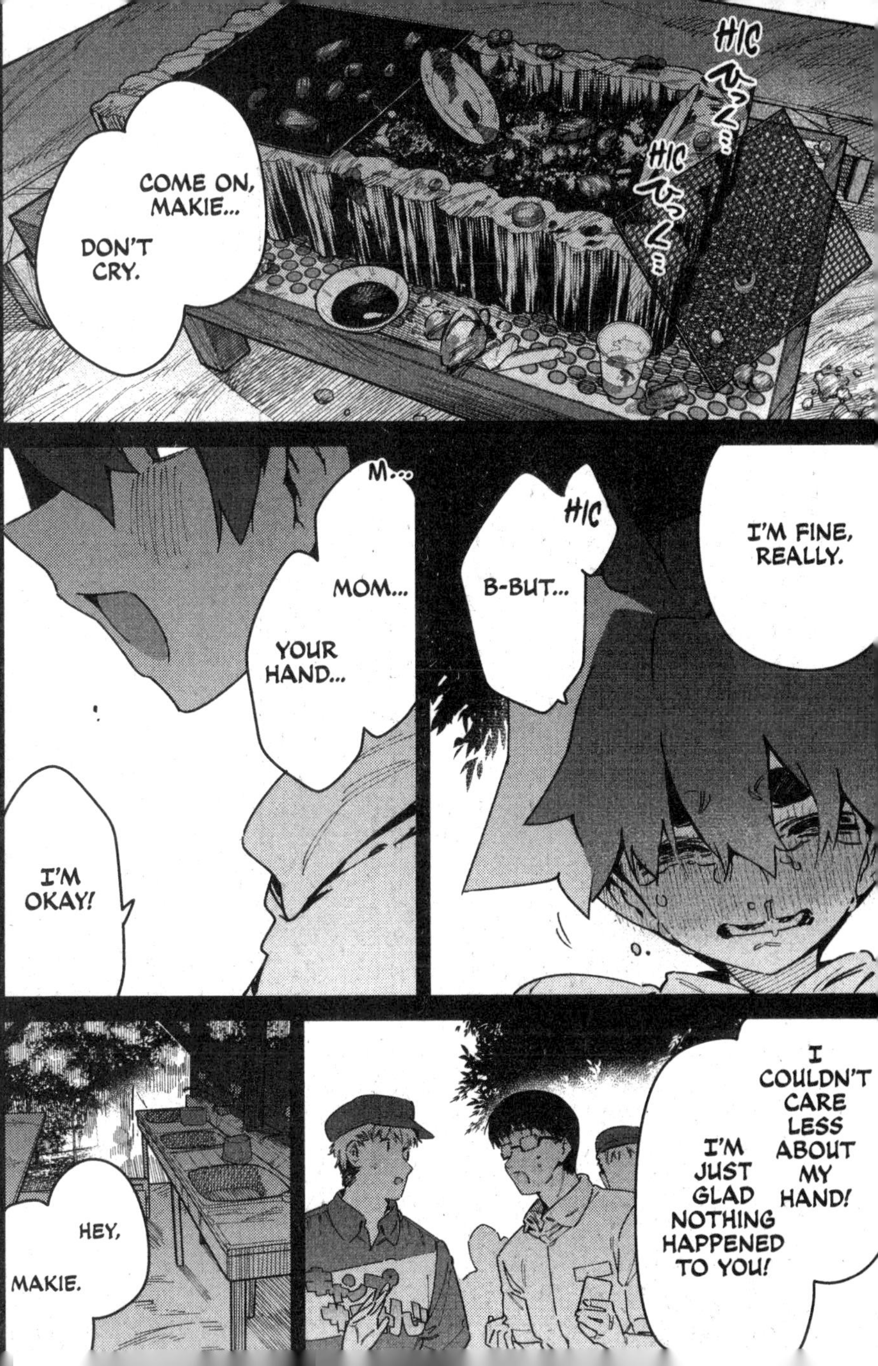
HIC ひっく…
HIC ひっく…
COME ON, MAKIE...
DON'T CRY.
I'M FINE, REALLY.
HIC
B-BUT...
M...
MOM...
YOUR HAND...
I'M OKAY!
I COULDN'T CARE LESS ABOUT MY HAND!
I'M JUST GLAD NOTHING HAPPENED TO YOU!
HEY,
MAKIE.

Chapter 27: Together Again

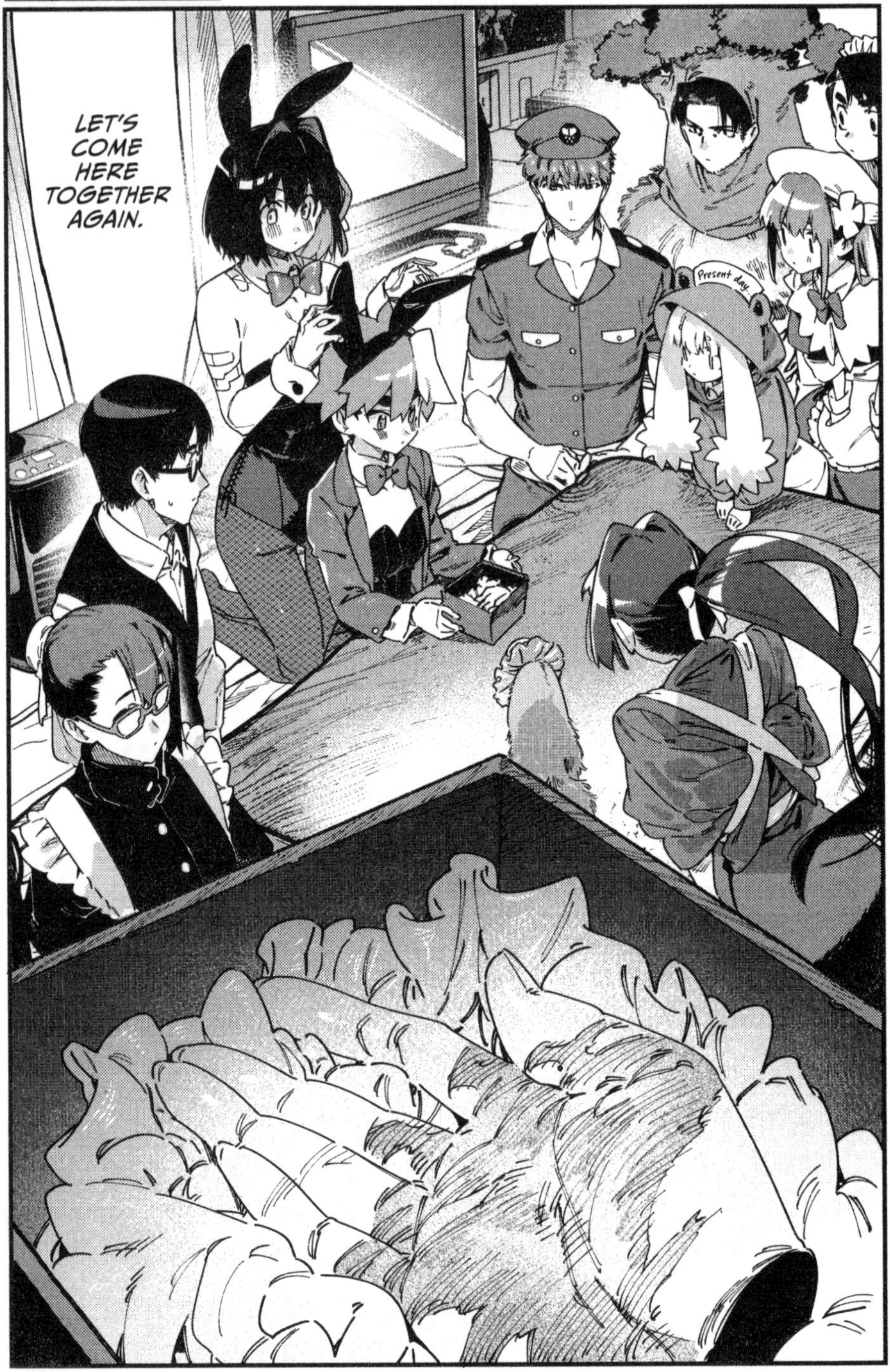
LET'S COME HERE TOGETHER AGAIN.
Present day.

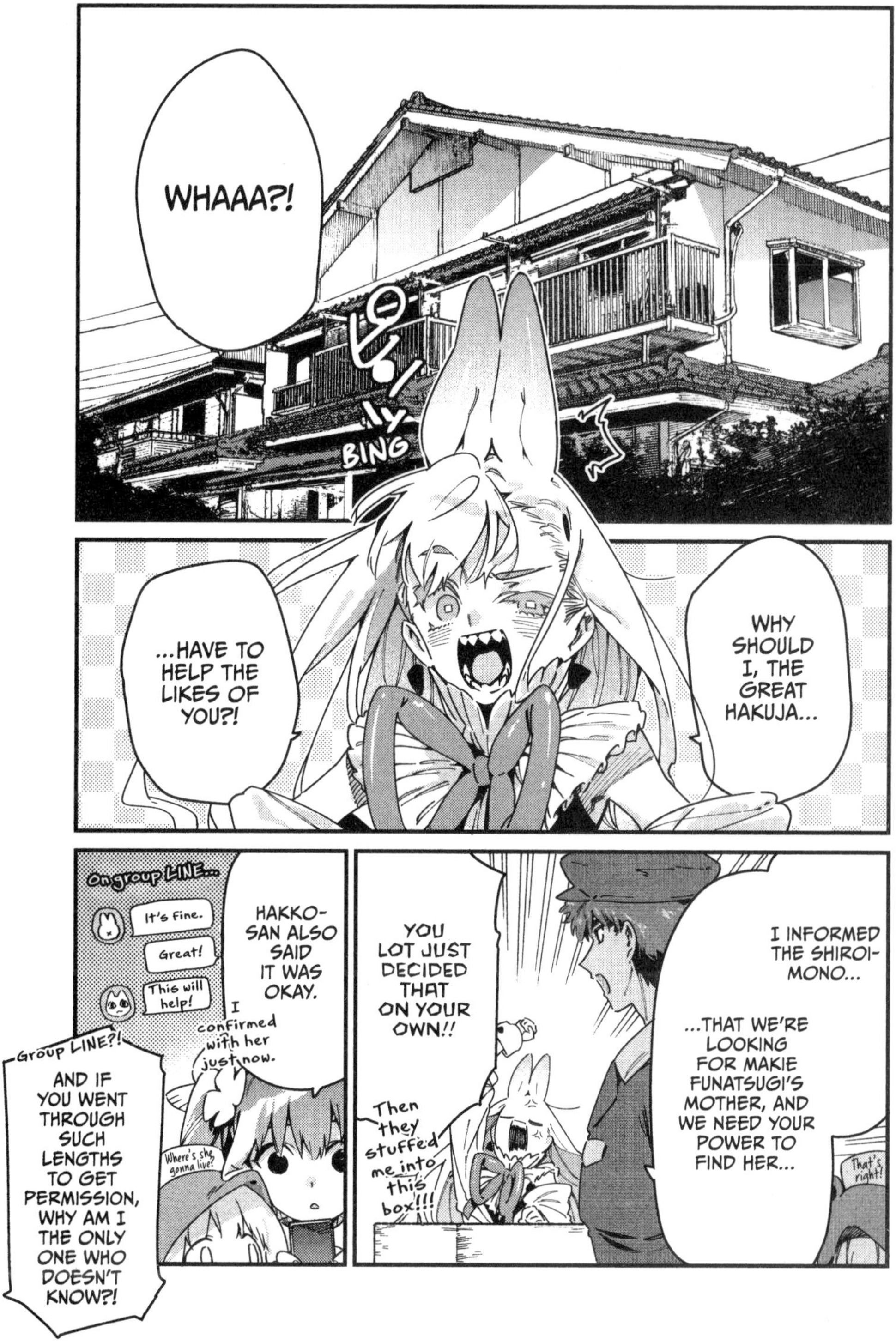
WHAAA?!
BING
WHY SHOULD I, THE GREAT HAKUJA...
...HAVE TO HELP THE LIKES OF YOU?!
I INFORMED THE SHIROI-MONO...
...THAT WE'RE LOOKING FOR MAKIE FUNATSUGI'S MOTHER, AND WE NEED YOUR POWER TO FIND HER...
That's right!
YOU LOT JUST DECIDED THAT ON YOUR OWN!!
Then they stuffed me into this box!!!
HAKKO-SAN ALSO SAID IT WAS OKAY.
I confirmed with her just now.
On group LINE...
It's fine.
Great!
This will help!
Group LINE?!
AND IF YOU WENT THROUGH SUCH LENGTHS TO GET PERMISSION, WHY AM I THE ONLY ONE WHO DOESN'T KNOW?!
Where's she gonna live?

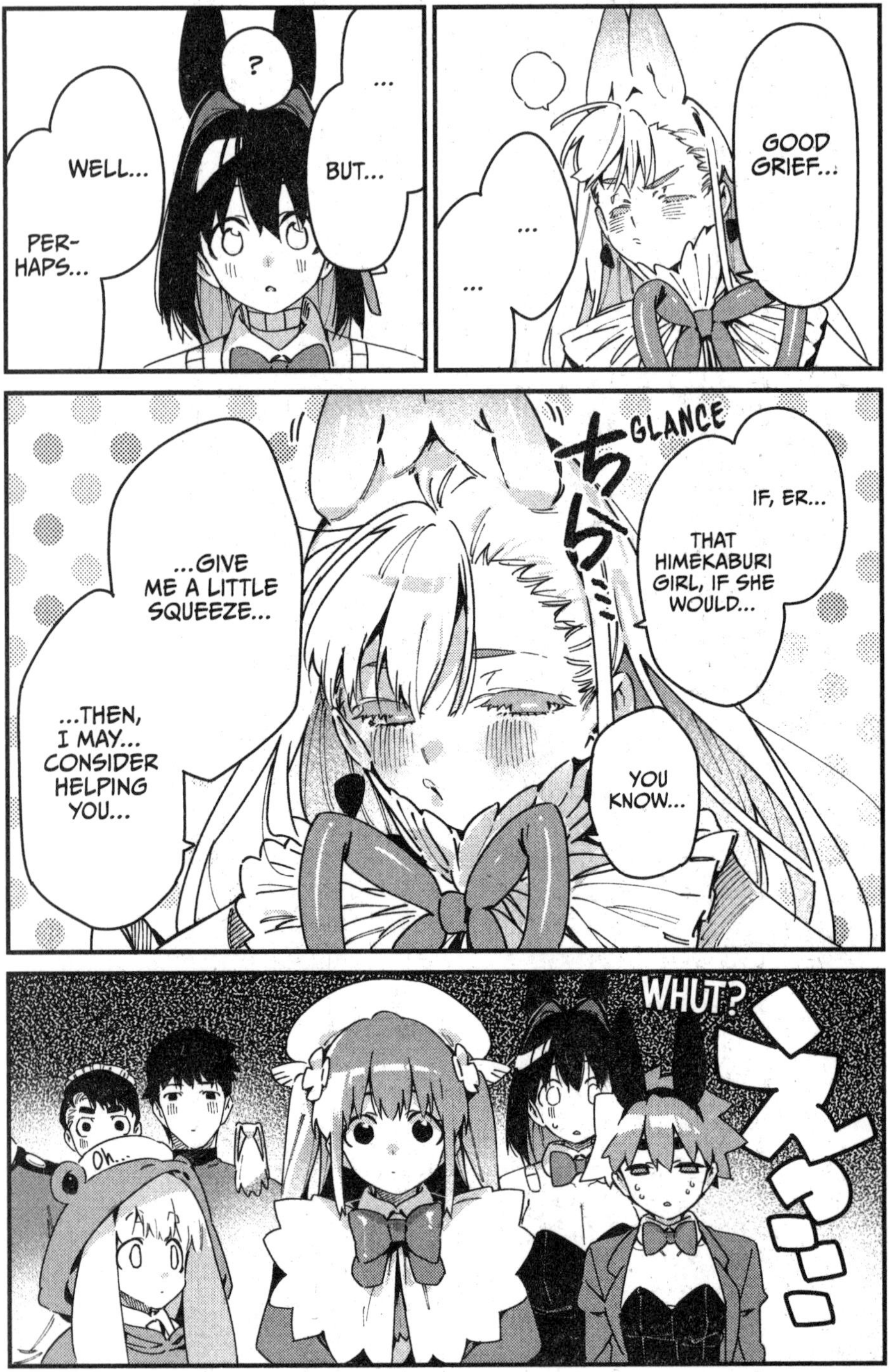
GOOD GRIEF...
...
...
?
...
BUT...
WELL...
PER-HAPS...
GLANCE
ちら
IF, ER...
THAT HIMEKABURI GIRL, IF SHE WOULD...
YOU KNOW...
...GIVE ME A LITTLE SQUEEZE...
...THEN, I MAY... CONSIDER HELPING YOU...
WHUT?
Oh...

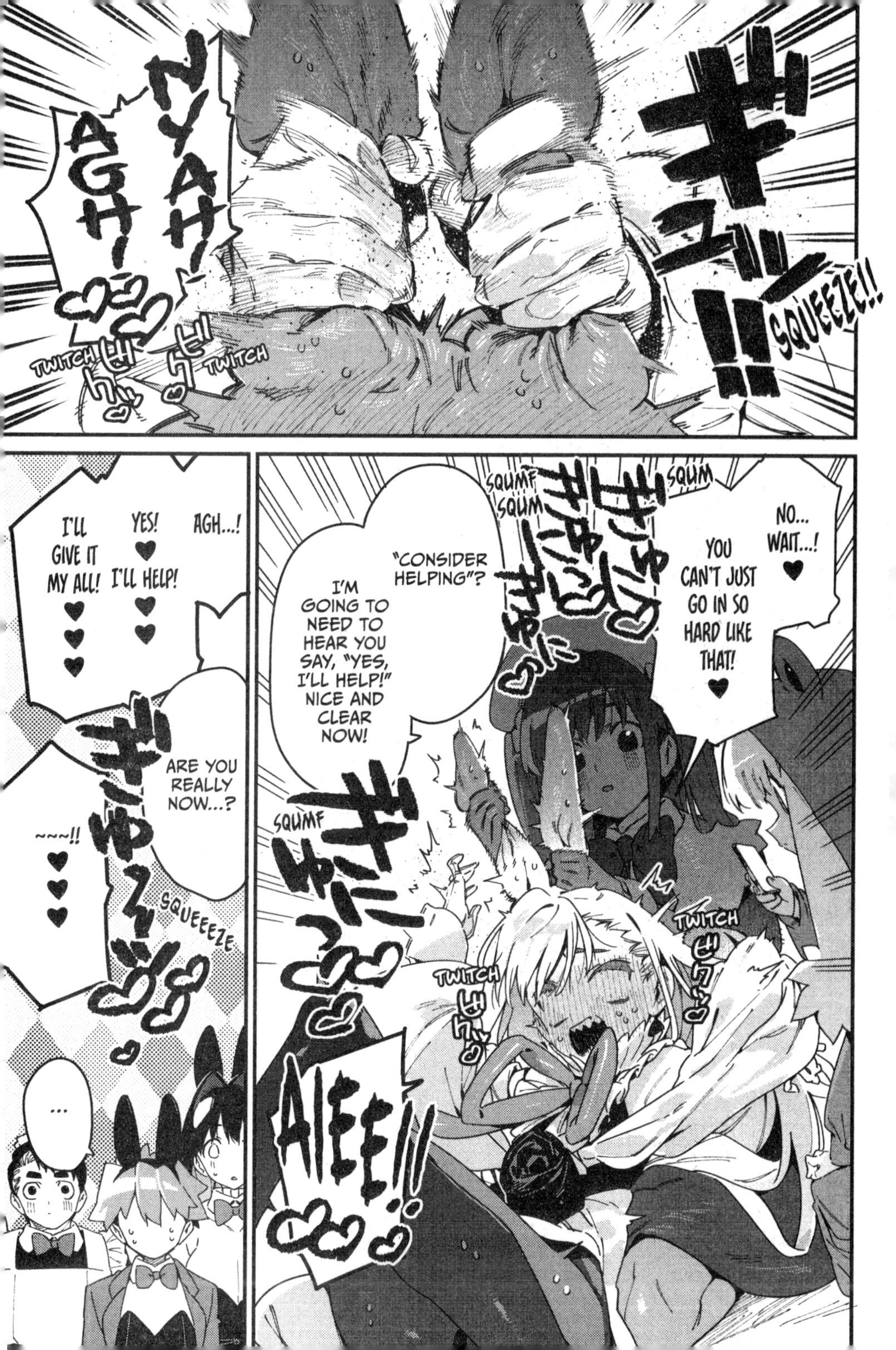
SQUEEZE!!
NYAH! AGH!~♥
TWITCH
TWITCH
SQUM
NO... WAIT...! ♥
YOU CAN'T JUST GO IN SO HARD LIKE THAT! ♥
SQUMF SQUM
"CONSIDER HELPING"?
I'M GOING TO NEED TO HEAR YOU SAY, "YES, I'LL HELP!" NICE AND CLEAR NOW!
SQUMF
TWITCH
TWITCH
AIEE!!
AGH...!
YES! ♥ I'LL HELP! ♥ ♥
I'LL GIVE IT MY ALL! ♥ ♥ ♥
ARE YOU REALLY NOW...?
SQUEEEEZE
~~~!! ♥ ♥ ♥
...
~~~

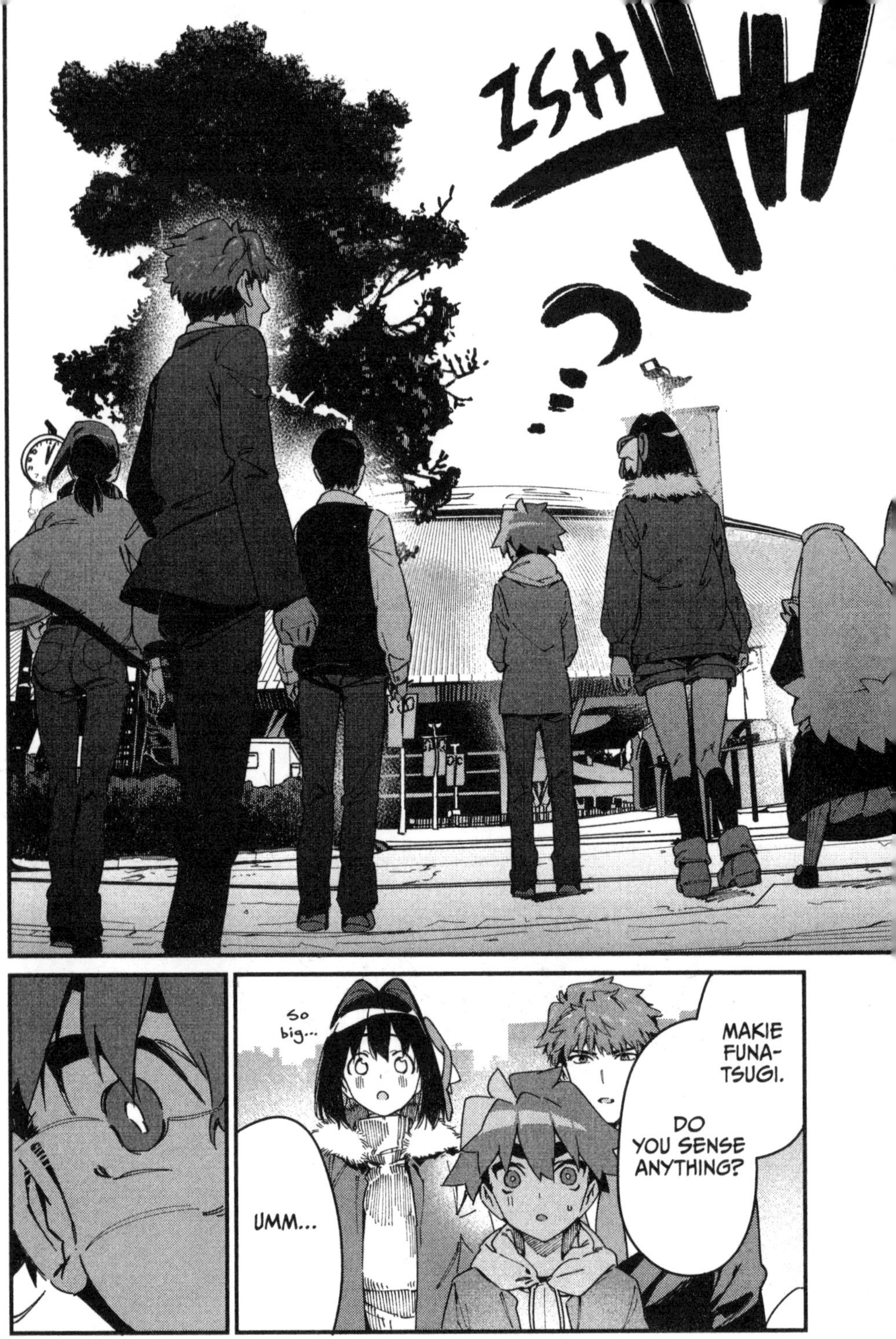
ZSH
MAKIE FUNA-TSUGI.
DO YOU SENSE ANYTHING?
So big...
UMM...

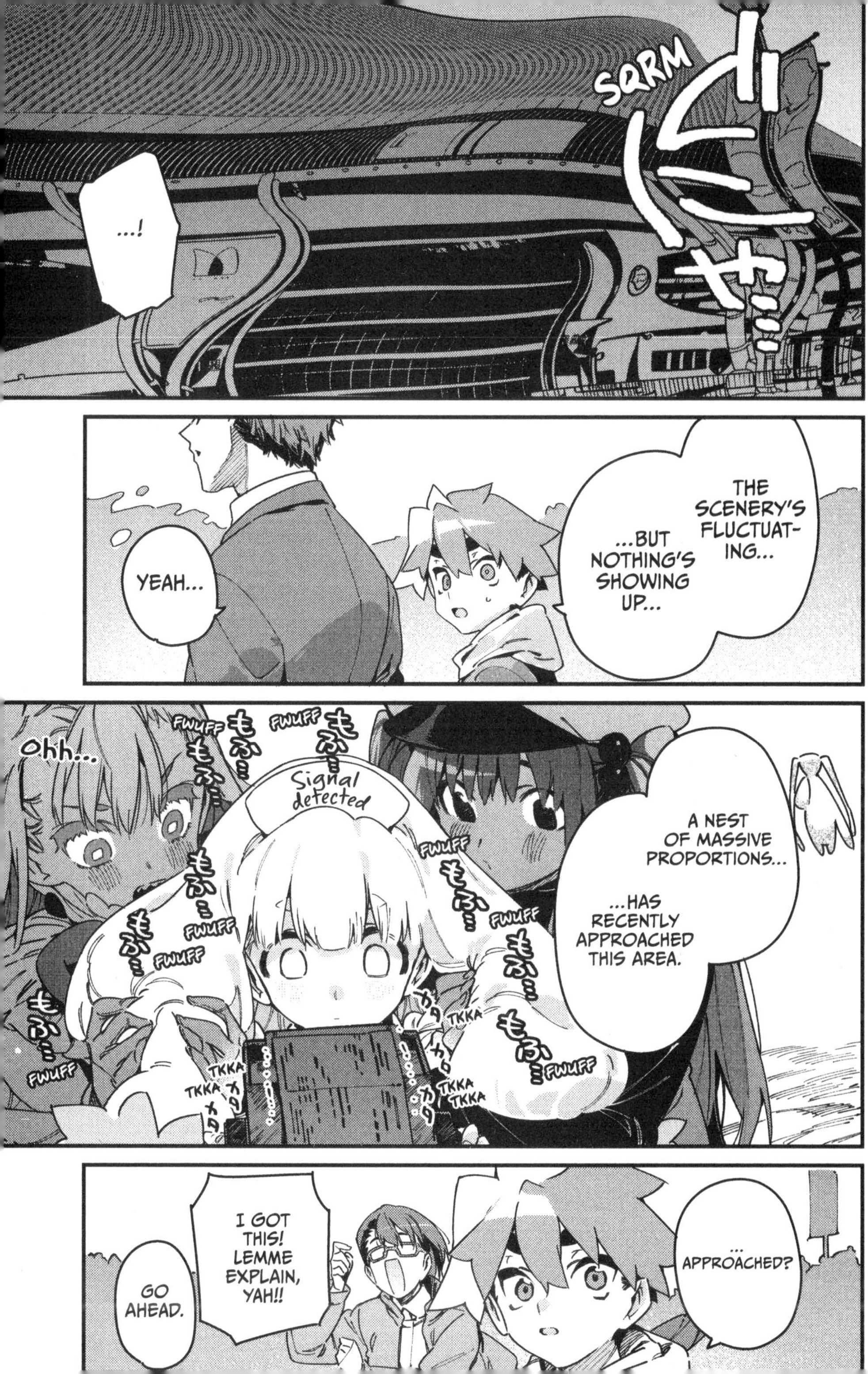
SQRM
...!
THE SCENERY'S FLUCTUATING... ...BUT NOTHING'S SHOWING UP...
YEAH...
A NEST OF MASSIVE PROPORTIONS... ...HAS RECENTLY APPROACHED THIS AREA.
FWUFF
FWUFF
Signal detected
Ohh...
FWUFF
FWUFF
TKKA
TKKA TKKA
TKKA TKKA
...APPROACHED?
I GOT THIS! LEMME EXPLAIN, YAH!!
GO AHEAD.

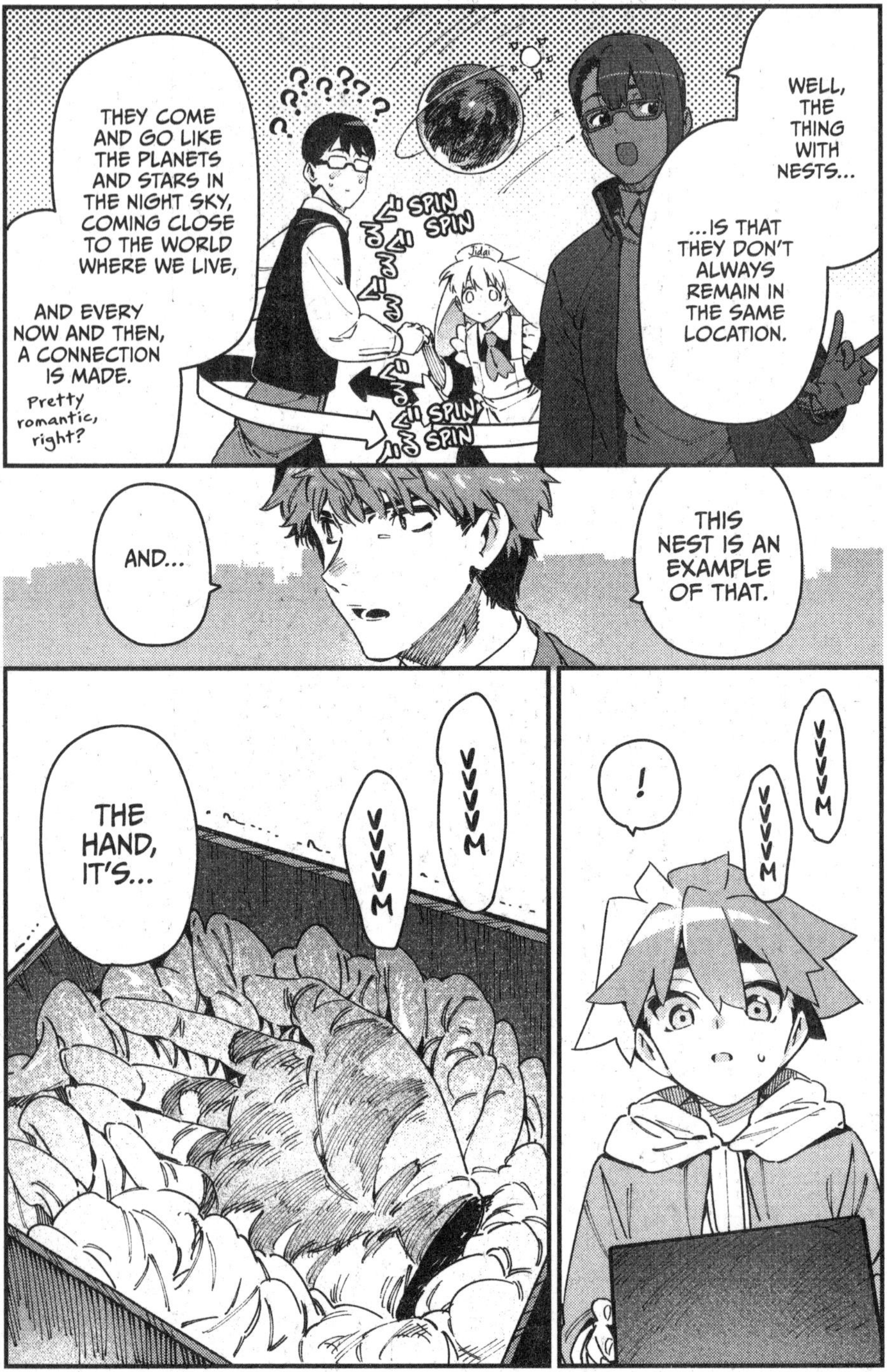
WELL, THE THING WITH NESTS...
...IS THAT THEY DON'T ALWAYS REMAIN IN THE SAME LOCATION.
THEY COME AND GO LIKE THE PLANETS AND STARS IN THE NIGHT SKY, COMING CLOSE TO THE WORLD WHERE WE LIVE,
AND EVERY NOW AND THEN, A CONNECTION IS MADE.
Pretty romantic, right?
SPIN SPIN
Jidai
SPIN SPIN
THIS NEST IS AN EXAMPLE OF THAT.
AND...
VVVVM
VVVVM
!
VVVVM
VVVVM
THE HAND, IT'S...

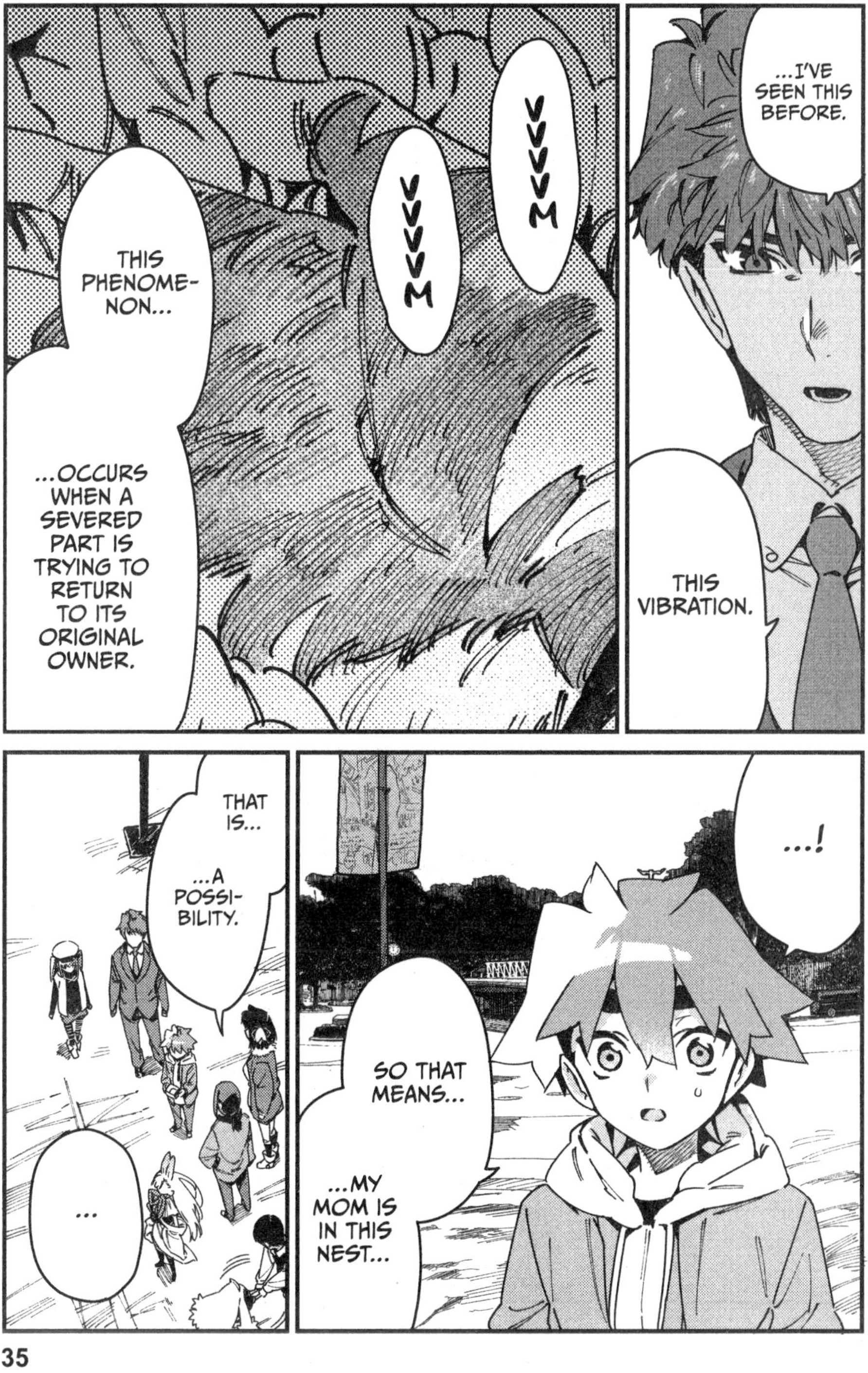

...I'VE SEEN THIS BEFORE.
THIS VIBRATION.
VVVVM
VVVVM
THIS PHENOME-NON...
...OCCURS WHEN A SEVERED PART IS TRYING TO RETURN TO ITS ORIGINAL OWNER.
...!
SO THAT MEANS...
...MY MOM IS IN THIS NEST...
THAT IS...
...A POSSI-BILITY.
...

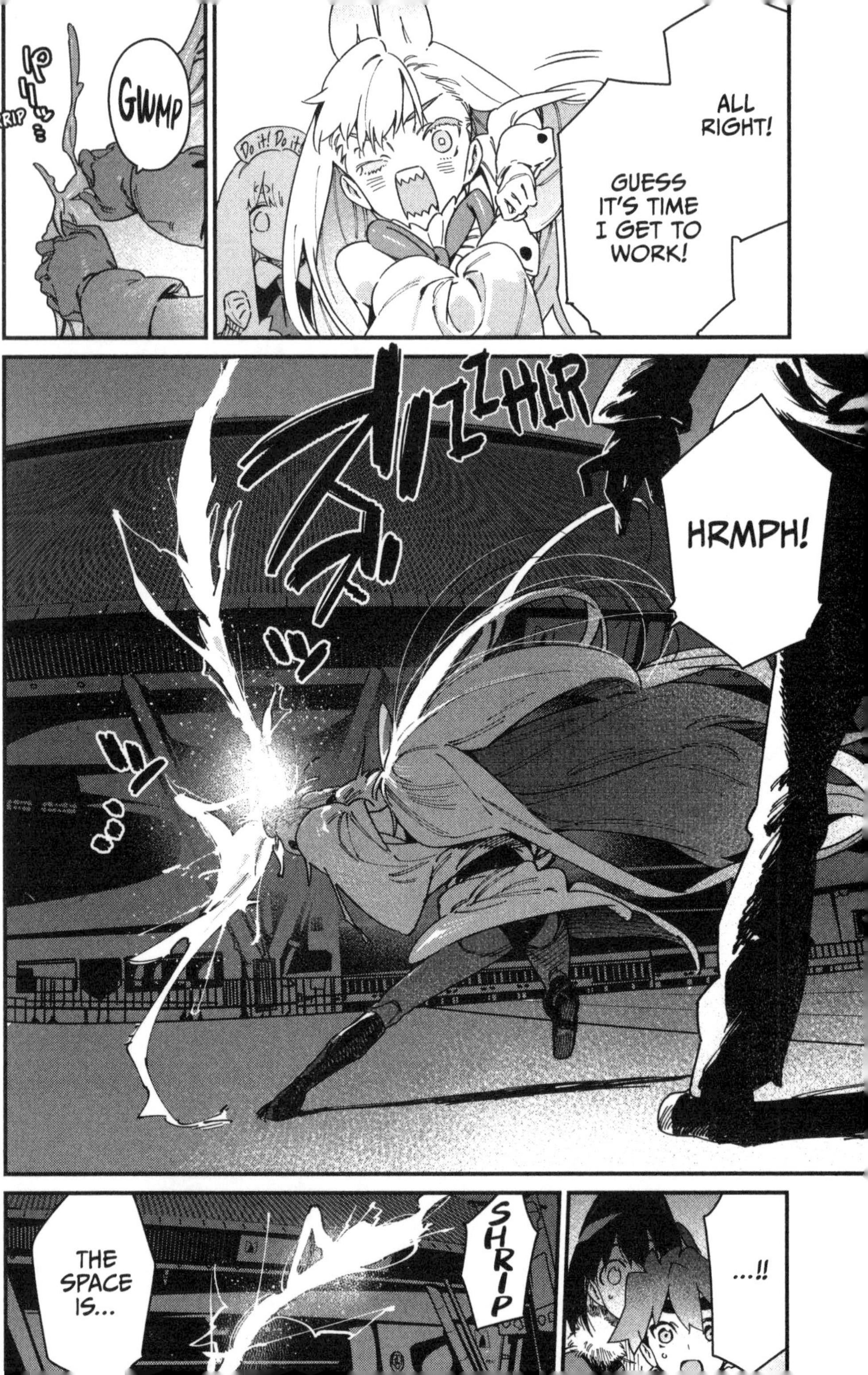
ALL RIGHT!
GUESS IT'S TIME I GET TO WORK!
Do it! Do it!
GWUMP
RRIP
HRMPH!
ZZHIR
...!!
SHRIP
THE SPACE IS...

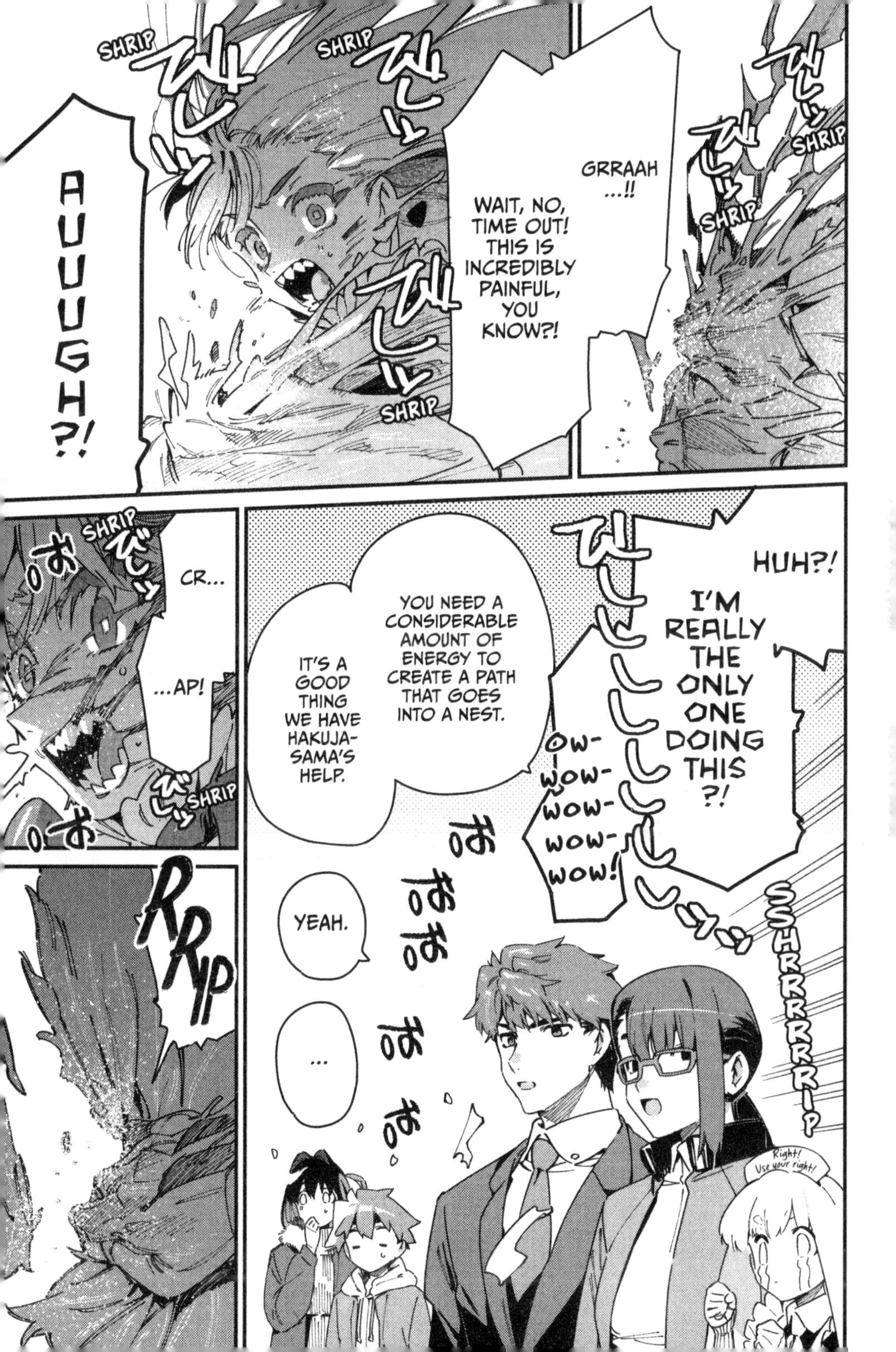
SHRIP
SHRIP
GRRAAH ...!!
SHRIP
SHRIP
WAIT, NO, TIME OUT! THIS IS INCREDIBLY PAINFUL, YOU KNOW?!
AUUUUGH?!
SHRIP
HUH?!
I'M REALLY THE ONLY ONE DOING THIS?!
YOU NEED A CONSIDERABLE AMOUNT OF ENERGY TO CREATE A PATH THAT GOES INTO A NEST.
IT'S A GOOD THING WE HAVE HAKUJA-SAMA'S HELP.
OW-WOW-WOW-WOW-WOW!
SSHRRRRRRIP
YEAH.
...
Right! Use your right!
SHRIP
CR...
...AP!
SHRIP
RRYIP

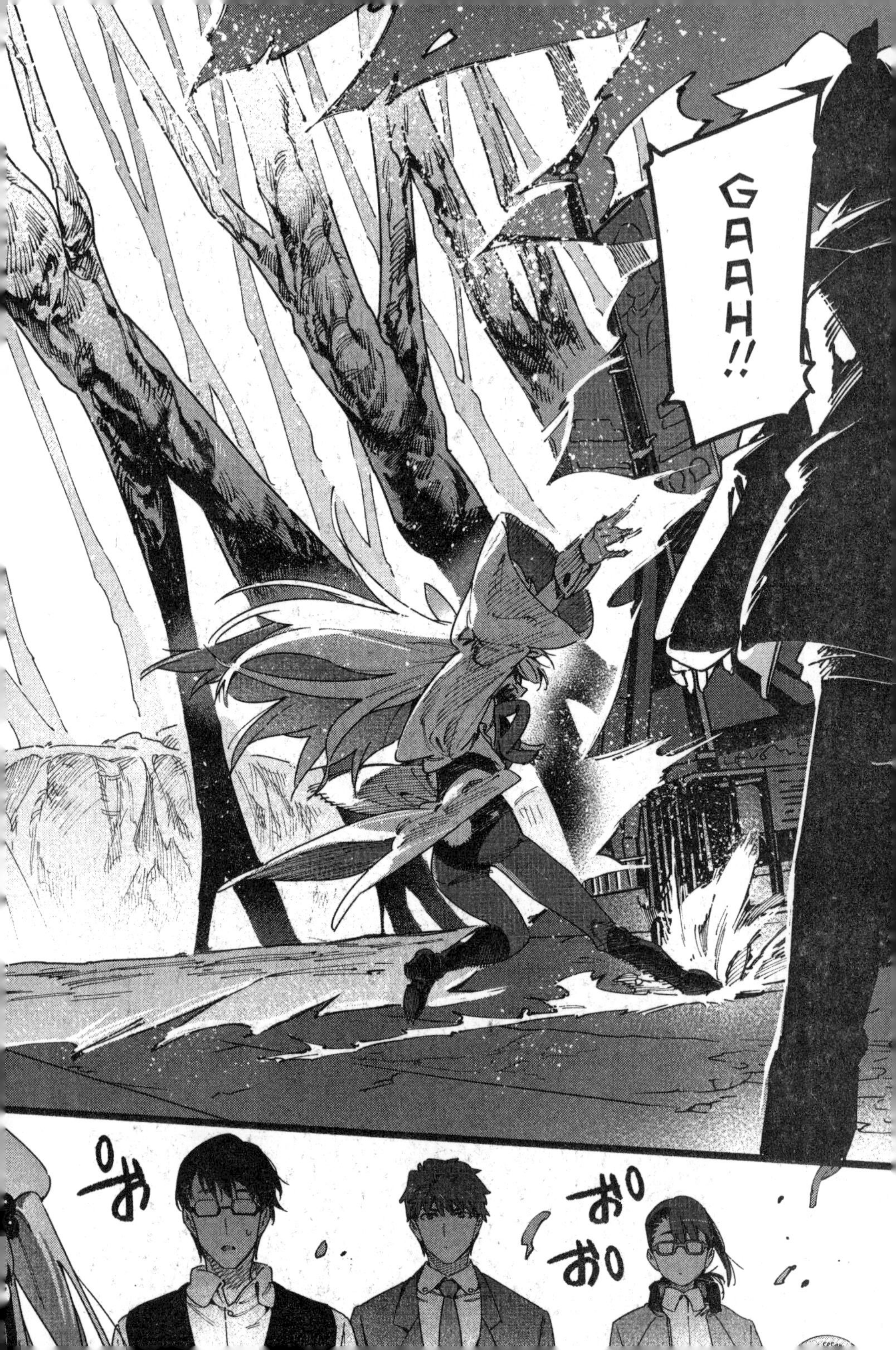
GAAAH!!
おおお
お

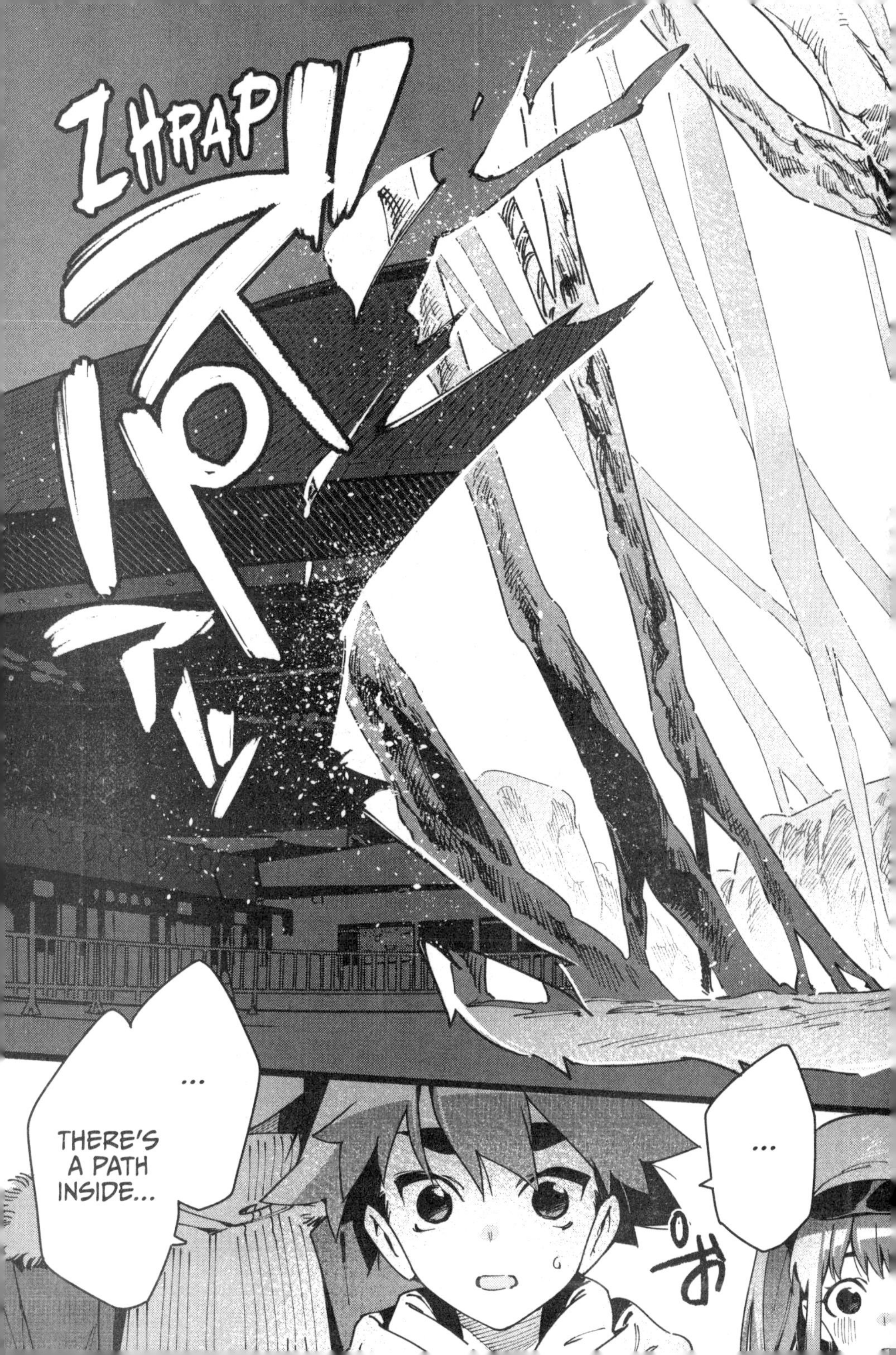
ZHRAP
...
...
THERE'S A PATH INSIDE...

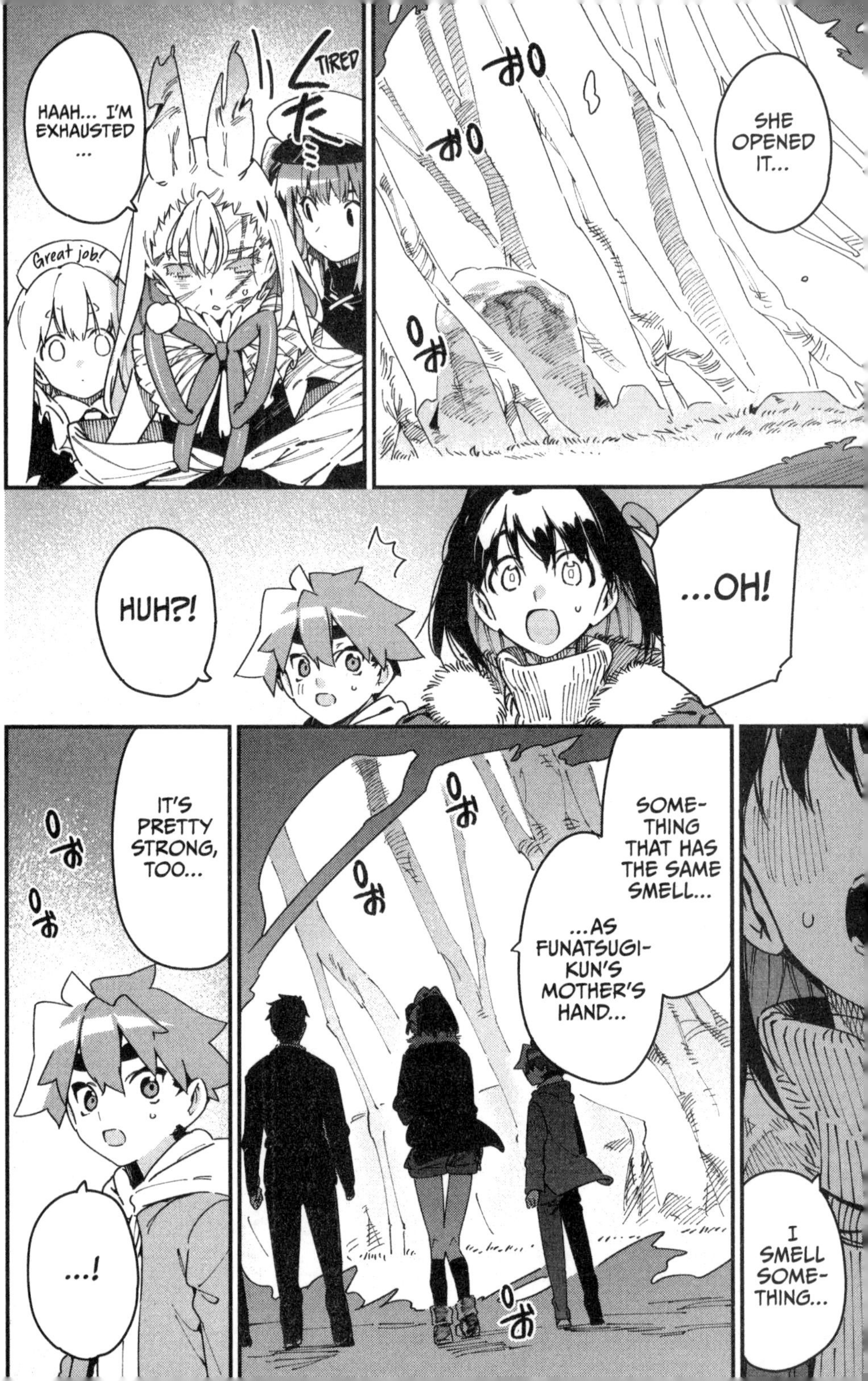
SHE OPENED IT...
TIRED
HAAH... I'M EXHAUSTED ...
Great job!
...OH!
HUH?!
I SMELL SOME-THING...
SOME-THING THAT HAS THE SAME SMELL...
...AS FUNATSUGI-KUN'S MOTHER'S HAND...
IT'S PRETTY STRONG, TOO...
...!

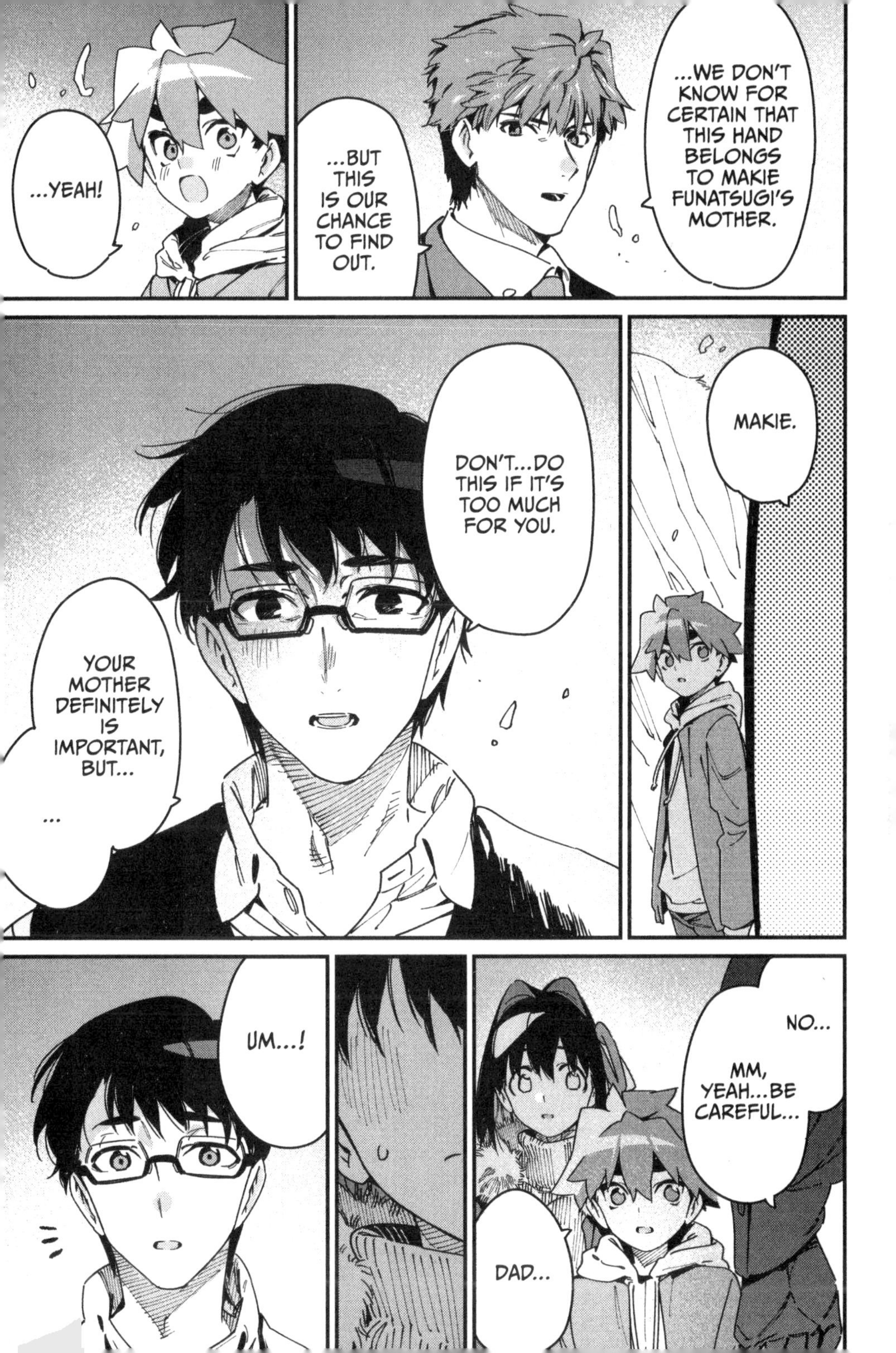
...WE DON'T KNOW FOR CERTAIN THAT THIS HAND BELONGS TO MAKIE FUNATSUGI'S MOTHER.
...BUT THIS IS OUR CHANCE TO FIND OUT.
...YEAH!
MAKIE.
DON'T...DO THIS IF IT'S TOO MUCH FOR YOU.
YOUR MOTHER DEFINITELY IS IMPORTANT, BUT...
...
NO...
MM, YEAH...BE CAREFUL...
DAD...
UM...!

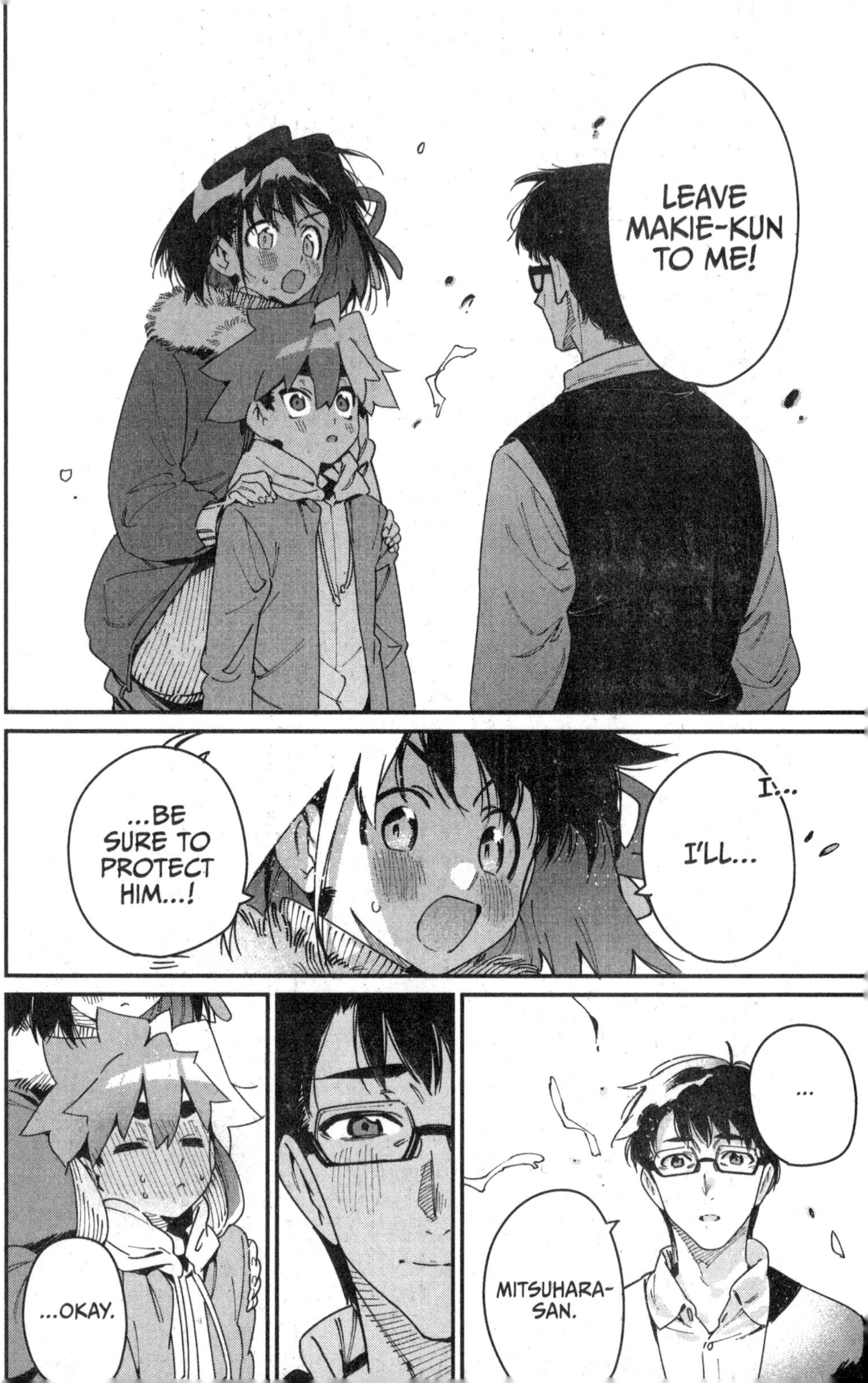
LEAVE MAKIE-KUN TO ME!
I... I'LL...
...BE SURE TO PROTECT HIM...!
...
MITSUHARA-SAN.
...OKAY.

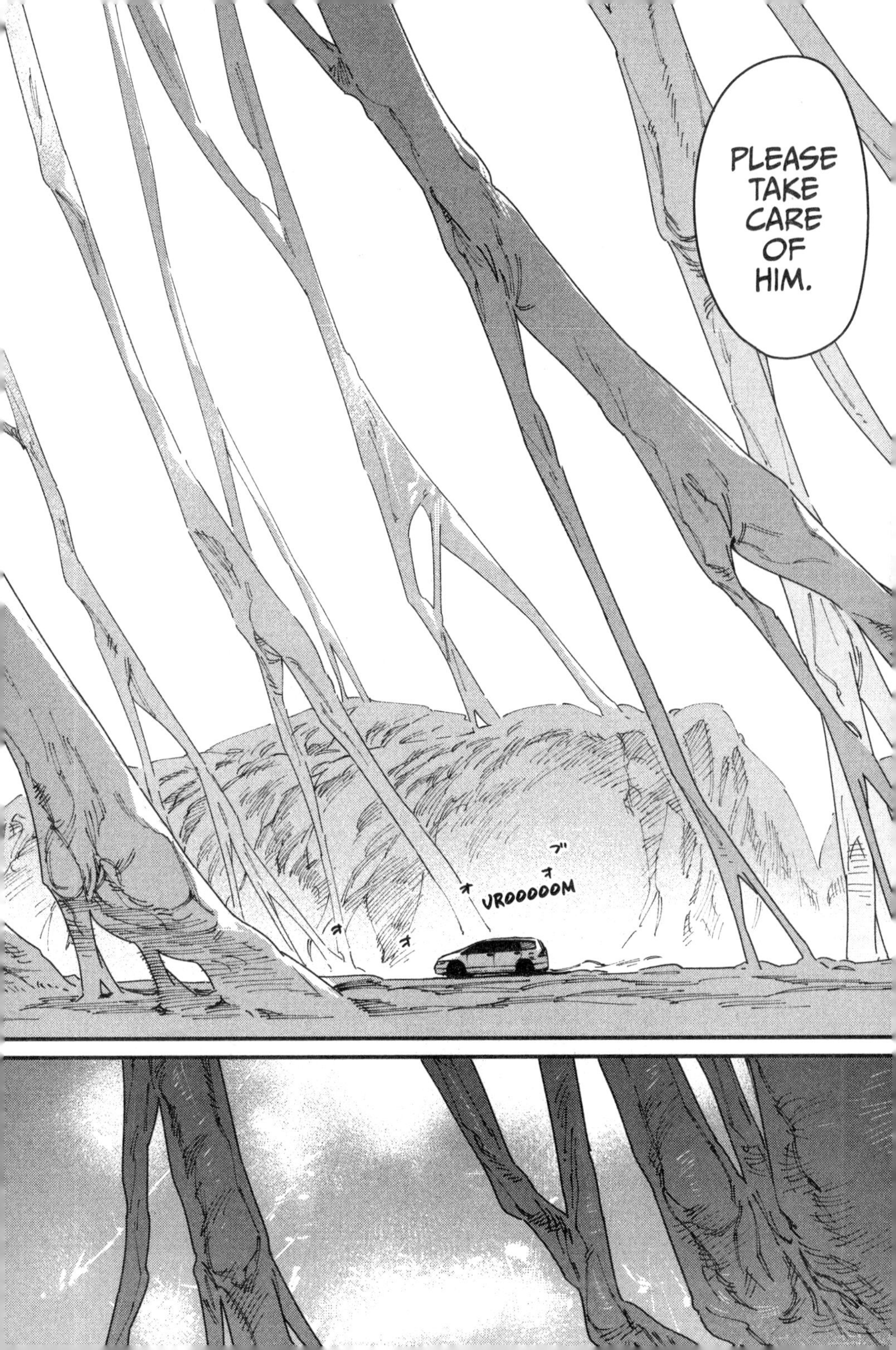
PLEASE TAKE CARE OF HIM.
VROOOOOM

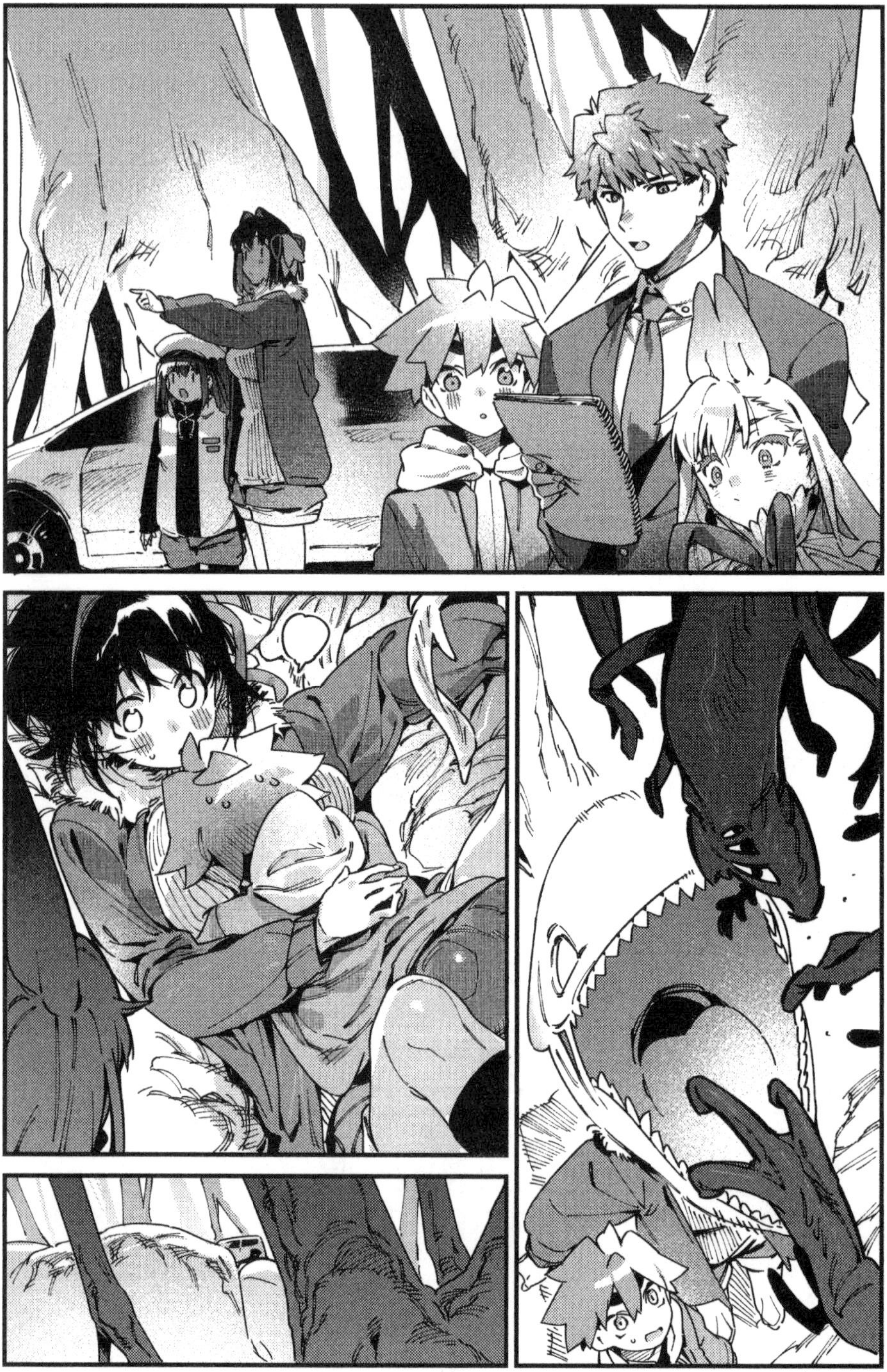

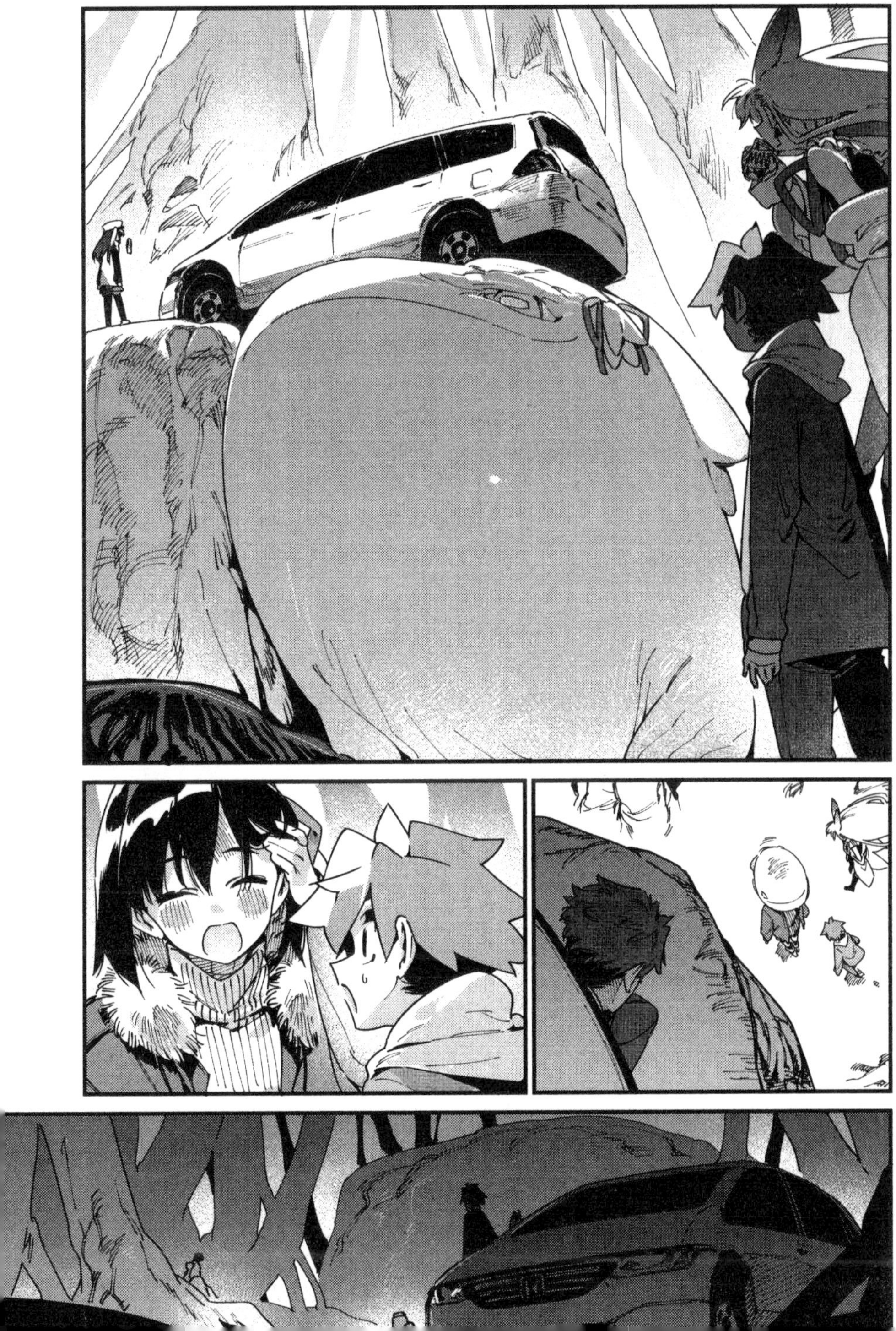

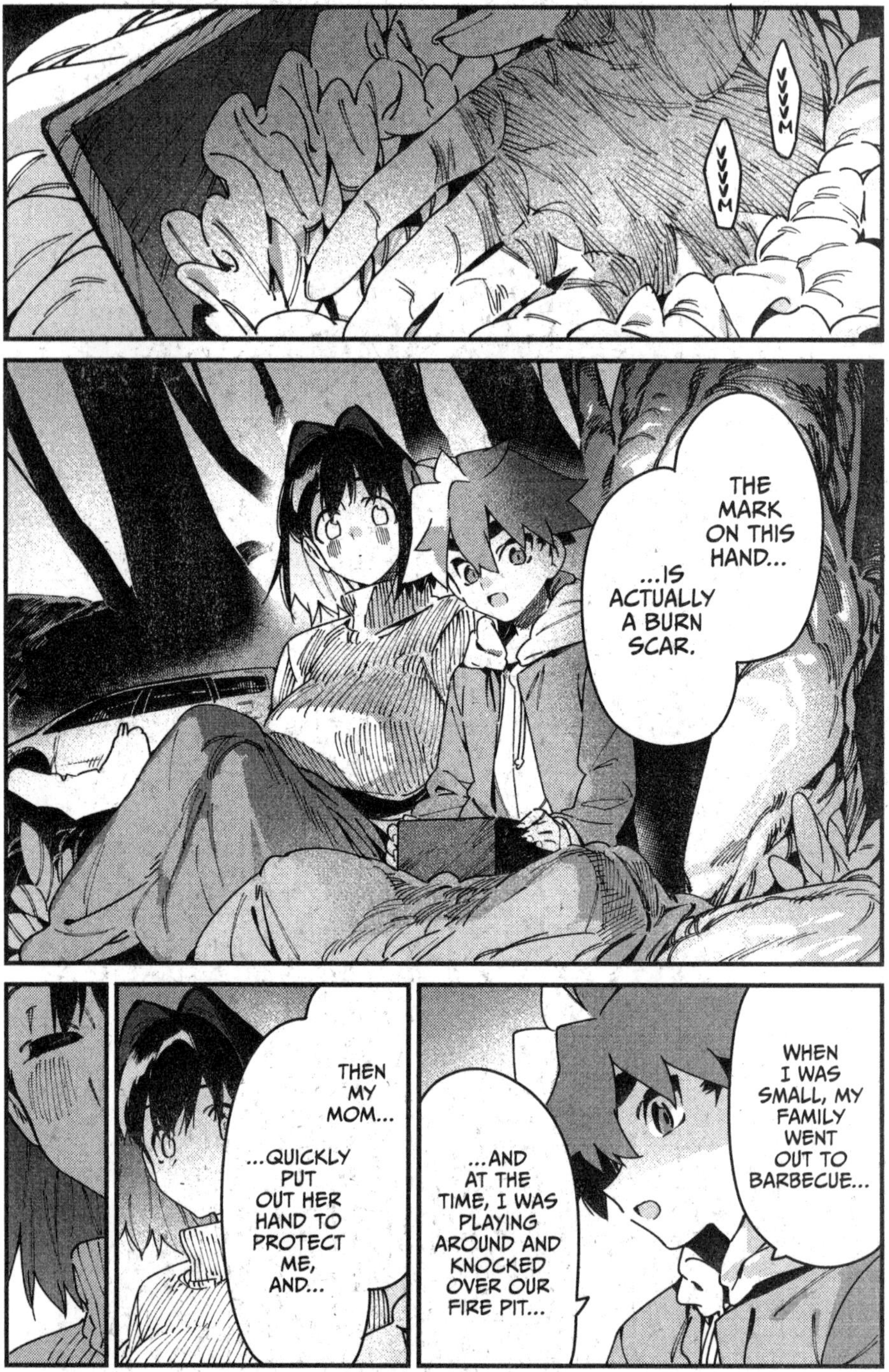
VVVVM
VVVVM
THE MARK ON THIS HAND...
...IS ACTUALLY A BURN SCAR.
WHEN I WAS SMALL, MY FAMILY WENT OUT TO BARBECUE...
...AND AT THE TIME, I WAS PLAYING AROUND AND KNOCKED OVER OUR FIRE PIT...
THEN MY MOM...
...QUICKLY PUT OUT HER HAND TO PROTECT ME, AND...

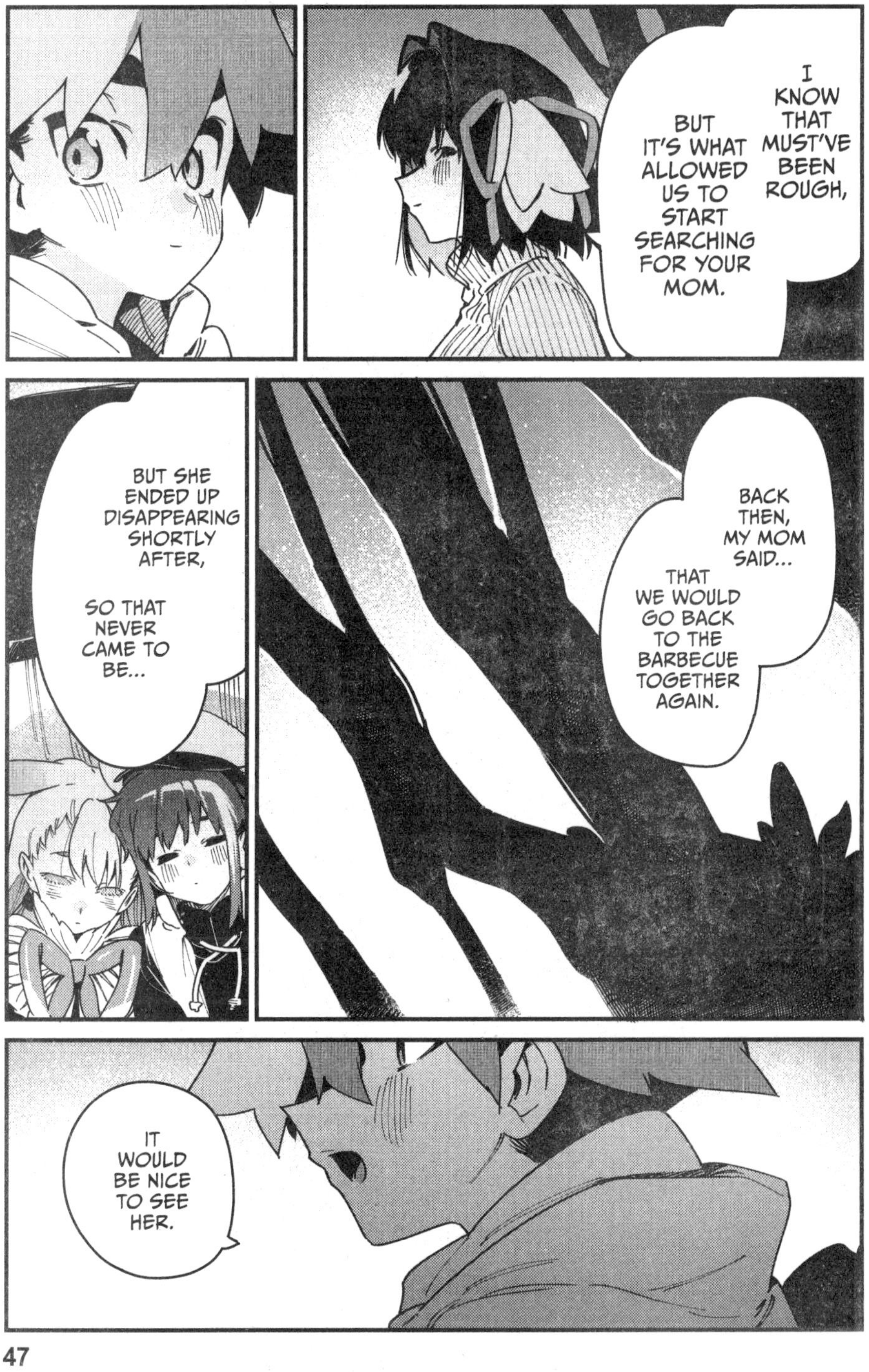
I KNOW THAT MUST'VE BEEN ROUGH,
BUT IT'S WHAT ALLOWED US TO START SEARCHING FOR YOUR MOM.
BACK THEN, MY MOM SAID...
THAT WE WOULD GO BACK TO THE BARBECUE TOGETHER AGAIN.
BUT SHE ENDED UP DISAPPEARING SHORTLY AFTER,
SO THAT NEVER CAME TO BE...
IT WOULD BE NICE TO SEE HER.

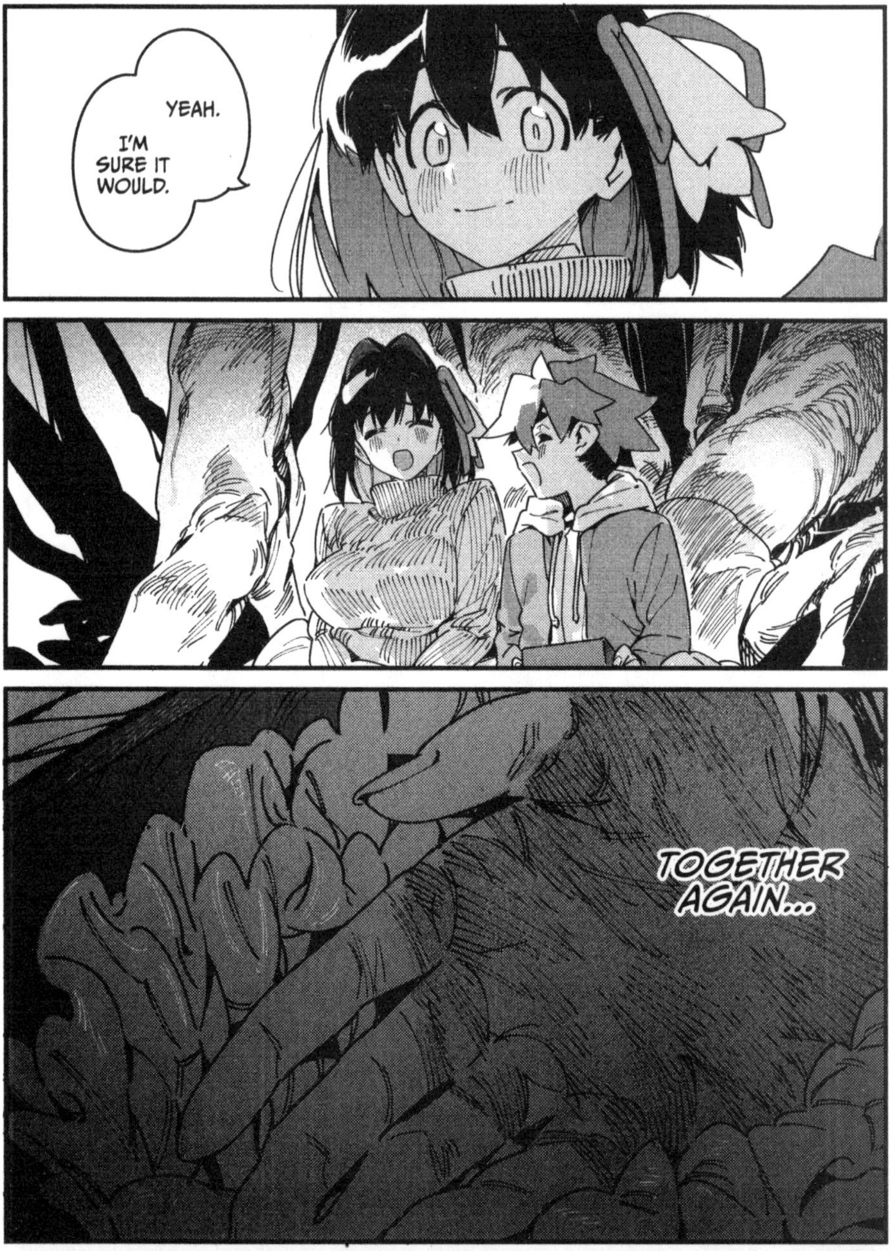
YEAH. I'M SURE IT WOULD.
TOGETHER AGAIN...

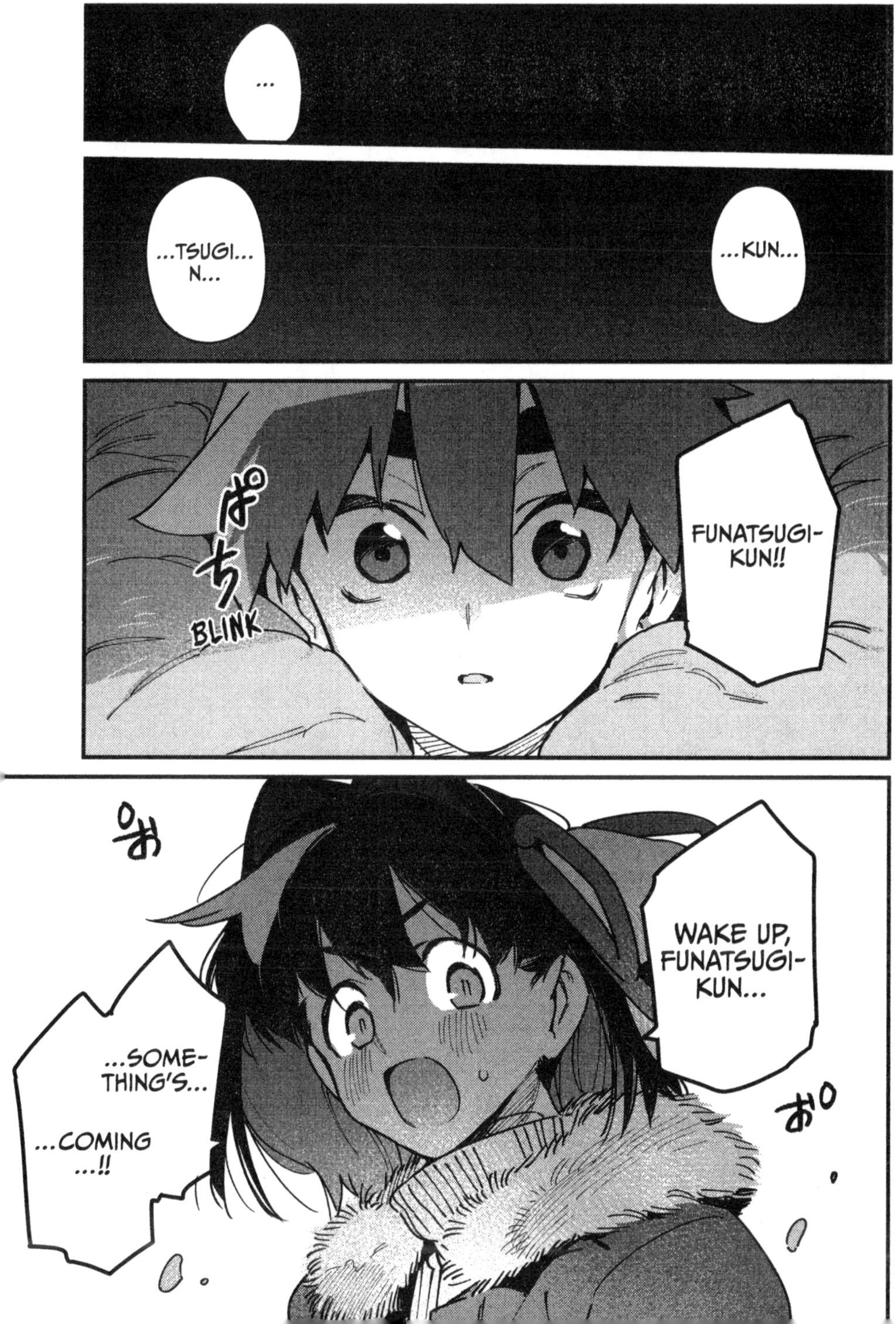
...
...KUN...
...TSUGI... N...
FUNATSUGI-KUN!!
ぱち
BLINK
WAKE UP, FUNATSUGI-KUN...
...SOME-THING'S...
...COMING ...!!

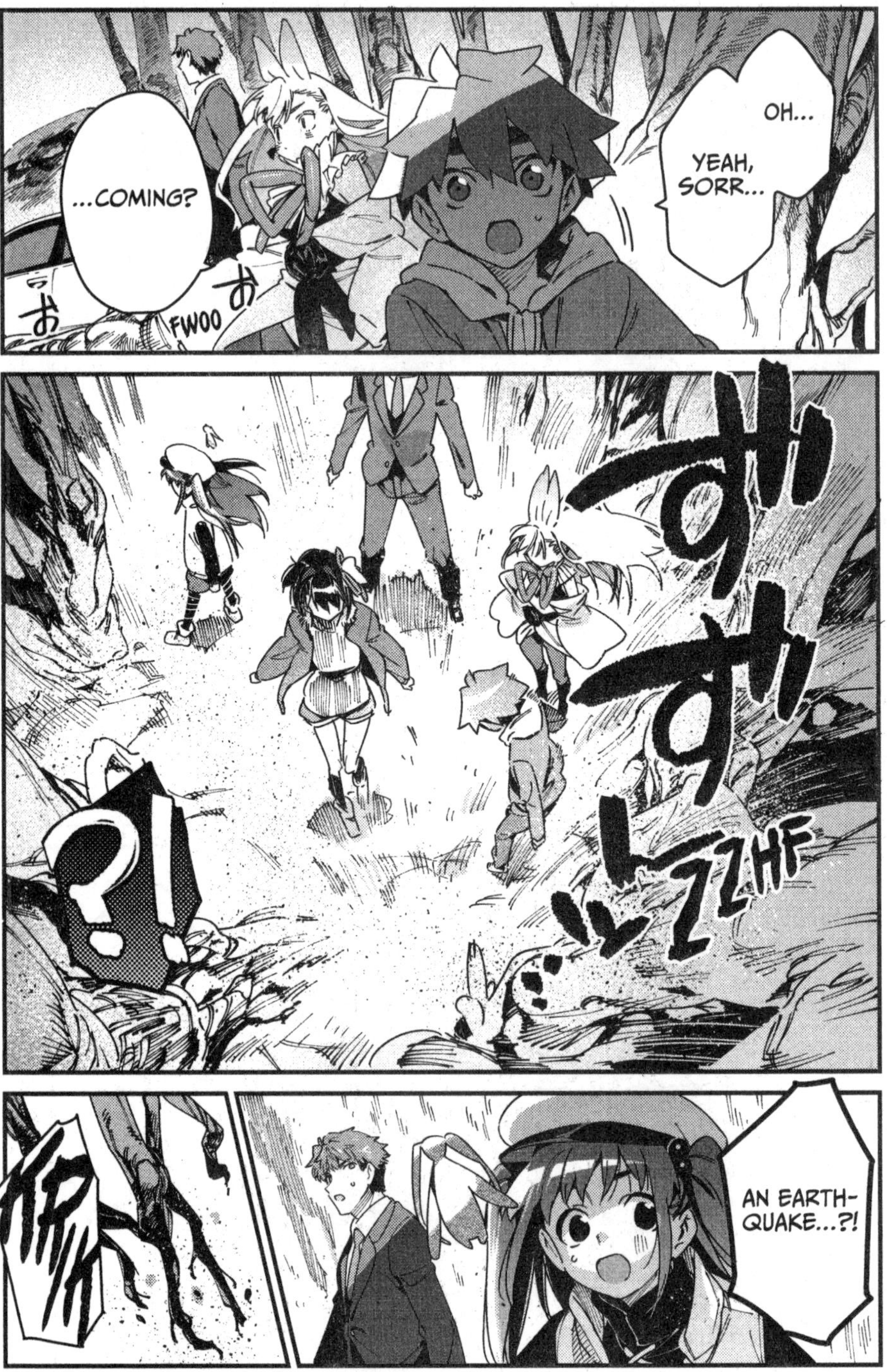
OH...
YEAH, SORR...
...COMING?
FWOO
ZZHF
?!
AN EARTH-QUAKE...?!
KRIK

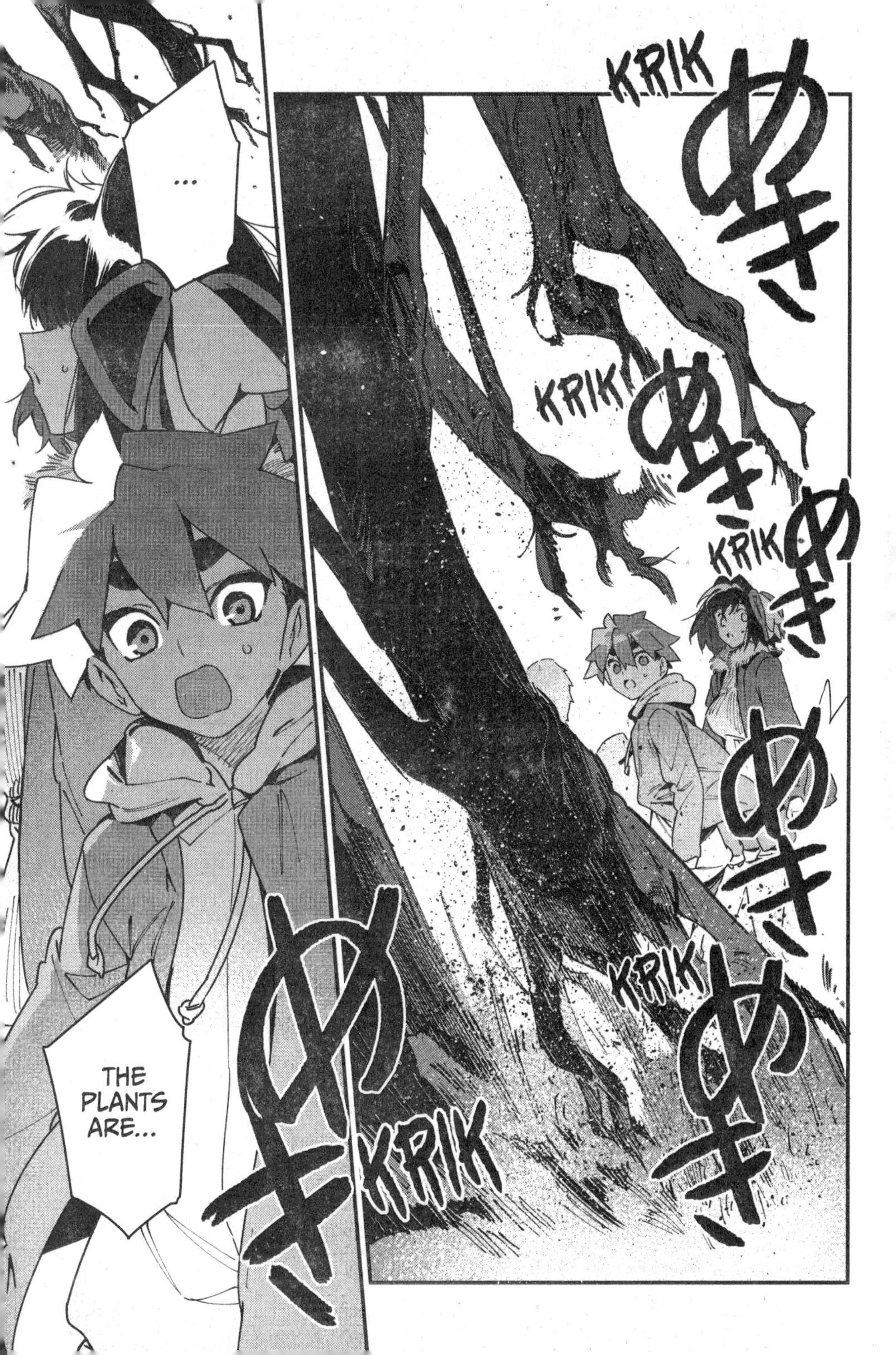

KRIK
めき
KRIK
めき
KRIK
めき
めき
KRIK
めき
KRIK
めき
...
THE PLANTS ARE...

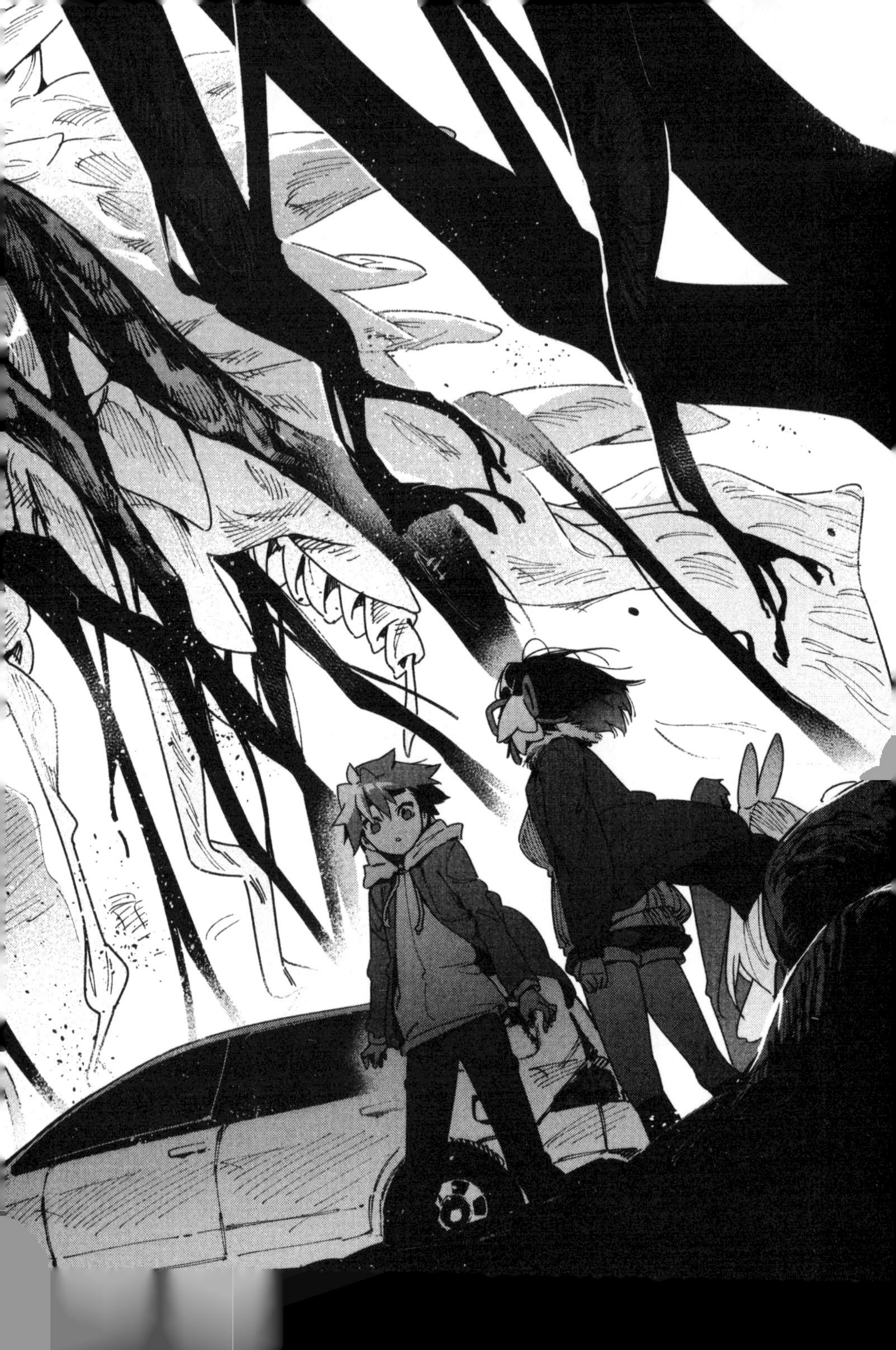

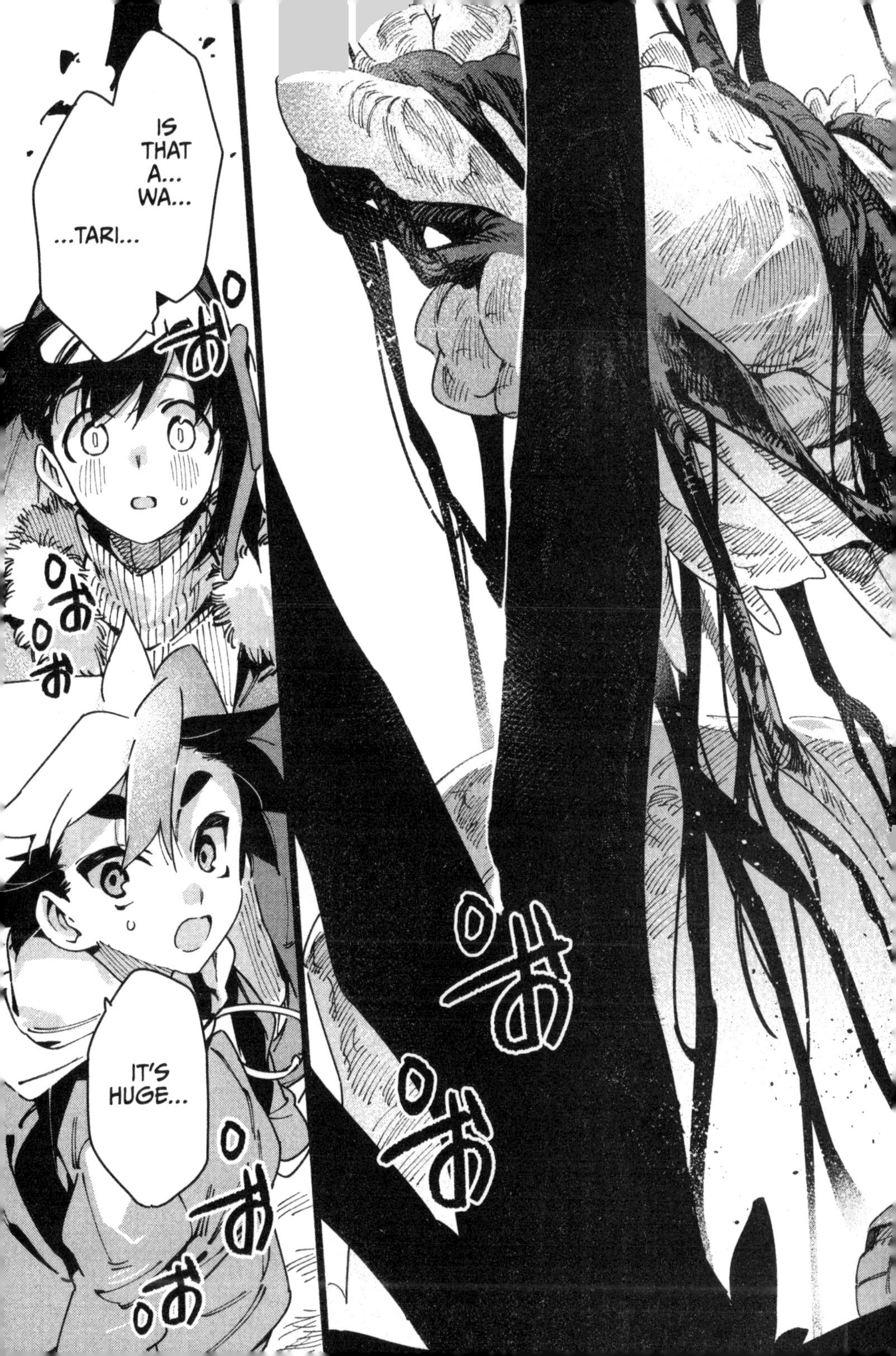

おお
おお
IS THAT A... WA...
...TARI...
お
おお
おお
IT'S HUGE...
おお
おお

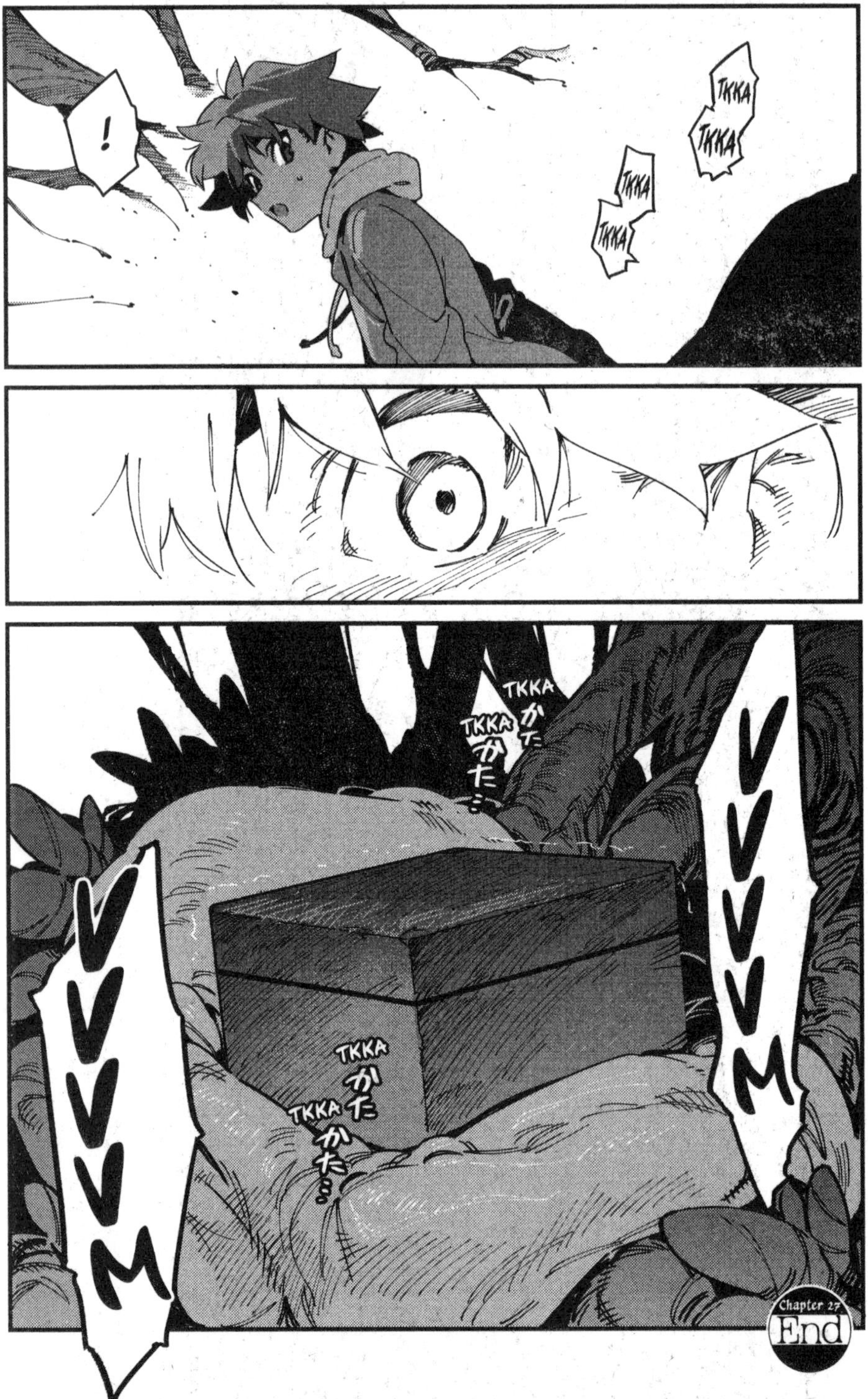
TKKA
TKKA
TKKA
TKKA
!
VVVVVM
TKKA かた
TKKA かた…
TKKA かた
TKKA かた…
VVVVVM
Chapter 27 End

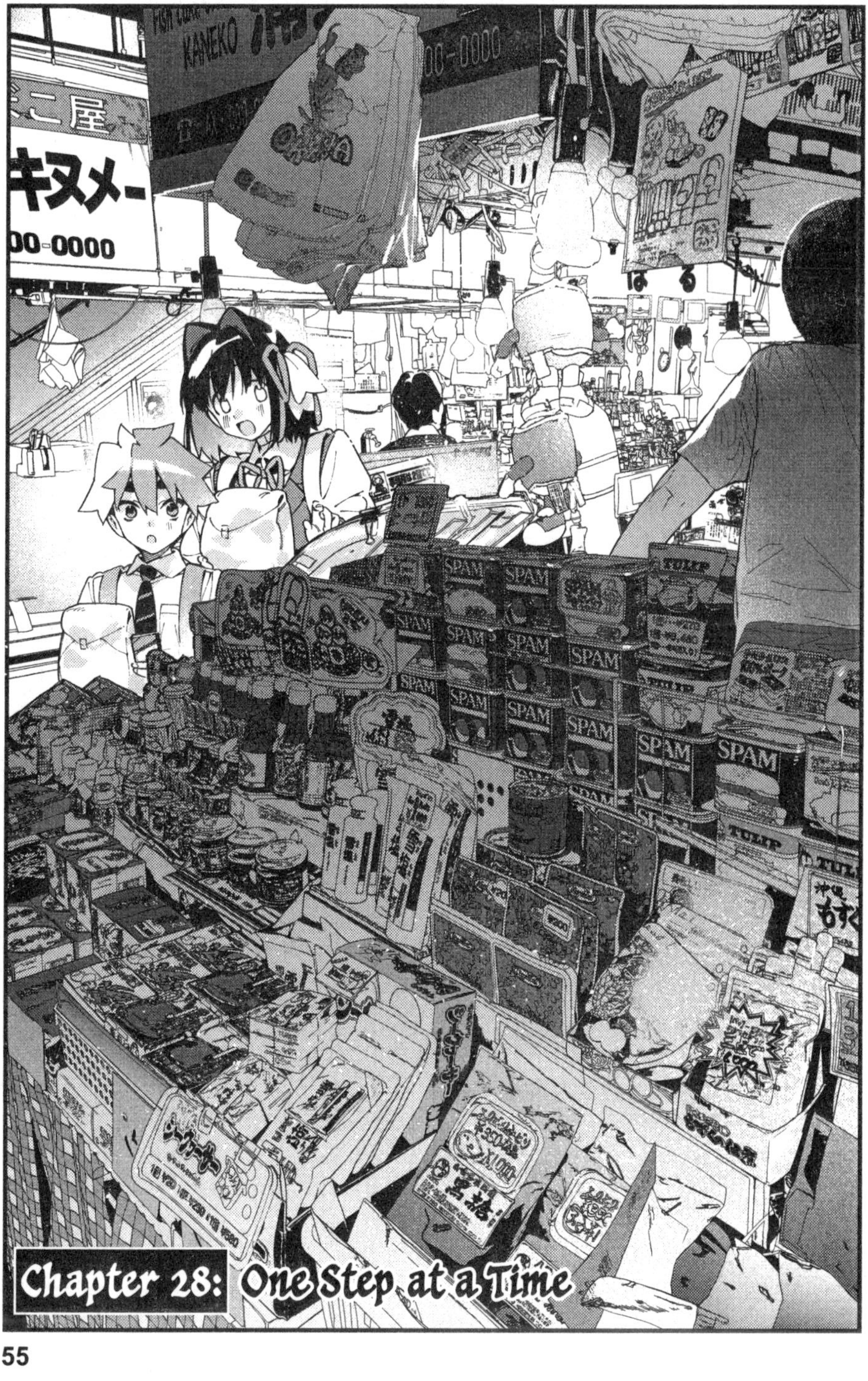
KANEKO
キヌメー
00-0000
はる
SPAM
TULIP
Chapter 28: One Step at a Time

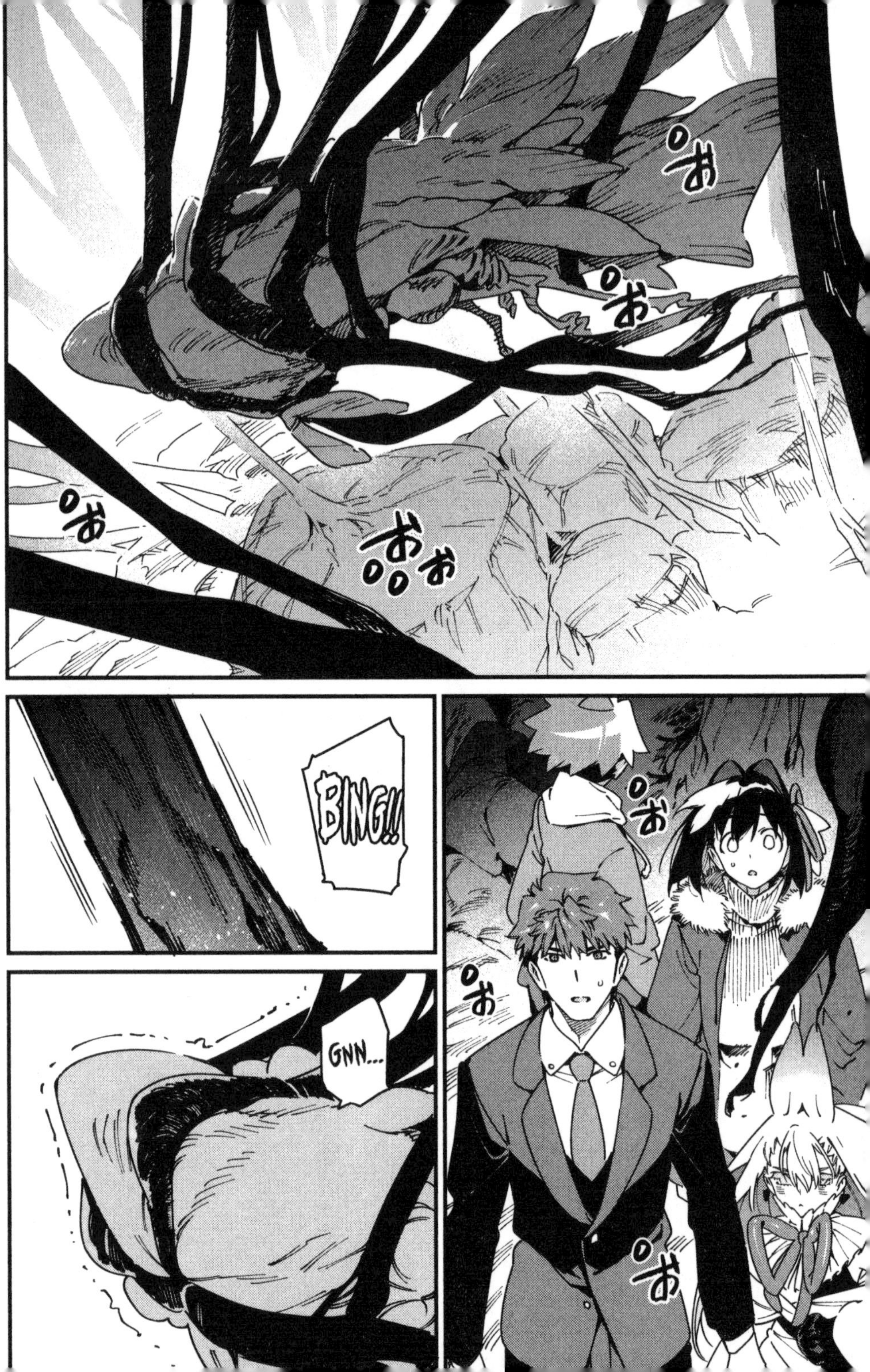
ぉお
ぉお
おぉぉお
ぉお
ぉお
ぉお
ぉお
BING!!
GNN...

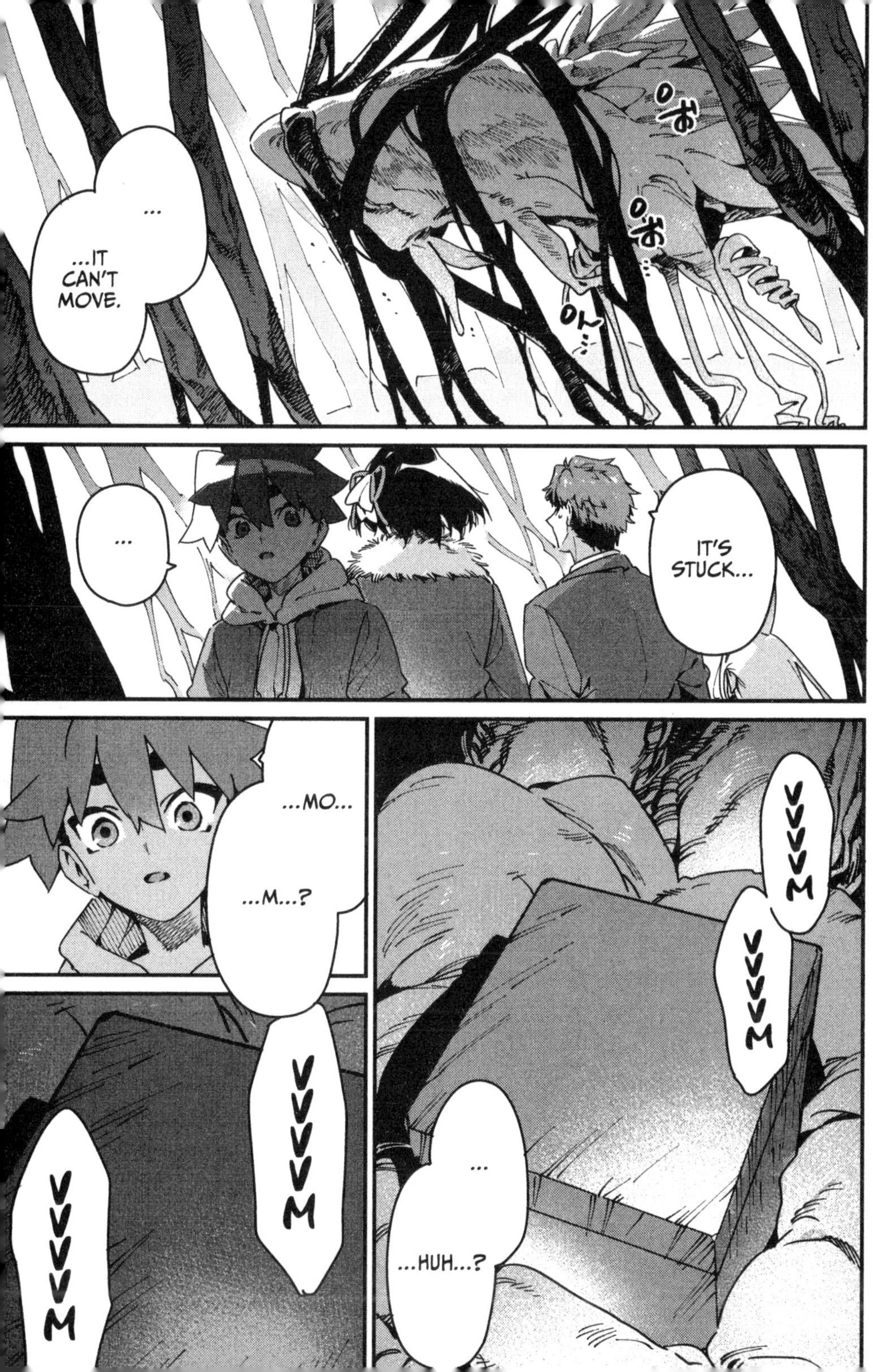
...
...IT CAN'T MOVE.
IT'S STUCK...
...
VVVVM
VVVVM
...
...HUH...?
...MO...
...M...?
VVVVM
VVVVM

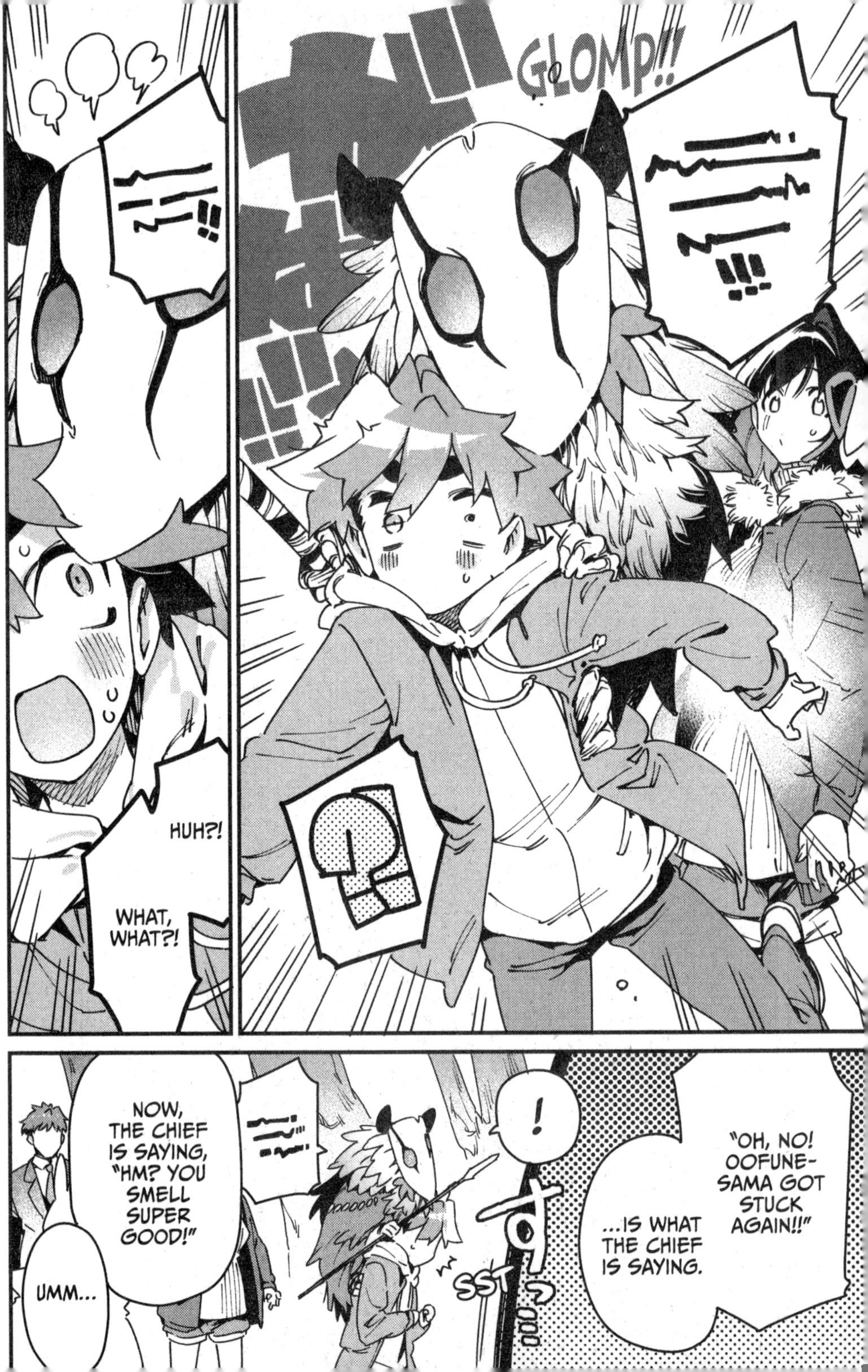
GLOMP!!
?!
HUH?!
WHAT, WHAT?!
"OH, NO! OOFUNE-SAMA GOT STUCK AGAIN!!"
...IS WHAT THE CHIEF IS SAYING.
SST
!
NOW, THE CHIEF IS SAYING, "HM? YOU SMELL SUPER GOOD!"
UMM...

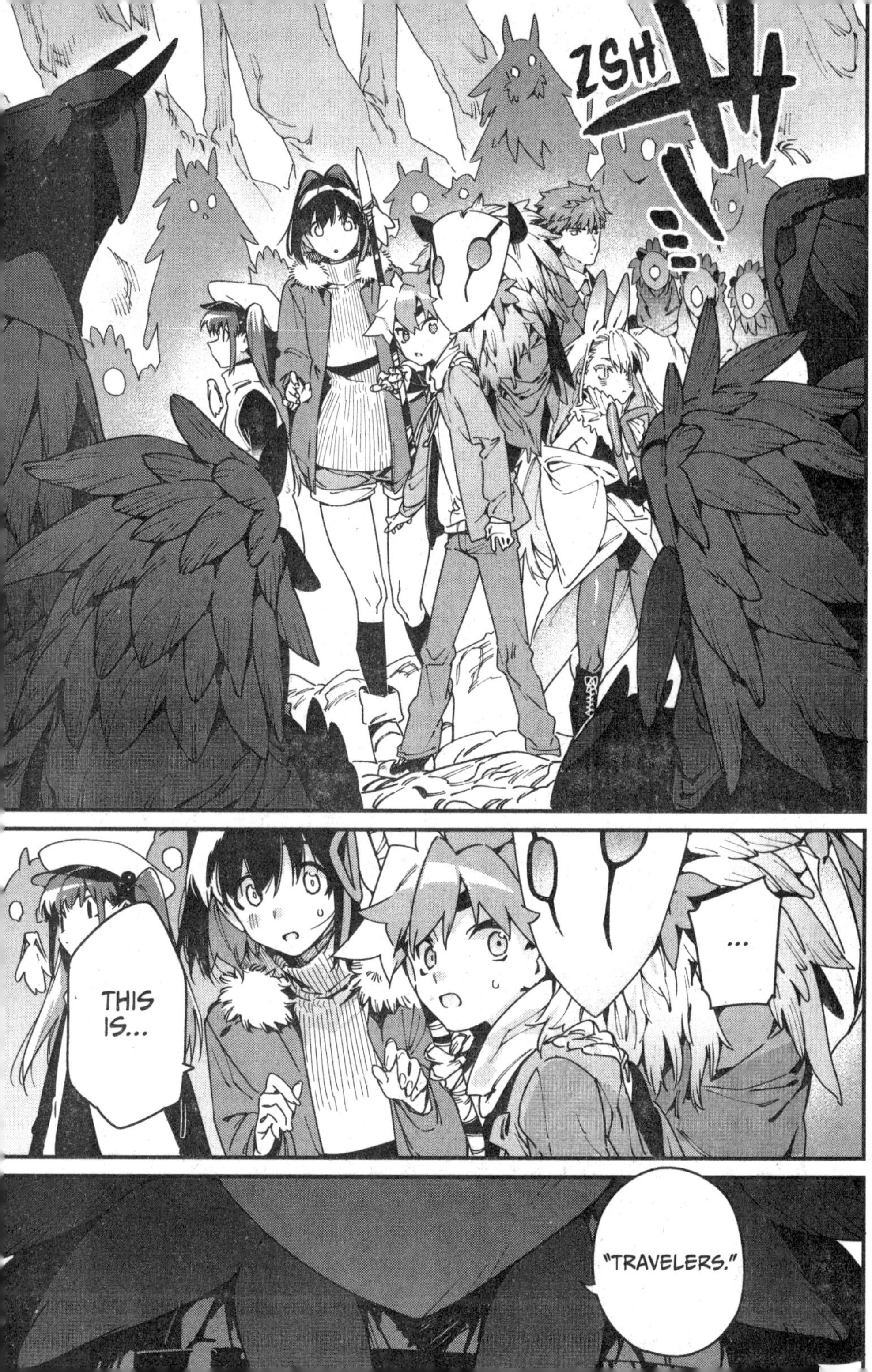
ZSH
...
THIS IS...
"TRAVELERS."

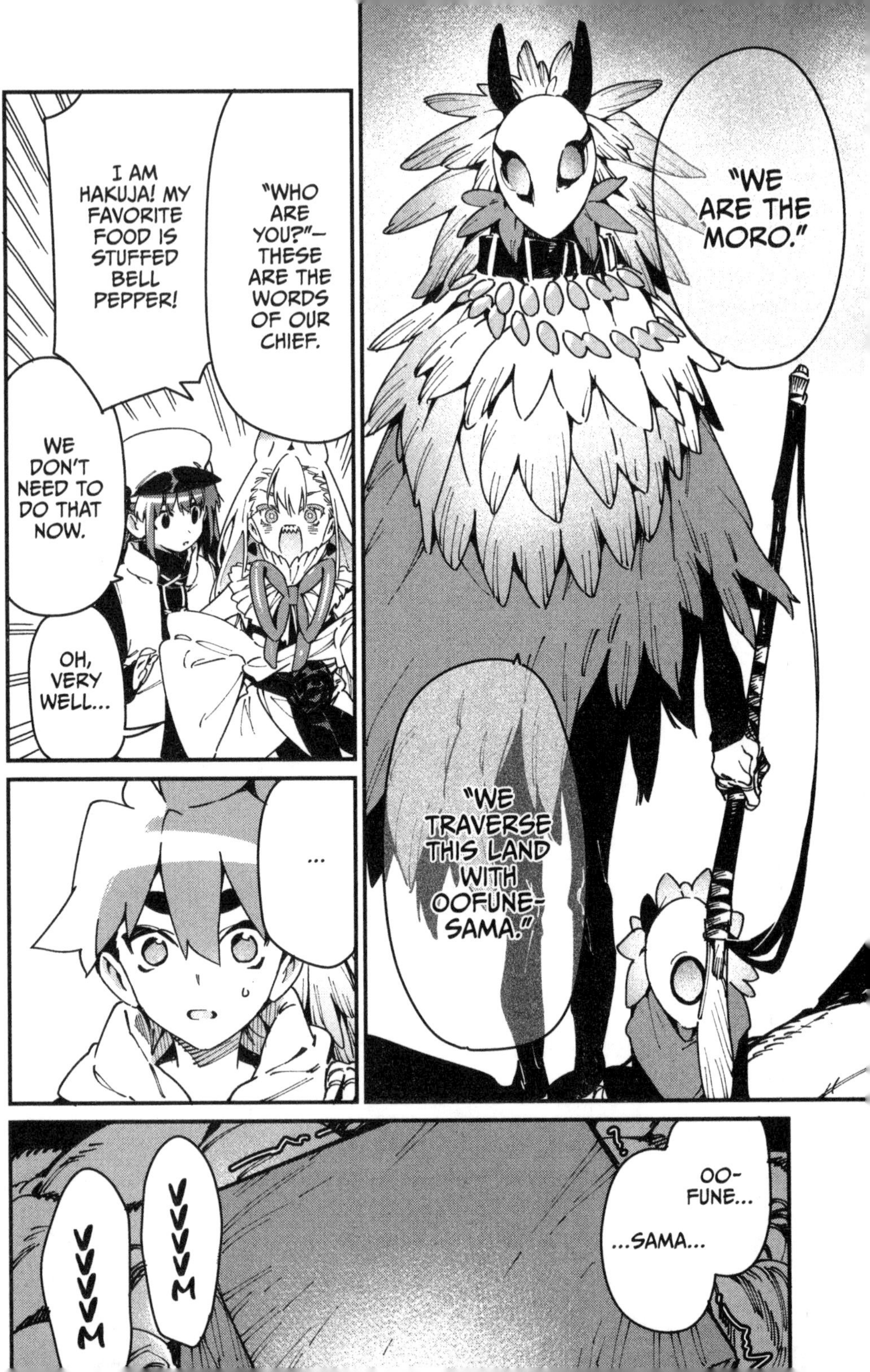
"WE ARE THE MORO."
"WE TRAVERSE THIS LAND WITH OOFUNE-SAMA."
"WHO ARE YOU?"—THESE ARE THE WORDS OF OUR CHIEF.
I AM HAKUJA! MY FAVORITE FOOD IS STUFFED BELL PEPPER!
WE DON'T NEED TO DO THAT NOW.
OH, VERY WELL...
...
OO-FUNE...
...SAMA...
VVVVM
VVVVVM

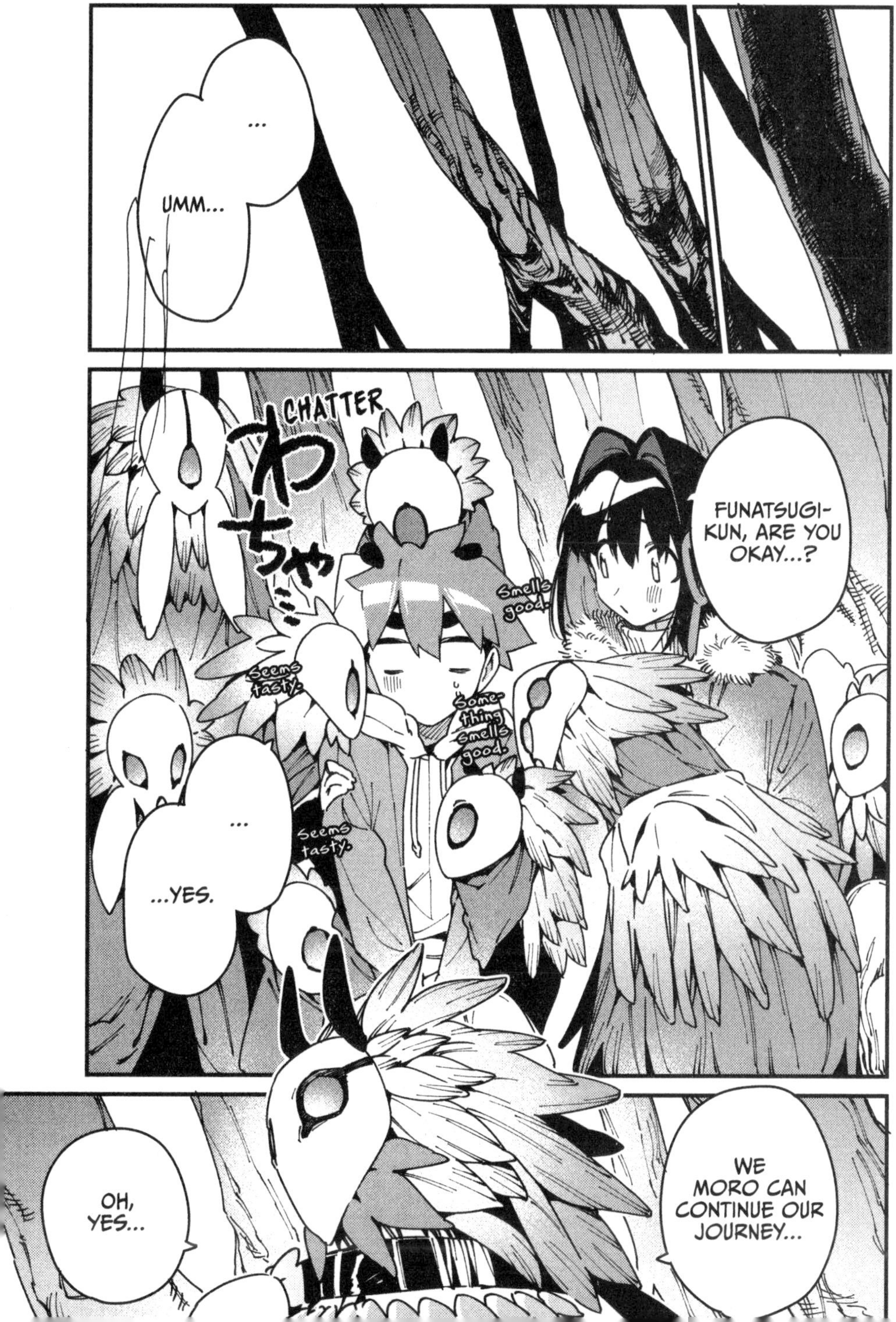
...
UMM...
FUNATSUGI-KUN, ARE YOU OKAY...?
CHATTER
わちゃ
Smells good.
Something smells good.
Seems tasty.
Seems tasty.
...
...YES.
WE MORO CAN CONTINUE OUR JOURNEY...
OH, YES...

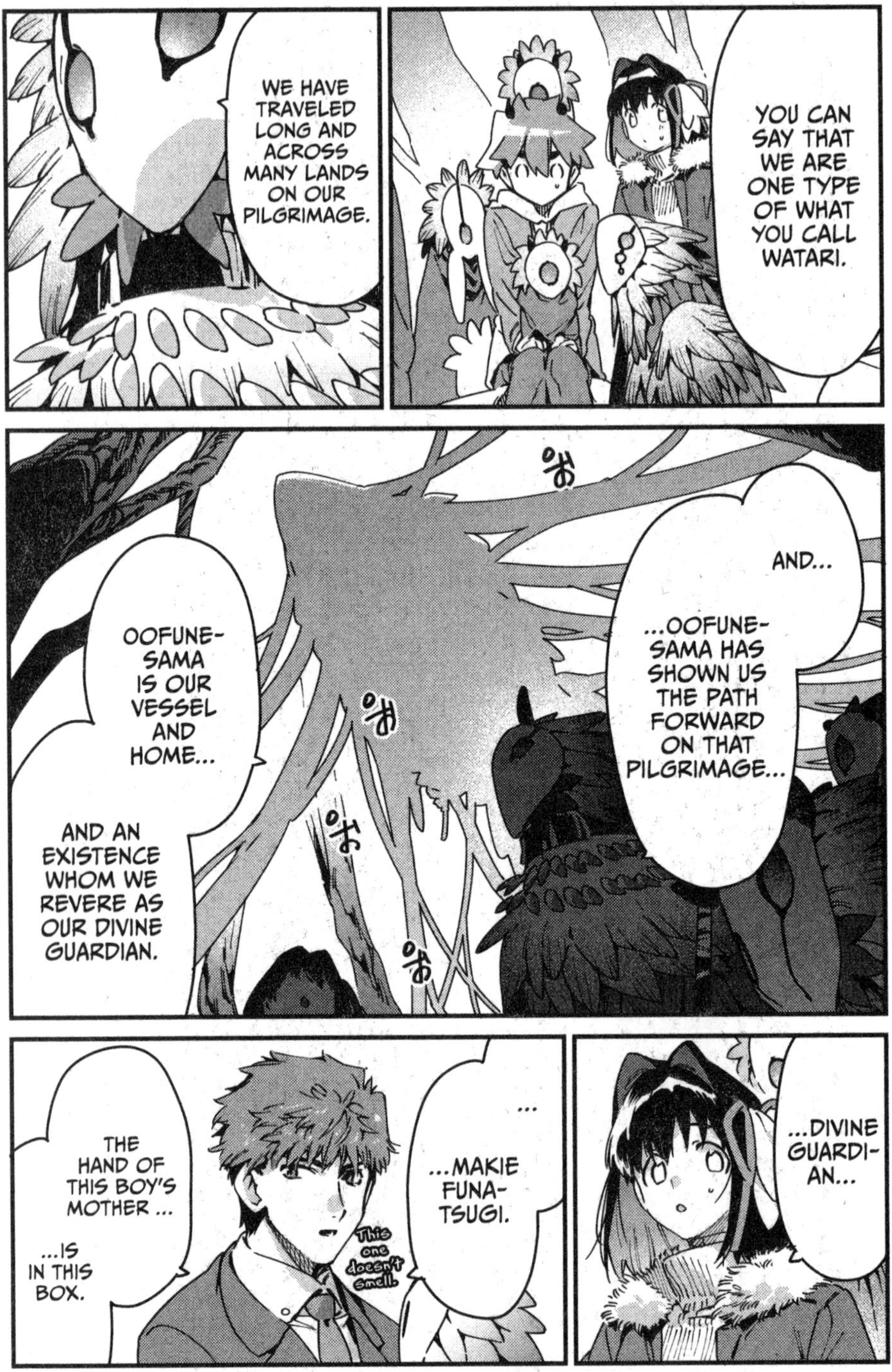
YOU CAN SAY THAT WE ARE ONE TYPE OF WHAT YOU CALL WATARI.
WE HAVE TRAVELED LONG AND ACROSS MANY LANDS ON OUR PILGRIMAGE.
AND...
...OOFUNE-SAMA HAS SHOWN US THE PATH FORWARD ON THAT PILGRIMAGE...
OOFUNE-SAMA IS OUR VESSEL AND HOME...
AND AN EXISTENCE WHOM WE REVERE AS OUR DIVINE GUARDIAN.
...DIVINE GUARDI-AN...
...
...MAKIE FUNA-TSUGI.
This one doesn't smell.
THE HAND OF THIS BOY'S MOTHER ...
...IS IN THIS BOX.

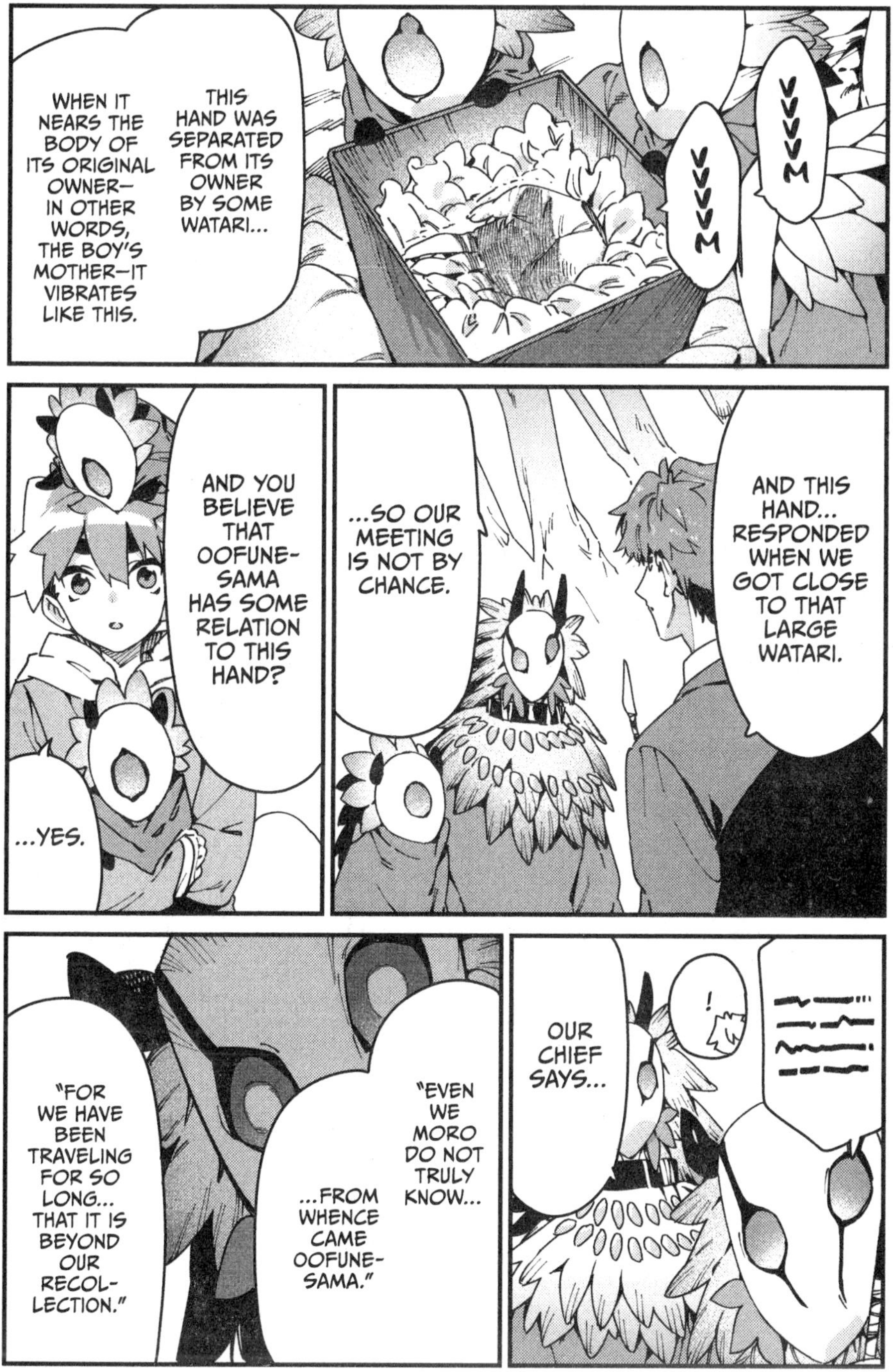
VVVVM
VVVVM
THIS HAND WAS SEPARATED FROM ITS OWNER BY SOME WATARI...
WHEN IT NEARS THE BODY OF ITS ORIGINAL OWNER—IN OTHER WORDS, THE BOY'S MOTHER—IT VIBRATES LIKE THIS.
AND THIS HAND... RESPONDED WHEN WE GOT CLOSE TO THAT LARGE WATARI.
...SO OUR MEETING IS NOT BY CHANCE.
AND YOU BELIEVE THAT OOFUNE-SAMA HAS SOME RELATION TO THIS HAND?
...YES.
!
OUR CHIEF SAYS...
"EVEN WE MORO DO NOT TRULY KNOW...
...FROM WHENCE CAME OOFUNE-SAMA."
"FOR WE HAVE BEEN TRAVELING FOR SO LONG... THAT IT IS BEYOND OUR RECOL-LECTION."

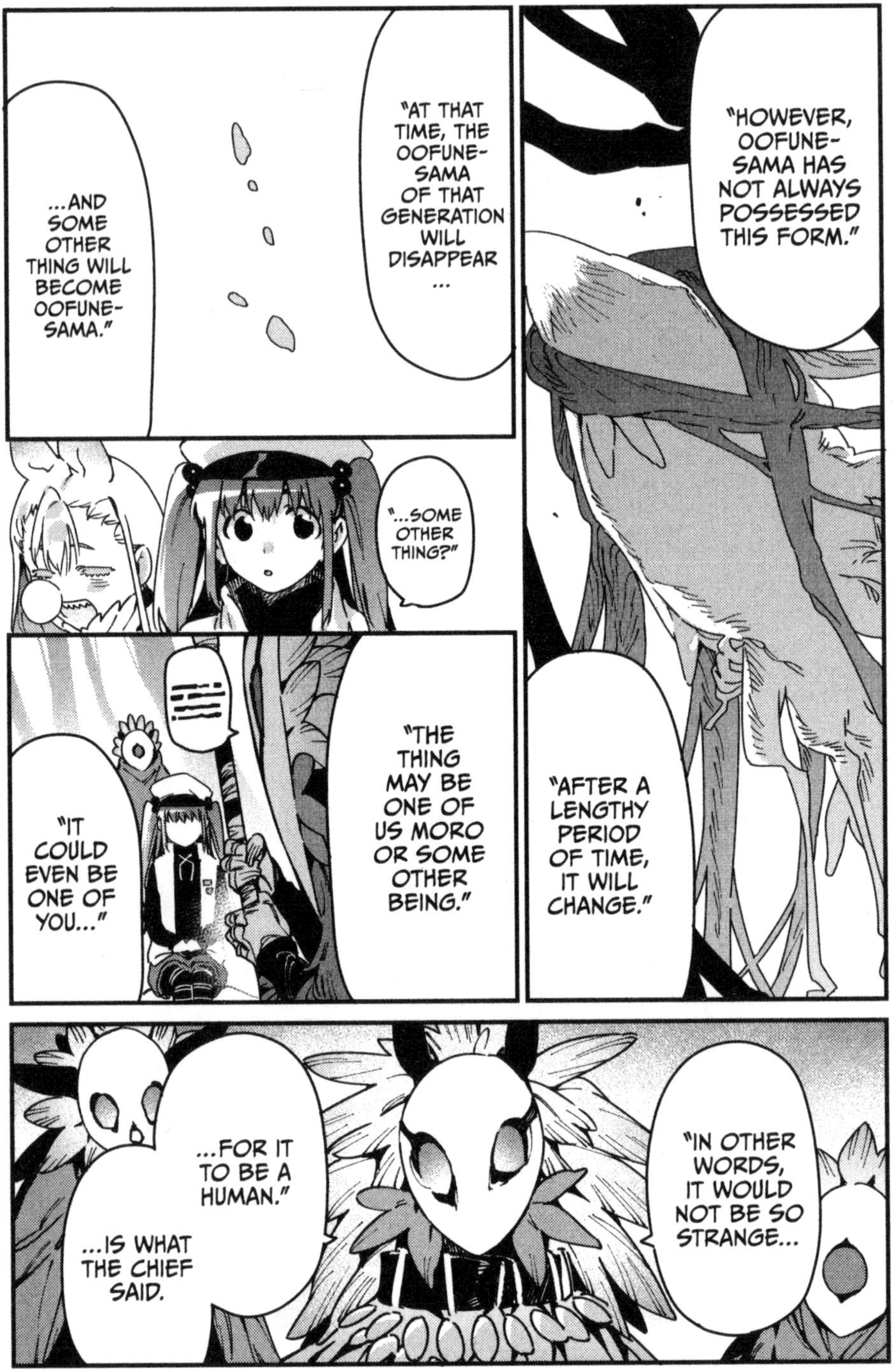
"HOWEVER, OOFUNE-SAMA HAS NOT ALWAYS POSSESSED THIS FORM."
"AFTER A LENGTHY PERIOD OF TIME, IT WILL CHANGE."
"AT THAT TIME, THE OOFUNE-SAMA OF THAT GENERATION WILL DISAPPEAR ...
...AND SOME OTHER THING WILL BECOME OOFUNE-SAMA."
"...SOME OTHER THING?"
"THE THING MAY BE ONE OF US MORO OR SOME OTHER BEING."
"IT COULD EVEN BE ONE OF YOU..."
"IN OTHER WORDS, IT WOULD NOT BE SO STRANGE...
...FOR IT TO BE A HUMAN."
...IS WHAT THE CHIEF SAID.

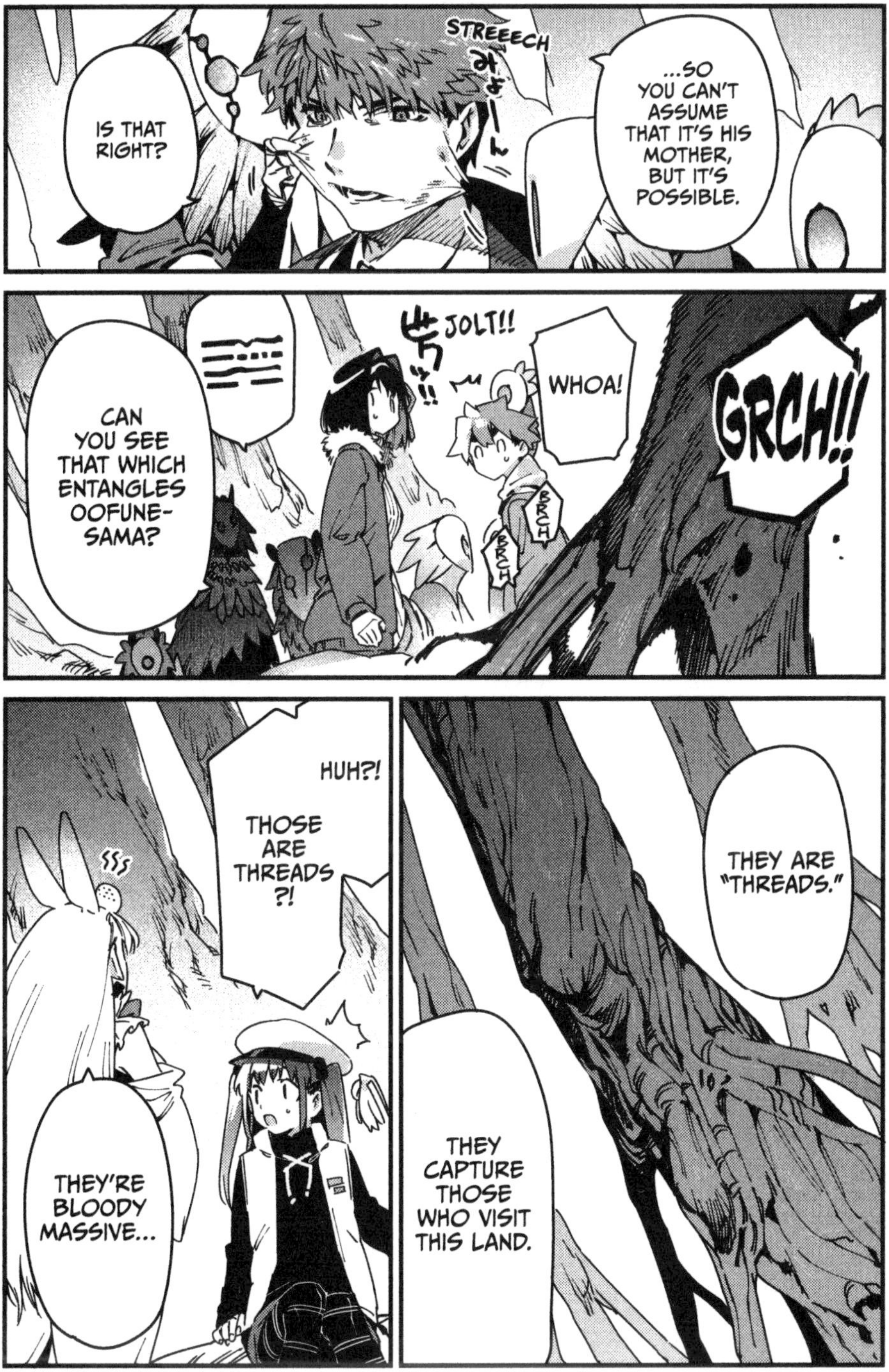

...SO YOU CAN'T ASSUME THAT IT'S HIS MOTHER, BUT IT'S POSSIBLE.
STREEECH
IS THAT RIGHT?
GRCH!!
WHOA!
JOLT!!
CAN YOU SEE THAT WHICH ENTANGLES OOFUNE-SAMA?
BRCH
BRCH
THEY ARE "THREADS."
THEY CAPTURE THOSE WHO VISIT THIS LAND.
HUH?!
THOSE ARE THREADS?!
THEY'RE BLOODY MASSIVE...

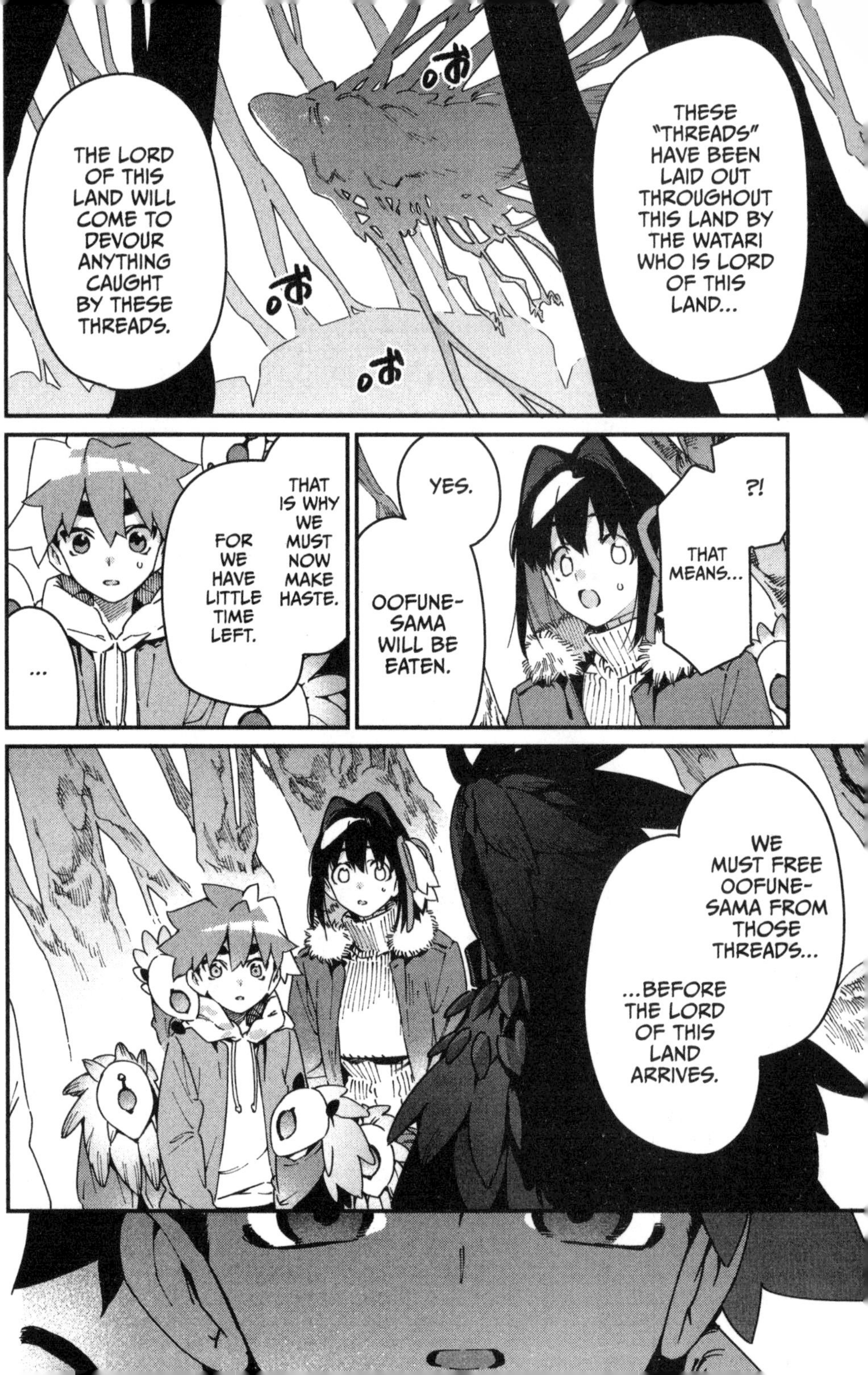
THESE "THREADS" HAVE BEEN LAID OUT THROUGHOUT THIS LAND BY THE WATARI WHO IS LORD OF THIS LAND...
THE LORD OF THIS LAND WILL COME TO DEVOUR ANYTHING CAUGHT BY THESE THREADS.
?!
THAT MEANS...
YES.
OOFUNE-SAMA WILL BE EATEN.
THAT IS WHY WE MUST NOW MAKE HASTE.
FOR WE HAVE LITTLE TIME LEFT.
...
WE MUST FREE OOFUNE-SAMA FROM THOSE THREADS...
...BEFORE THE LORD OF THIS LAND ARRIVES.

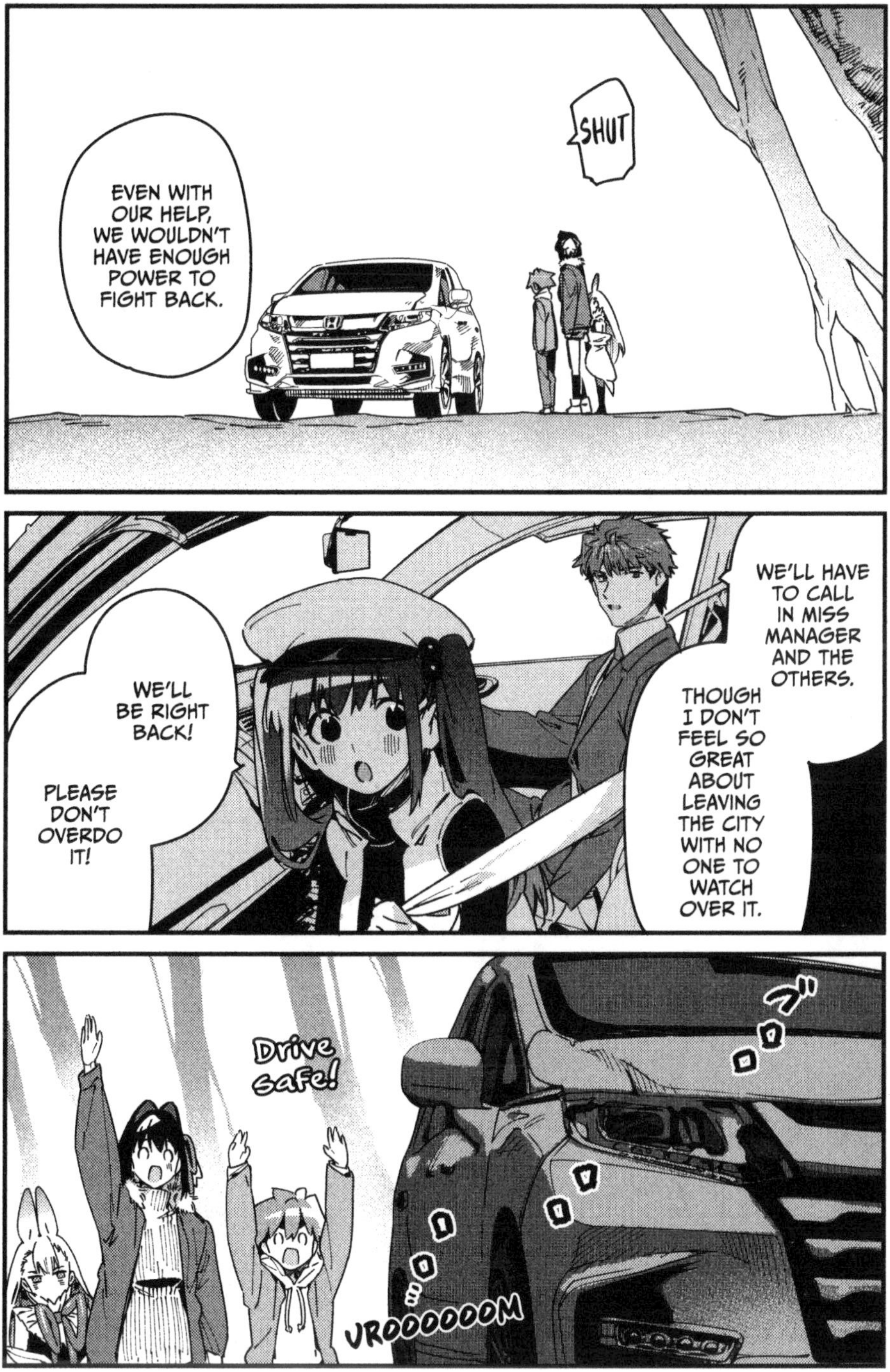
SHUT
EVEN WITH OUR HELP, WE WOULDN'T HAVE ENOUGH POWER TO FIGHT BACK.
WE'LL HAVE TO CALL IN MISS MANAGER AND THE OTHERS.
THOUGH I DON'T FEEL SO GREAT ABOUT LEAVING THE CITY WITH NO ONE TO WATCH OVER IT.
WE'LL BE RIGHT BACK!
PLEASE DON'T OVERDO IT!
VROOOOOOM
Drive safe!

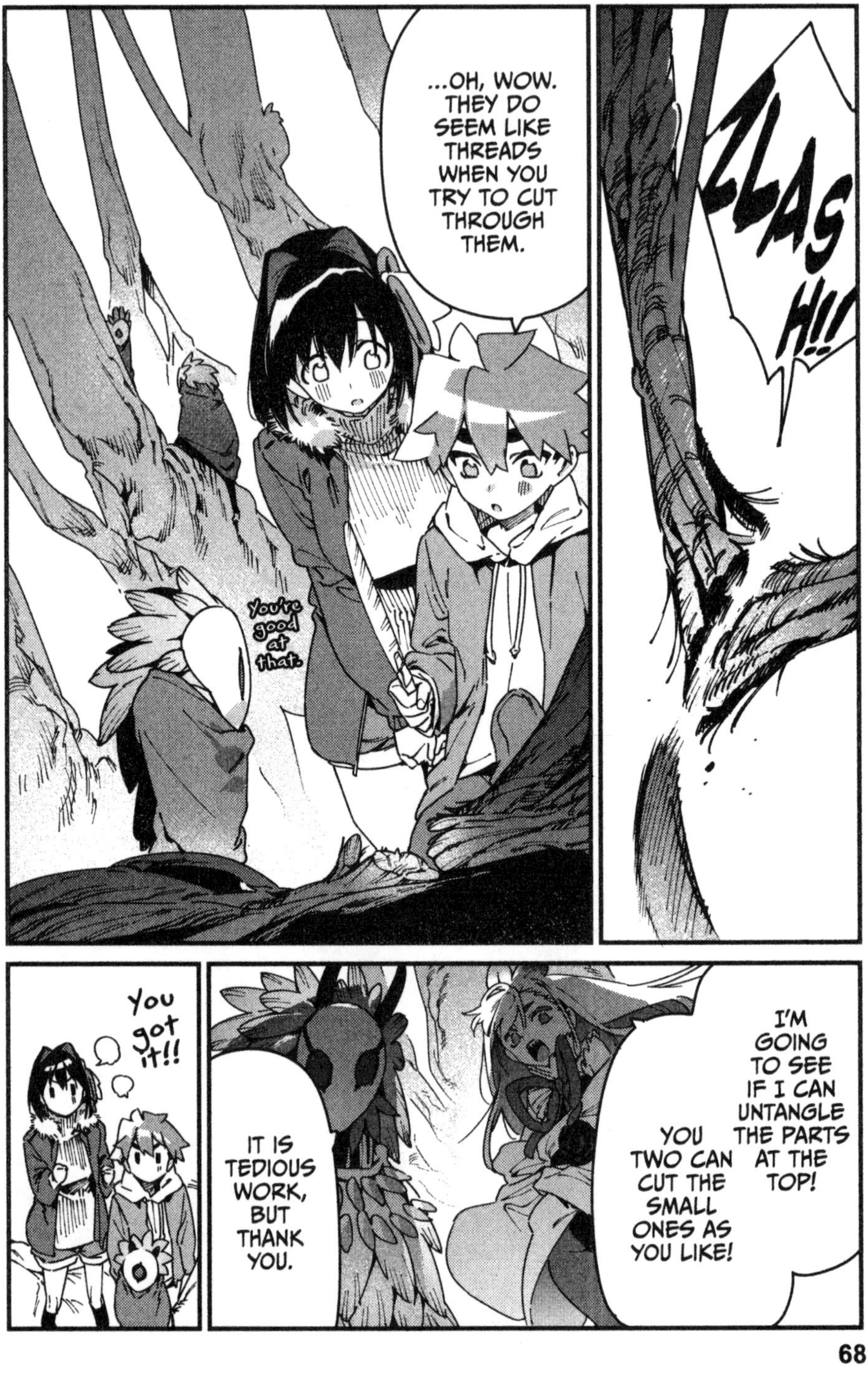
ZZLASH!!
...OH, WOW. THEY DO SEEM LIKE THREADS WHEN YOU TRY TO CUT THROUGH THEM.
You're good at that.
I'M GOING TO SEE IF I CAN UNTANGLE THE PARTS AT THE TOP!
YOU TWO CAN CUT THE SMALL ONES AS YOU LIKE!
IT IS TEDIOUS WORK, BUT THANK YOU.
You got it!!

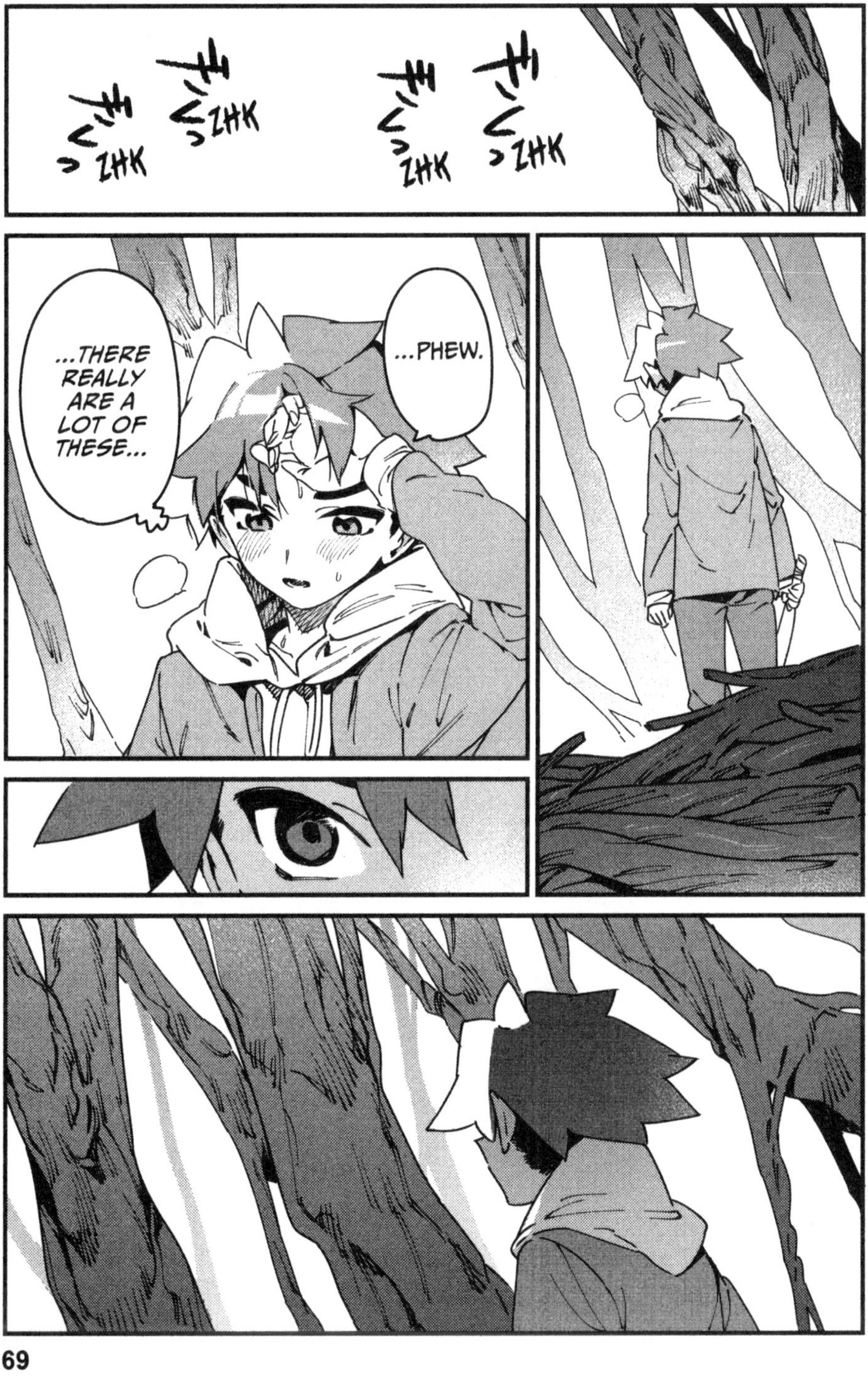
ZHK
ZHK
ZHK
ZHK
...PHEW.
...THERE REALLY ARE A LOT OF THESE...

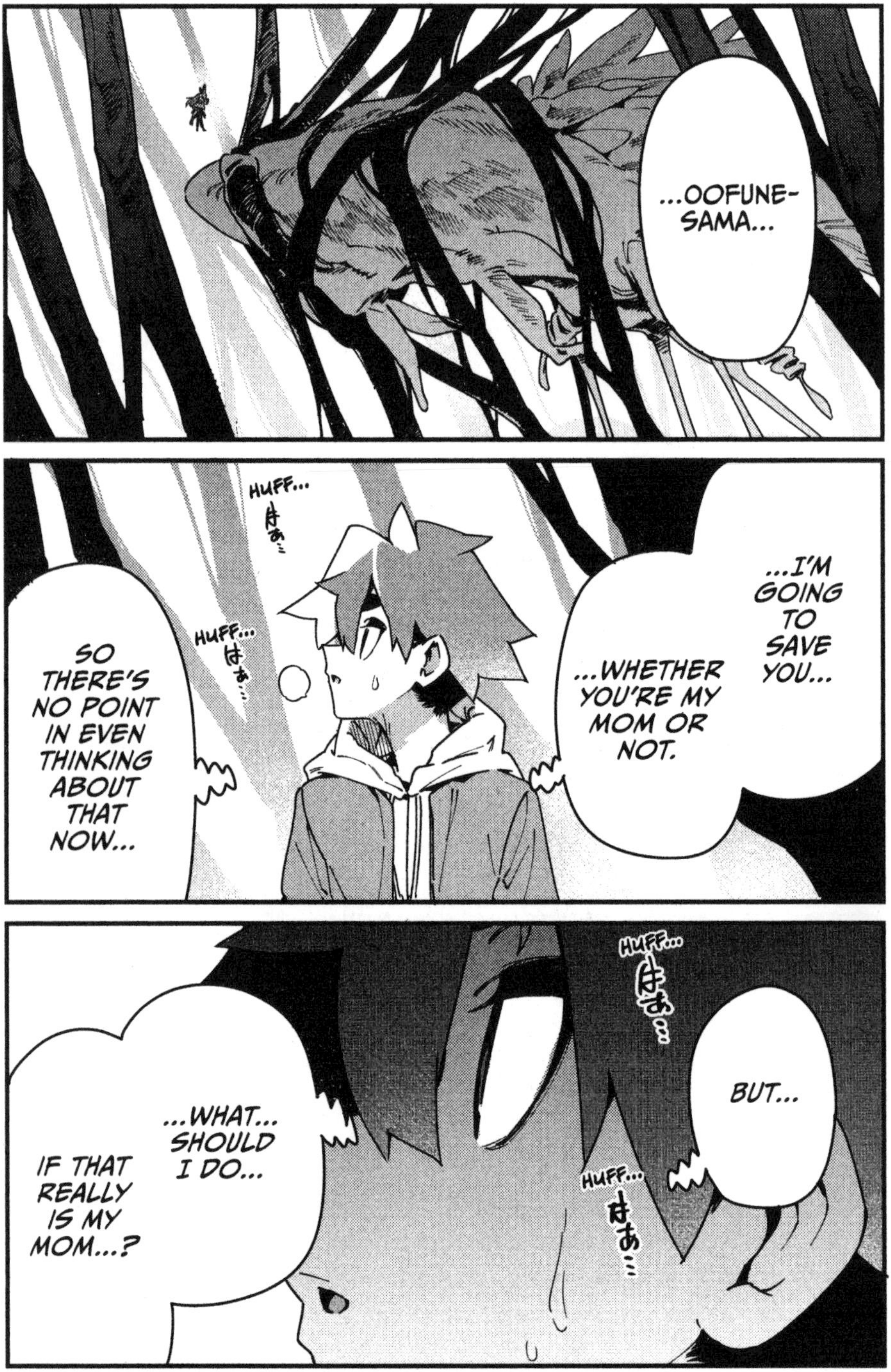
...OOFUNE-SAMA...
...I'M GOING TO SAVE YOU...
...WHETHER YOU'RE MY MOM OR NOT.
HUFF...
HUFF...
SO THERE'S NO POINT IN EVEN THINKING ABOUT THAT NOW...
HUFF...
BUT...
HUFF...
...WHAT... SHOULD I DO...
IF THAT REALLY IS MY MOM...?

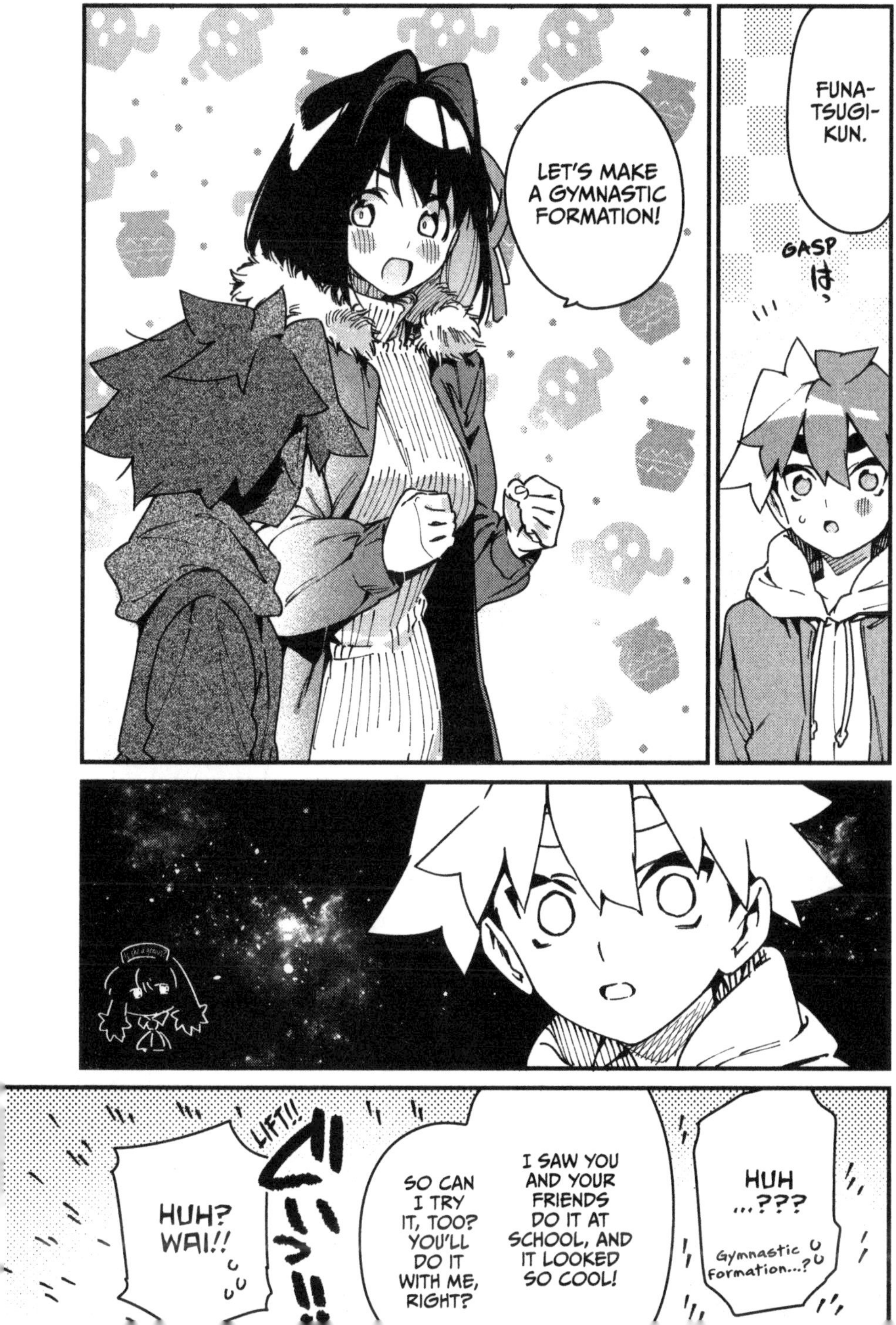
FUNA-TSUGI-KUN.
GASP
は、
LET'S MAKE A GYMNASTIC FORMATION!
HUH ...???
Gymnastic Formation...?
I SAW YOU AND YOUR FRIENDS DO IT AT SCHOOL, AND IT LOOKED SO COOL!
SO CAN I TRY IT, TOO? YOU'LL DO IT WITH ME, RIGHT?
LIFT!!
HUH? WAI!!

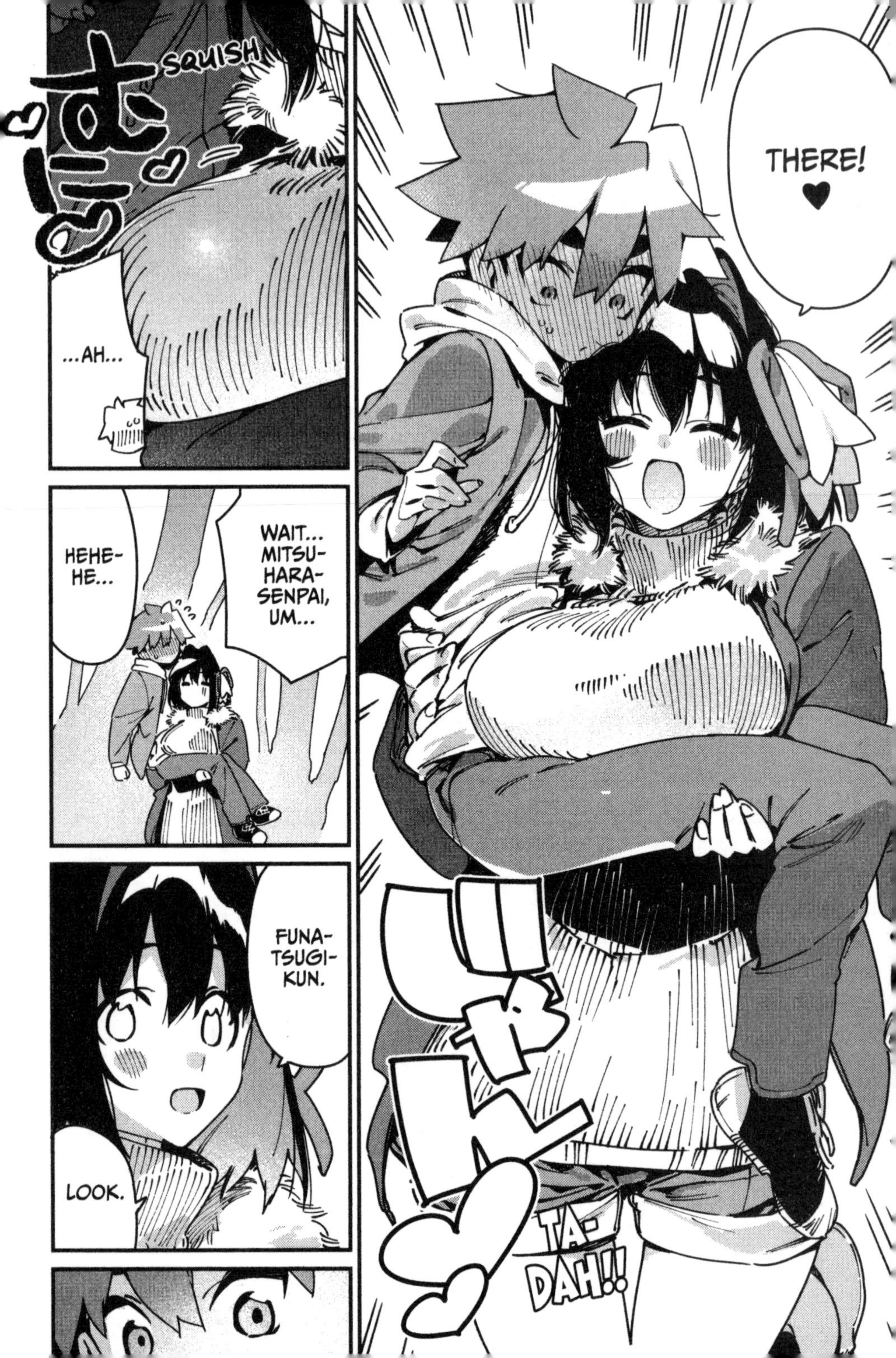
THERE! ♥
TA-DAH!!
SQUISH
...AH...
WAIT... MITSUHARA-SENPAI, UM...
HEHEHE...
FUNATSUGI-KUN.
LOOK.

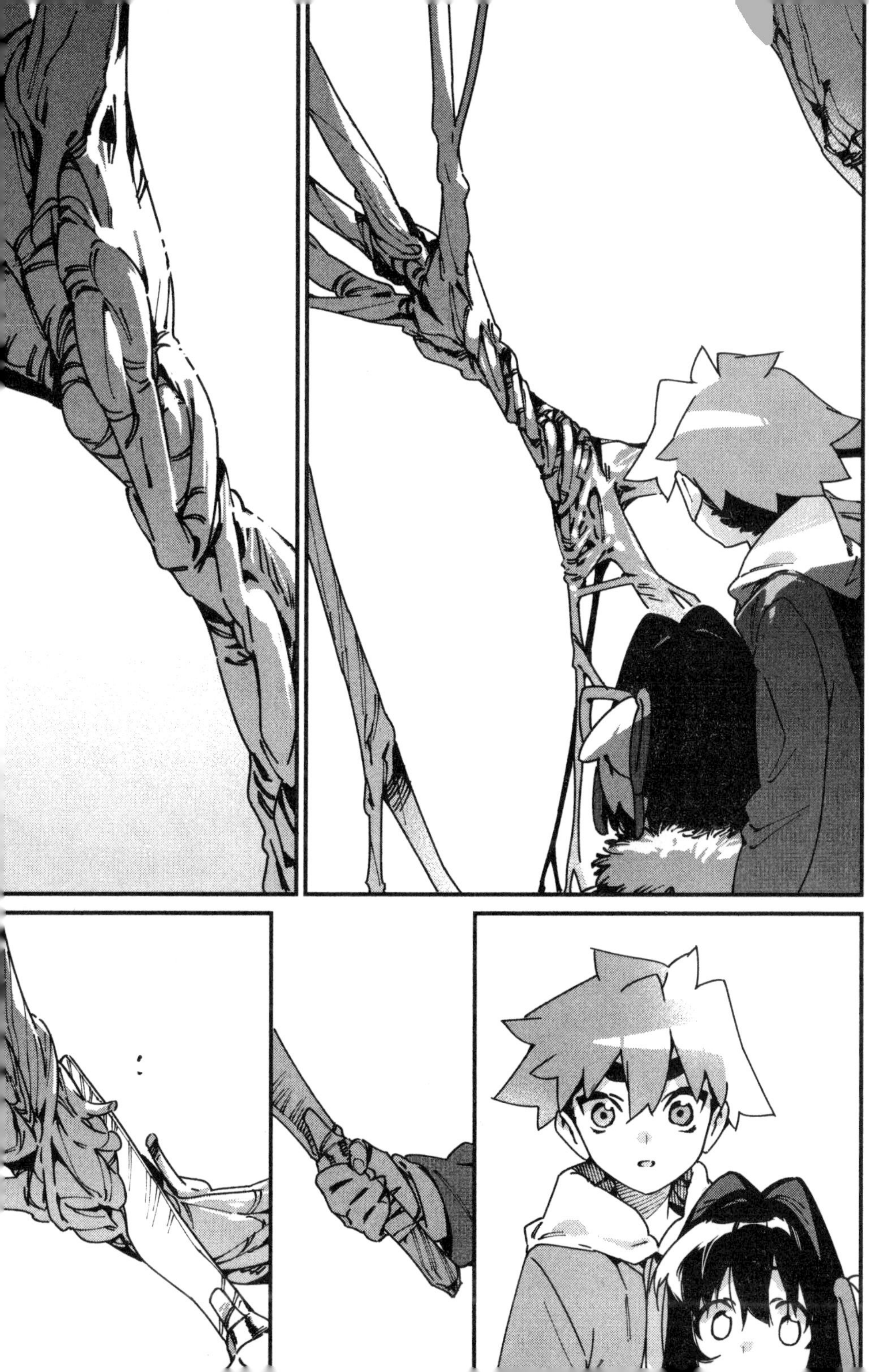

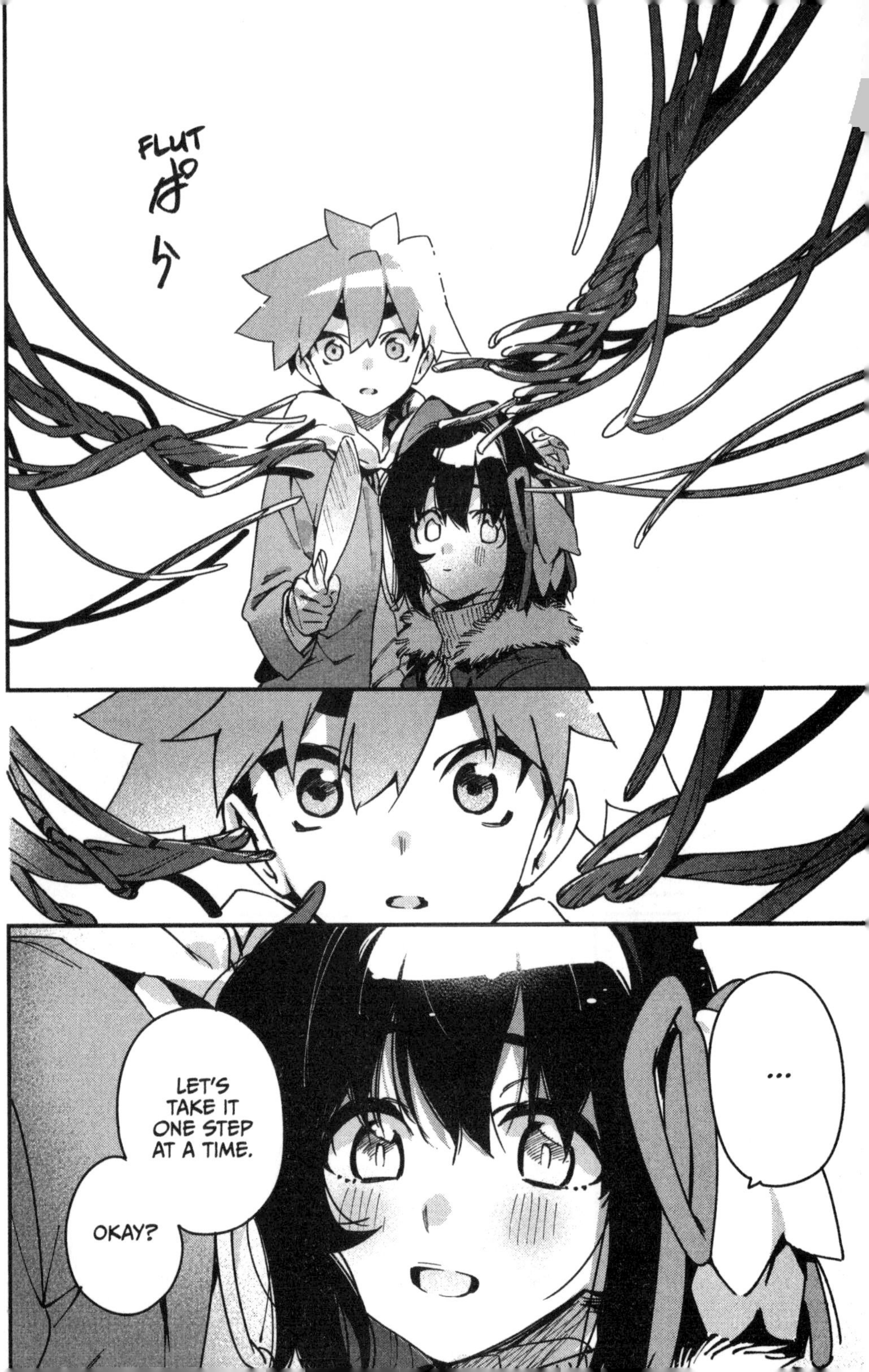
FLUT
ぱら
...
LET'S TAKE IT ONE STEP AT A TIME.
OKAY?

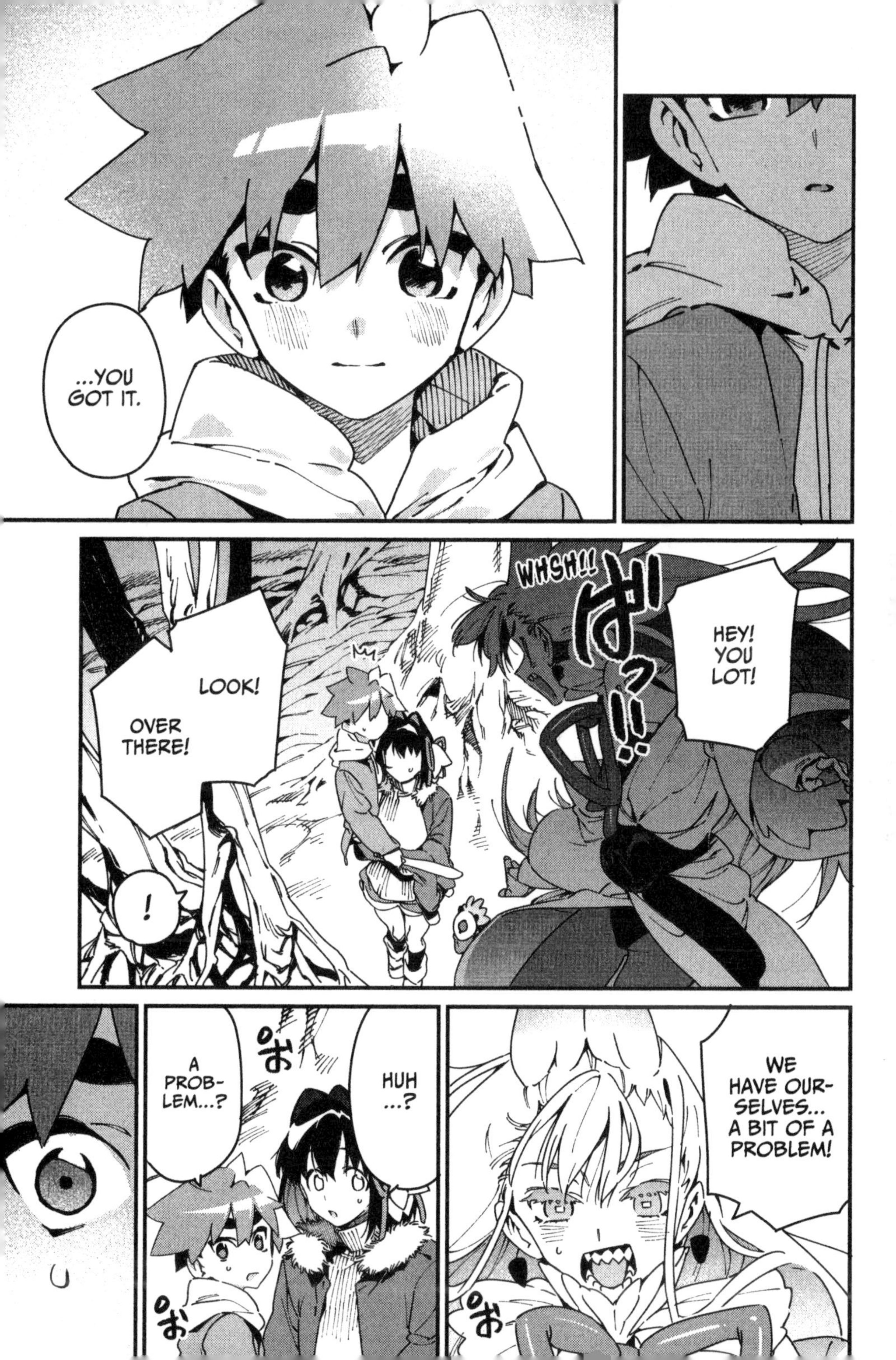
...YOU GOT IT.
HEY! YOU LOT!
WHSH!!
ぱっ!!
LOOK!
OVER THERE!
!
WE HAVE OUR-SELVES... A BIT OF A PROBLEM!
ぉ
HUH ...?
A PROB-LEM...?
ぉ
ぉ

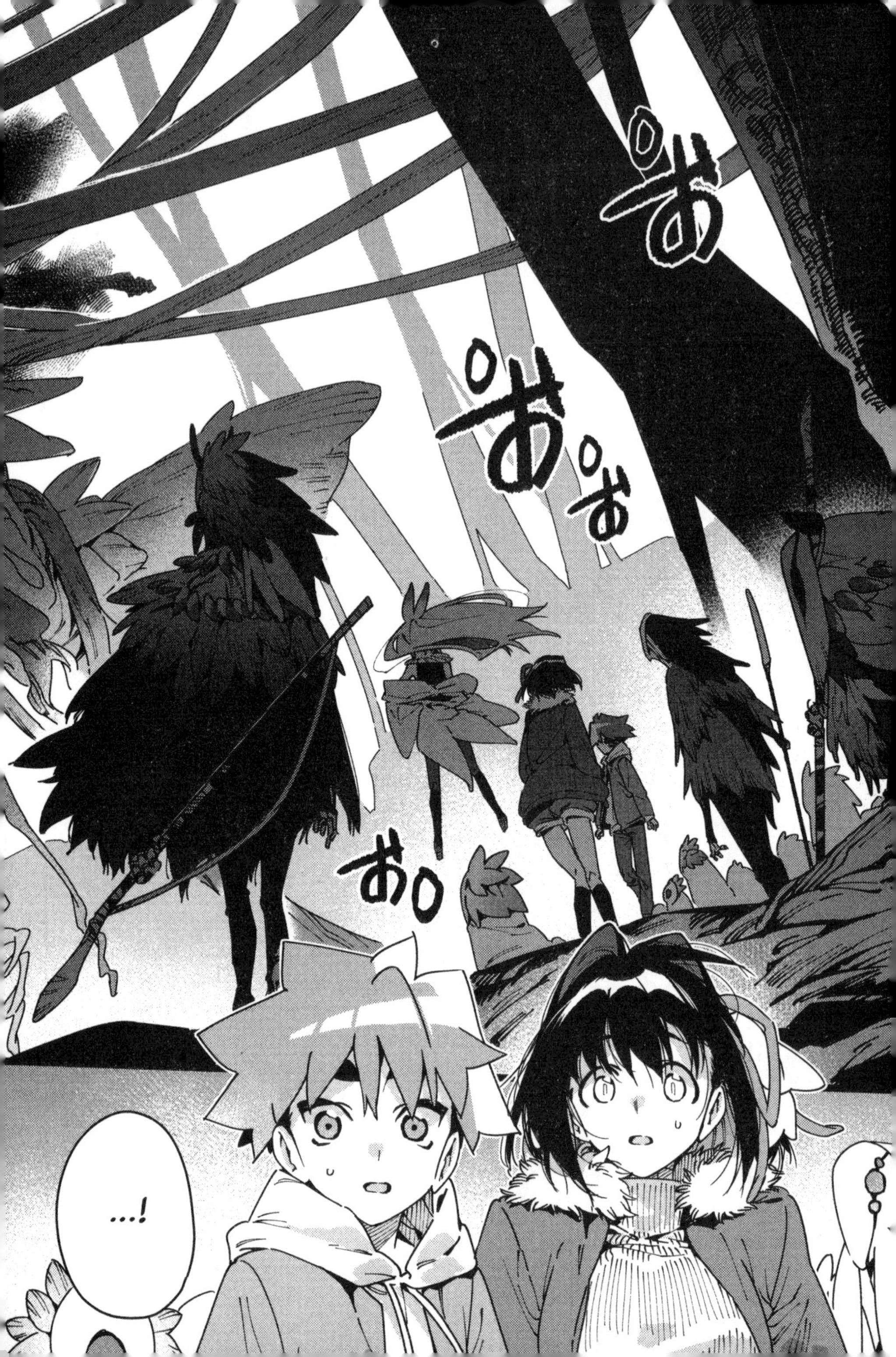
おおおお
...!

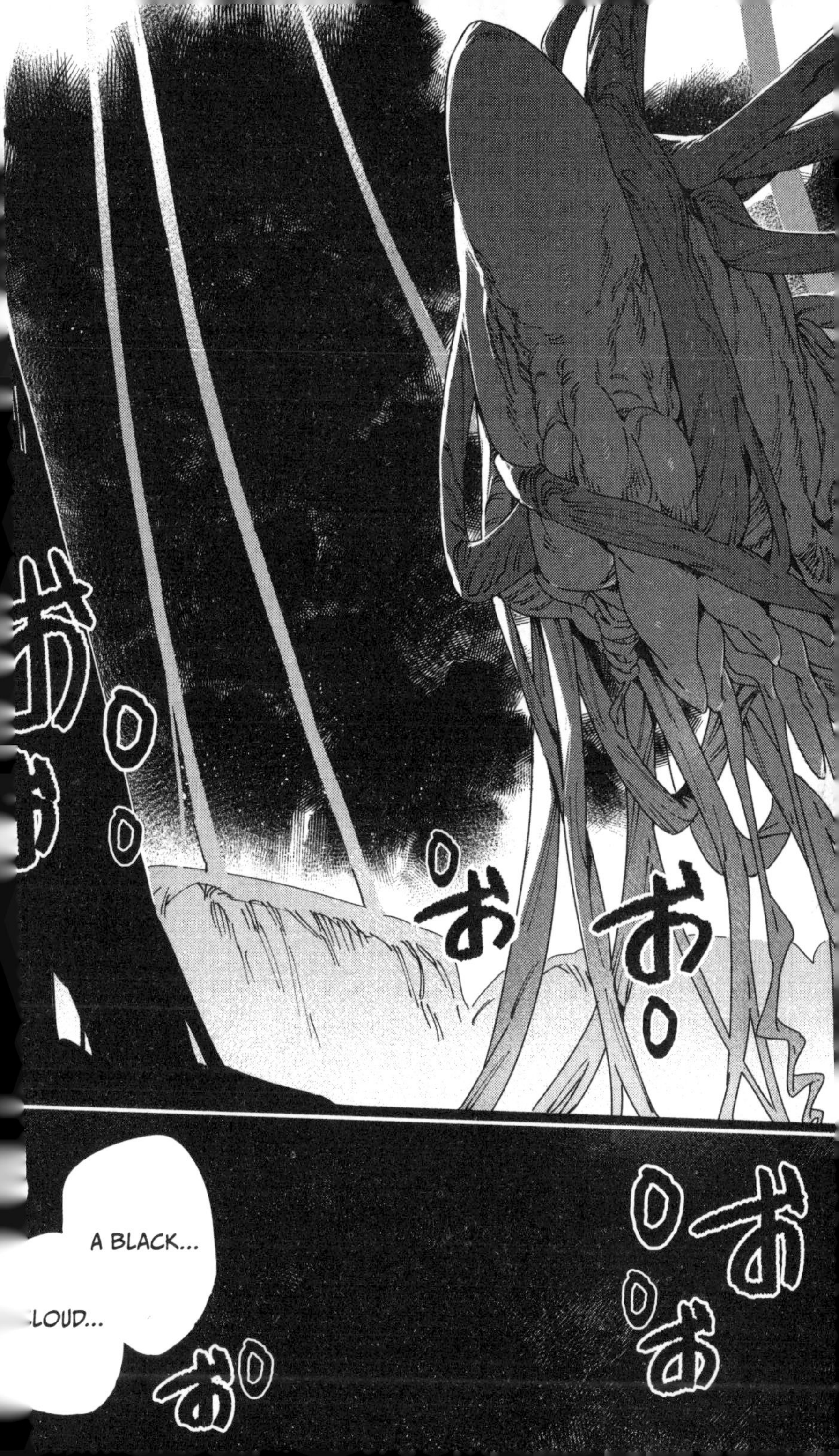

おぉ
おぉ
おぉぉ
おぉぉ
A BLACK...
CLOUD...
おぉ

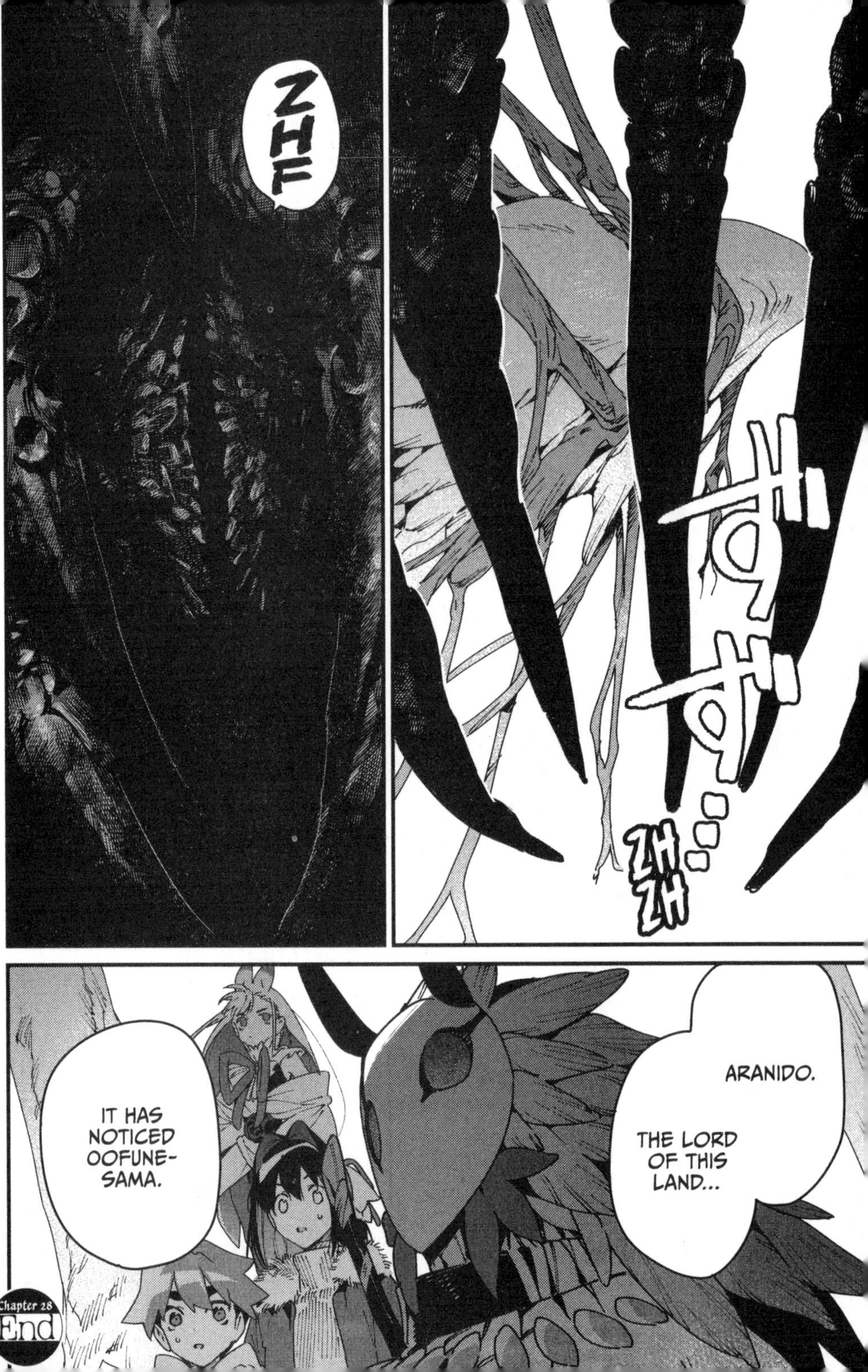
ずず…
ZH ZH
ZHF
ARANIDO.
THE LORD OF THIS LAND...
IT HAS NOTICED OOFUNE-SAMA.
Chapter 28 End

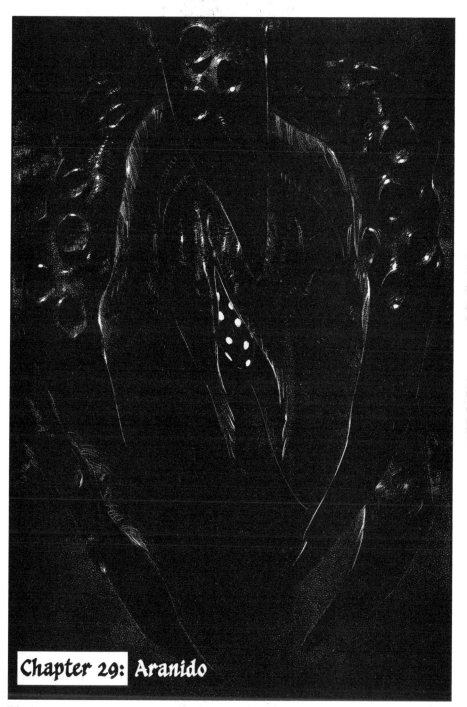

Chapter 29: Aranido

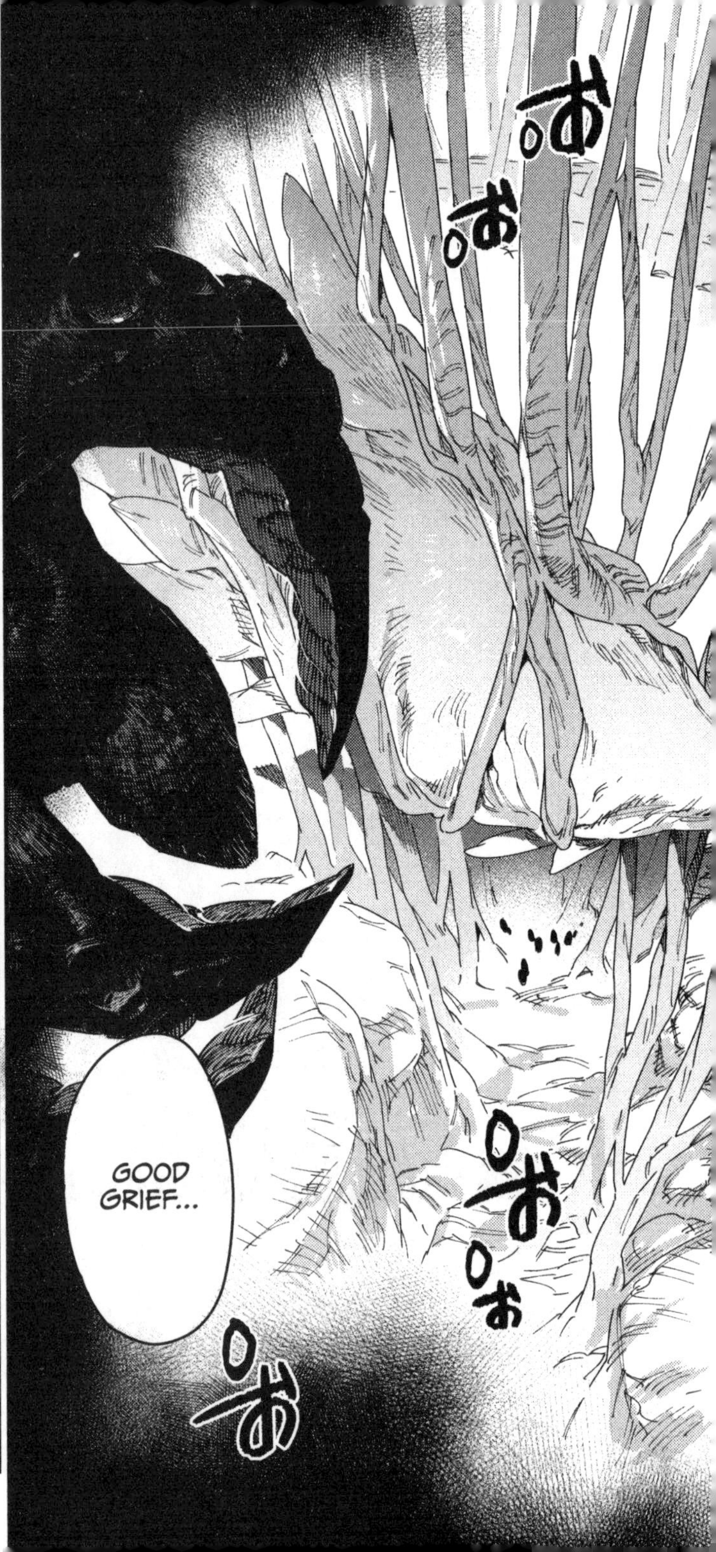
GOOD GRIEF...
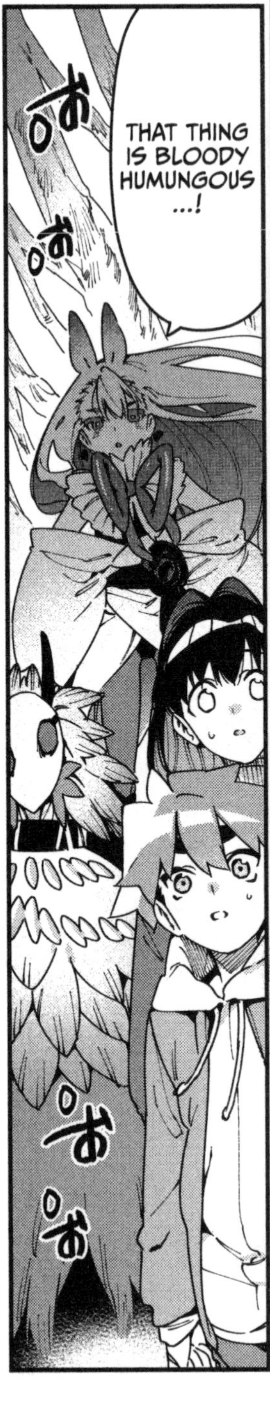
THAT THING IS BLOODY HUMUNGOUS ...!

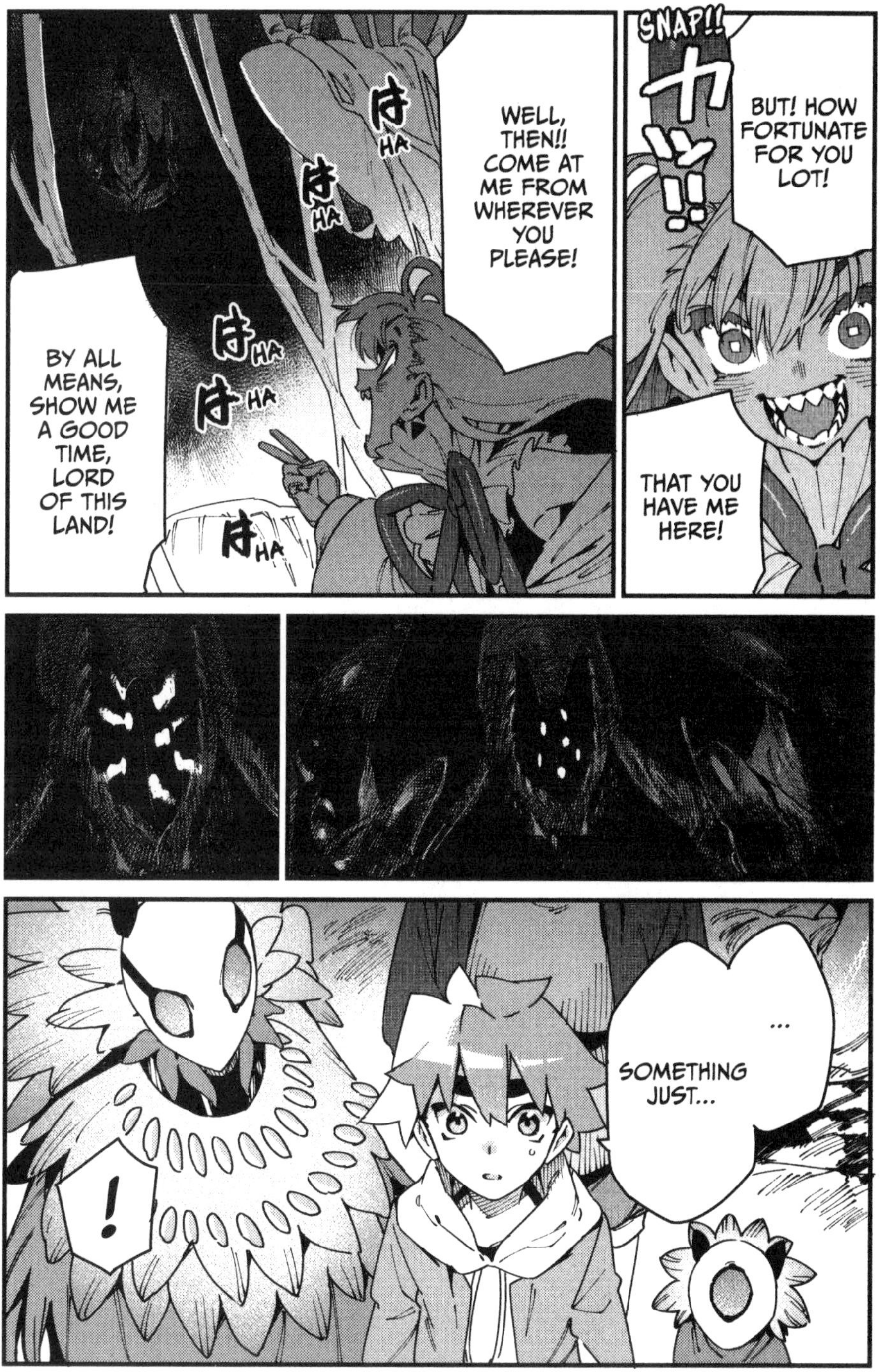
SNAP!!
カッ!!
BUT! HOW FORTUNATE FOR YOU LOT!
THAT YOU HAVE ME HERE!
WELL, THEN!! COME AT ME FROM WHEREVER YOU PLEASE!
は HA
は HA
は HA
は HA
は HA
BY ALL MEANS, SHOW ME A GOOD TIME, LORD OF THIS LAND!
... SOMETHING JUST...
!

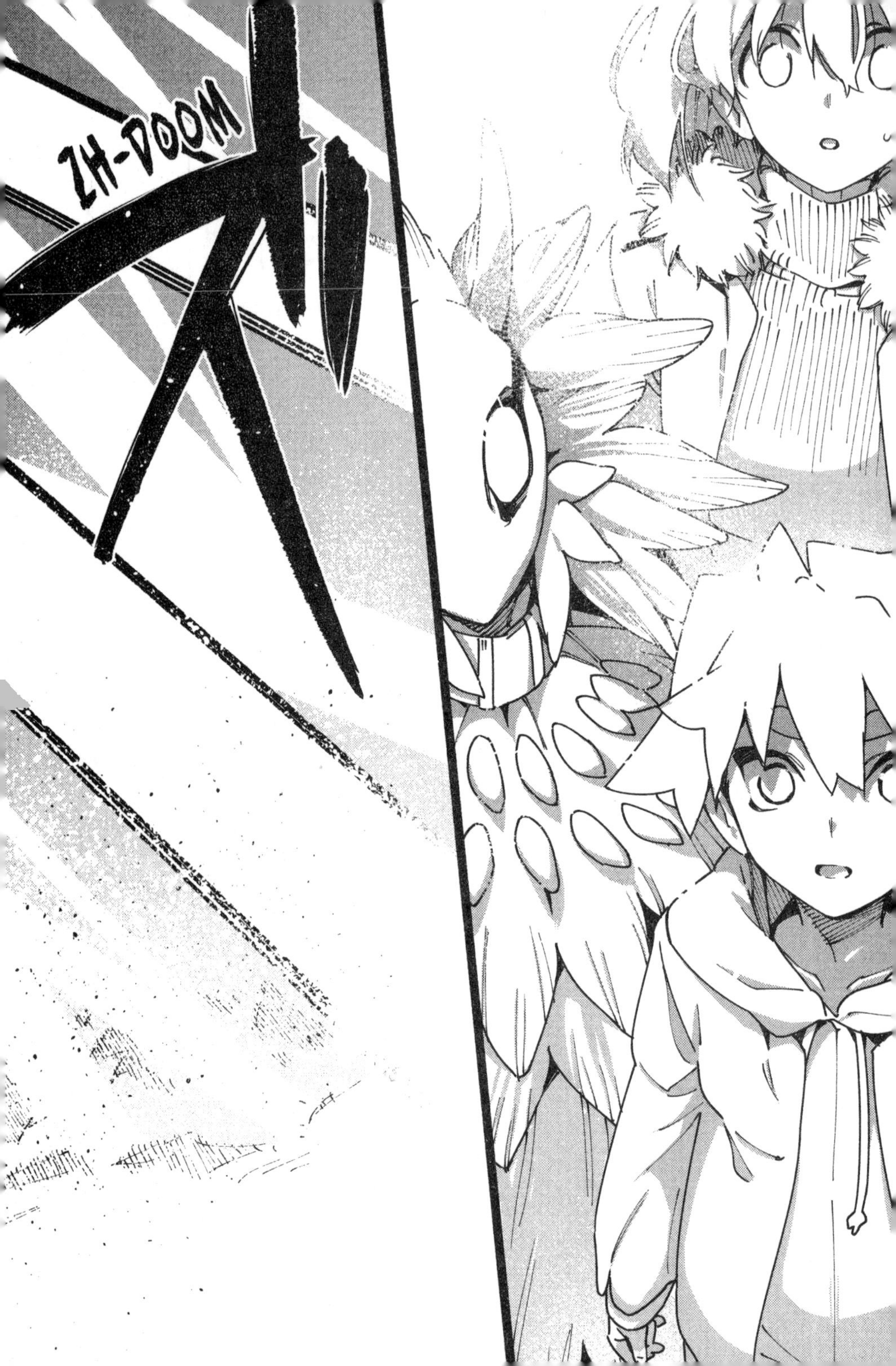
ZH-DOOM

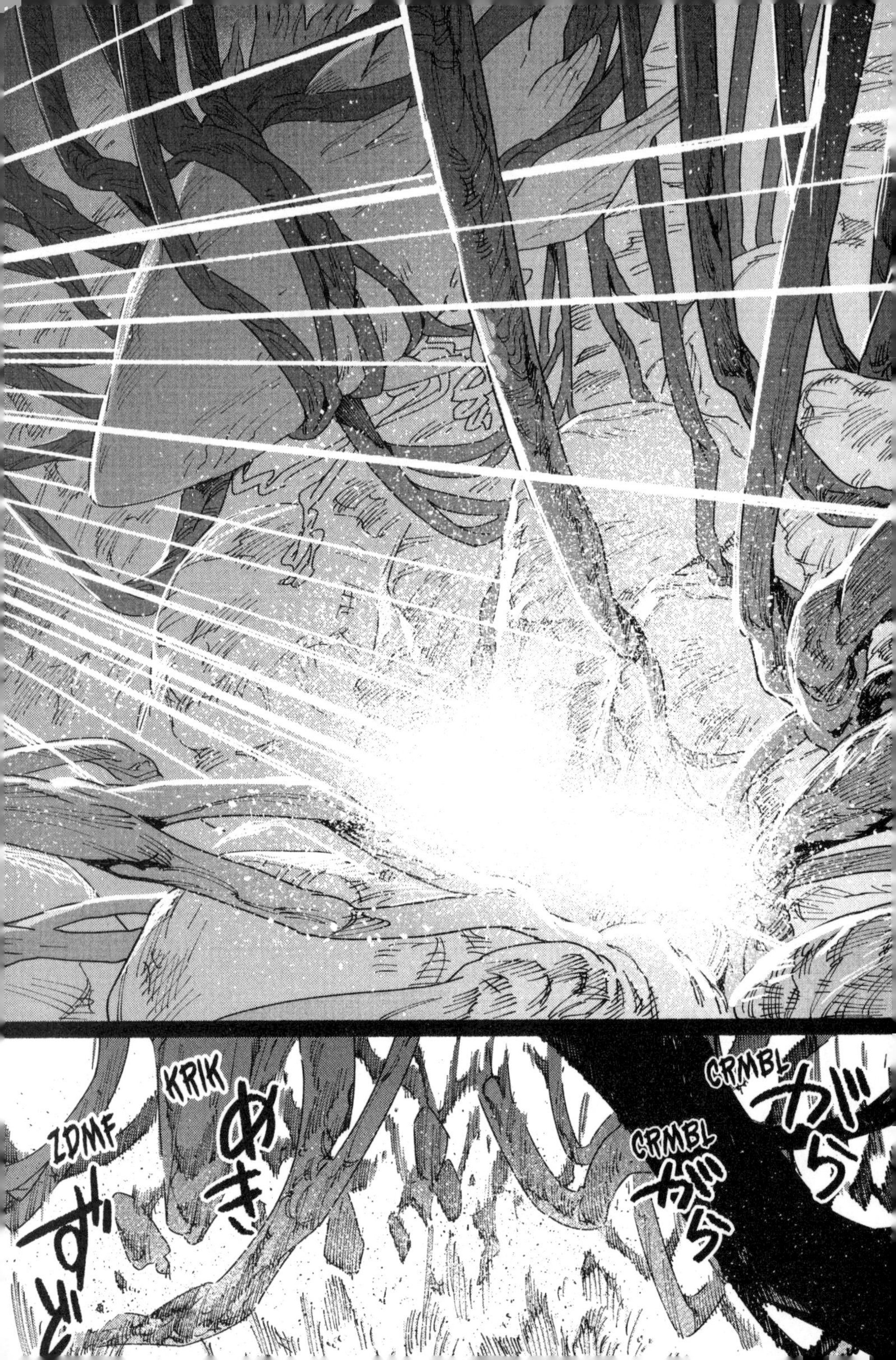
CRMBL
がら
CRMBL
がら
KRIK
めき
ZDMF
ずズ

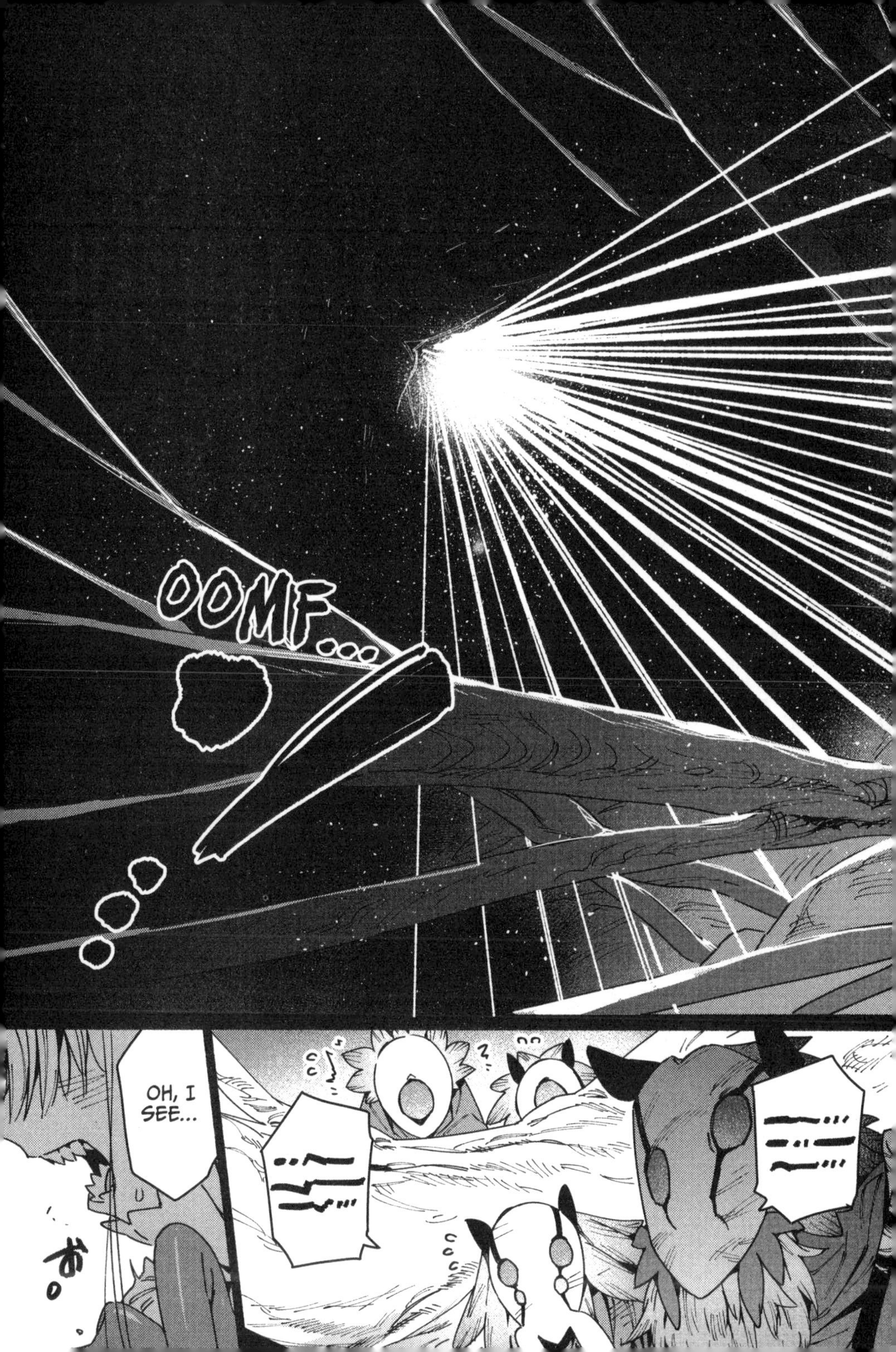
OOMF...
OH, I SEE...
お。

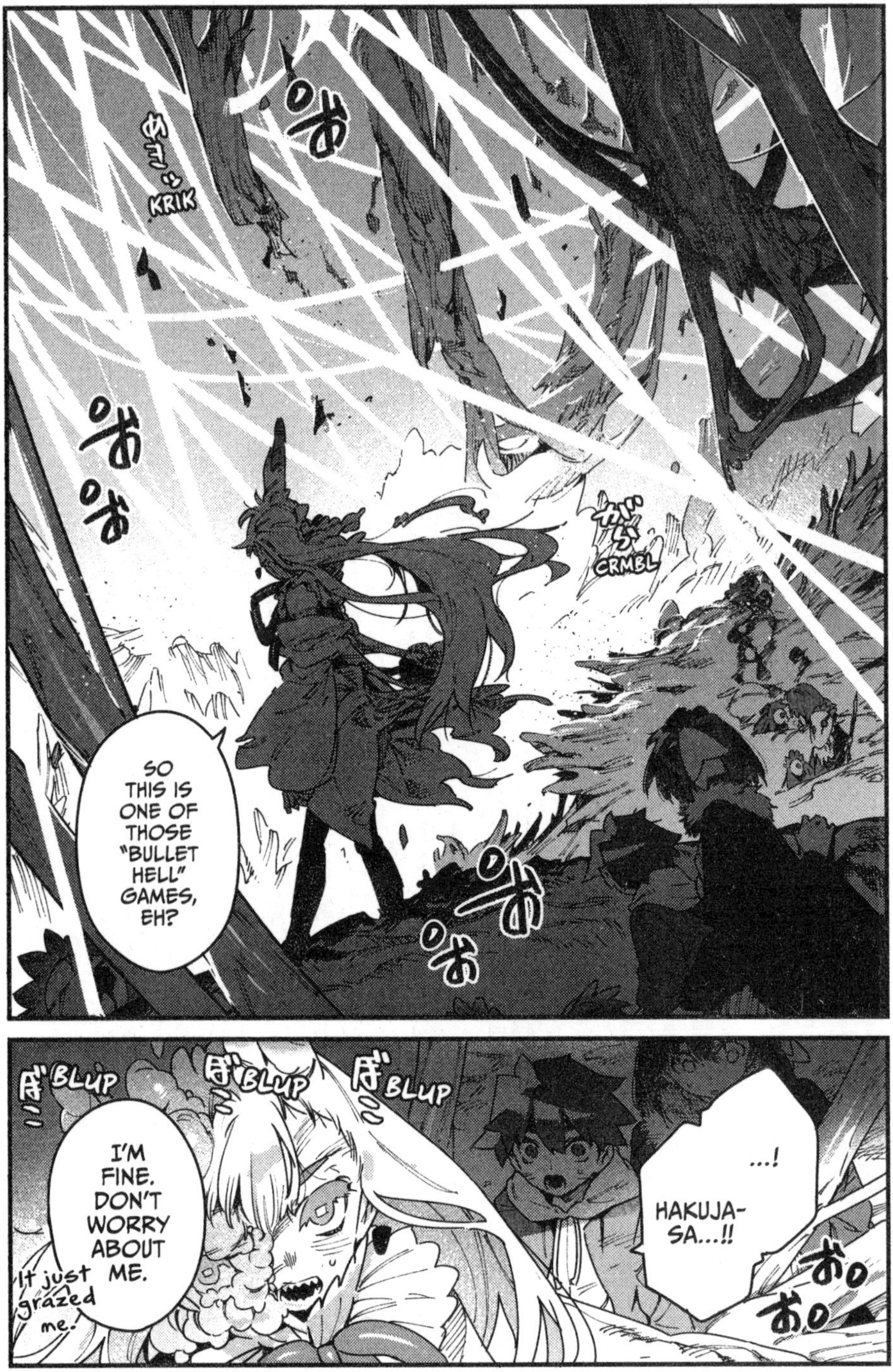

ぉお
がら CRMBL
めきっ KRIK
ぉお ぉお
SO THIS IS ONE OF THOSE "BULLET HELL" GAMES, EH?
ぉお ぉお
...! HAKUJA-SA...!!
おぉ おぉ
ぼこ BLUP
ぼこ BLUP
ぼこ BLUP
I'M FINE. DON'T WORRY ABOUT ME.
It just grazed me.

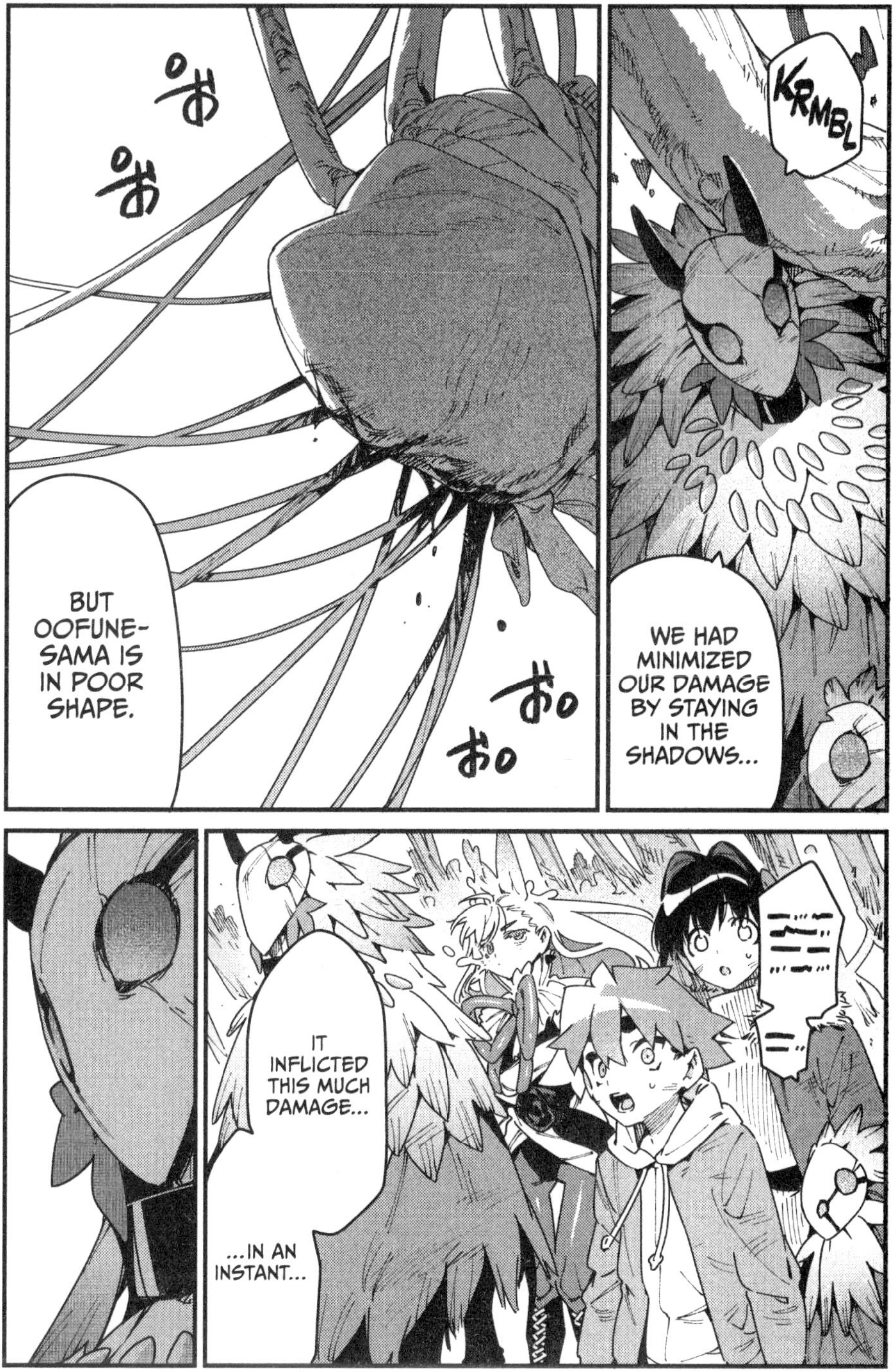
KRMBL
WE HAD MINIMIZED OUR DAMAGE BY STAYING IN THE SHADOWS...
BUT OOFUNE-SAMA IS IN POOR SHAPE.
IT INFLICTED THIS MUCH DAMAGE...
...IN AN INSTANT...

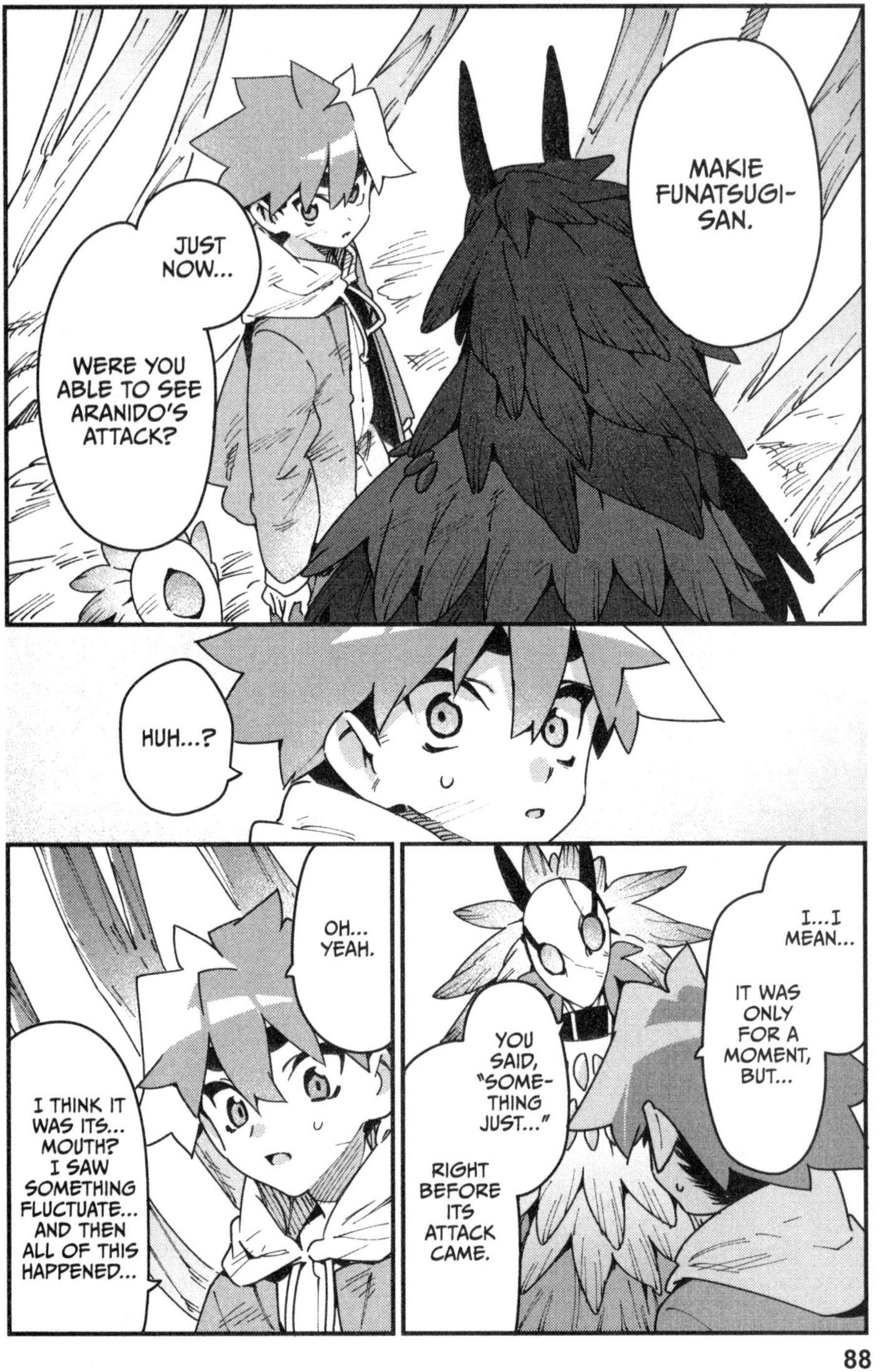
MAKIE FUNATSUGI-SAN.
JUST NOW...
WERE YOU ABLE TO SEE ARANIDO'S ATTACK?
HUH...?
I...I MEAN...
IT WAS ONLY FOR A MOMENT, BUT...
YOU SAID, "SOME-THING JUST..."
RIGHT BEFORE ITS ATTACK CAME.
OH... YEAH.
I THINK IT WAS ITS... MOUTH? I SAW SOMETHING FLUCTUATE... AND THEN ALL OF THIS HAPPENED...

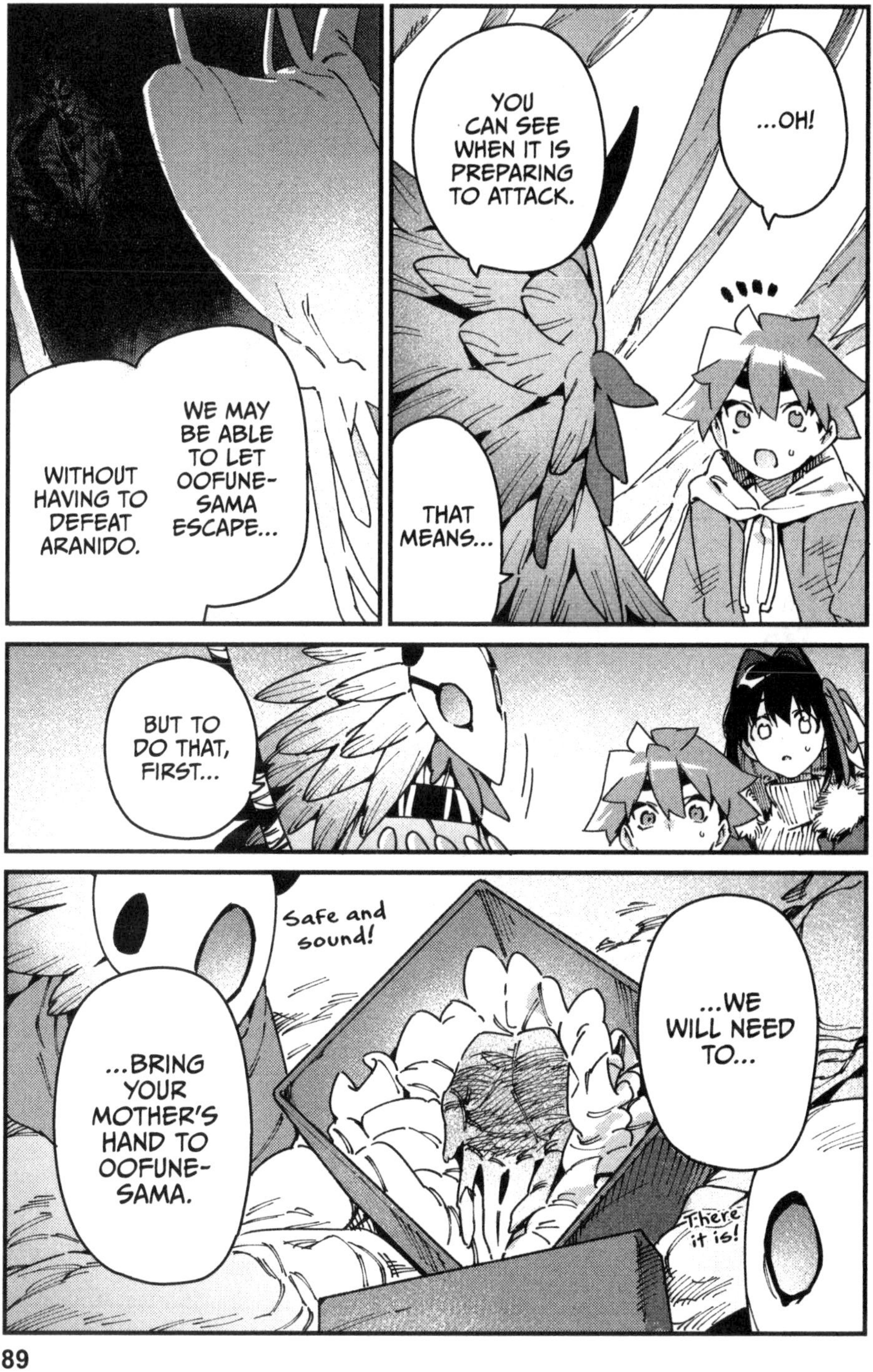
...OH!
YOU CAN SEE WHEN IT IS PREPARING TO ATTACK.
THAT MEANS...
WE MAY BE ABLE TO LET OOFUNE-SAMA ESCAPE...
WITHOUT HAVING TO DEFEAT ARANIDO.
BUT TO DO THAT, FIRST...
...WE WILL NEED TO...
There it is!
Safe and sound!
...BRING YOUR MOTHER'S HAND TO OOFUNE-SAMA.

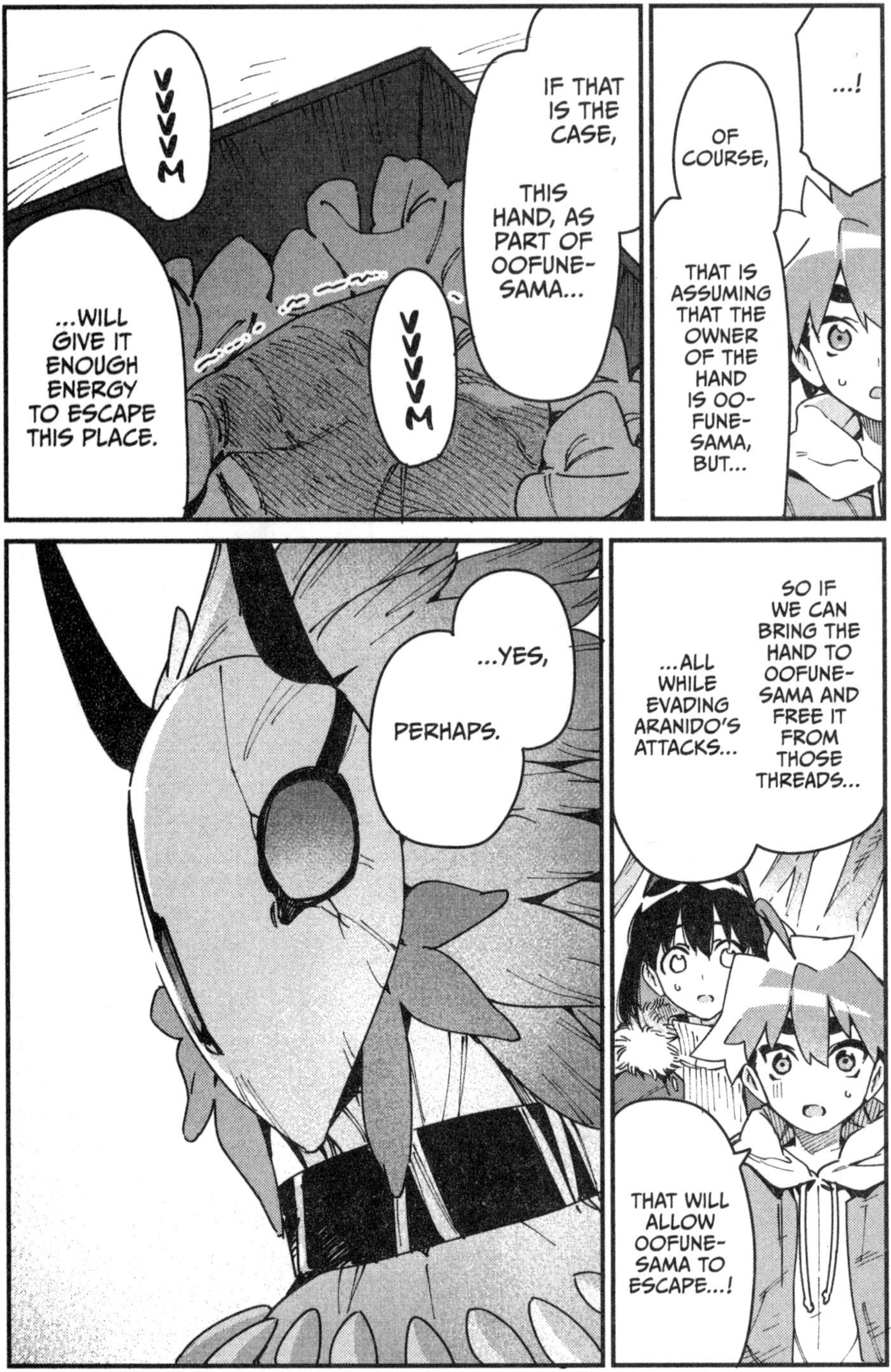
...!
OF COURSE,
THAT IS ASSUMING THAT THE OWNER OF THE HAND IS OO-FUNE-SAMA, BUT...
IF THAT IS THE CASE,
THIS HAND, AS PART OF OOFUNE-SAMA...
VVVVM
VVVVM
...WILL GIVE IT ENOUGH ENERGY TO ESCAPE THIS PLACE.
SO IF WE CAN BRING THE HAND TO OOFUNE-SAMA AND FREE IT FROM THOSE THREADS...
...ALL WHILE EVADING ARANIDO'S ATTACKS...
THAT WILL ALLOW OOFUNE-SAMA TO ESCAPE...!
...YES,
PERHAPS.

IT'S ALMOST LIKE IT SMILED JUST NOW...

...BUT HOW DO WE GET OVER THERE...?

.... WHAT?

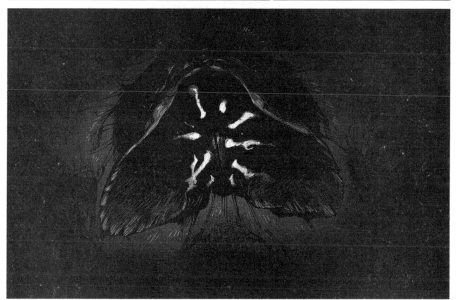

!!

IT FLUCTUATED AGAIN...

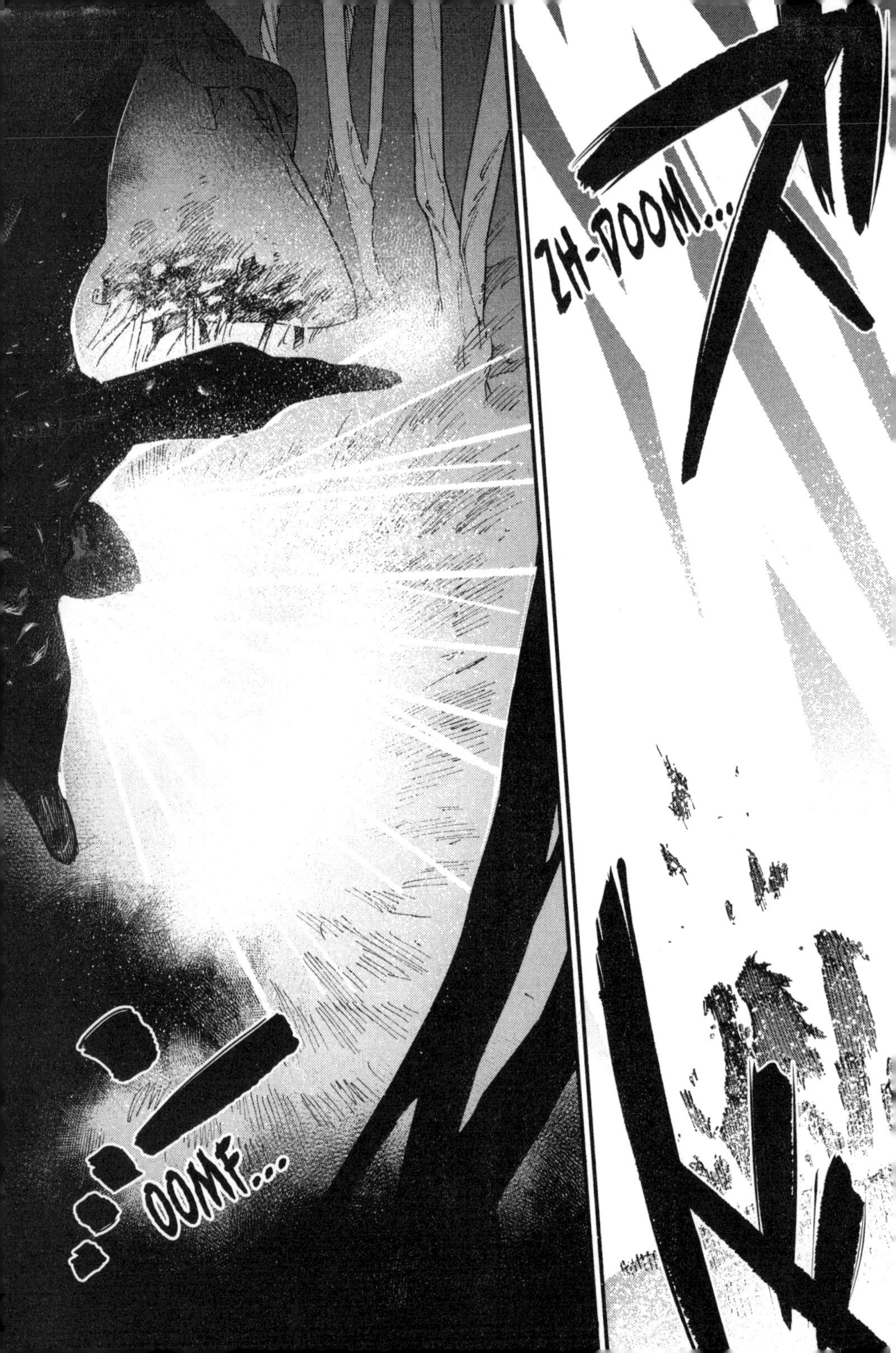
ZH-DOOM...
OOMF...

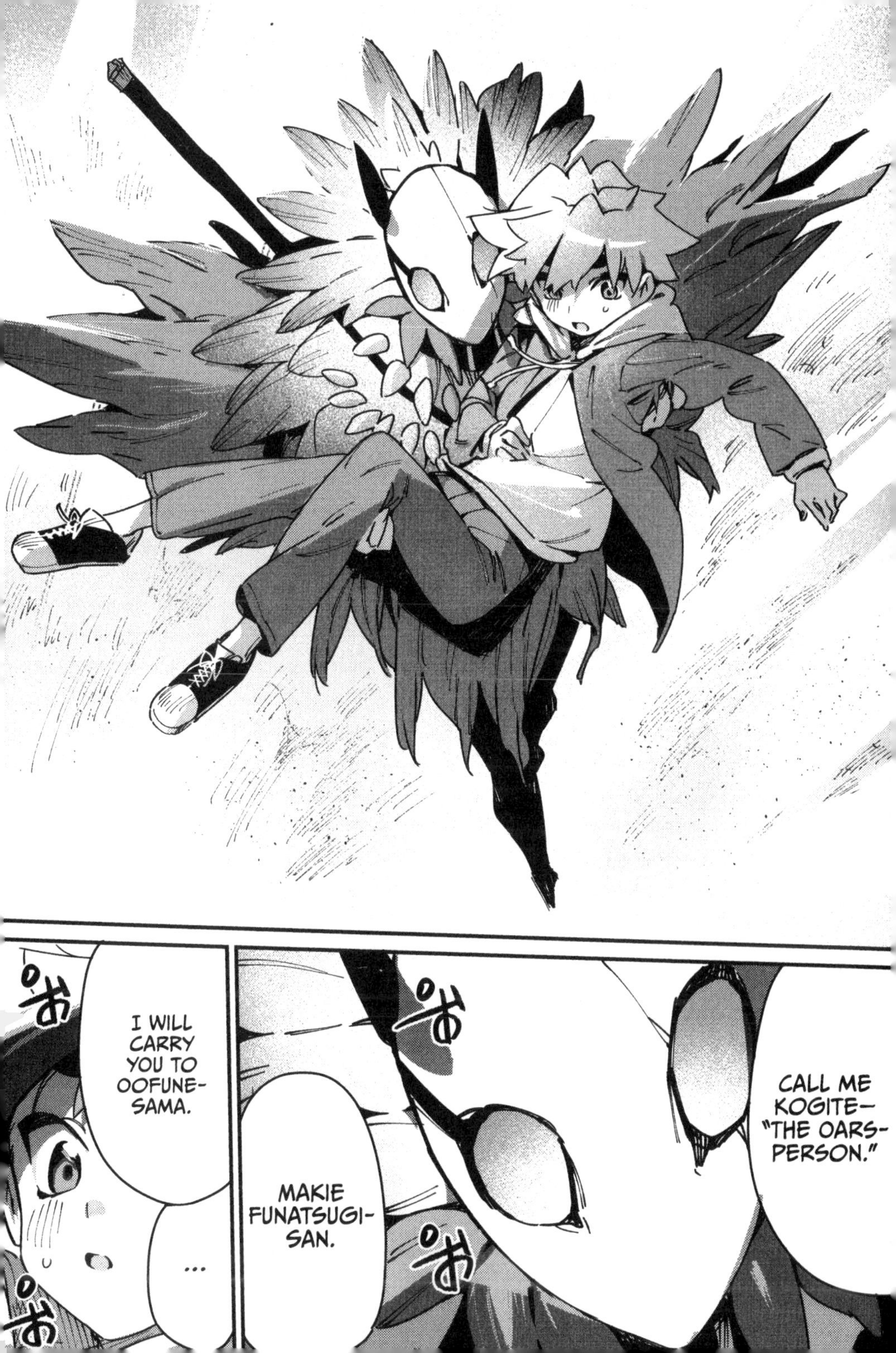
CALL ME KOGITE— "THE OARS-PERSON."
MAKIE FUNATSUGI-SAN.
I WILL CARRY YOU TO OOFUNE-SAMA.
...

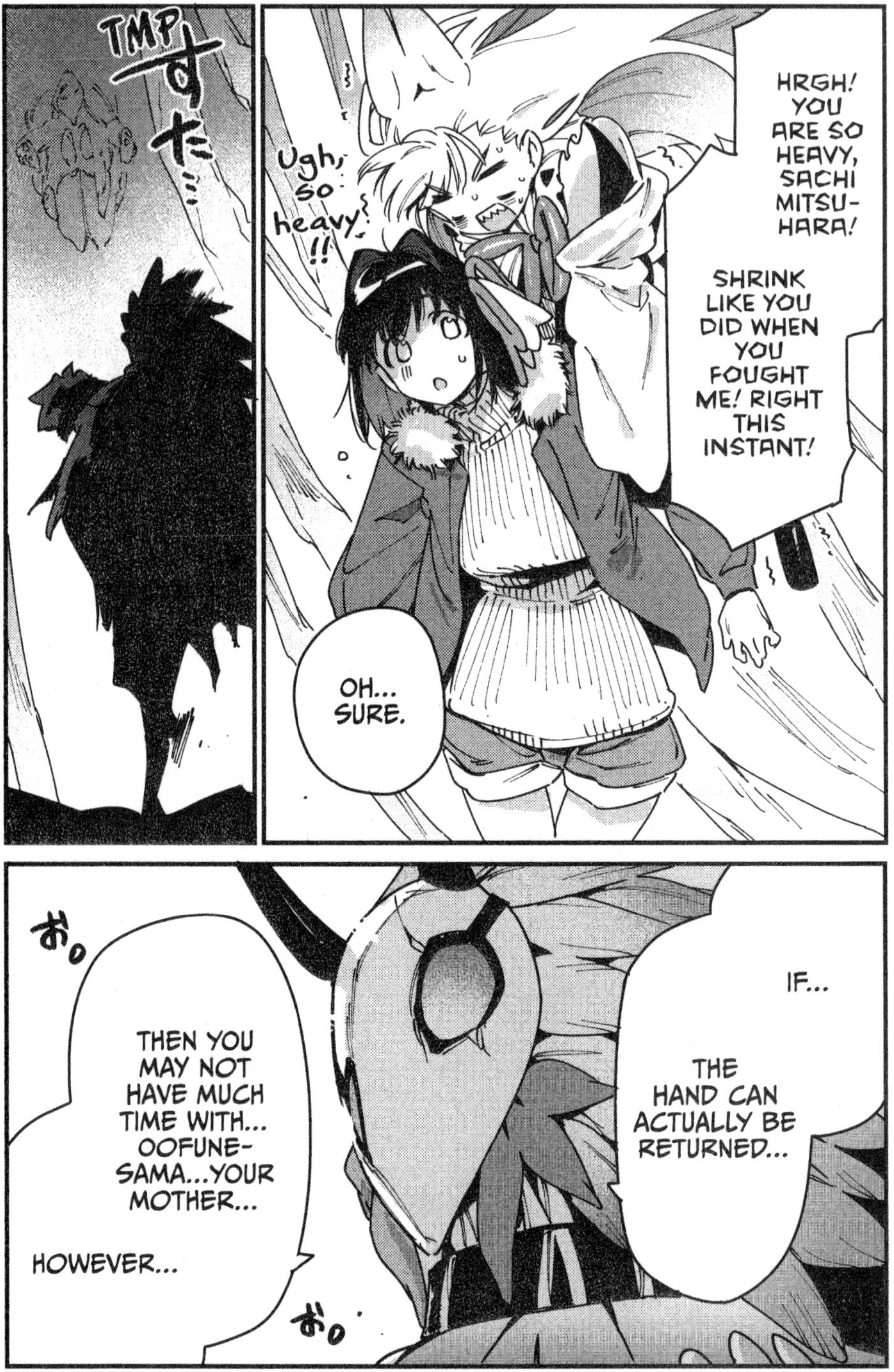
HRGH! YOU ARE SO HEAVY, SACHI MITSUHARA!
SHRINK LIKE YOU DID WHEN YOU FOUGHT ME! RIGHT THIS INSTANT!
Ugh, so heavy!!
OH... SURE.
TMP
すた
IF...
THE HAND CAN ACTUALLY BE RETURNED...
THEN YOU MAY NOT HAVE MUCH TIME WITH... OOFUNE-SAMA...YOUR MOTHER...
HOWEVER...
お。
お。

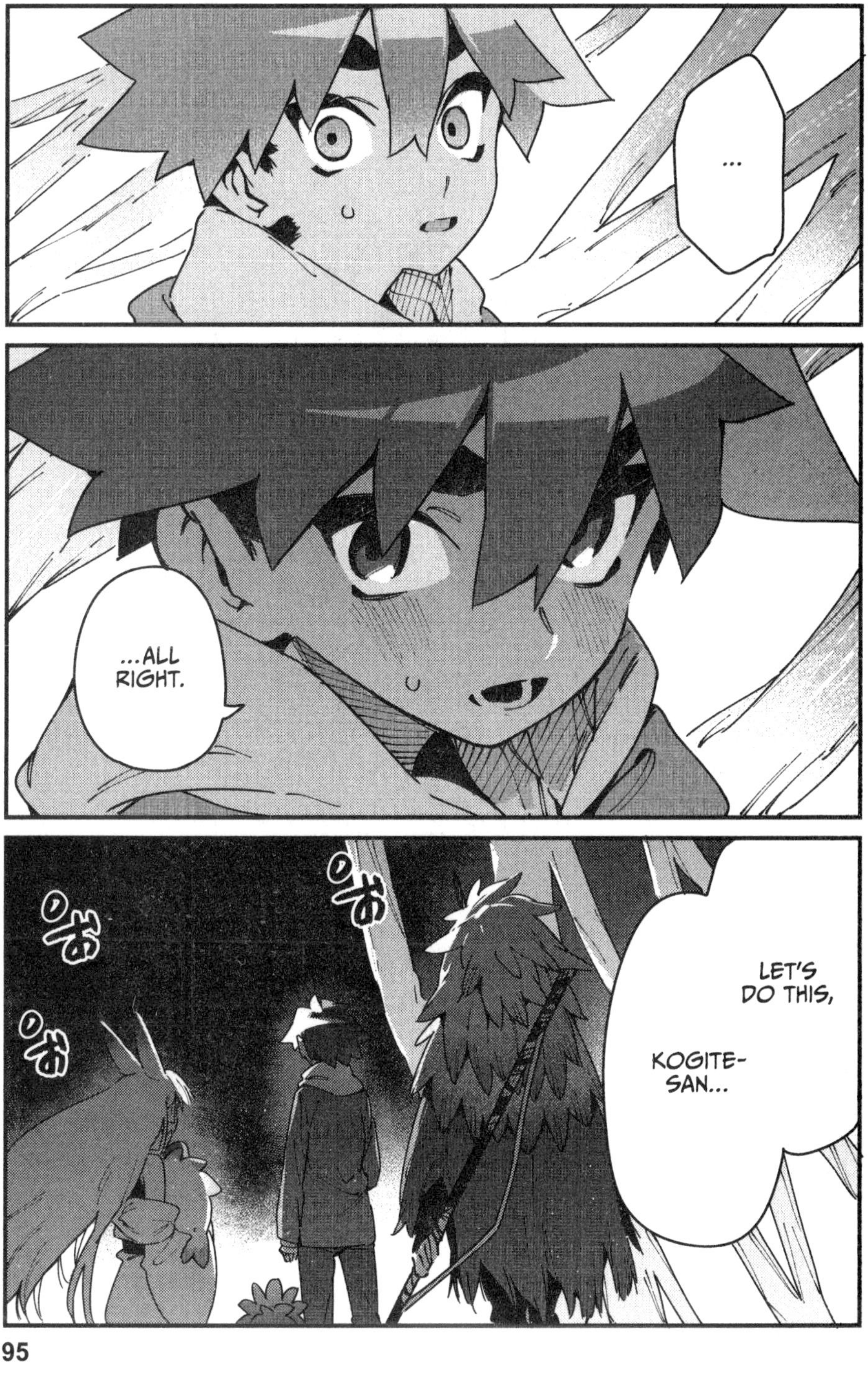
...
...ALL RIGHT.
LET'S DO THIS, KOGITE-SAN...

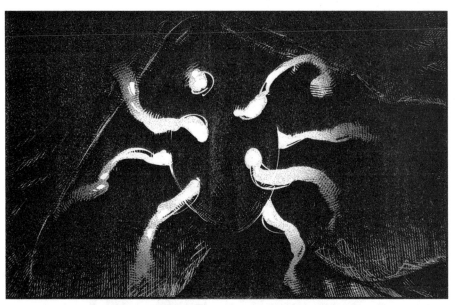

...I'M COMING!

ZH-DOOM

Chapter 29
End

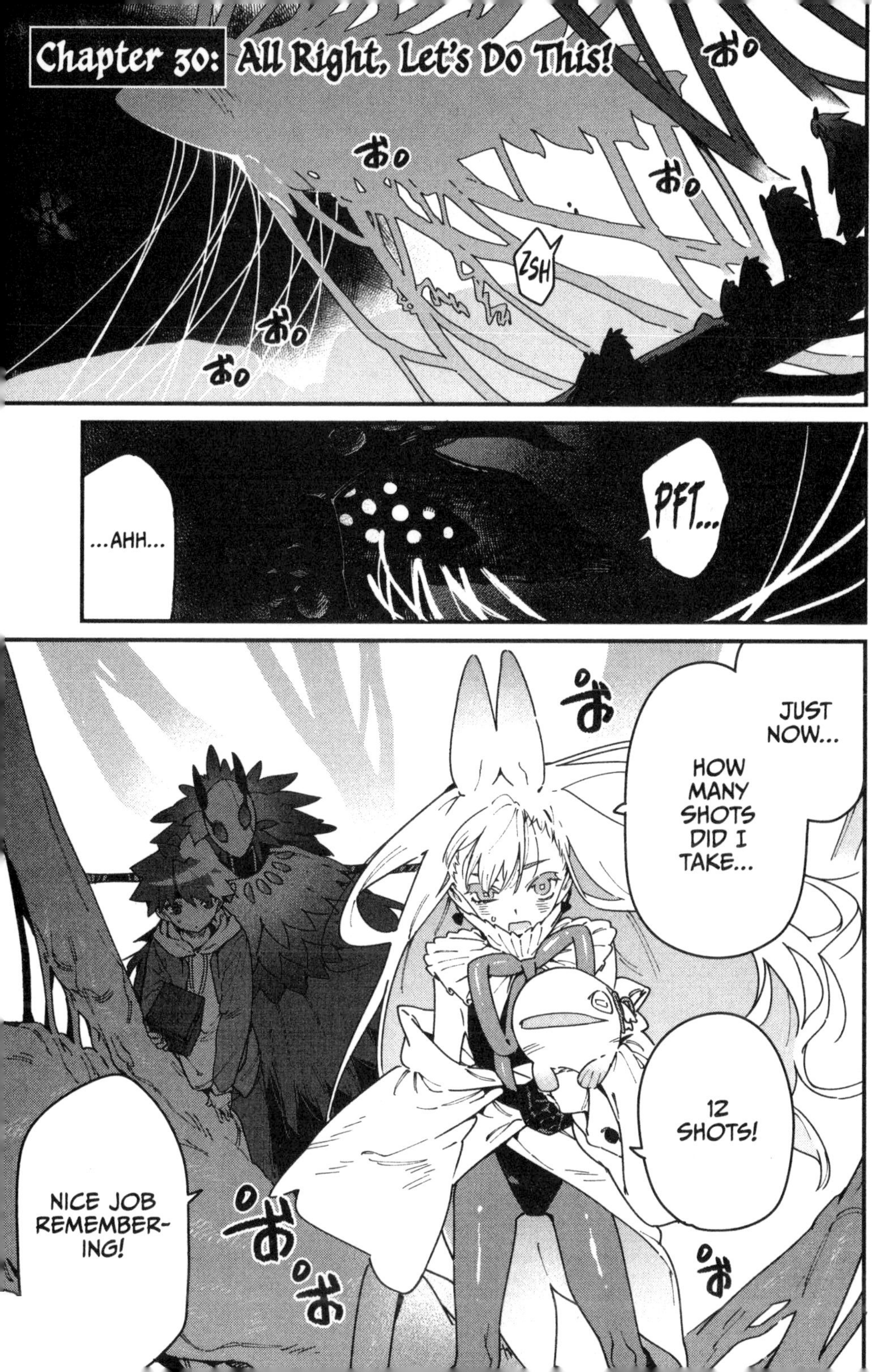

Chapter 30: All Right, Let's Do This!
お
お
お
ZSH
お
お
PFT...
...AHH...
お
JUST NOW...
HOW MANY SHOTS DID I TAKE...
12 SHOTS!
NICE JOB REMEMBERING!
おぉ
お

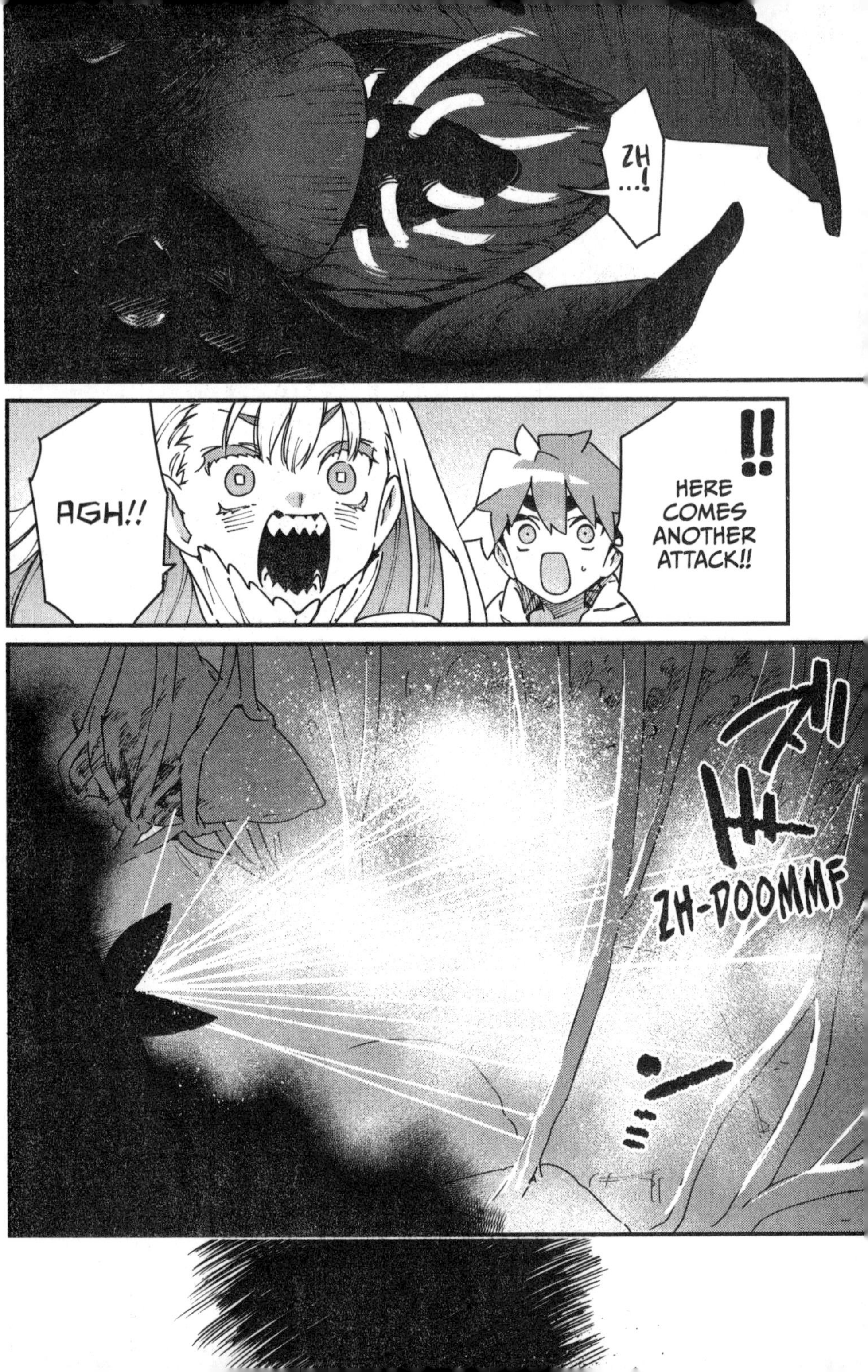
ZH...!
!!
HERE COMES ANOTHER ATTACK!!
AGH!!
ZH-DOOMMF

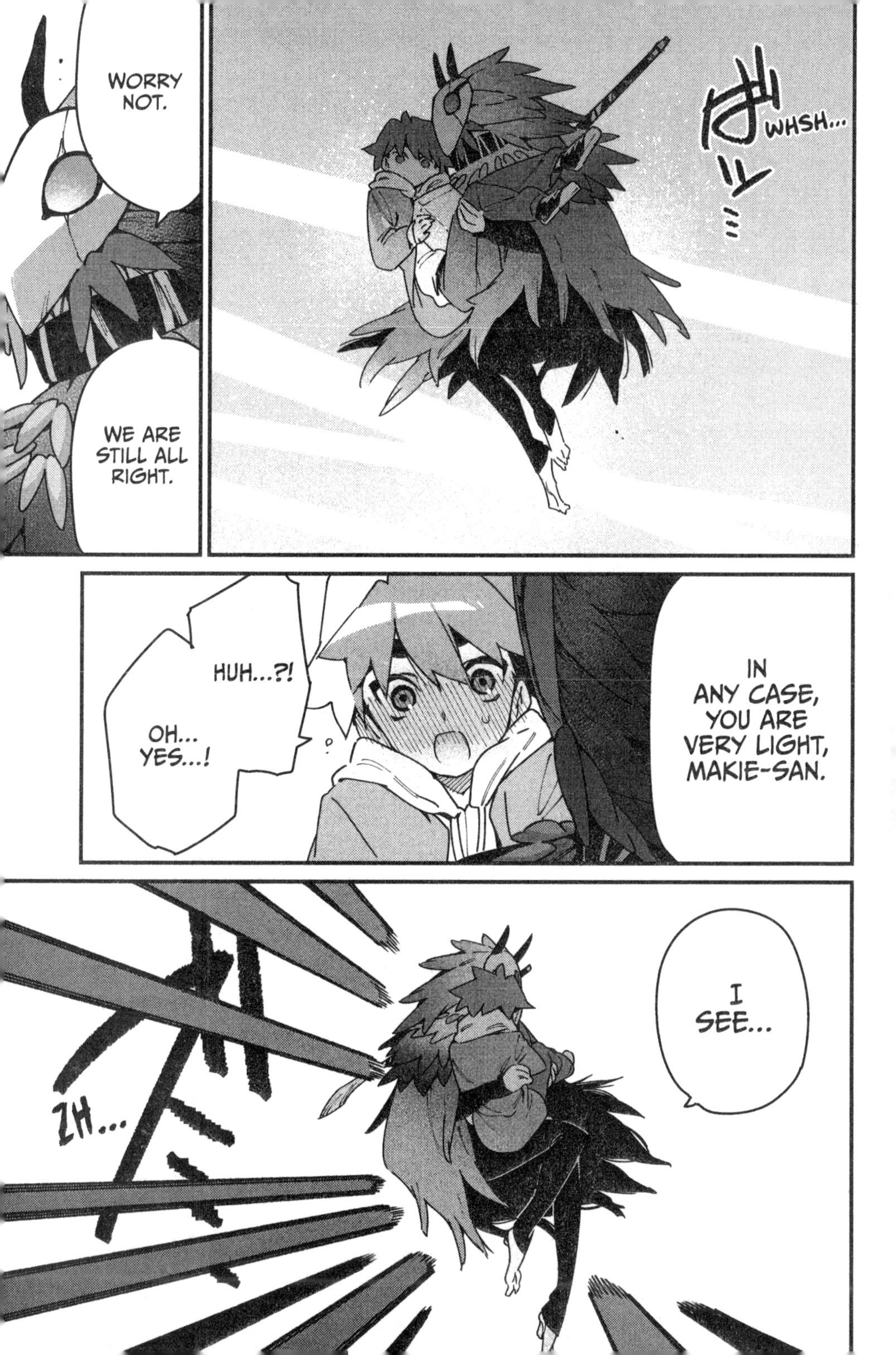
ぱッ
WHSH...
WORRY NOT.
WE ARE STILL ALL RIGHT.
IN ANY CASE, YOU ARE VERY LIGHT, MAKIE-SAN.
HUH...?!
OH... YES...!
I SEE...
ZH...

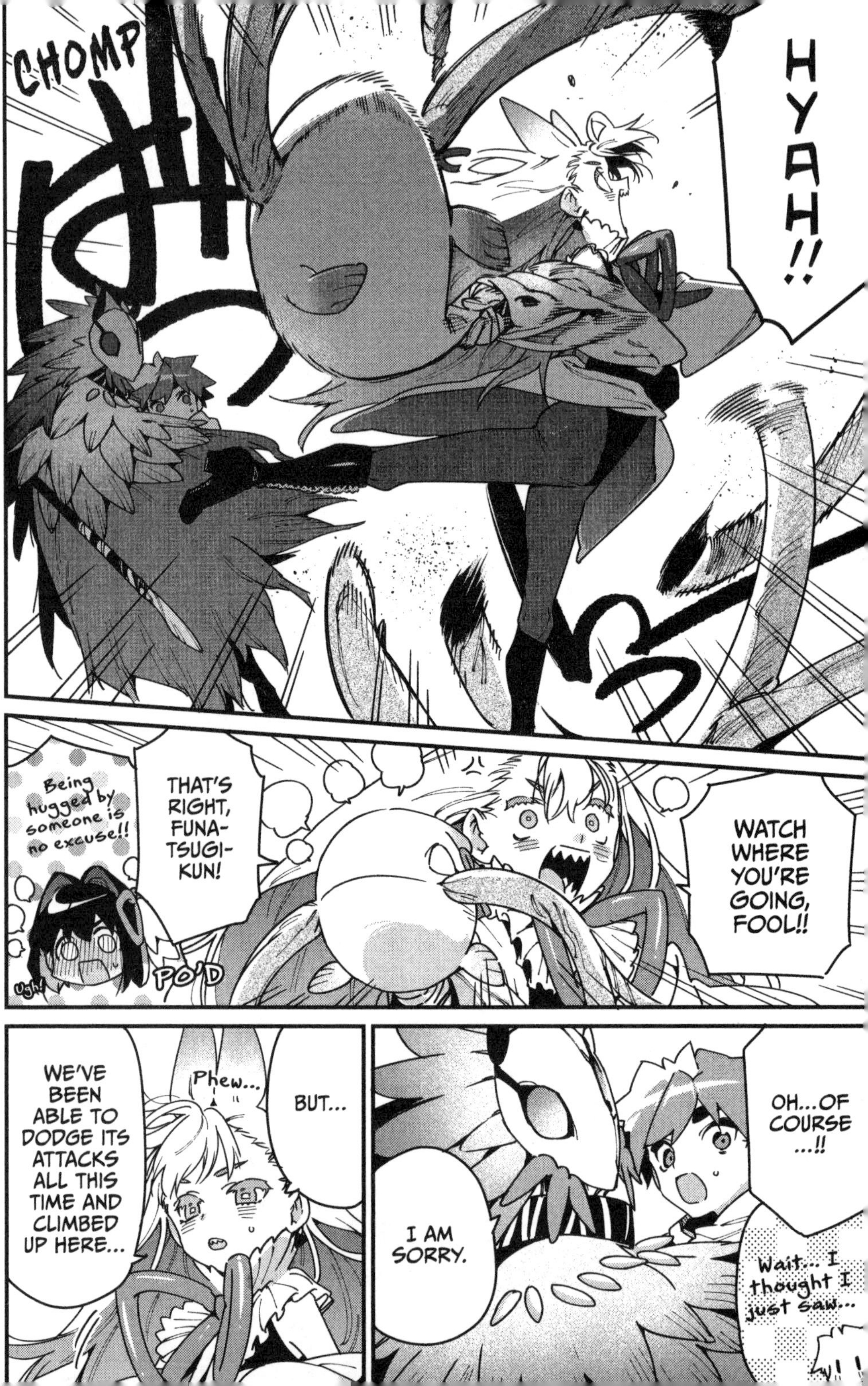
HYAH!!
CHOMP
WATCH WHERE YOU'RE GOING, FOOL!!
THAT'S RIGHT, FUNATSUGI-KUN!
Being hugged by someone is no excuse!!
PO'D
Ugh!
OH...OF COURSE...!!
Wait... I thought I just saw...
Phew...
WE'VE BEEN ABLE TO DODGE ITS ATTACKS ALL THIS TIME AND CLIMBED UP HERE...
BUT...
I AM SORRY.

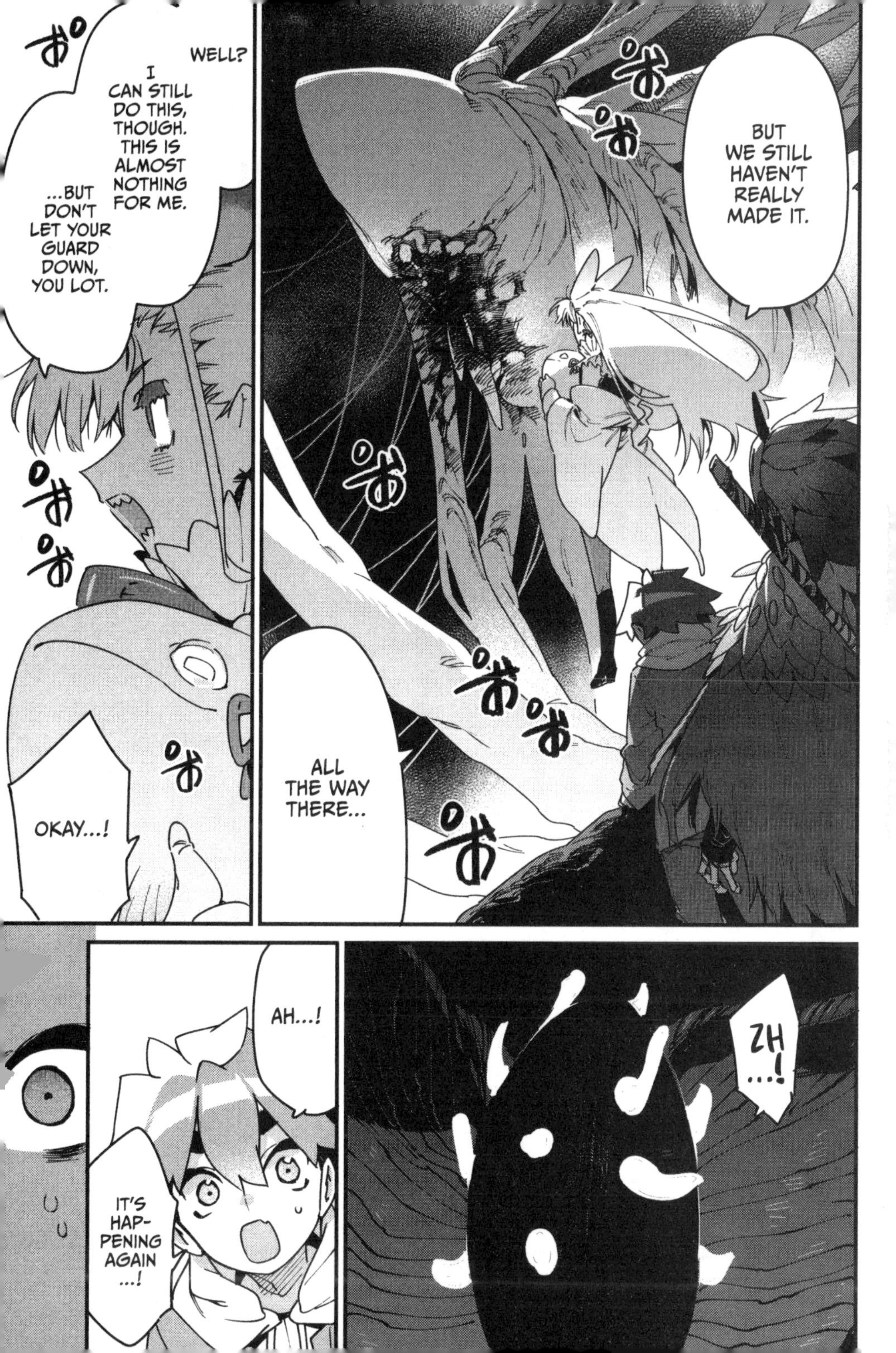

BUT WE STILL HAVEN'T REALLY MADE IT.
ALL THE WAY THERE...
WELL? I CAN STILL DO THIS, THOUGH. THIS IS ALMOST NOTHING FOR ME.
...BUT DON'T LET YOUR GUARD DOWN, YOU LOT.
OKAY...!
ZH...!
AH...!
IT'S HAP-PENING AGAIN...!

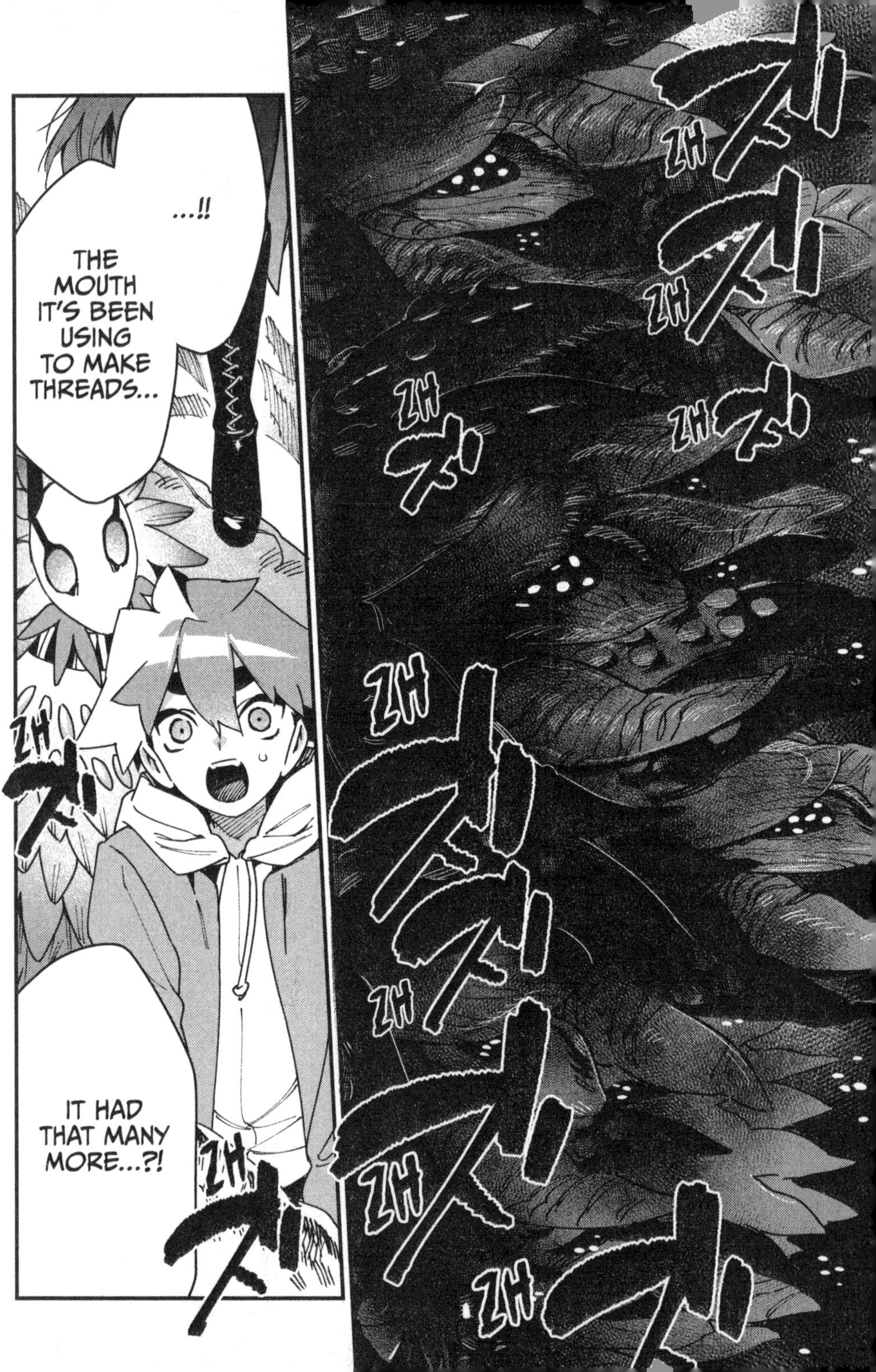
ZH
ZH
ZH
ZH
ZH
ZH
ZH
ZH
...!!
THE MOUTH IT'S BEEN USING TO MAKE THREADS...
ZH
IT HAD THAT MANY MORE...?!
ZH

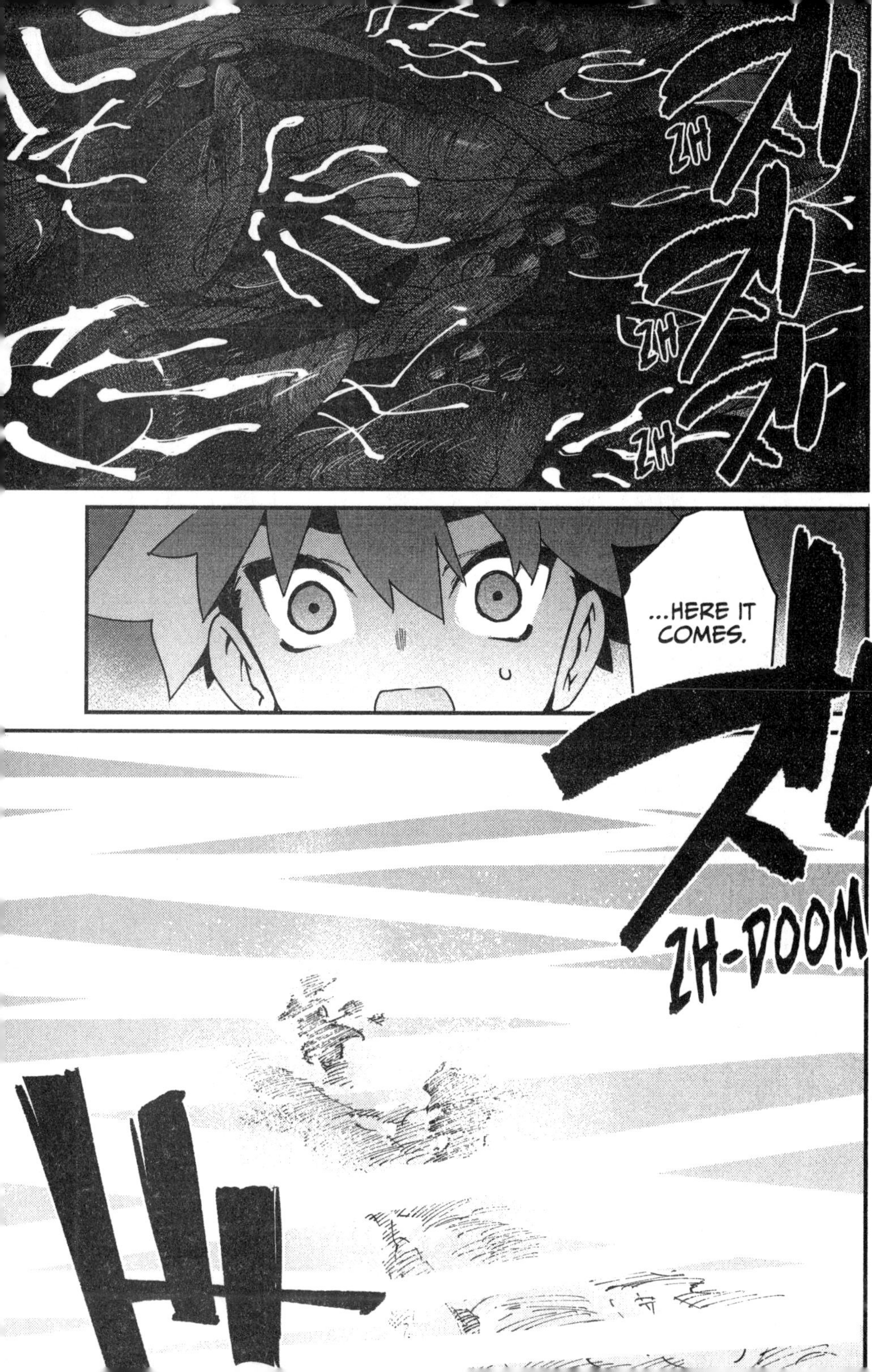
ZH
ZH
ZH
...HERE IT COMES.
ZH-DOOM

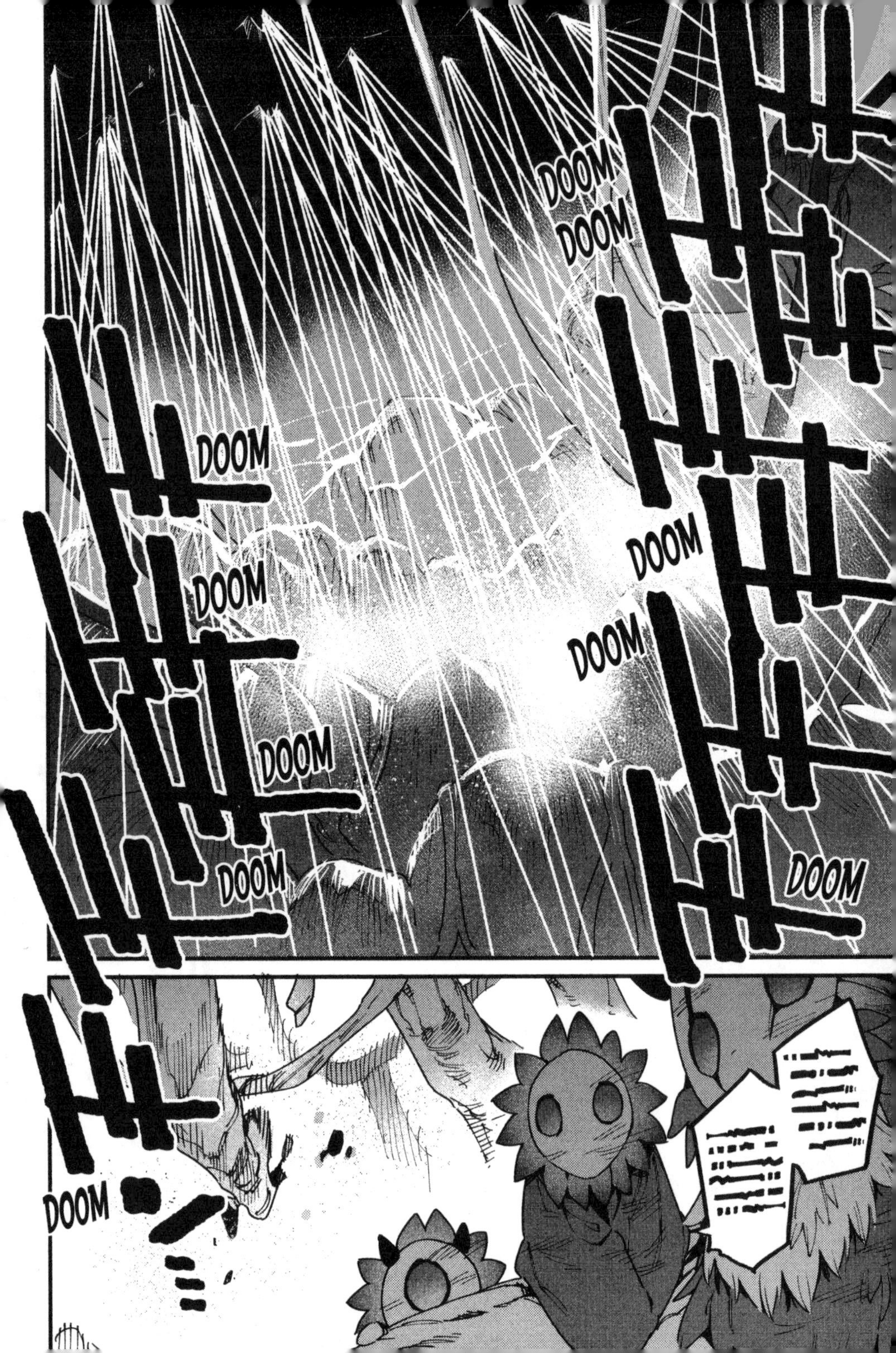
DOOM
DOOM
DOOM
DOOM
DOOM
DOOM
DOOM
DOOM
DOOM
DOOM

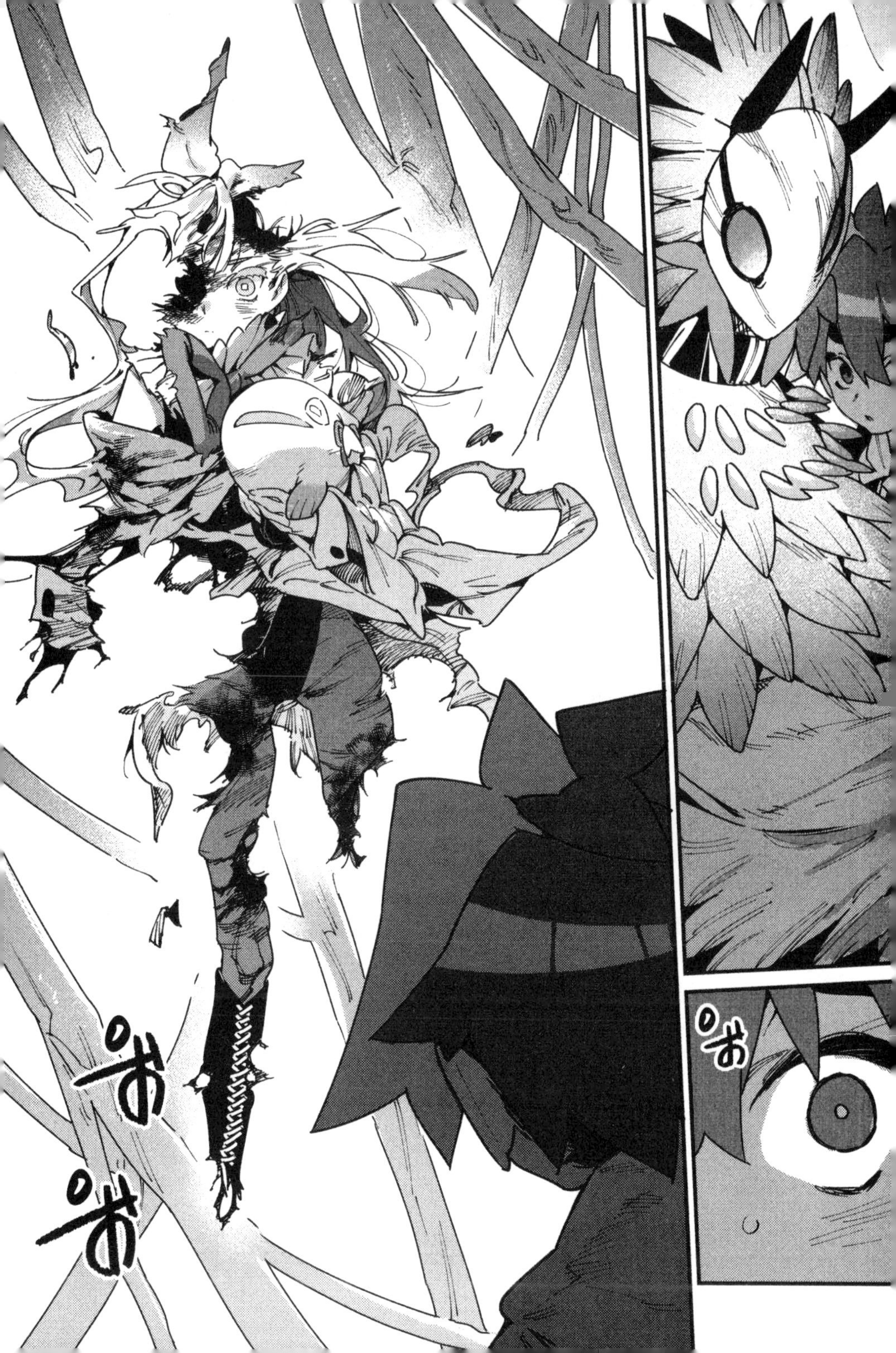
ぉお
ぉお
ぉお

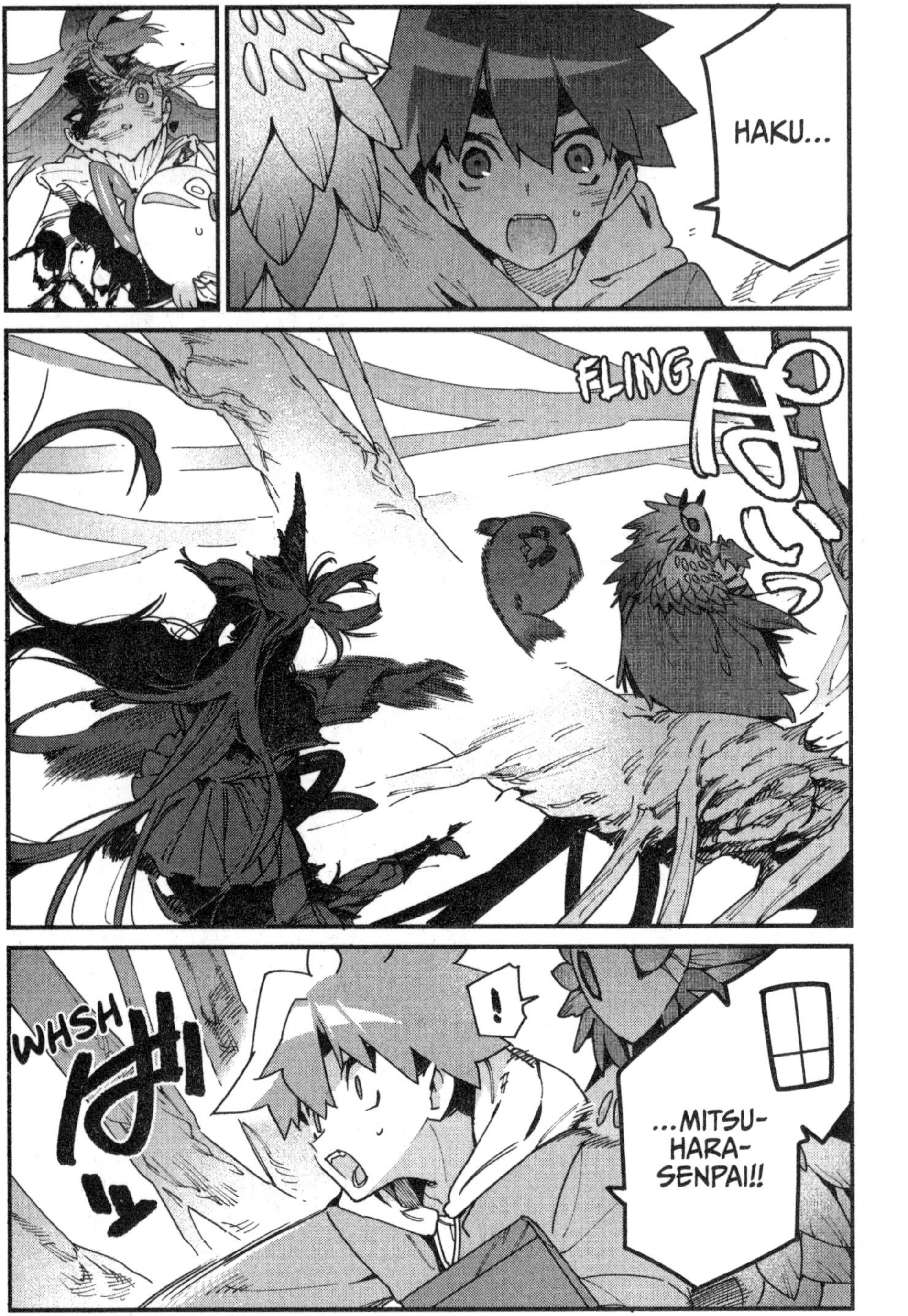
HAKU...
FLING
ぽいっ
!
...MITSU-
HARA-
SENPAI!!
WHSH
ばッ

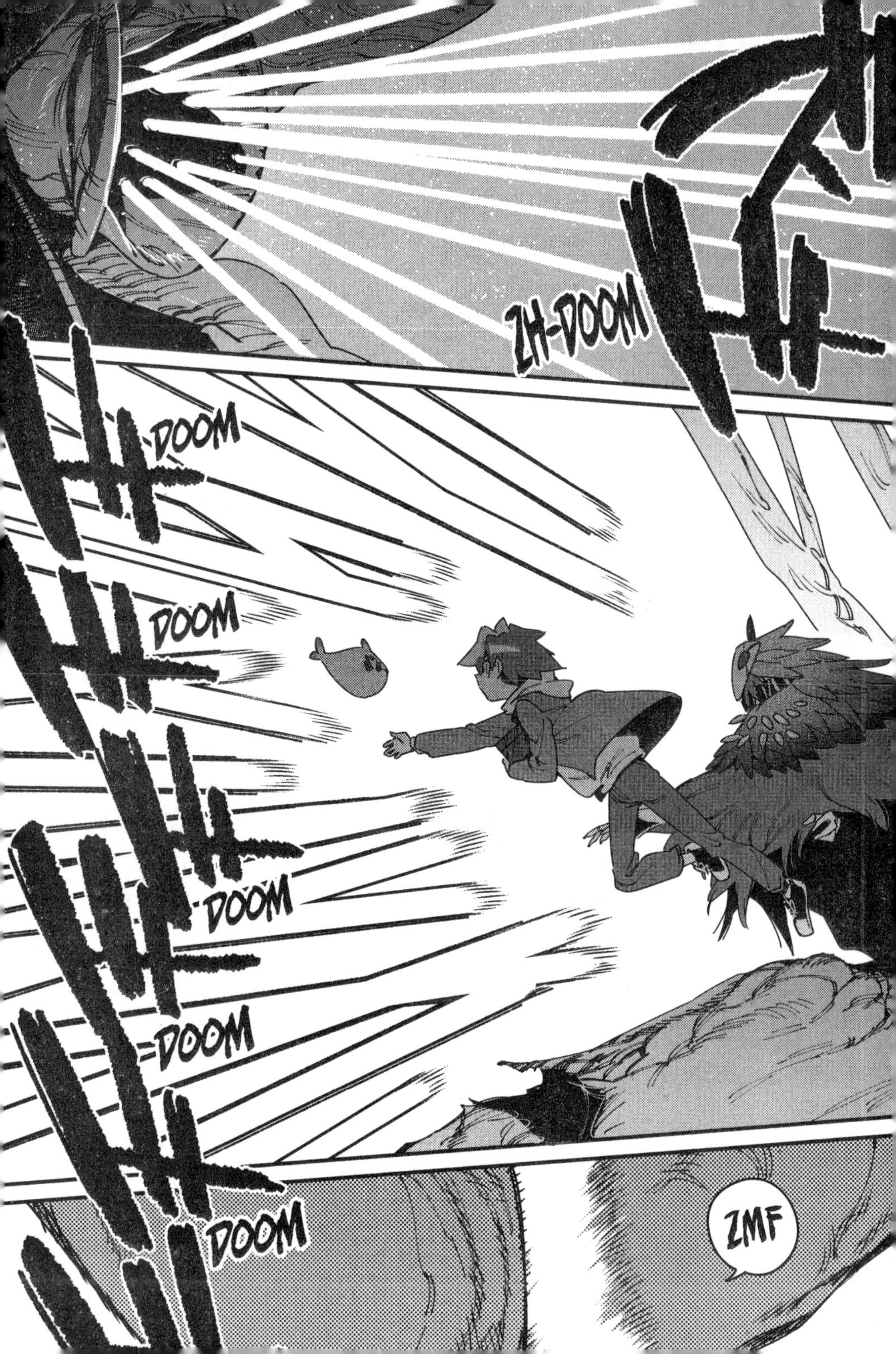
ZH-DOOM
DOOM
DOOM
DOOM
DOOM
ZMF
DOOM

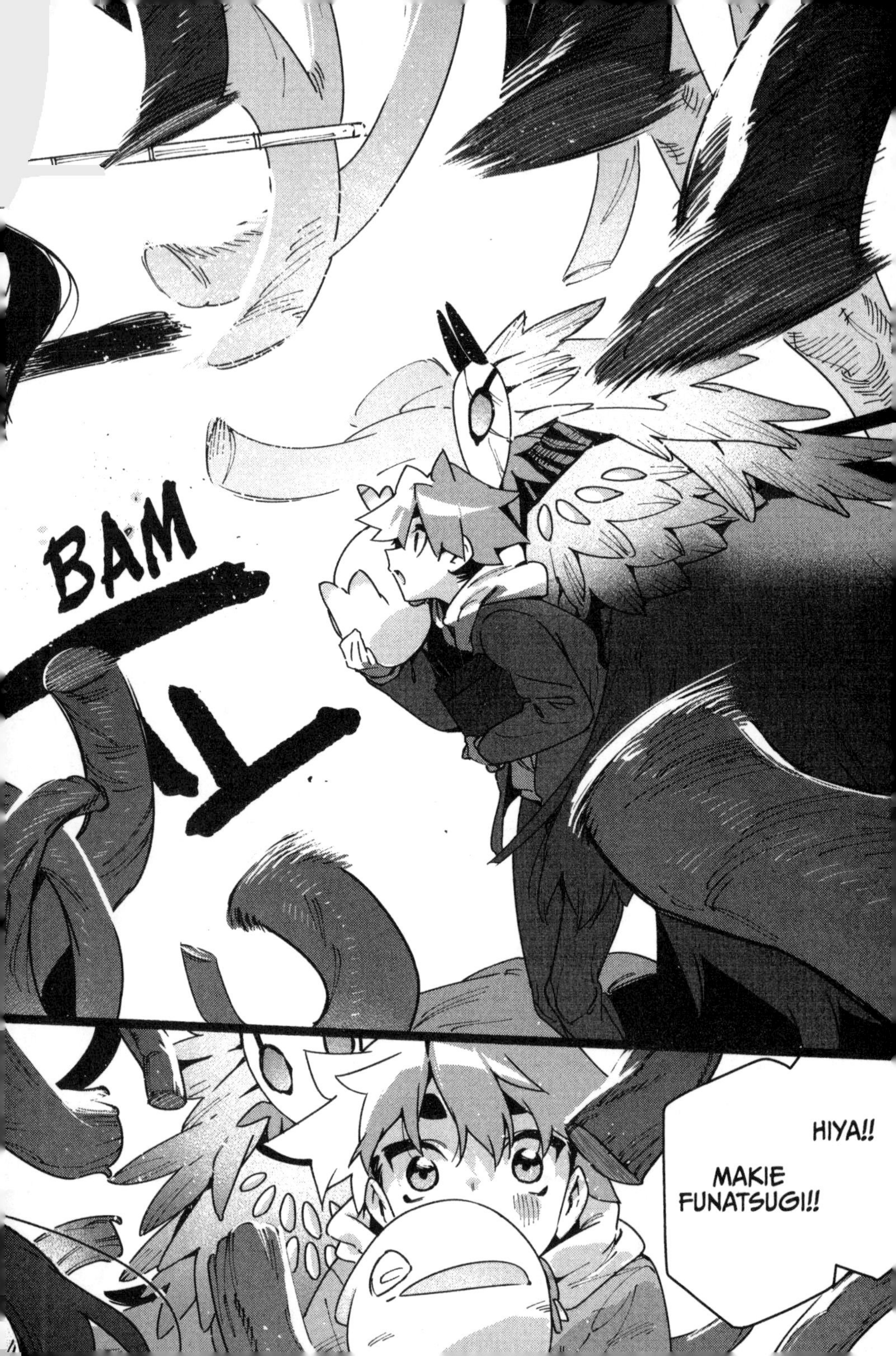
BAM
HIYA!!
MAKIE FUNATSUGI!!

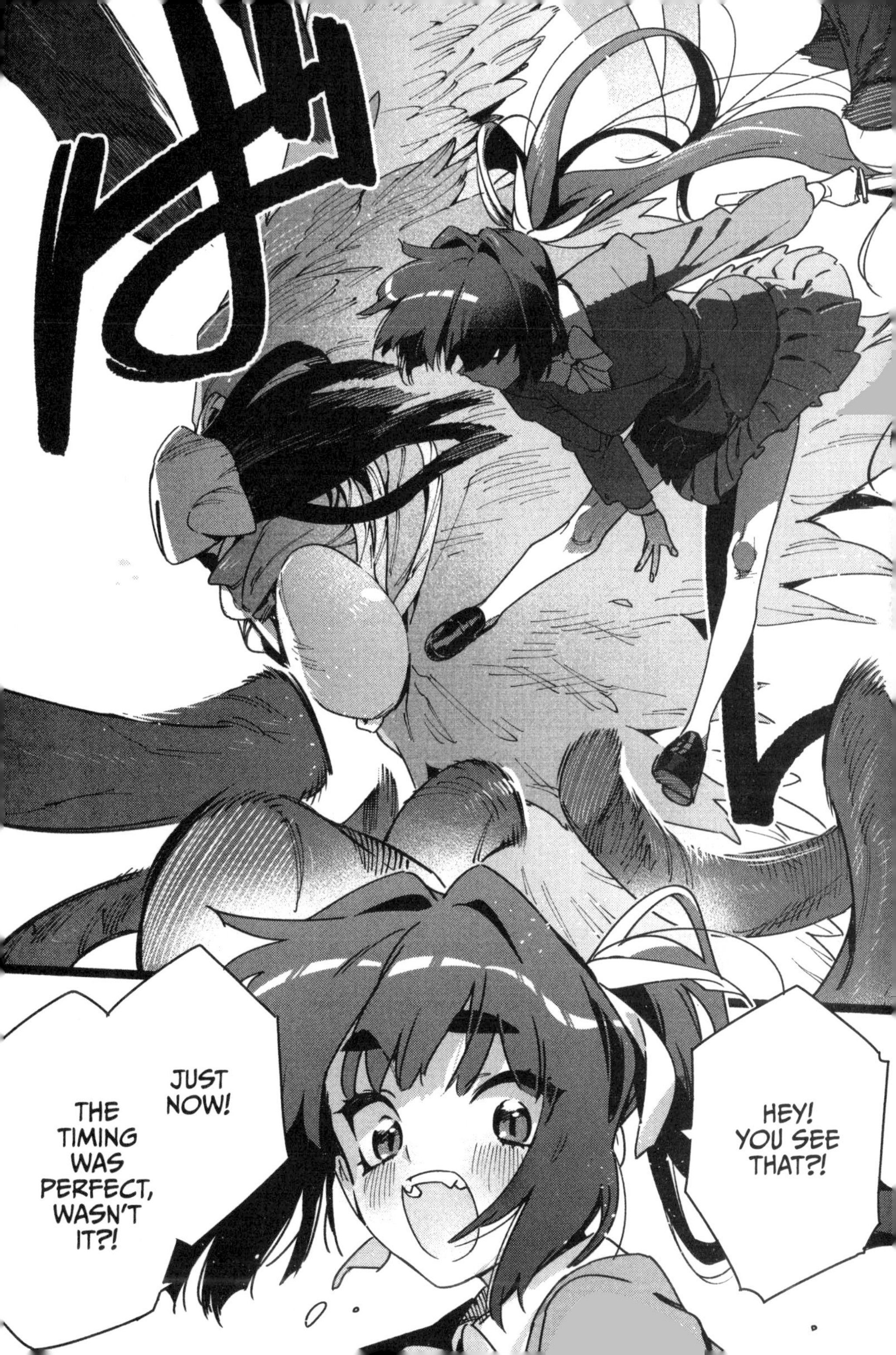
HEY! YOU SEE THAT?!
JUST NOW!
THE TIMING WAS PERFECT, WASN'T IT?!

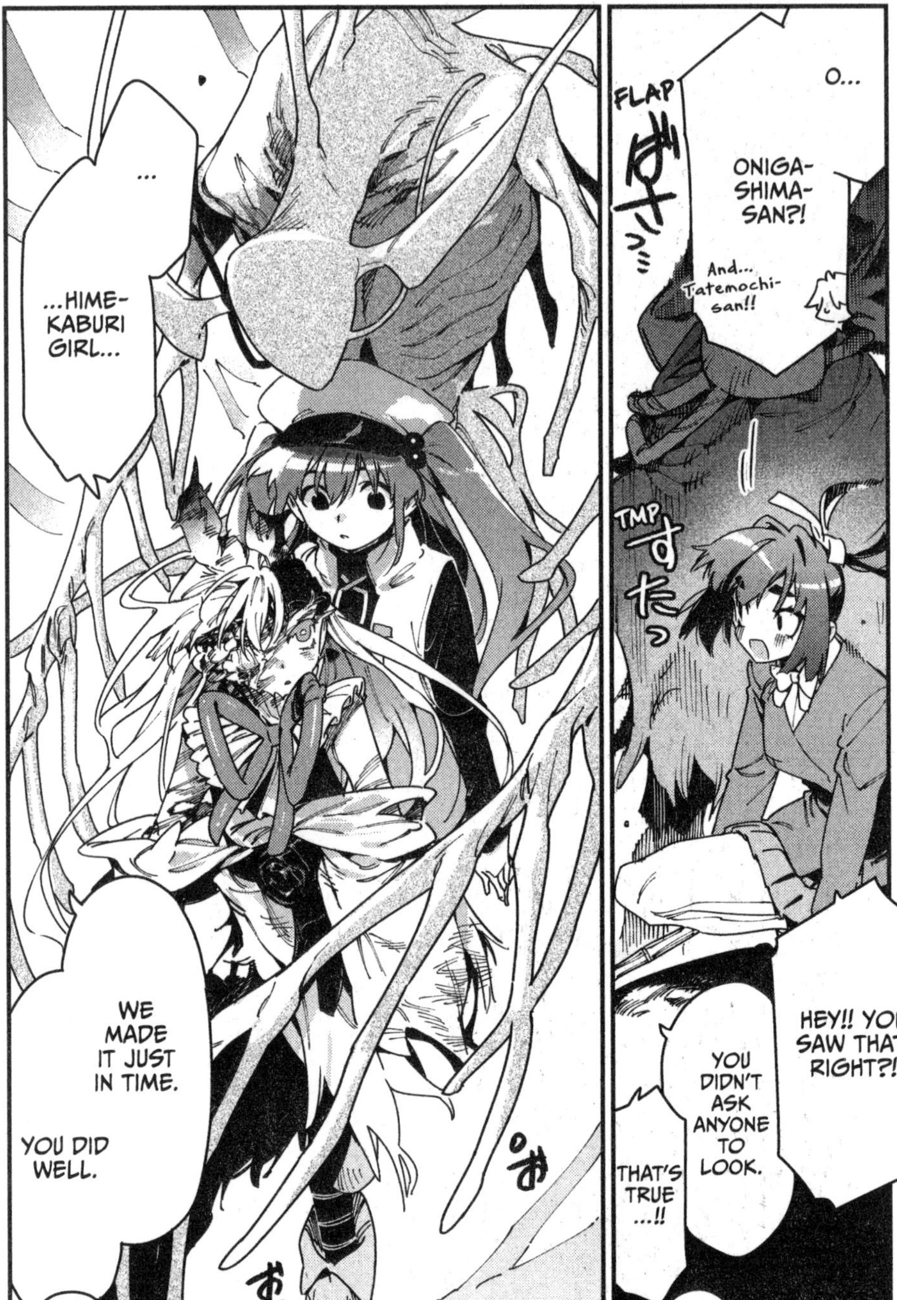

O...
FLAP
ONIGA-SHIMA-SAN?!
And... Tatemochi-san!!
TMP
すたっ
HEY!! YOU SAW THAT, RIGHT?!
YOU DIDN'T ASK ANYONE TO LOOK.
THAT'S TRUE ...!!
Uhh...
...
...HIME-KABURI GIRL...
WE MADE IT JUST IN TIME.
YOU DID WELL.
...

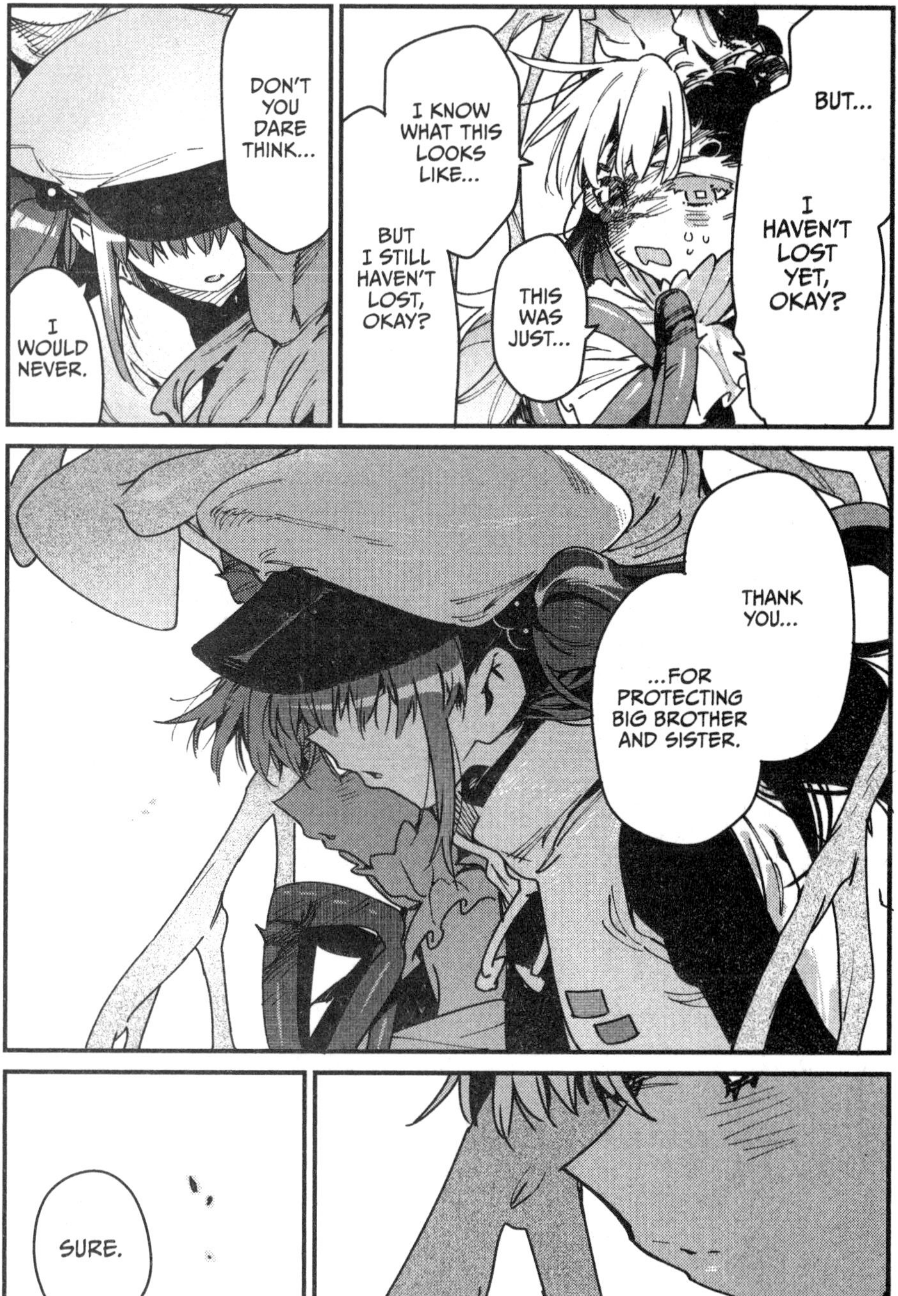
BUT...
I HAVEN'T LOST YET, OKAY?
I KNOW WHAT THIS LOOKS LIKE...
THIS WAS JUST...
BUT I STILL HAVEN'T LOST, OKAY?
DON'T YOU DARE THINK...
I WOULD NEVER.
THANK YOU...
...FOR PROTECTING BIG BROTHER AND SISTER.
SURE.

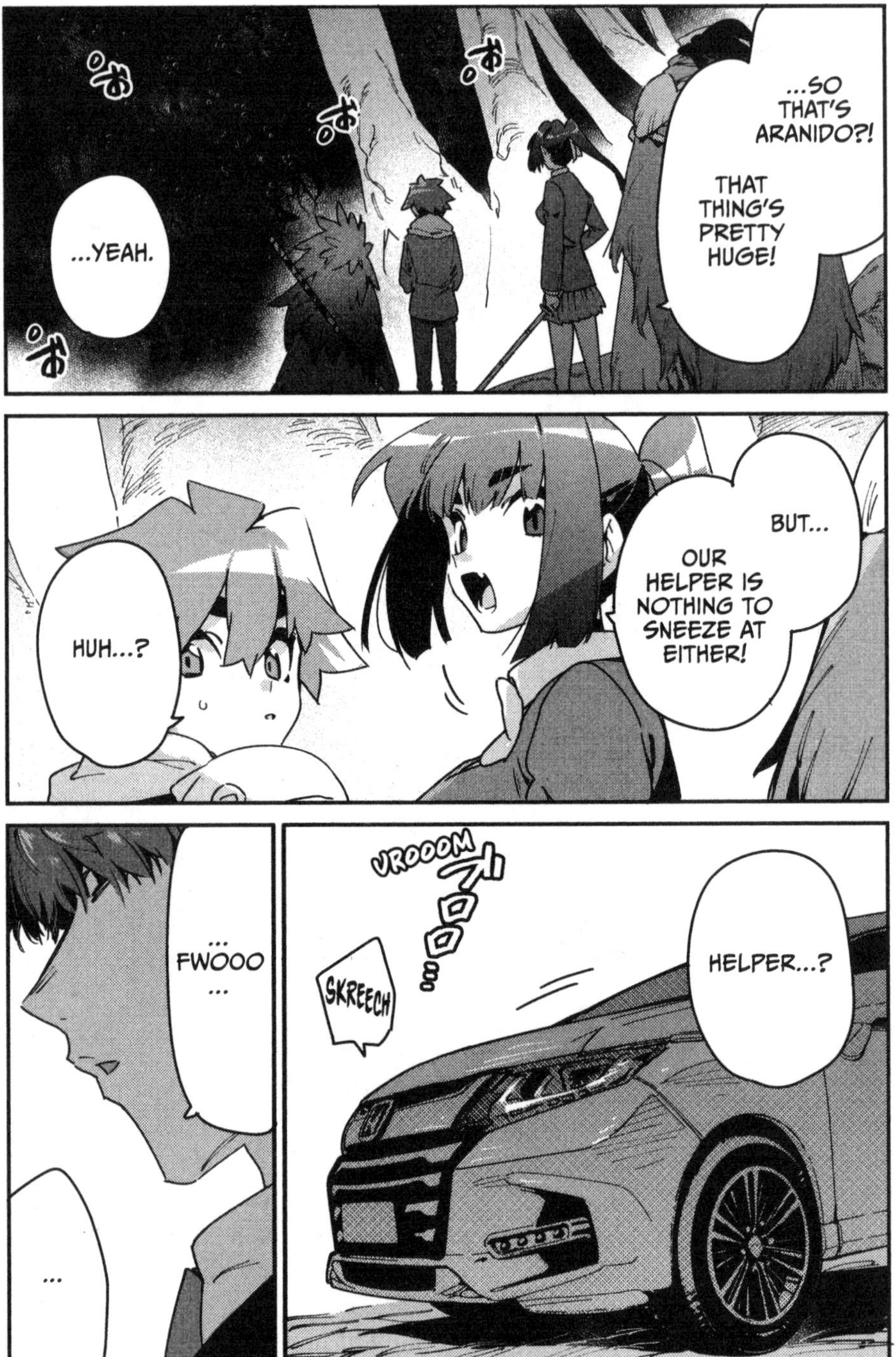

...SO THAT'S ARANIDO?!
THAT THING'S PRETTY HUGE!
...YEAH.
BUT...
OUR HELPER IS NOTHING TO SNEEZE AT EITHER!
HUH...?
HELPER...?
VROOOM
SKREECH
... FWOOO ...
...

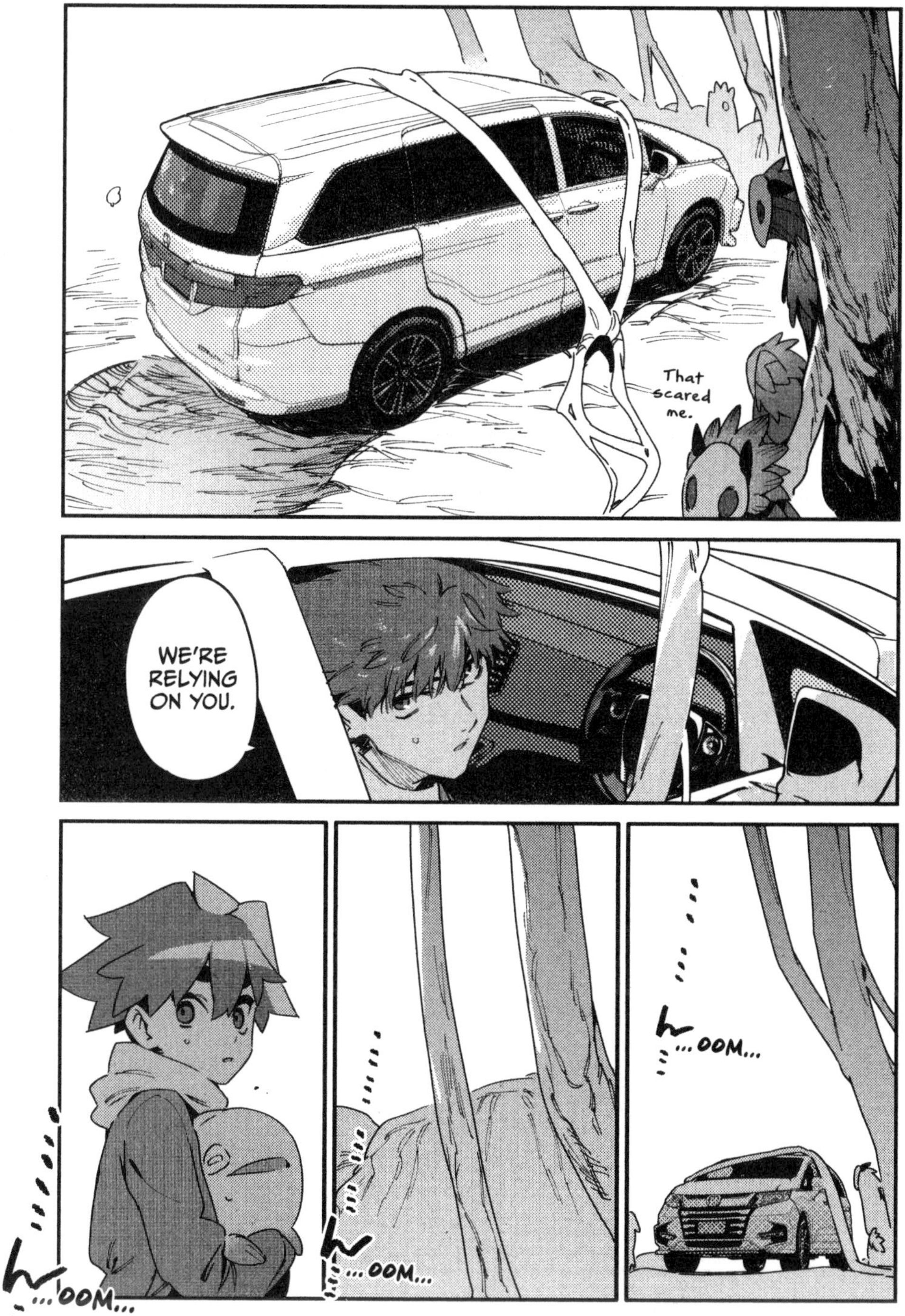
That scared me.
WE'RE RELYING ON YOU.
...
...OOM...
...OOM...
...OOM...

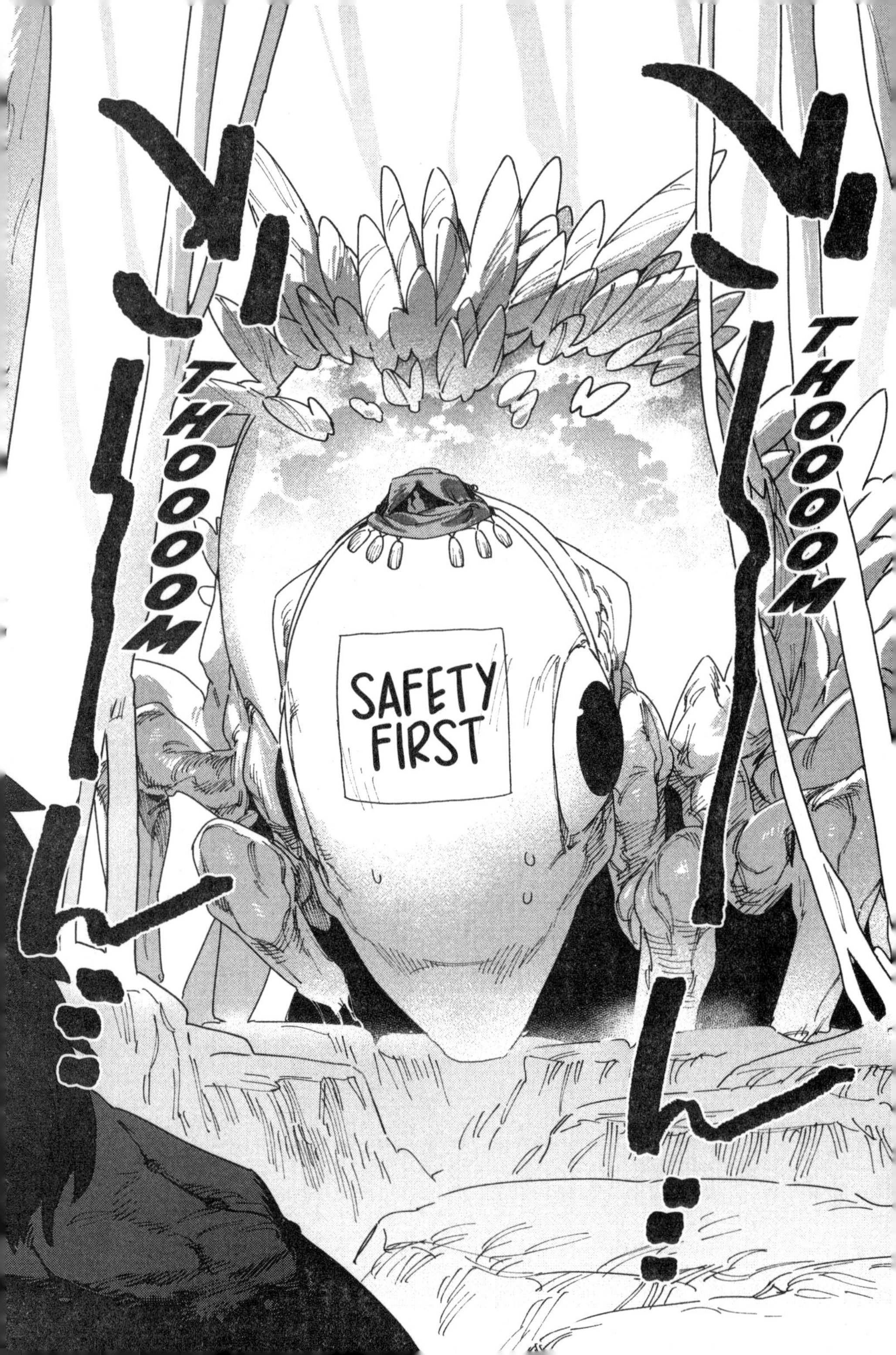
THOOOOOM
SAFETY FIRST
THOOOOOM

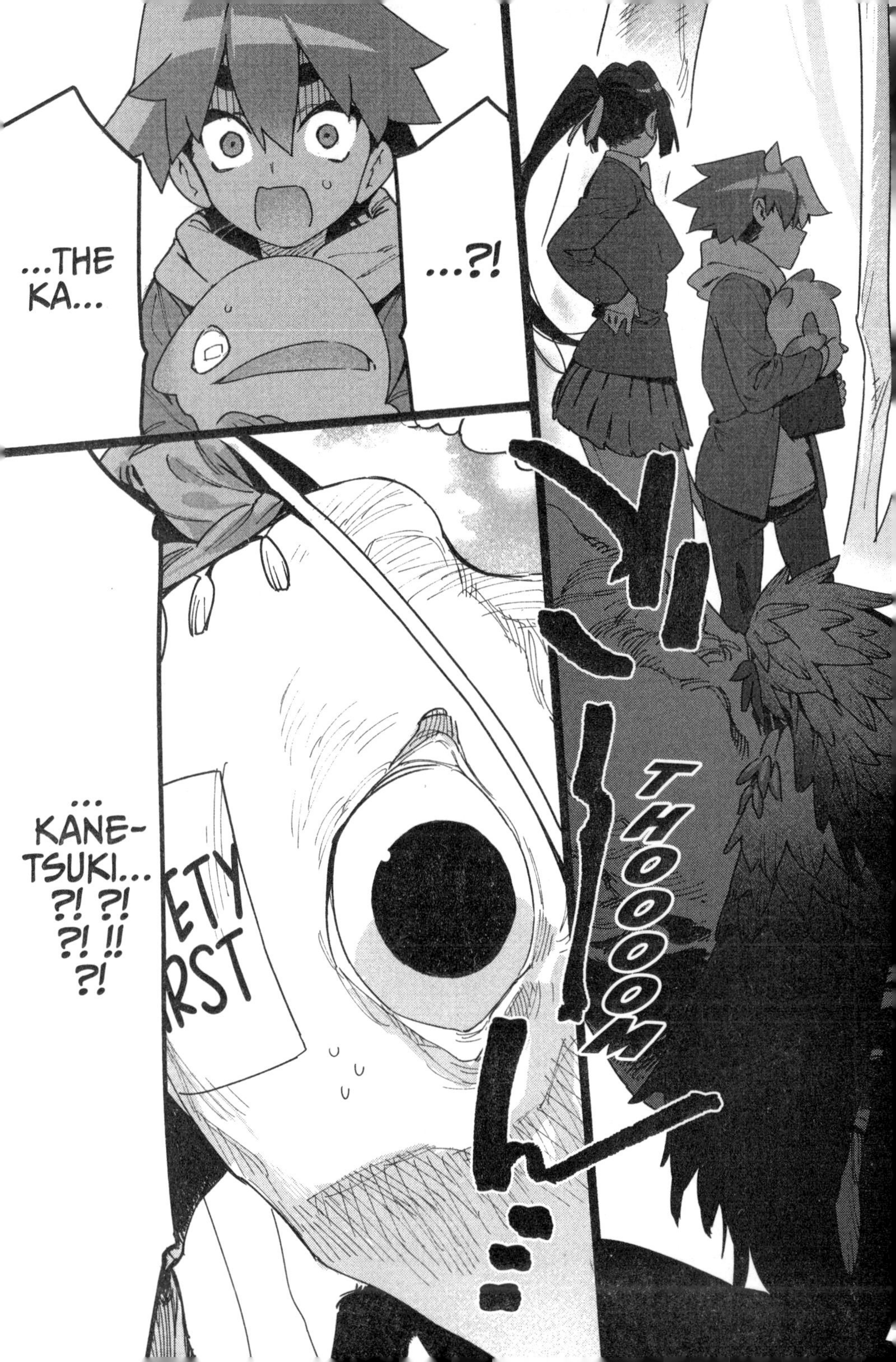
THOOOOOM
...?!
...THE KA...
... KANE-TSUKI...?! ?! ?! !! ?!

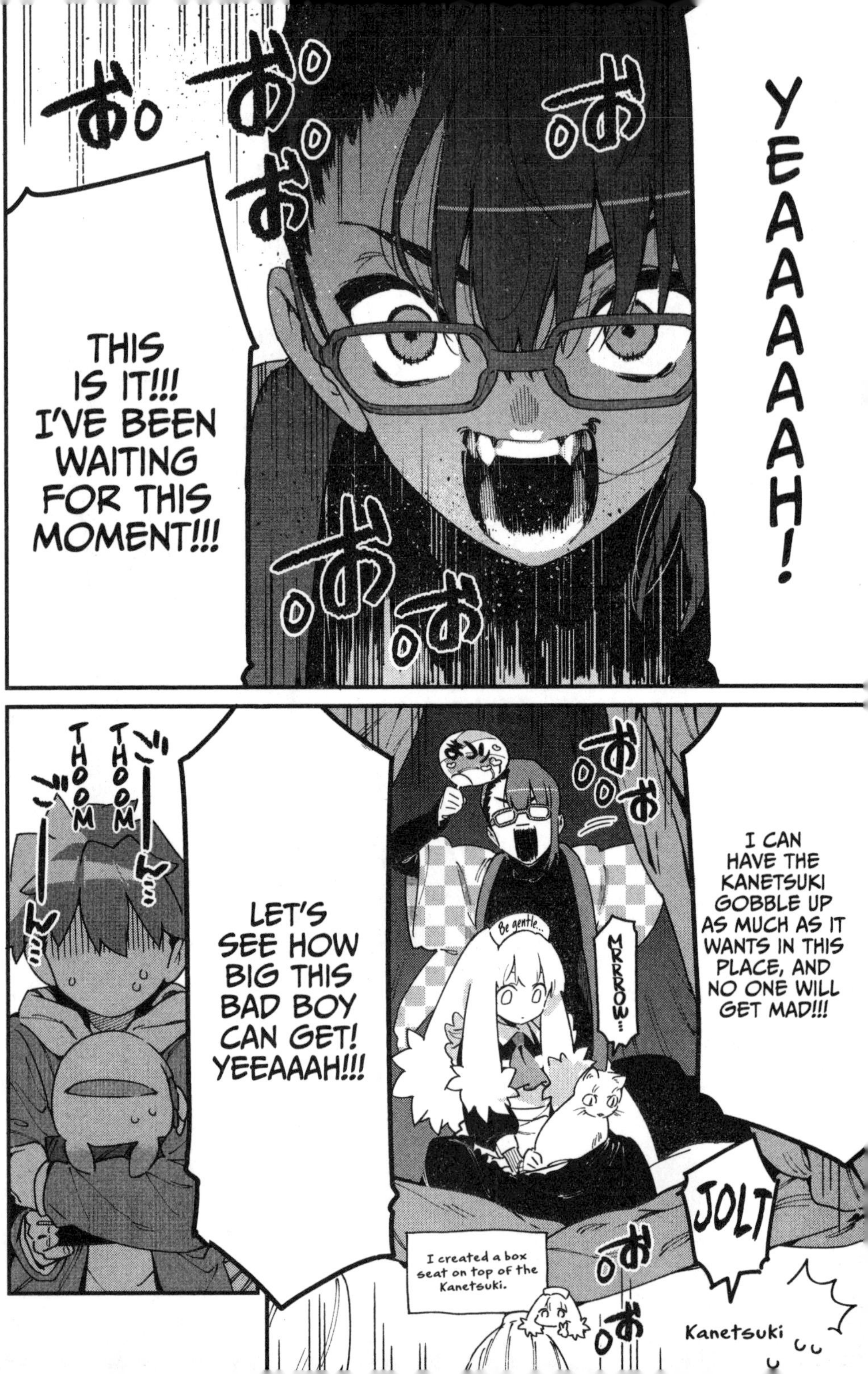
YEAAAAAH!
THIS IS IT!!! I'VE BEEN WAITING FOR THIS MOMENT!!!
I CAN HAVE THE KANETSUKI GOBBLE UP AS MUCH AS IT WANTS IN THIS PLACE, AND NO ONE WILL GET MAD!!!
MRRROW...
Be gentle...
LET'S SEE HOW BIG THIS BAD BOY CAN GET! YEEAAAH!!!
JOLT
I created a box seat on top of the Kanetsuki.
Kanetsuki
THOOM
THOOM

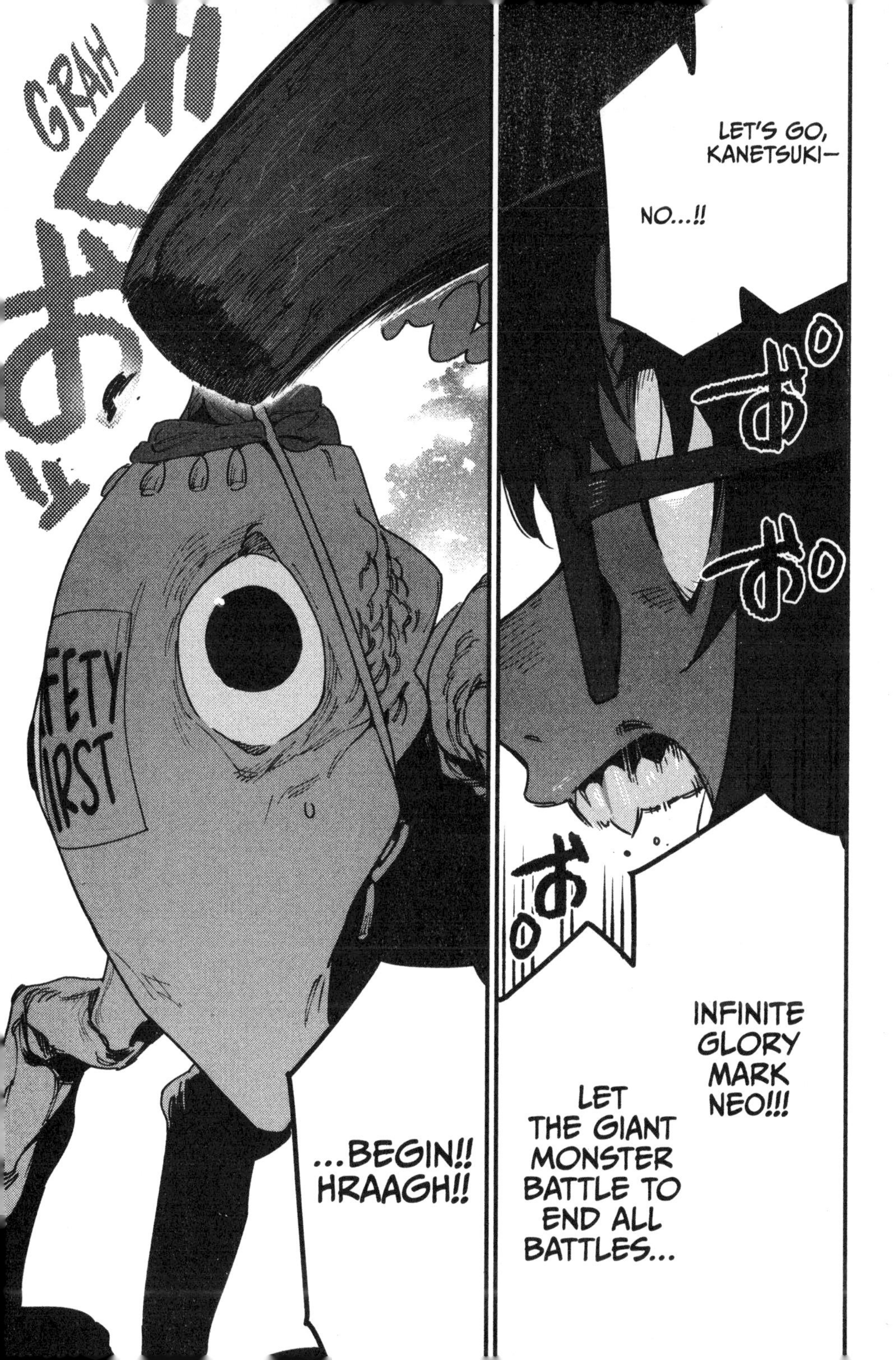
LET'S GO, KANETSUKI—
NO...!!
お。お。お。
INFINITE GLORY MARK NEO!!!
LET THE GIANT MONSTER BATTLE TO END ALL BATTLES...
GRAH
...BEGIN!! HRAAGH!!

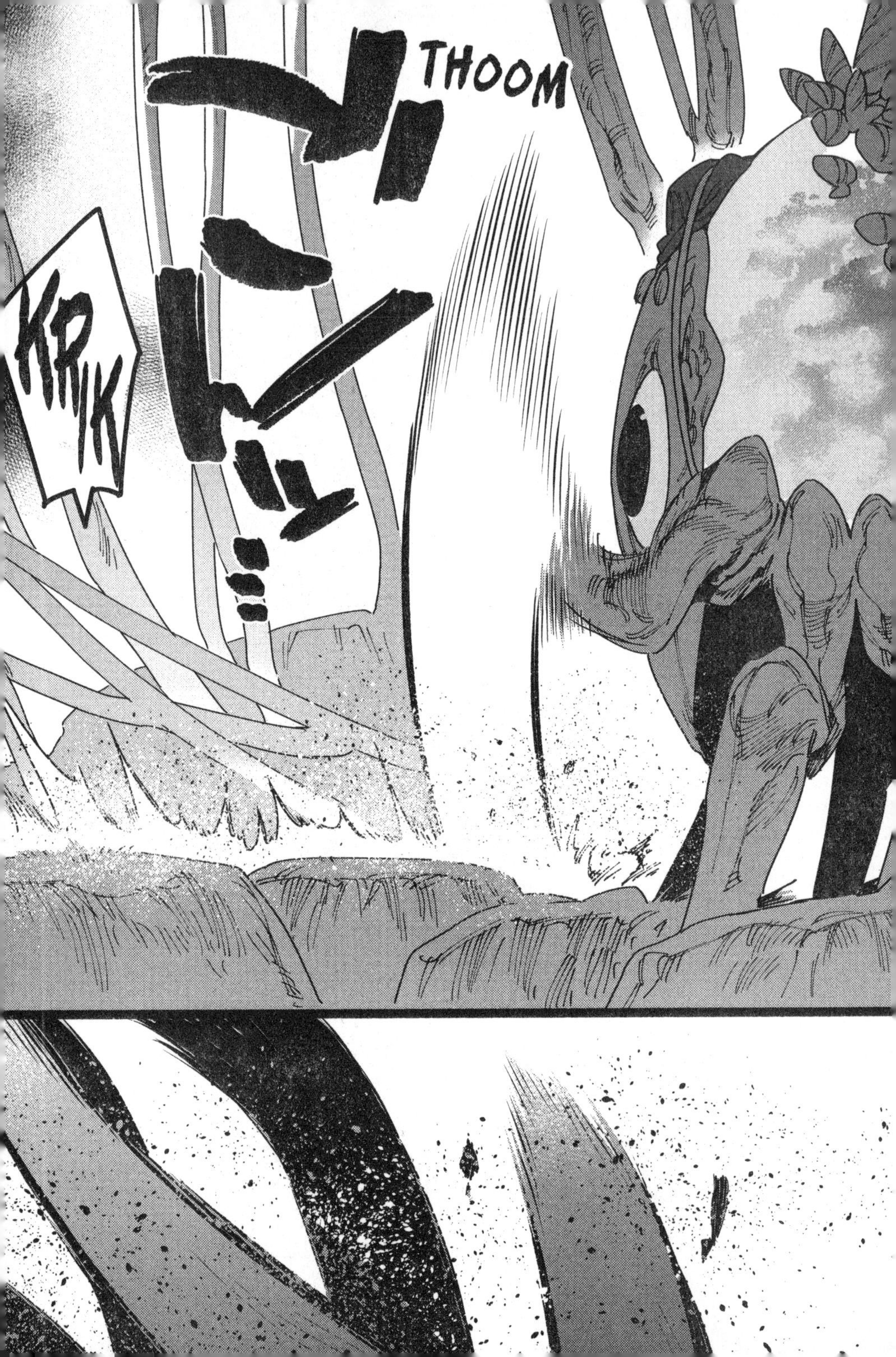
THOOM
KRIK

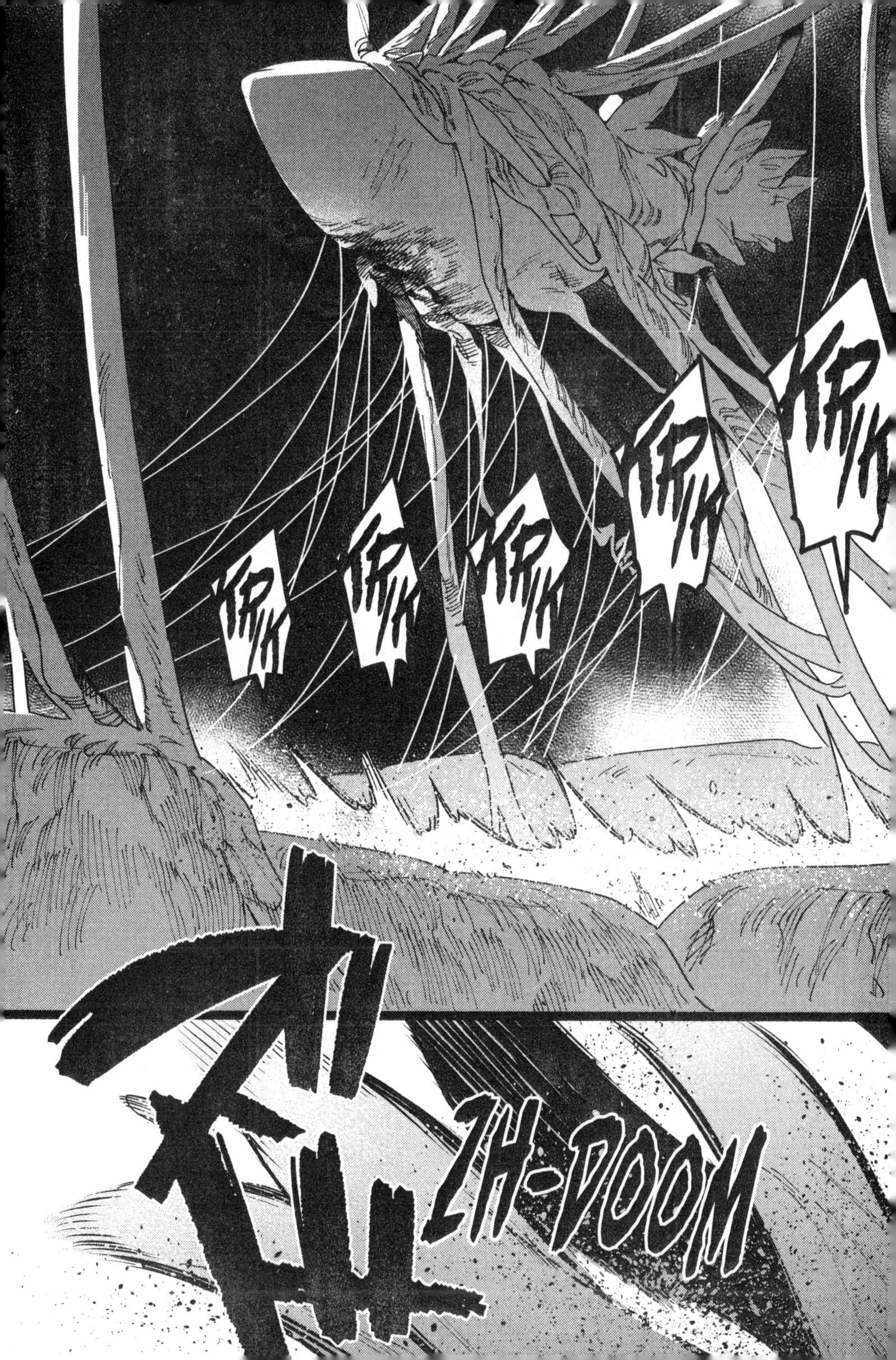
KRIK
KRIK
KRIK
KRIK
KRIK
ZH-DOOM

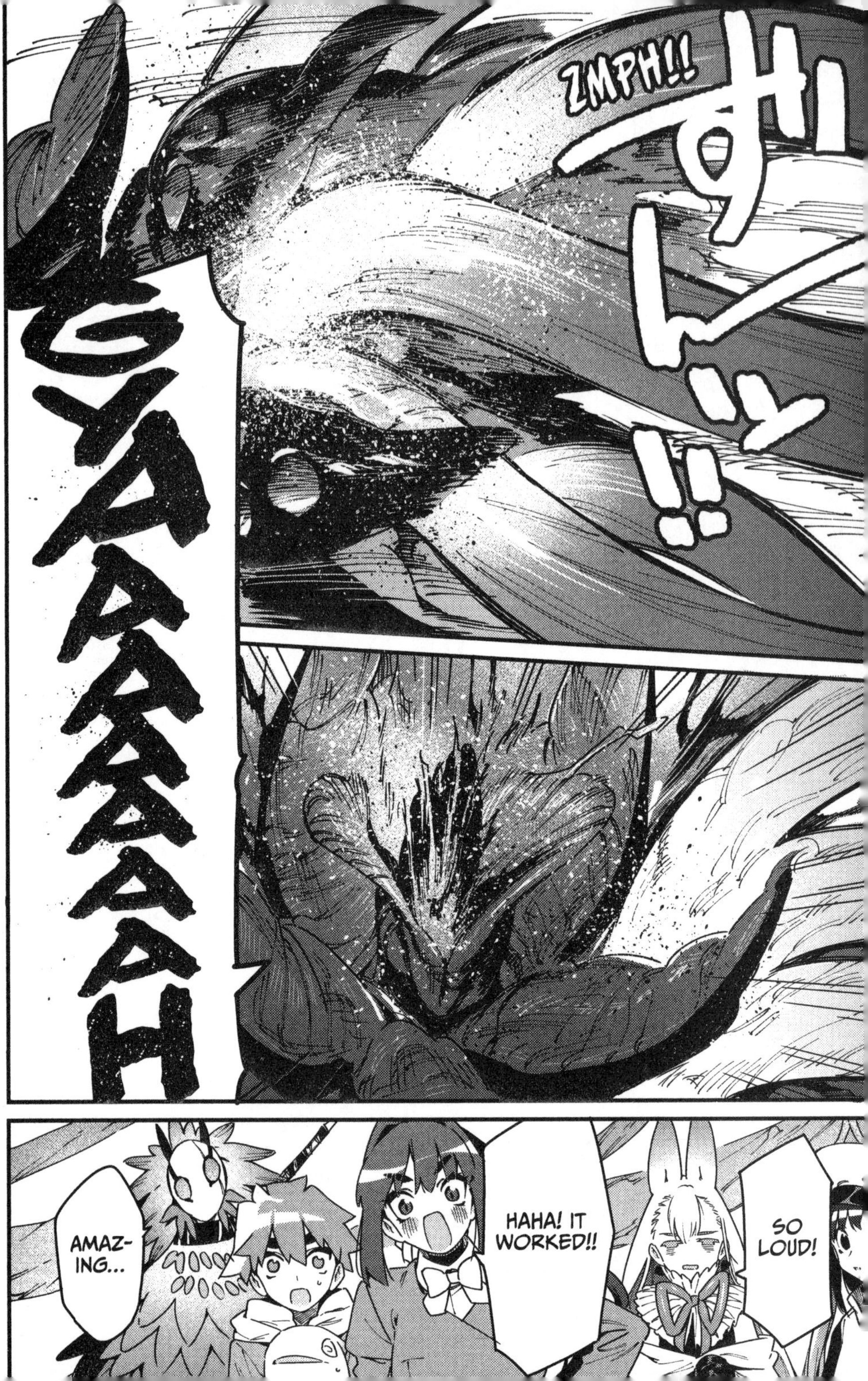
ZMPH!!
ずんッ!!
GYAAAAAAH
SO LOUD!
HAHA! IT WORKED!!
AMAZ-ING...

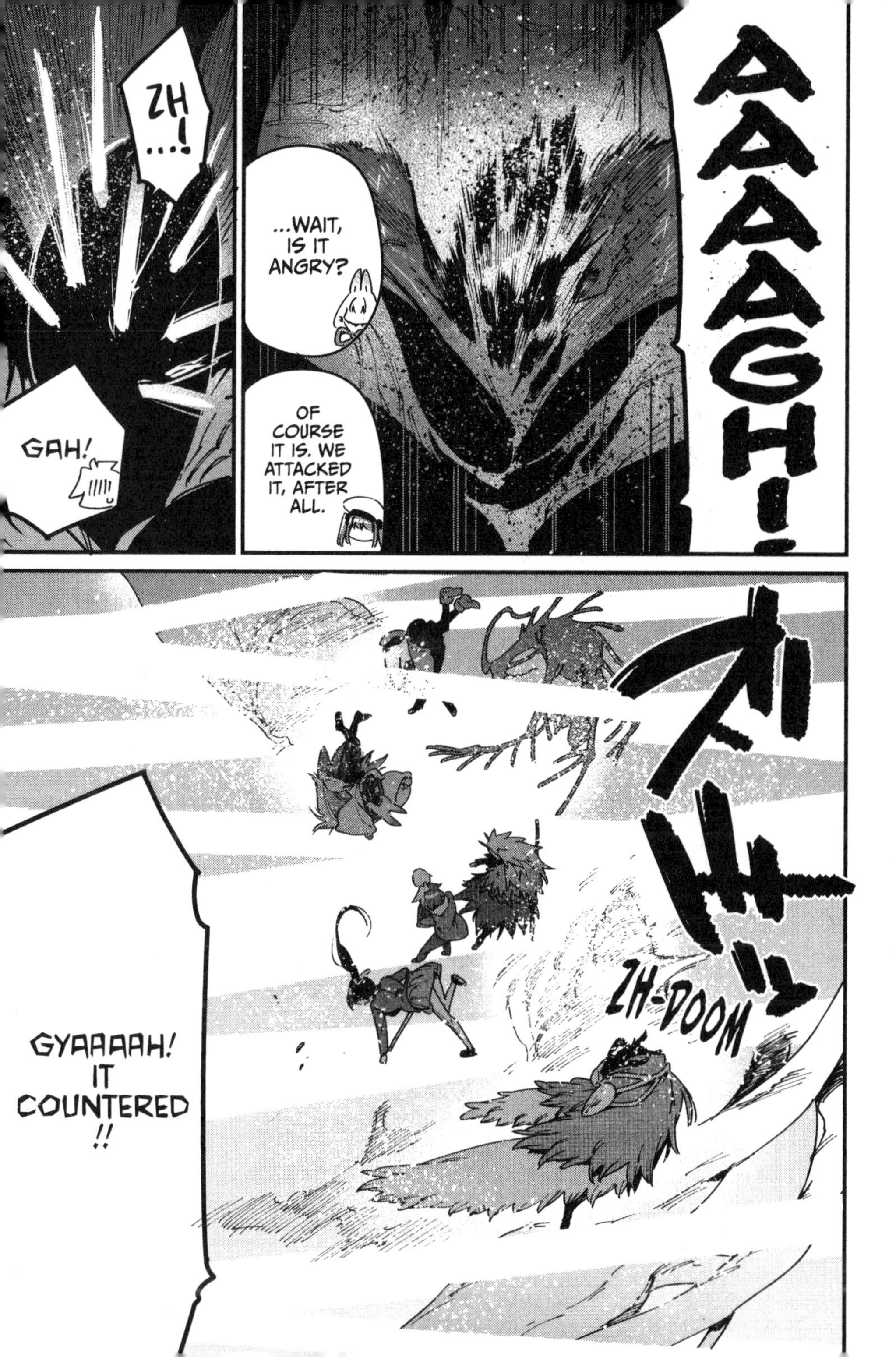
AAAAGH!
...WAIT, IS IT ANGRY?
OF COURSE IT IS. WE ATTACKED IT, AFTER ALL.
ZH...!
GAH!
ZH-DOOM
GYAAAAH! IT COUNTERED!!

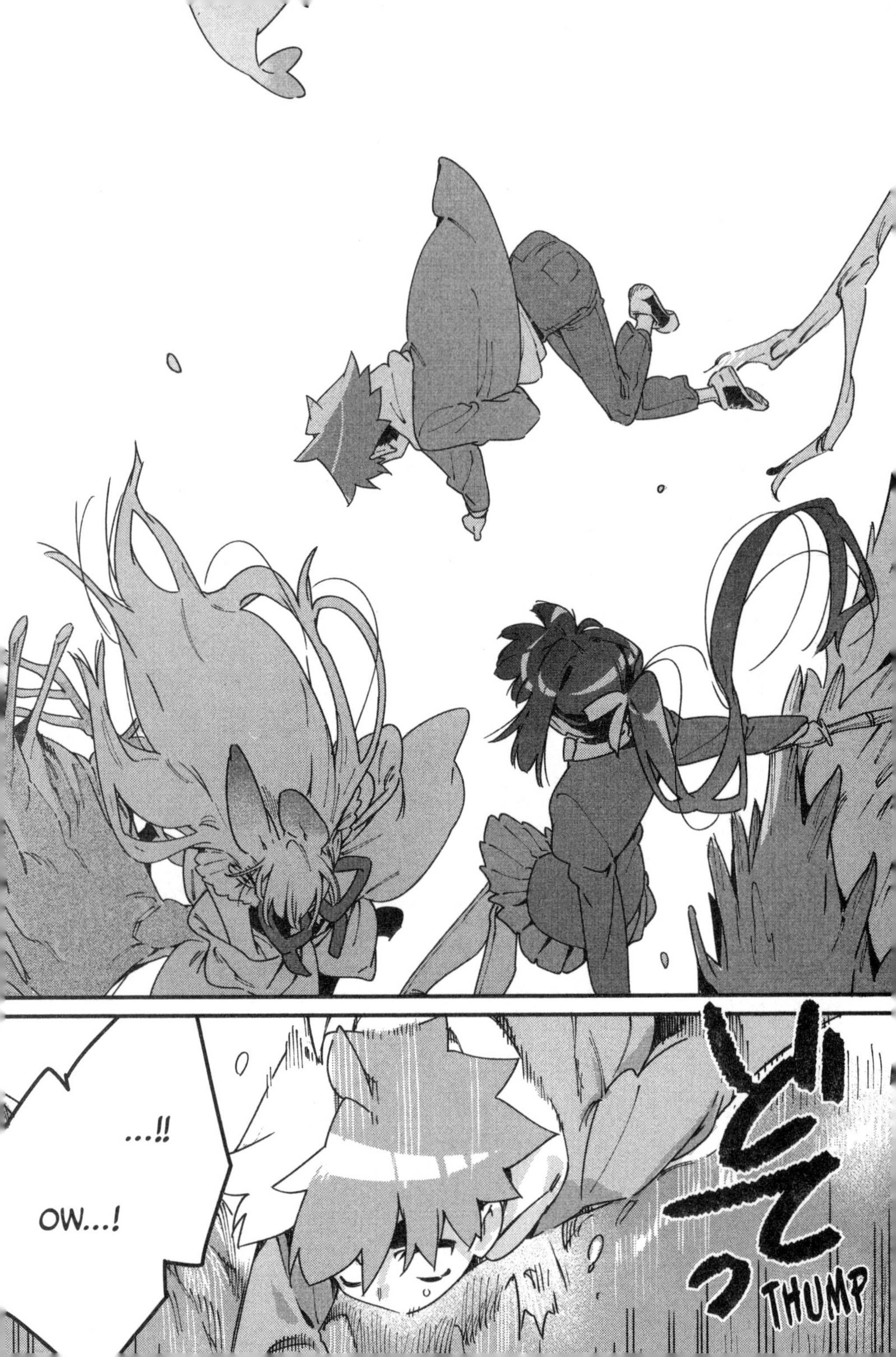
どっ
THUMP
...!!
OW...!

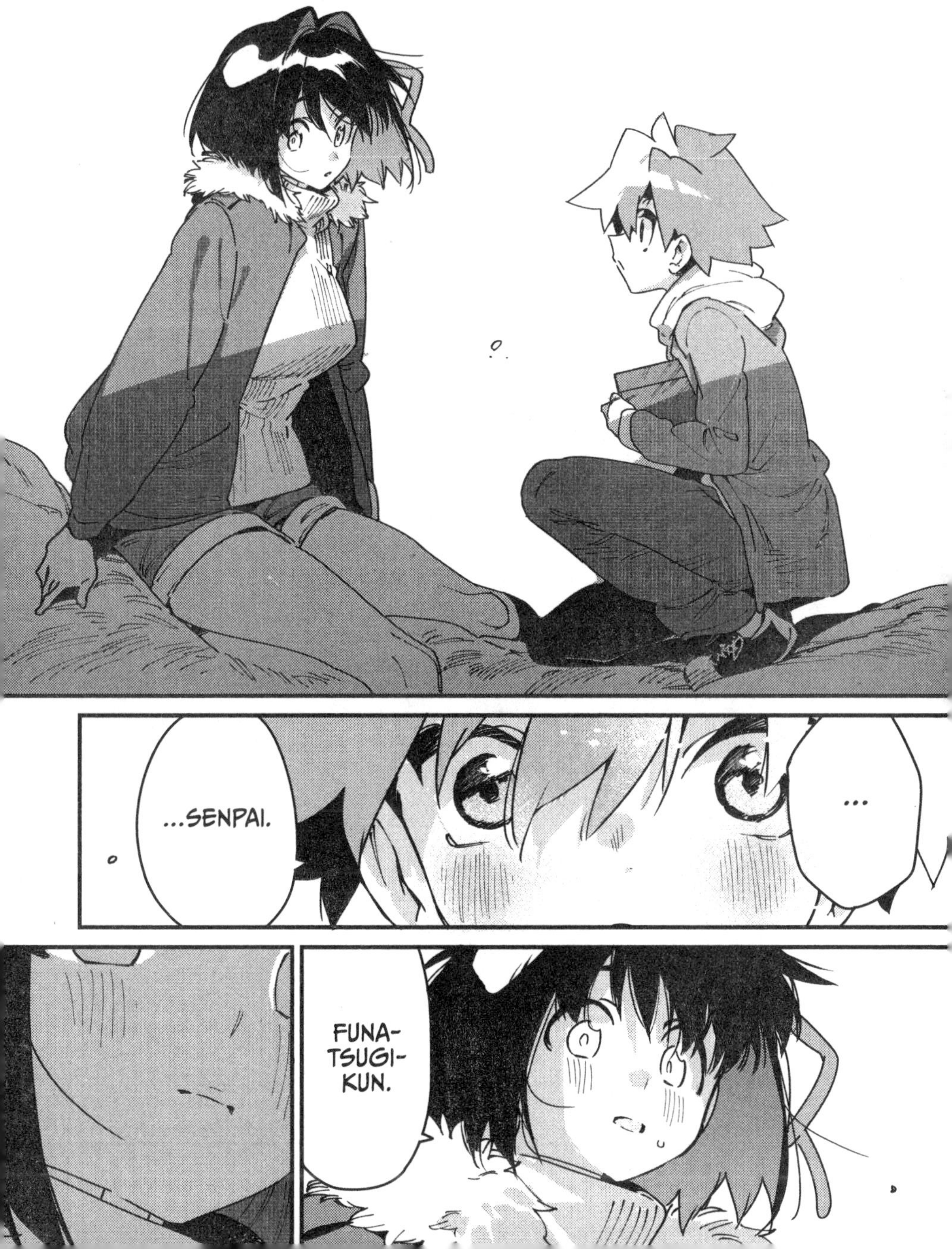
...
...SENPAI.
FUNA-TSUGI-KUN.

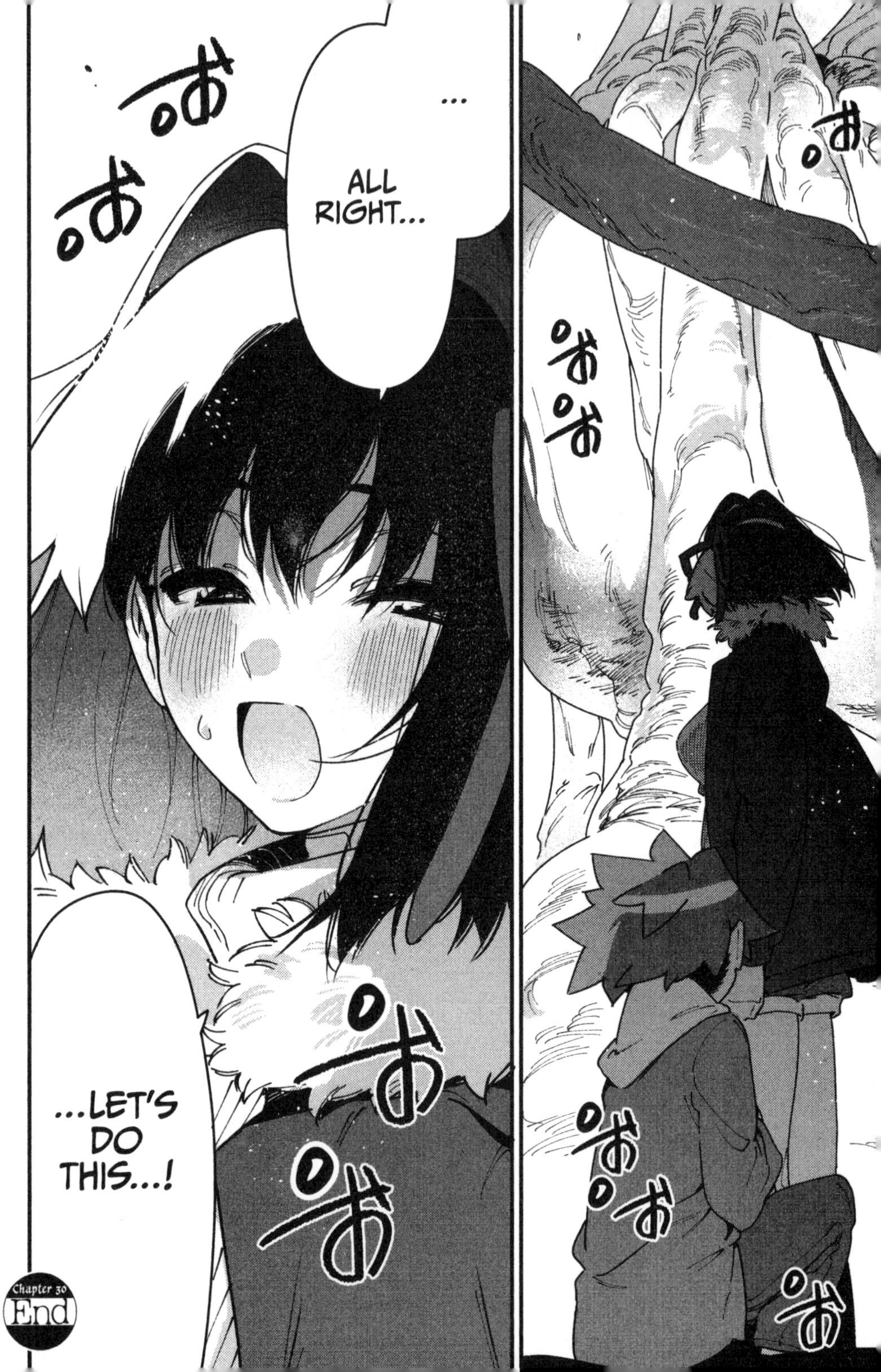
ぉ
ぉぉ
ぉぉ
ぉ
...
ALL RIGHT...
ぉぉ
ぉぉ
...LET'S DO THIS...!
Chapter 30
End

Chapter 31: Hold

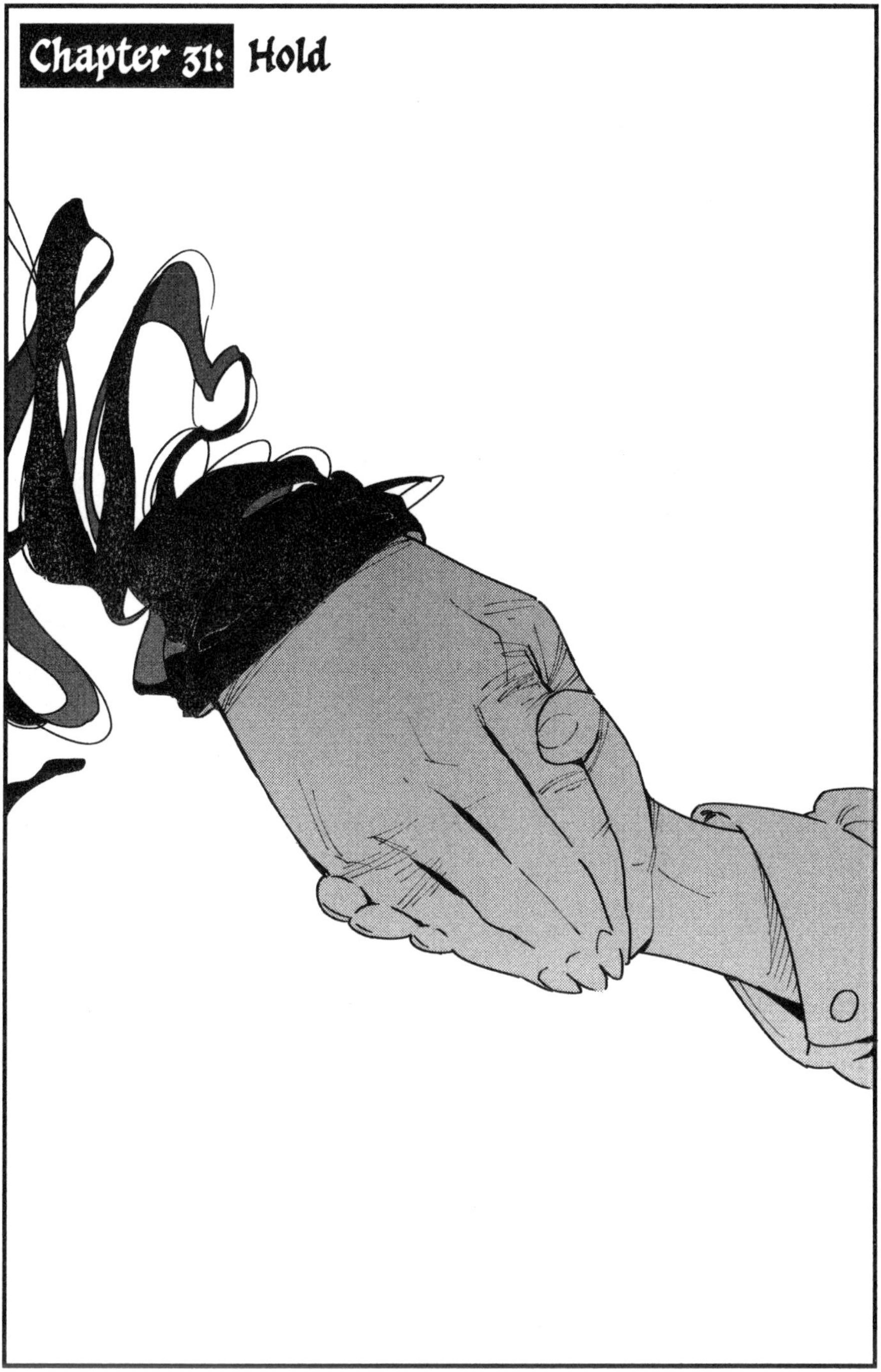

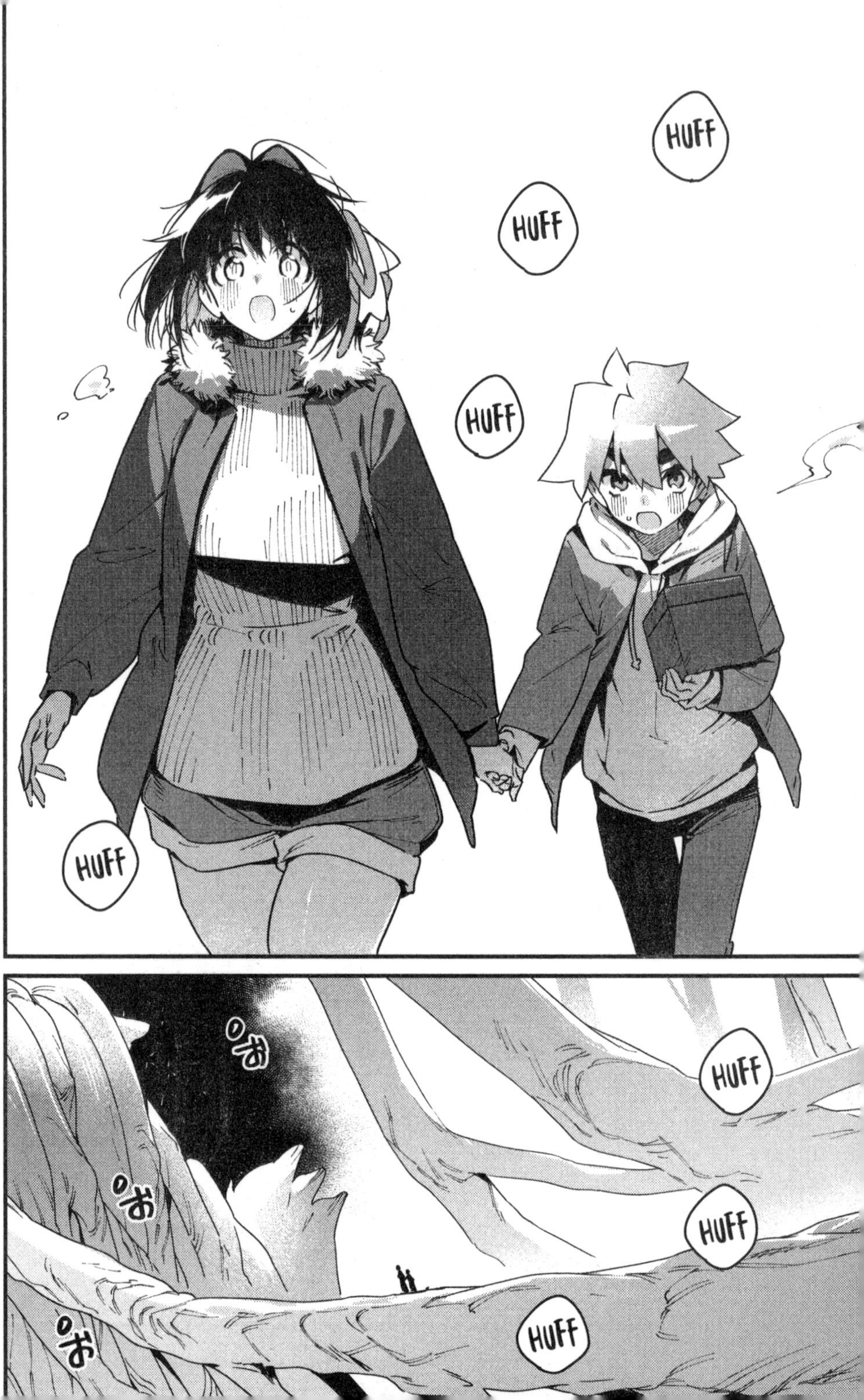
HUFF
HUFF
HUFF
HUFF
HUFF
HUFF
HUFF
お
お
お

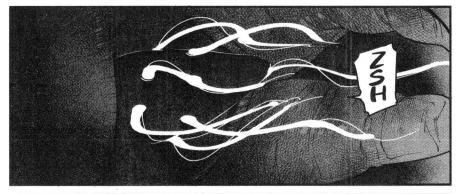

ZSH

MM!

IT'S COMING!!

CHOM...

ZH-DOOM

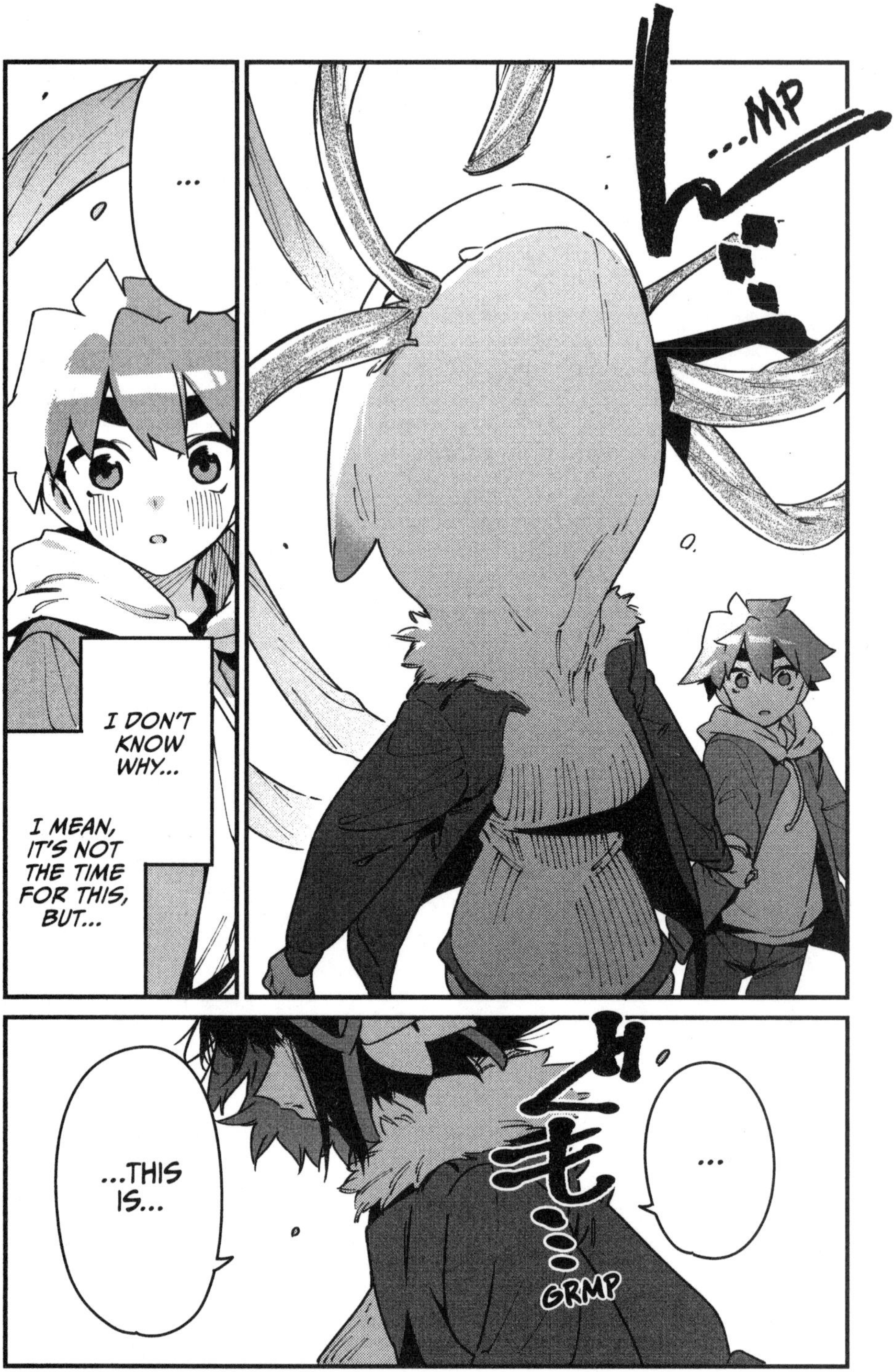
...MP
...
...
I DON'T KNOW WHY...
I MEAN, IT'S NOT THE TIME FOR THIS, BUT...
...
GRMP
...THIS IS...

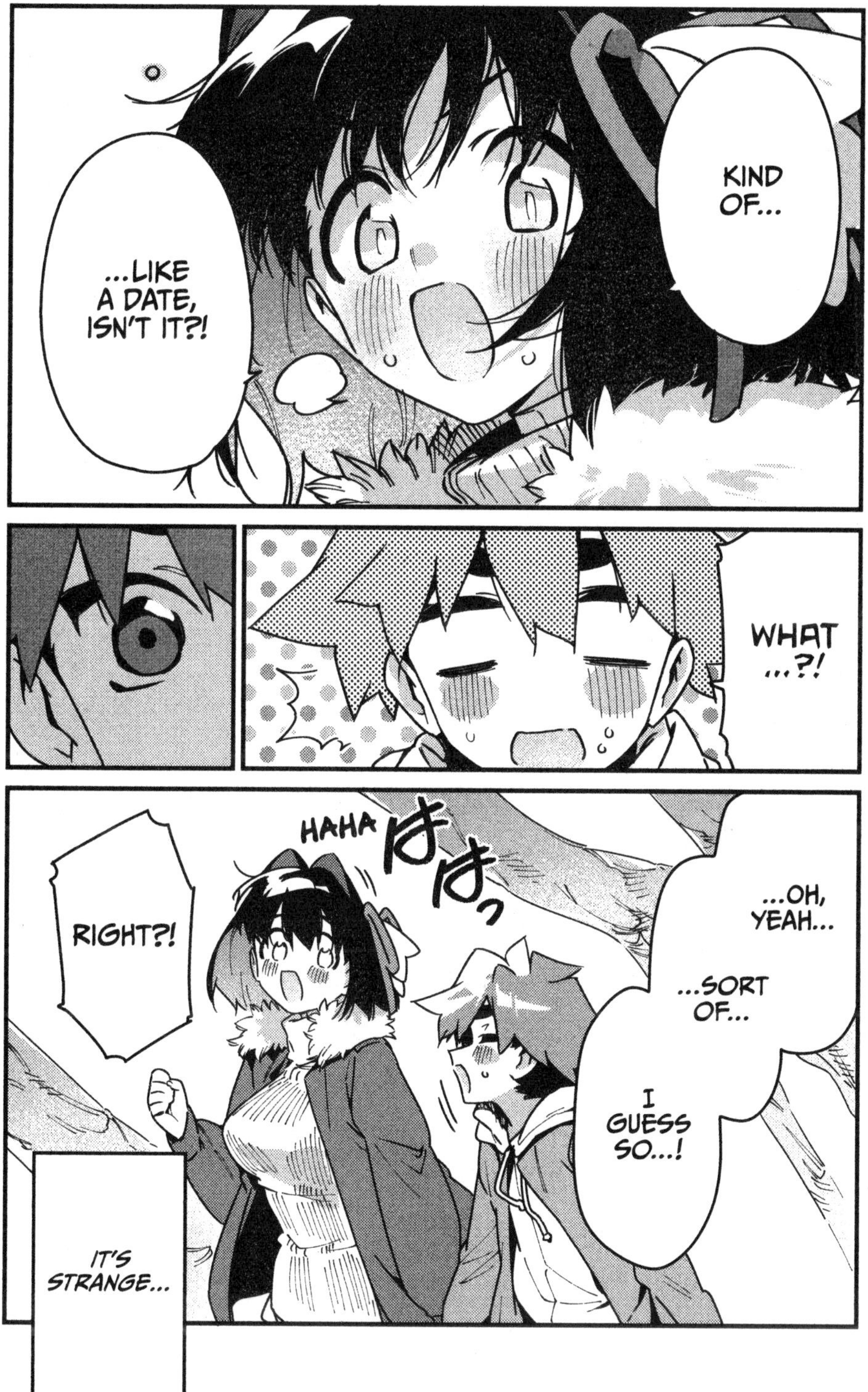
KIND OF...
...LIKE A DATE, ISN'T IT?!
WHAT ...?!
...OH, YEAH...
...SORT OF...
I GUESS SO...!
HAHA ははっ
RIGHT?!
IT'S STRANGE...

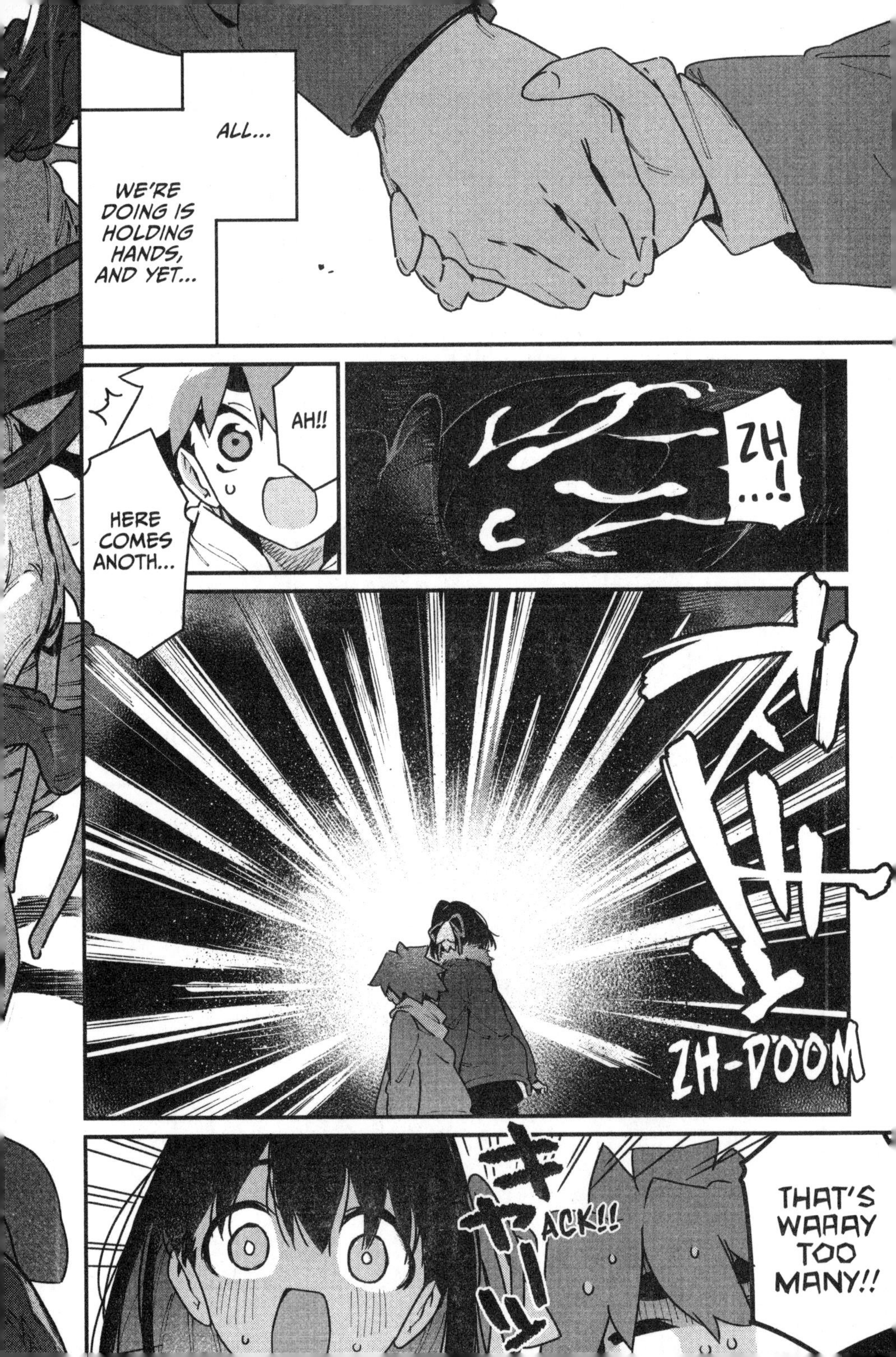
ALL...
WE'RE DOING IS HOLDING HANDS, AND YET...
ZH...!
AH!!
HERE COMES ANOTH...
ZH-DOOM
THAT'S WAAAY TOO MANY!!
ACK!!

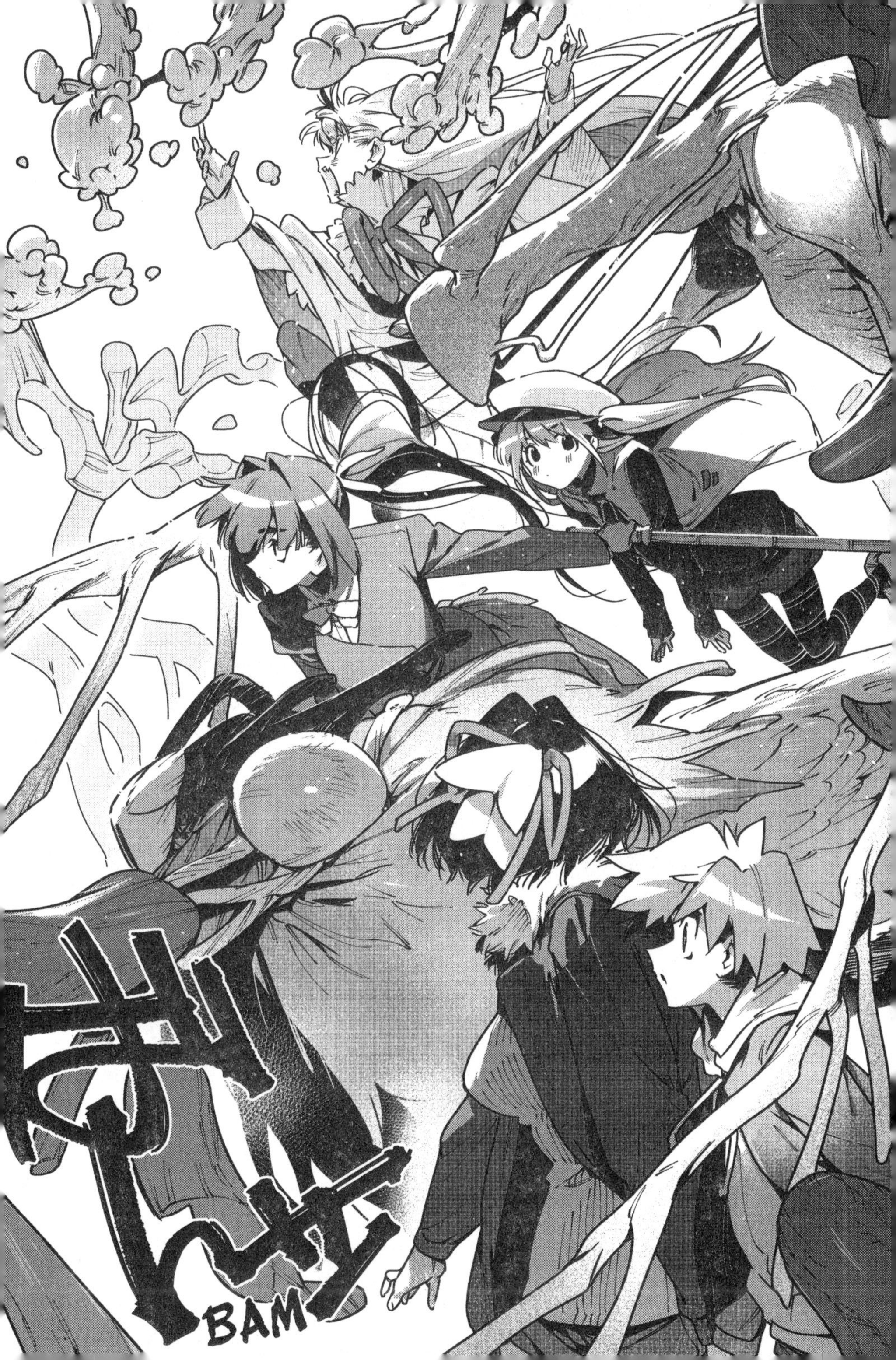
BAM

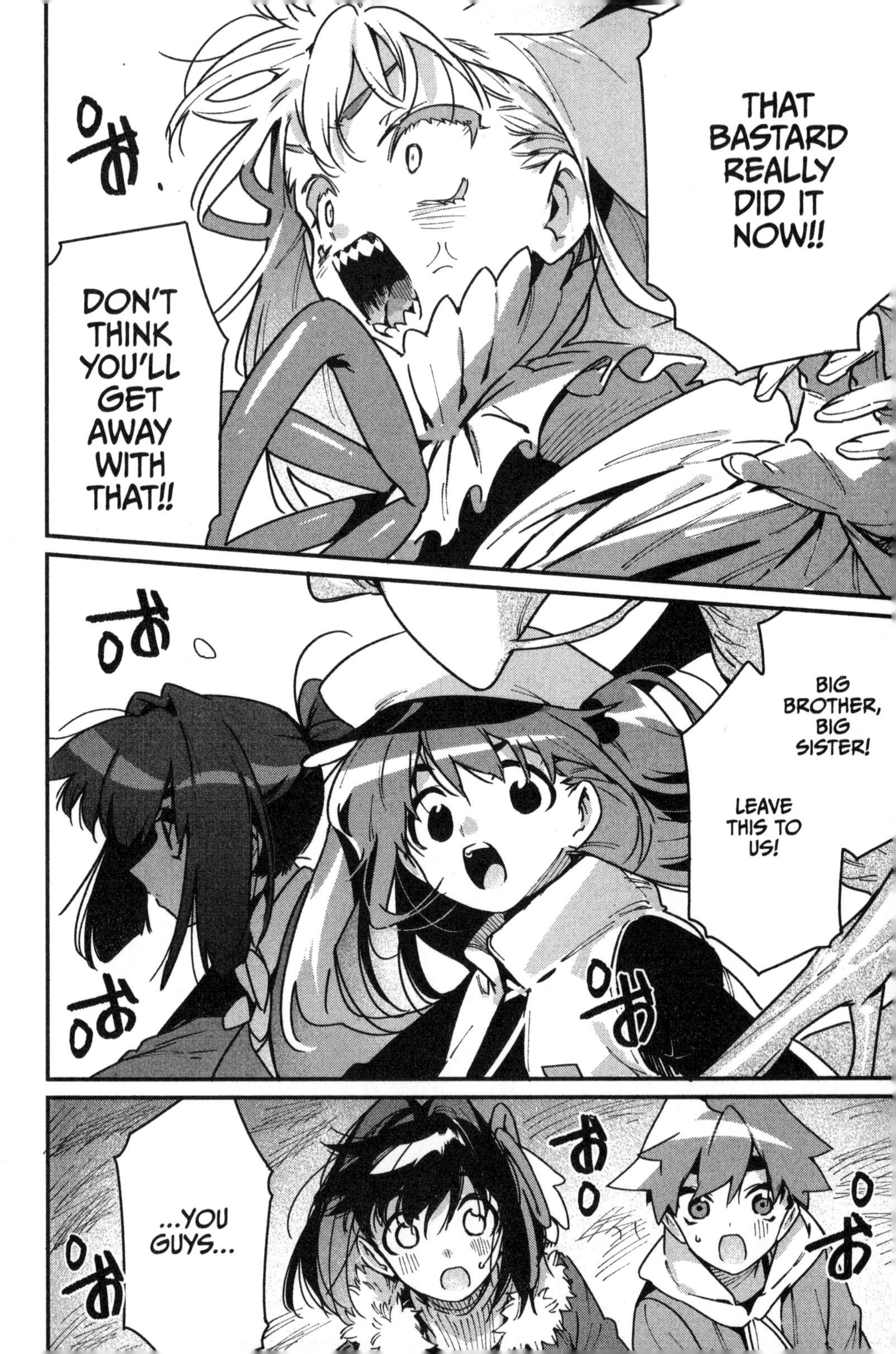
THAT BASTARD REALLY DID IT NOW!!
DON'T THINK YOU'LL GET AWAY WITH THAT!!
BIG BROTHER, BIG SISTER!
LEAVE THIS TO US!
...YOU GUYS...

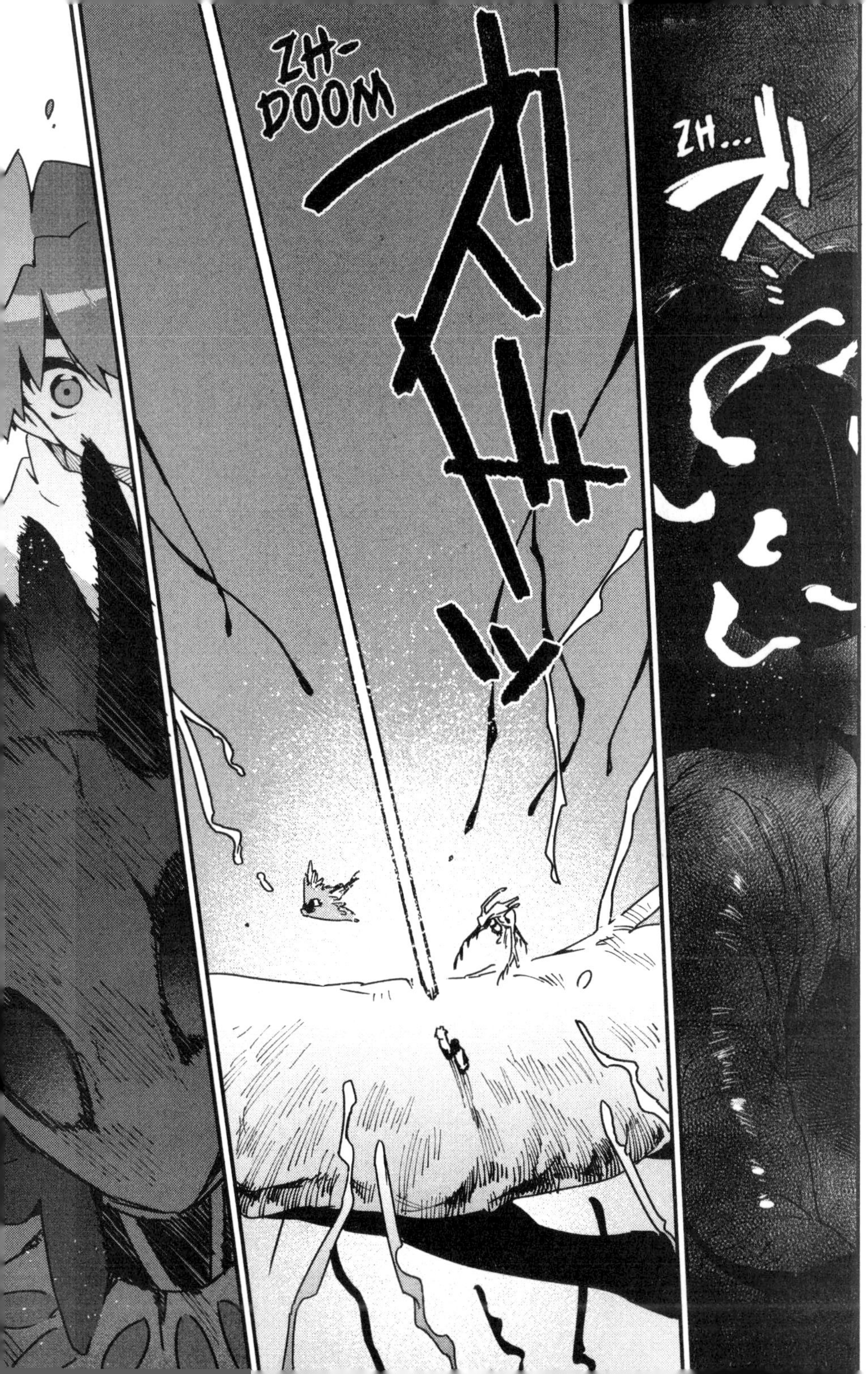
ZH...
ZH-
DOOM

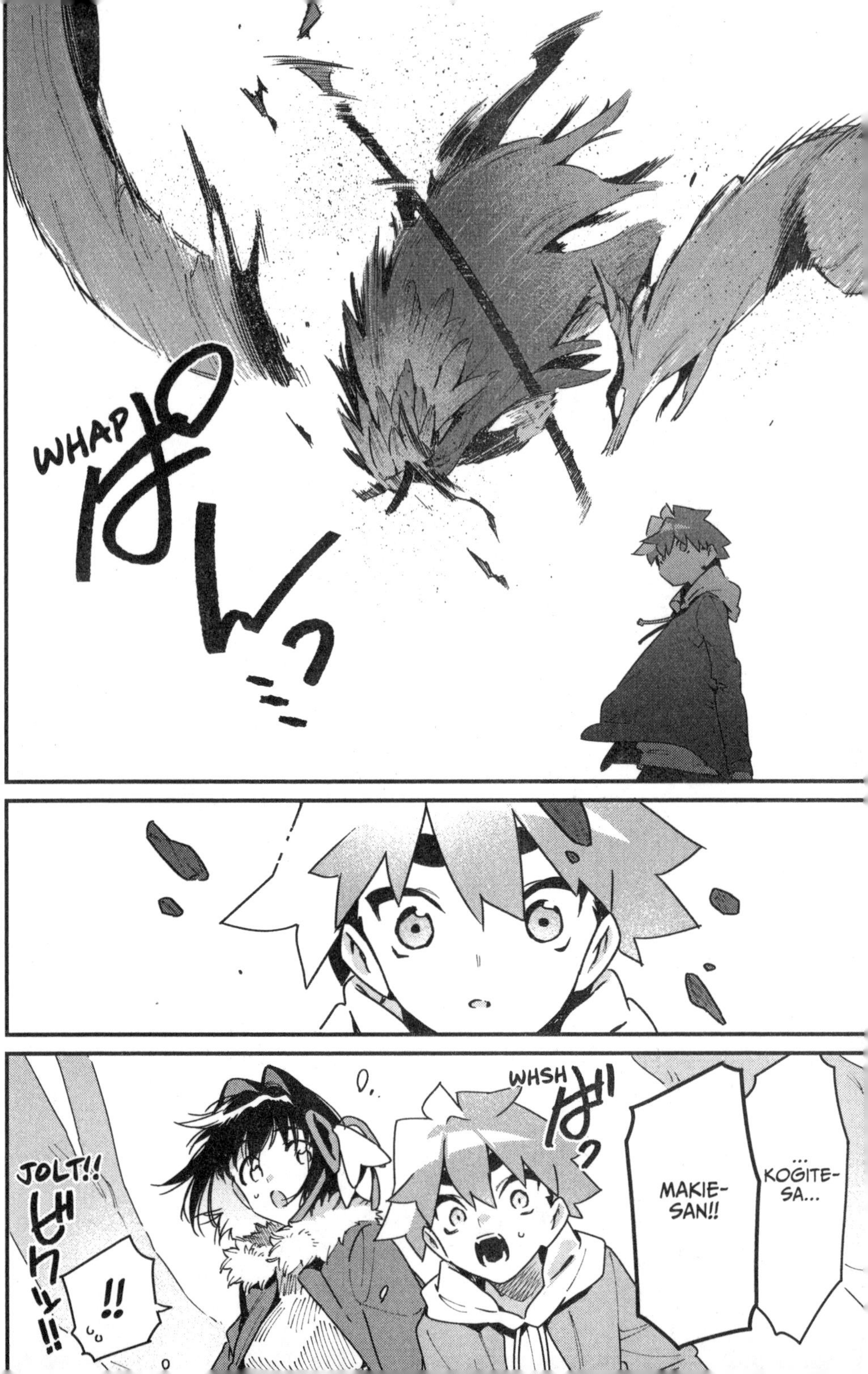
WHAP
ぱんっ
... KOGITE-SA...
MAKIE-SAN!!
WHSH
ばっ
JOLT!!
!!

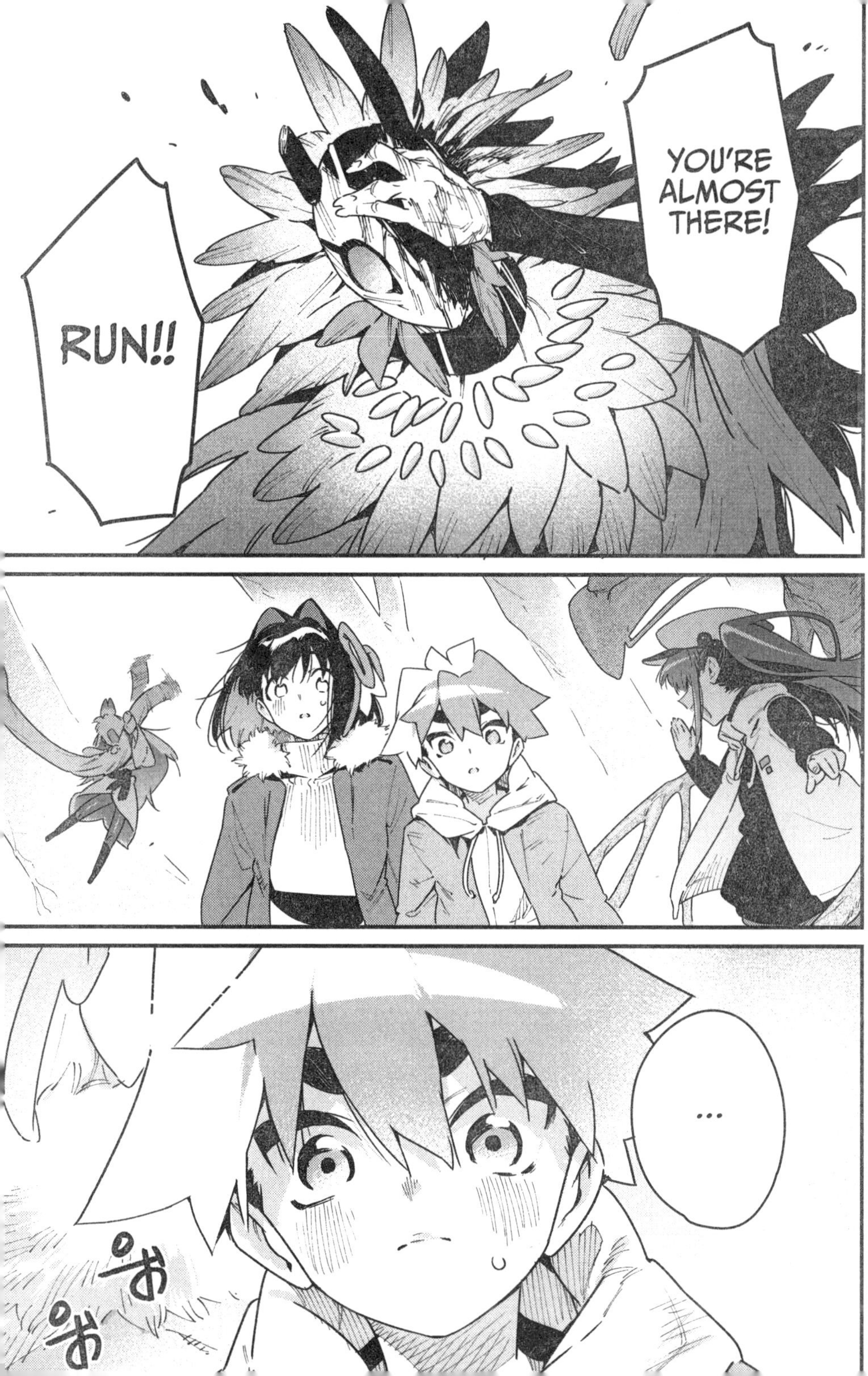

YOU'RE ALMOST THERE!
RUN!!
...

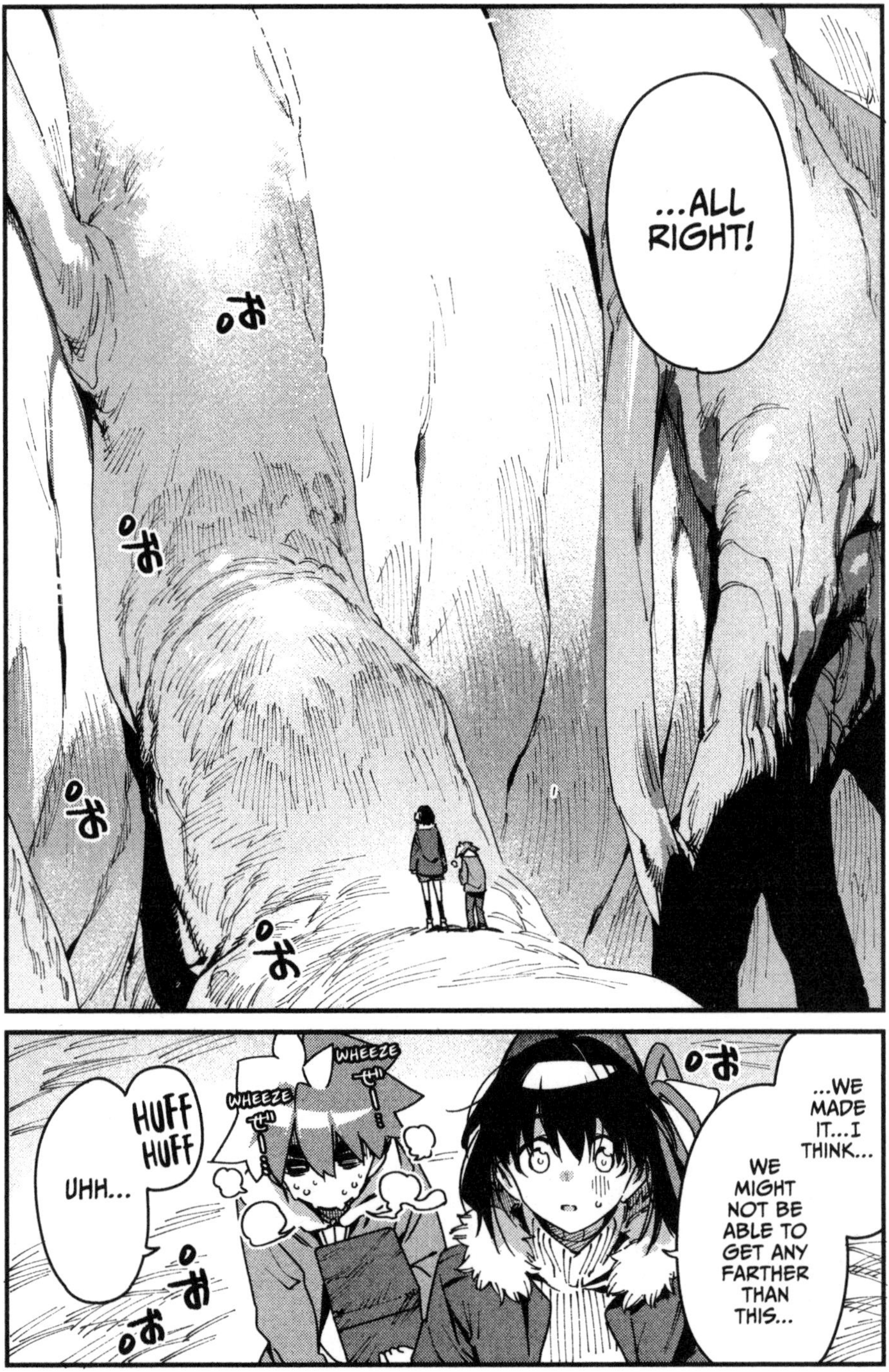
...ALL RIGHT!
お
ぉお
ぉお
ぉお
ぉお
...WE MADE IT...I THINK...
WE MIGHT NOT BE ABLE TO GET ANY FARTHER THAN THIS...
WHEEZE ぜー
WHEEZE ぜー
HUFF HUFF
UHH...
ぉお
ぉお

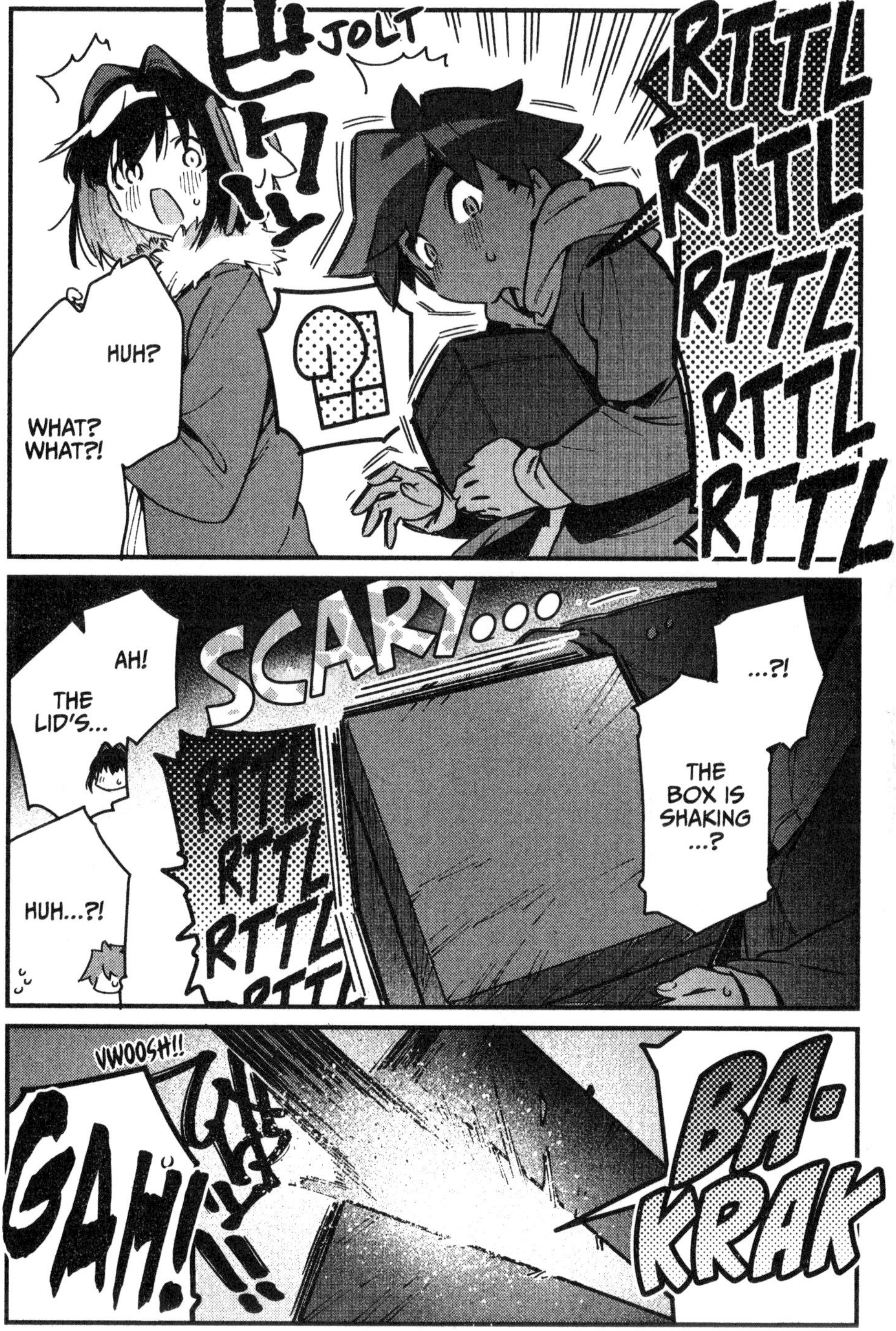

RTTL RTTL RTTL RTTL RTTL
JOLT
?
HUH?
WHAT? WHAT?!
...?!
THE BOX IS SHAKING ...?
SCARY...
RTTL RTTL RTTL
AH!
THE LID'S...
HUH...?!
BA-KRAK
GAH!!
VWOOSH!!

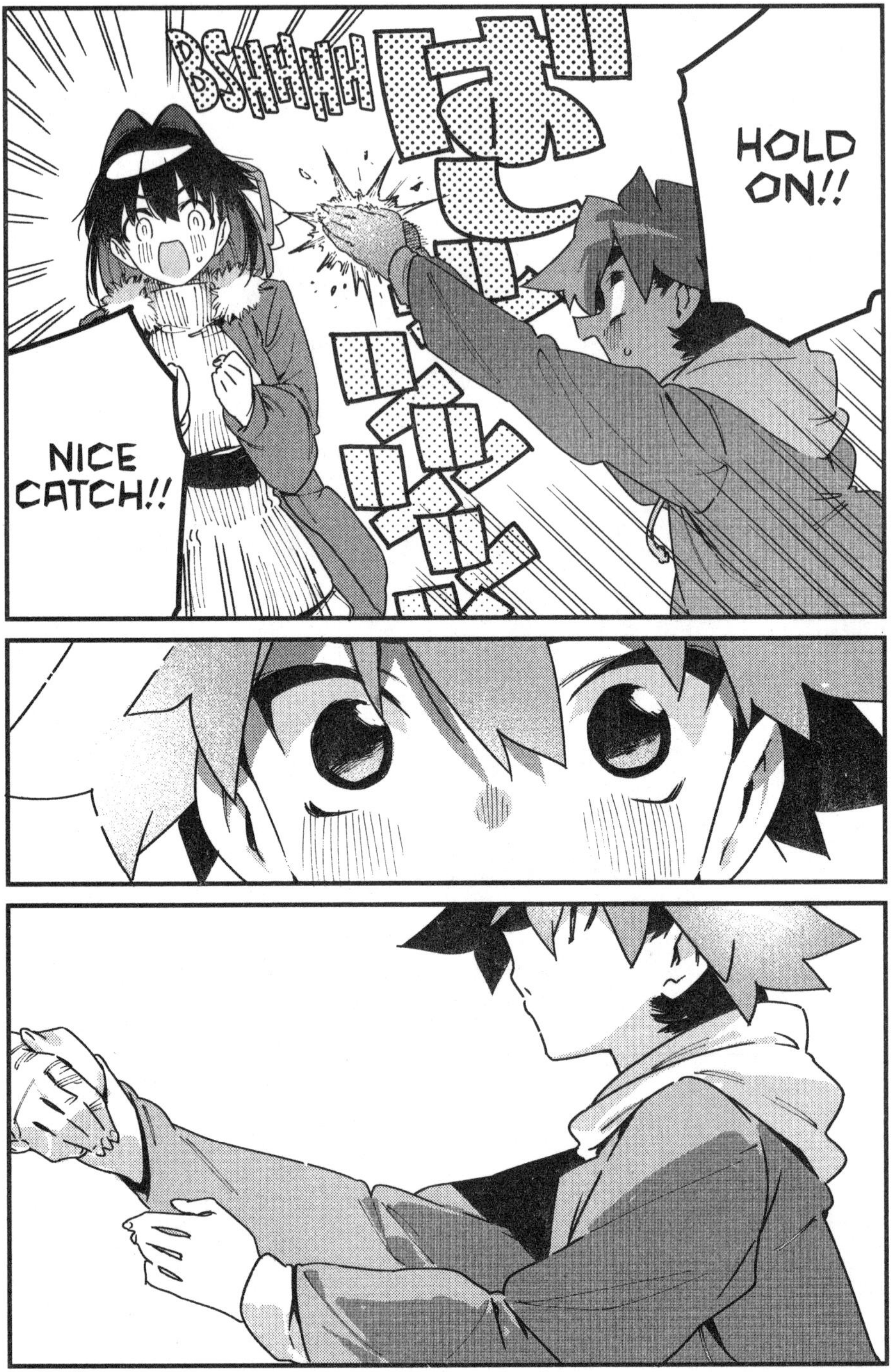
HOLD ON!!
BSHHHHH
NICE CATCH!!

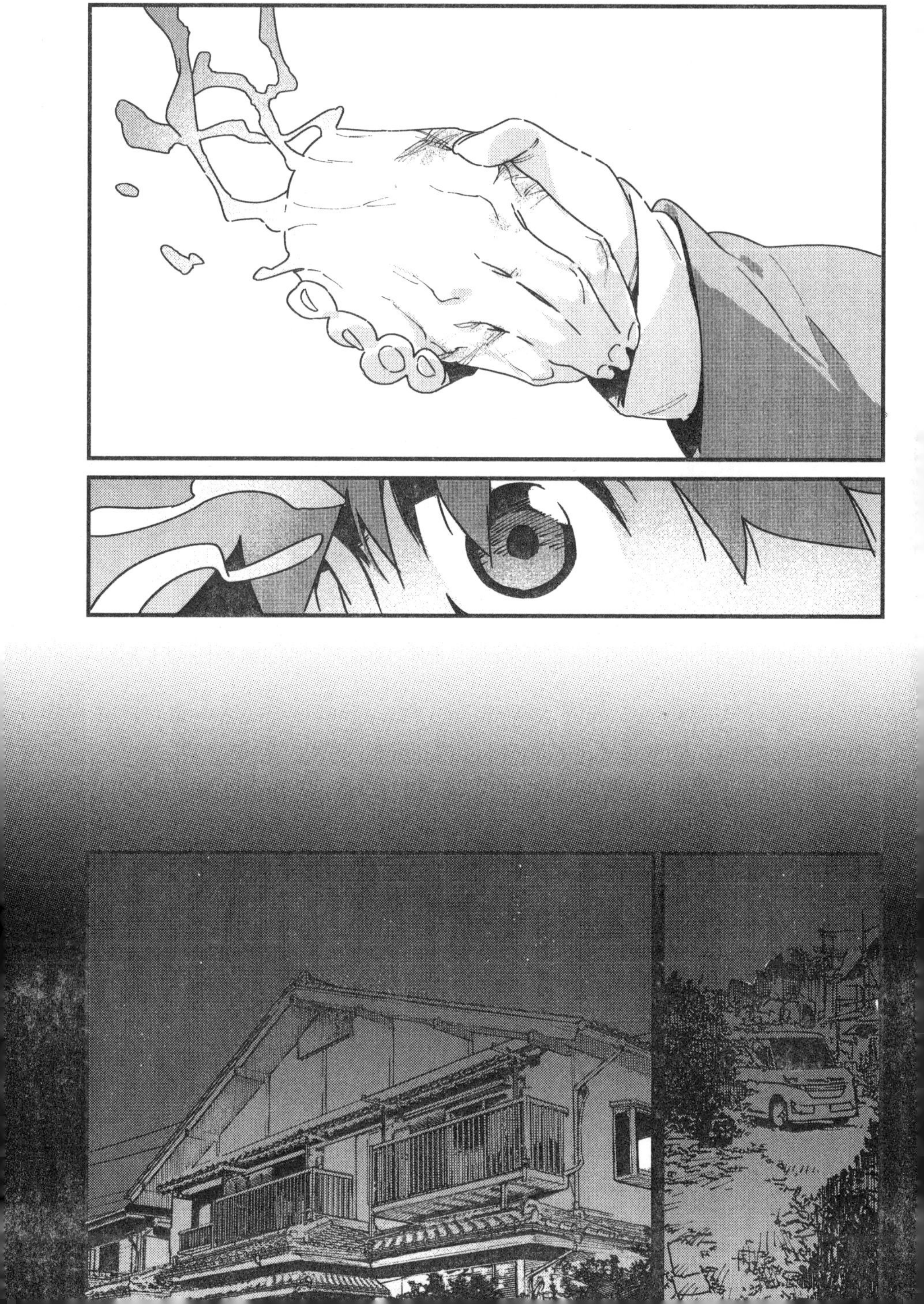

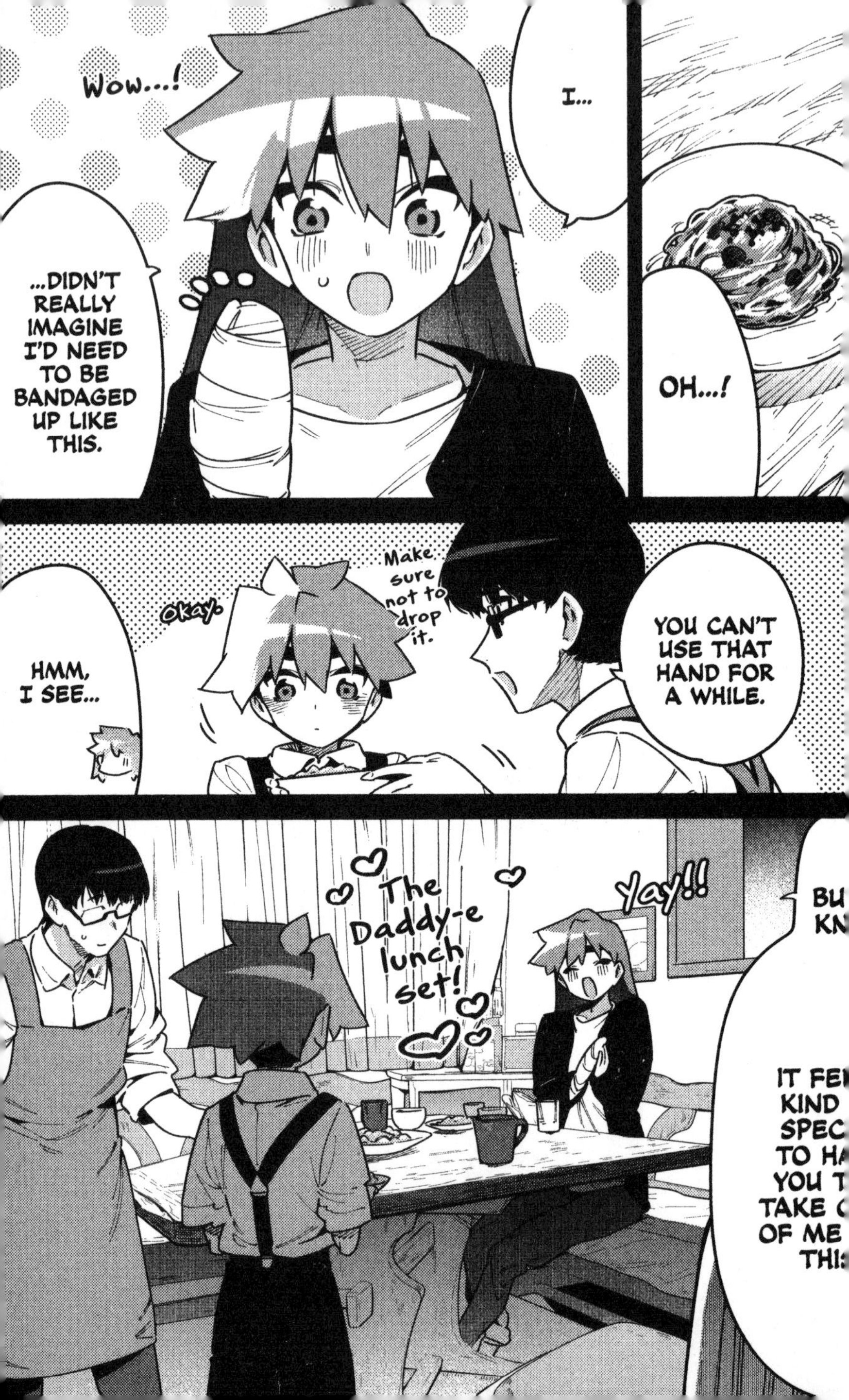
OH...!
I...
Wow...!
...DIDN'T REALLY IMAGINE I'D NEED TO BE BANDAGED UP LIKE THIS.
YOU CAN'T USE THAT HAND FOR A WHILE.
Make sure not to drop it.
Okay.
HMM, I SEE...
BU KN
IT FE KIND SPEC TO HA YOU T TAKE O OF ME THIS
Yay!!
The Daddy-e lunch set!

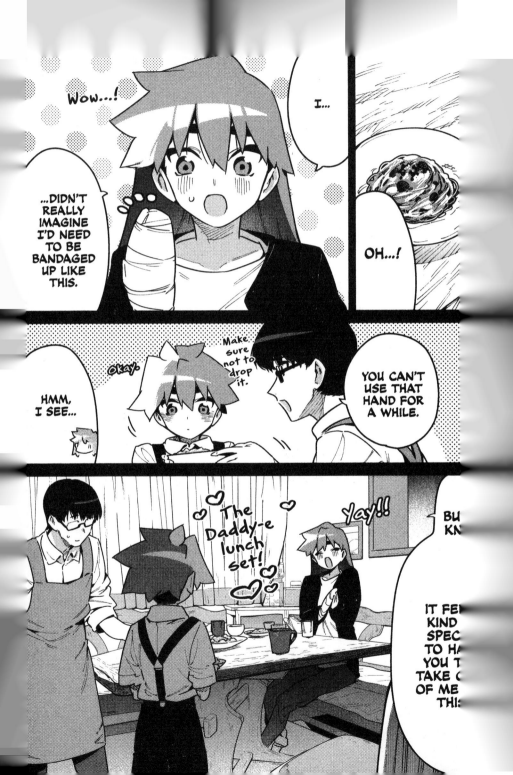

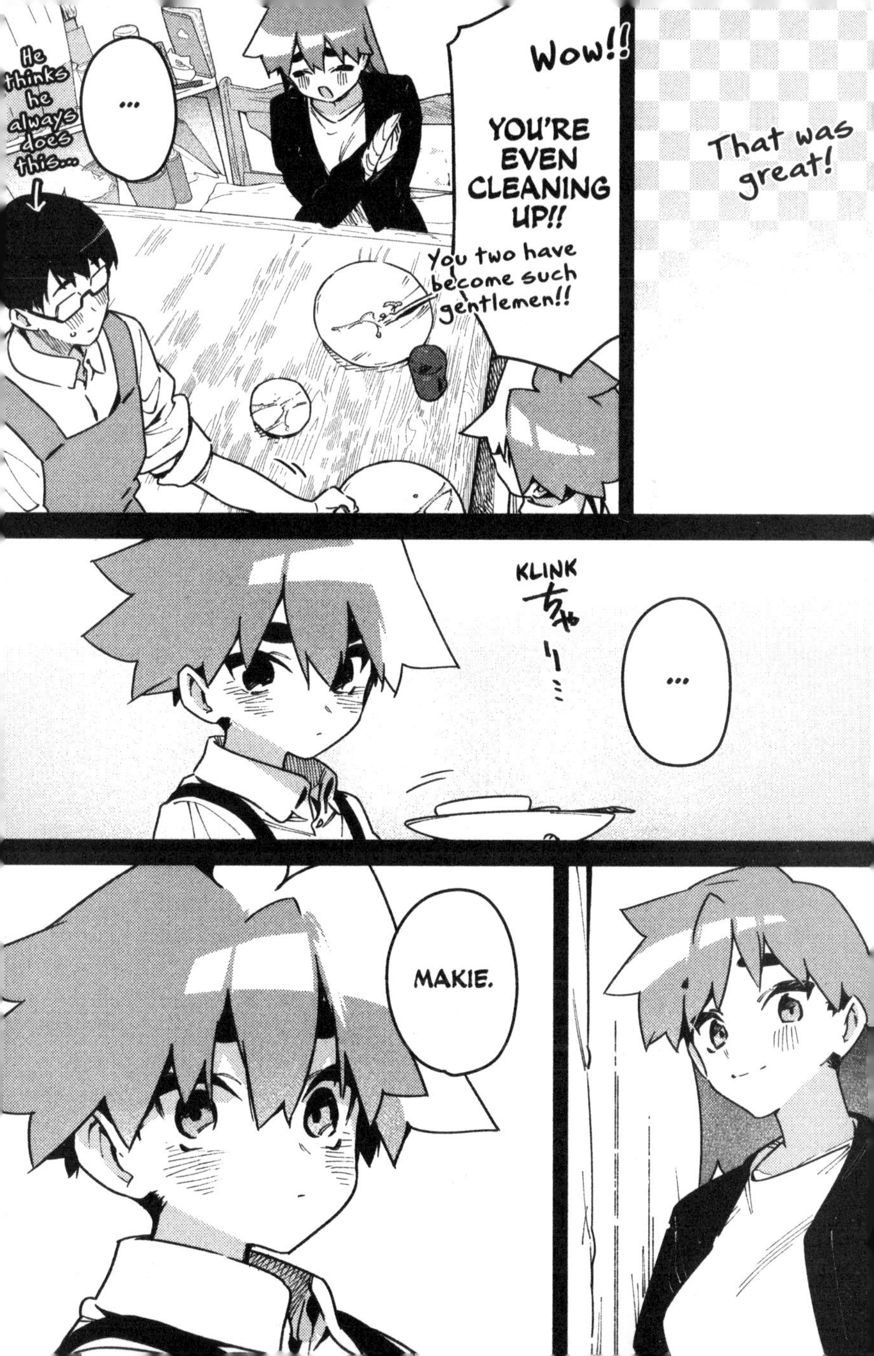
That was great!
Wow!!
YOU'RE EVEN CLEANING UP!!
You two have become such gentlemen!!
...
He thinks he always does this...
KLINK
...
MAKIE.

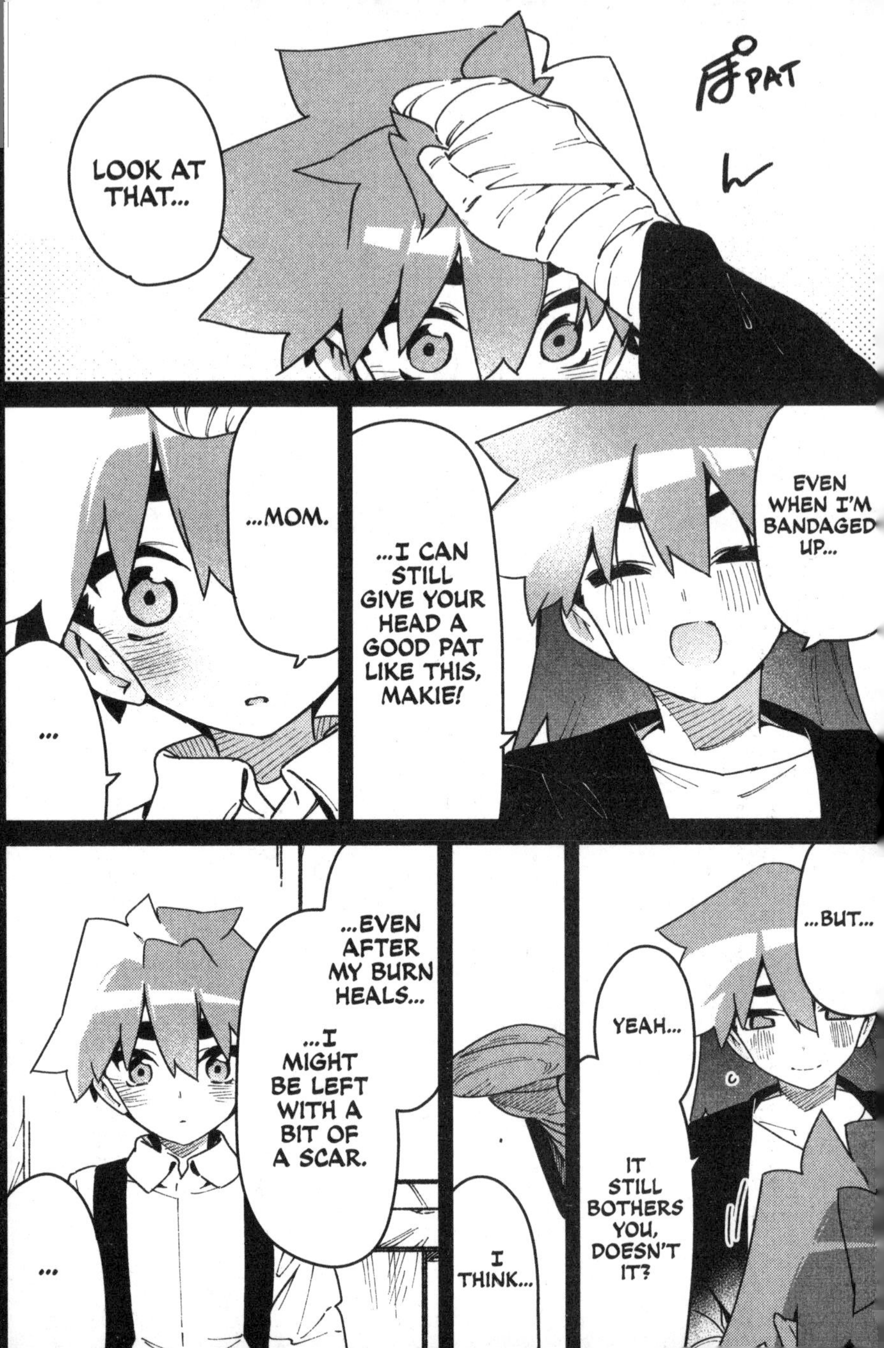
ぽ PAT
ん
LOOK AT THAT...
EVEN WHEN I'M BANDAGED UP...
...I CAN STILL GIVE YOUR HEAD A GOOD PAT LIKE THIS, MAKIE!
...MOM.
...
...BUT...
IT STILL BOTHERS YOU, DOESN'T IT?
YEAH...
I THINK...
...EVEN AFTER MY BURN HEALS...
...I MIGHT BE LEFT WITH A BIT OF A SCAR.
...

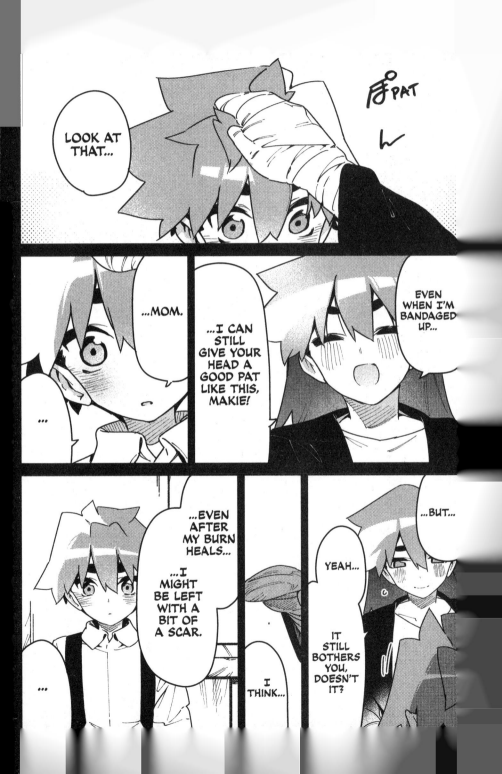

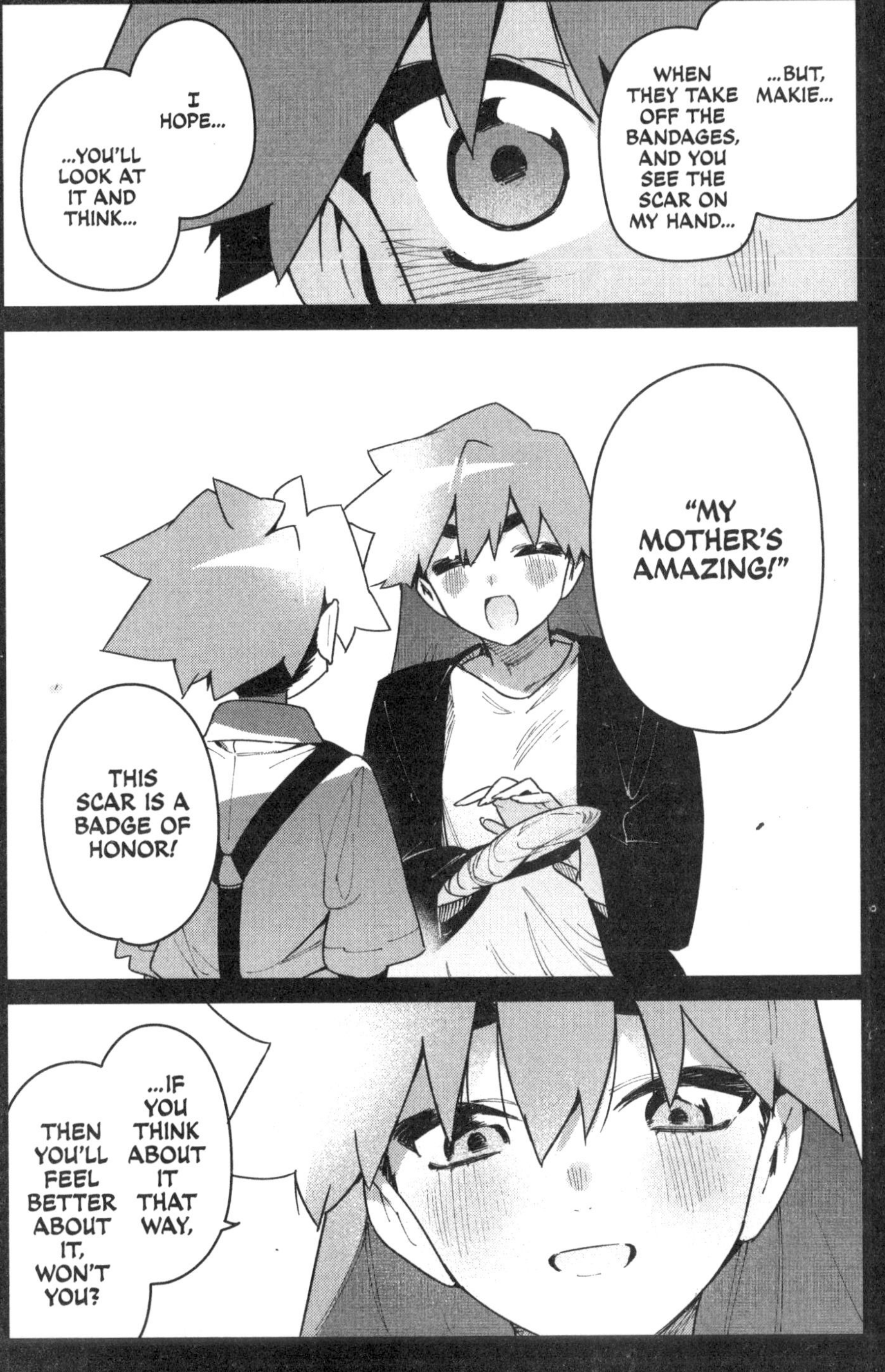
...BUT, MAKIE...
WHEN THEY TAKE OFF THE BANDAGES, AND YOU SEE THE SCAR ON MY HAND...
I HOPE...
...YOU'LL LOOK AT IT AND THINK...
"MY MOTHER'S AMAZING!"
THIS SCAR IS A BADGE OF HONOR!
...IF YOU THINK ABOUT IT THAT WAY,
THEN YOU'LL FEEL BETTER ABOUT IT, WON'T YOU?

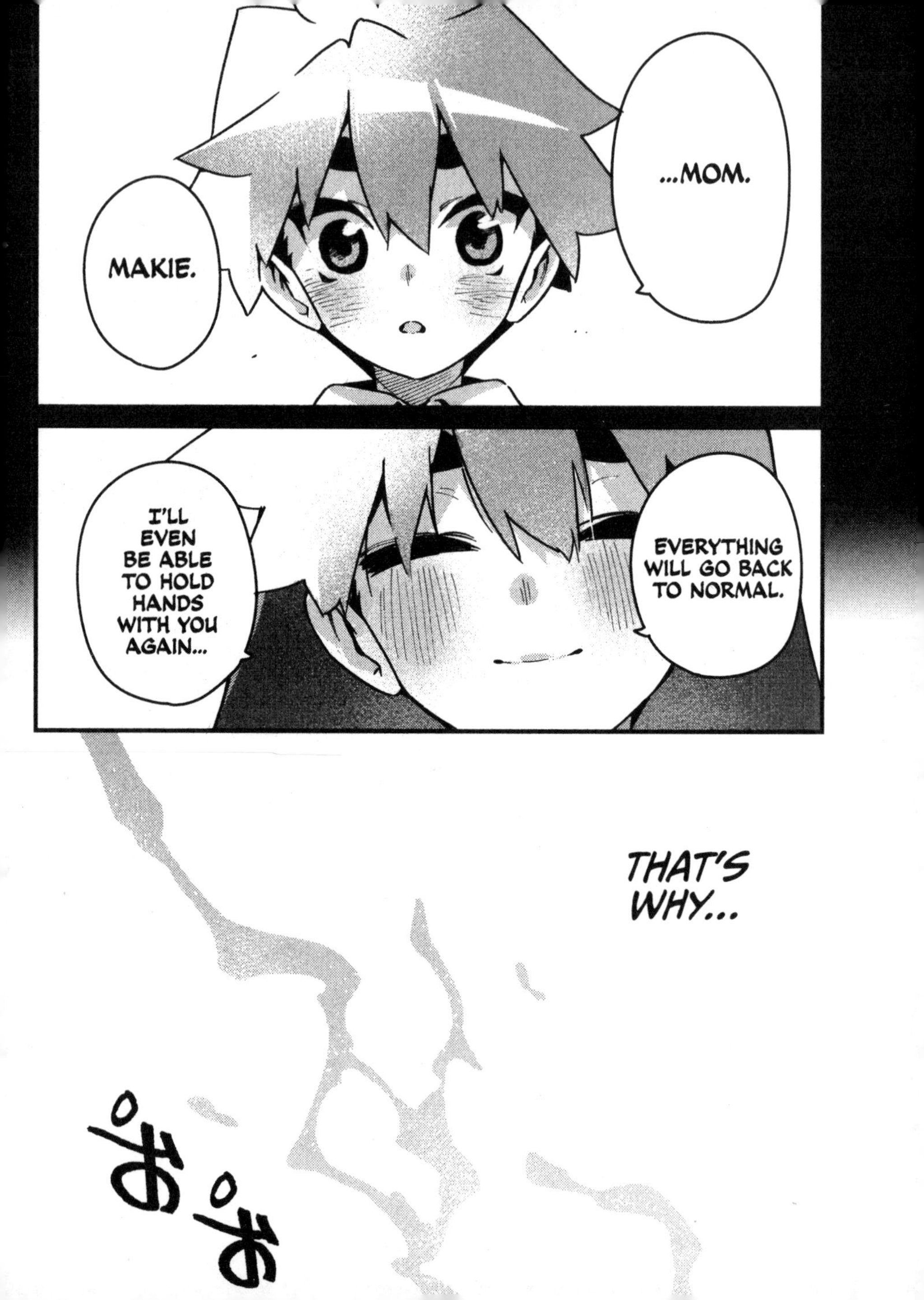
...MOM.
MAKIE.
EVERYTHING WILL GO BACK TO NORMAL.
I'LL EVEN BE ABLE TO HOLD HANDS WITH YOU AGAIN...
THAT'S WHY...

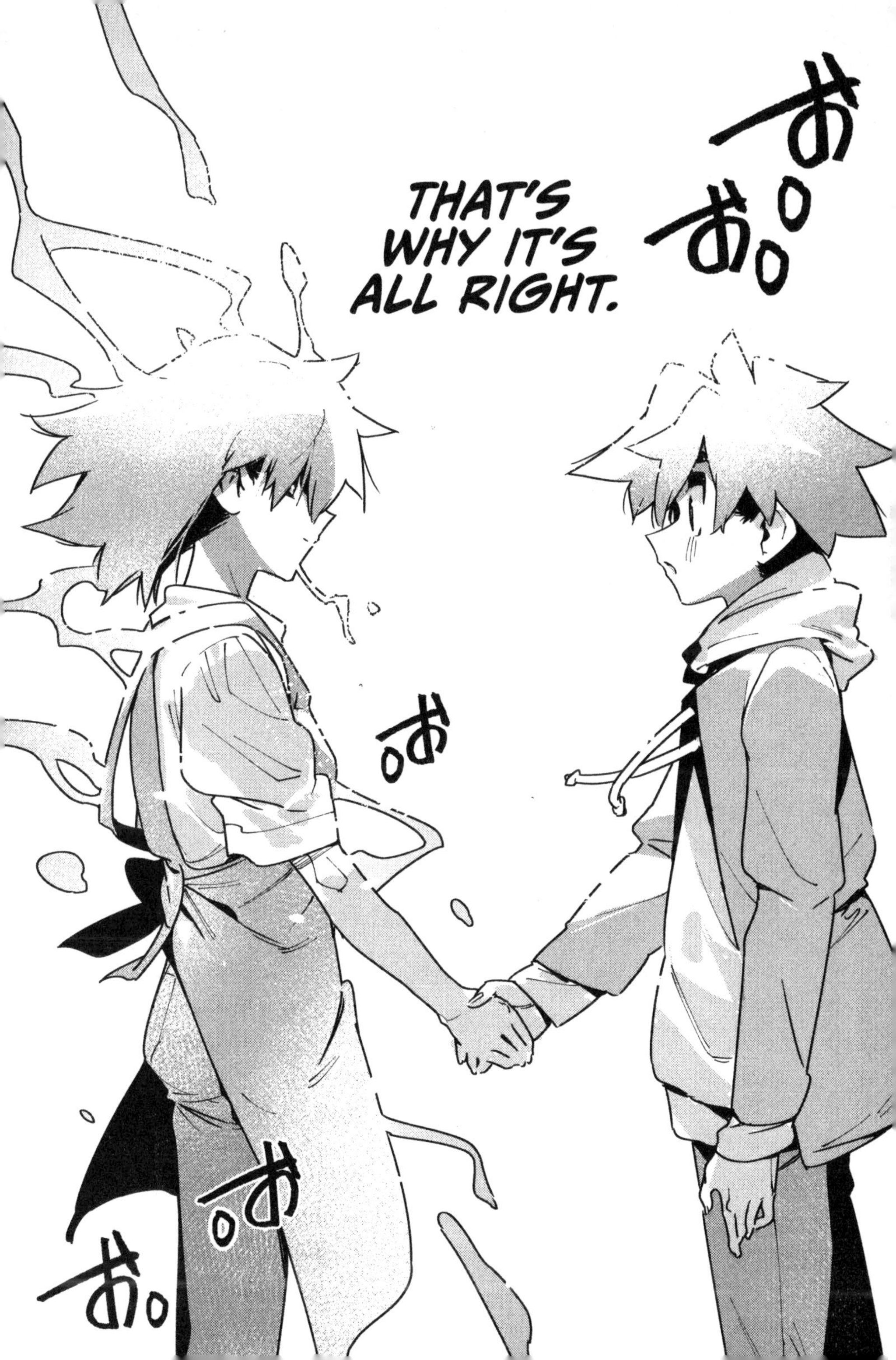

おお。。
THAT'S WHY IT'S ALL RIGHT.
お。
お。
お。

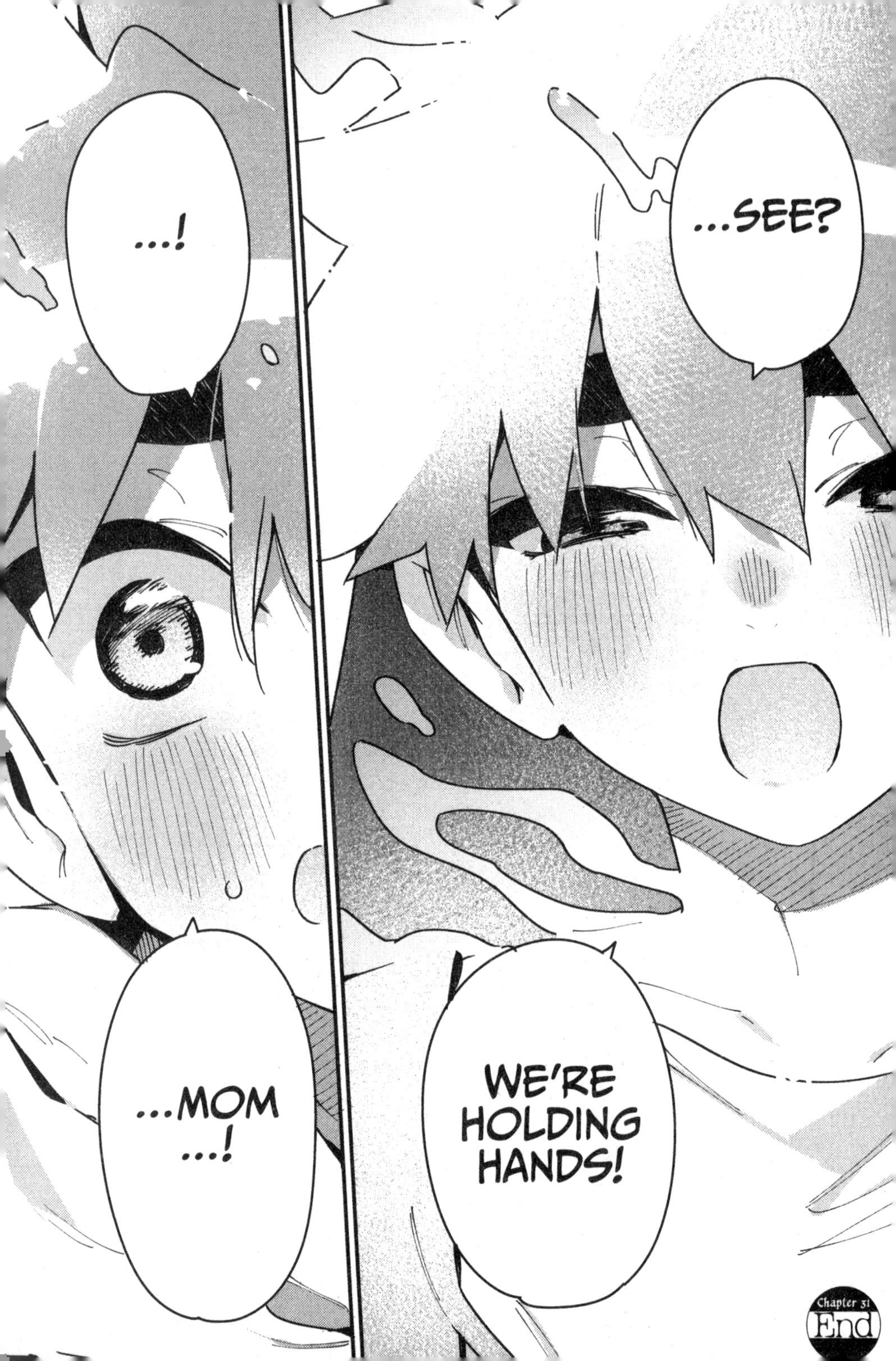
...SEE?
WE'RE HOLDING HANDS!
...!
...MOM ...!
Chapter 31 End

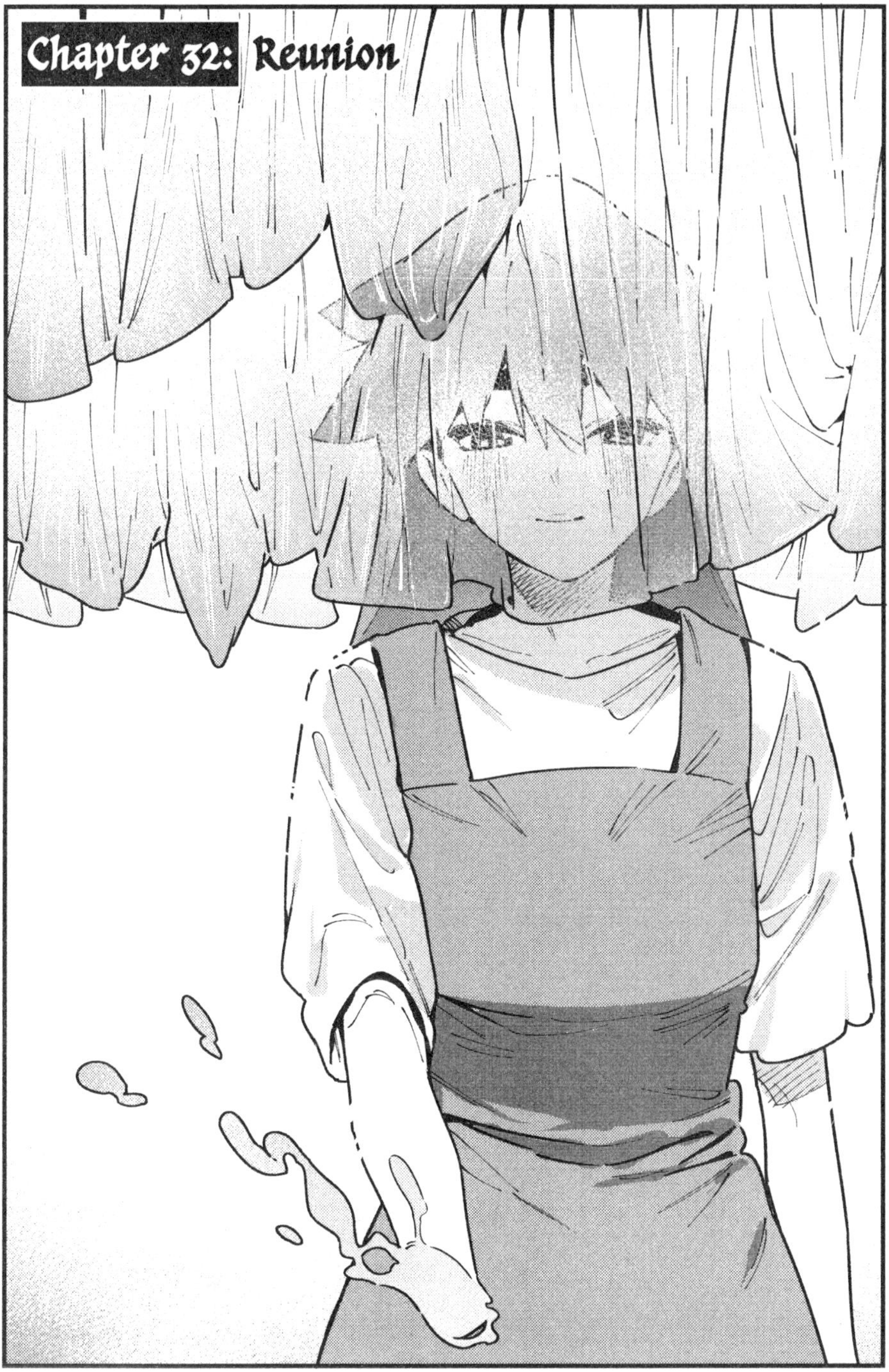
Chapter 32: Reunion

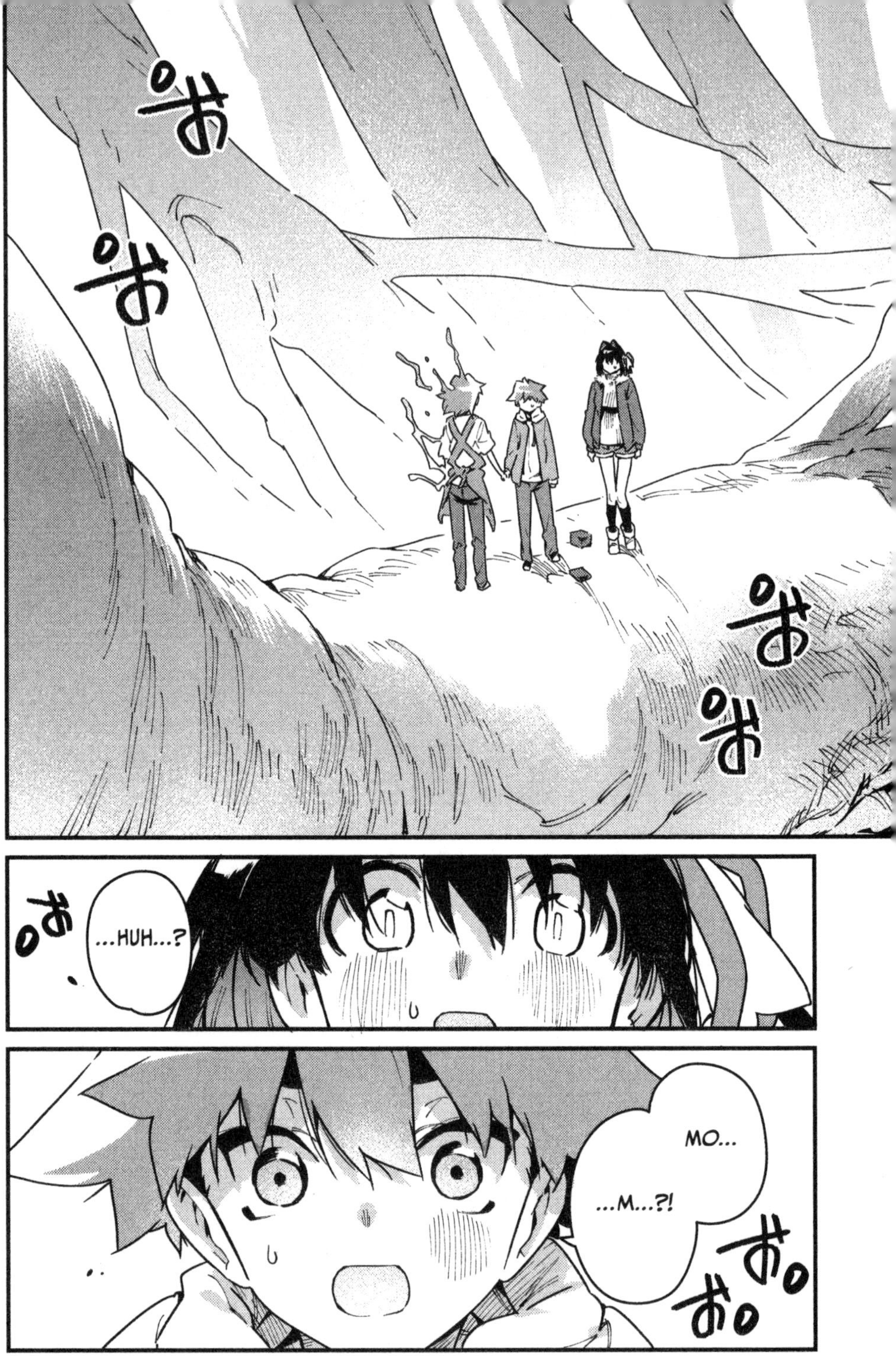

ぉぉ
ぉぉ
ぉ
...HUH...?
MO...
...M...?!
ぉぉ

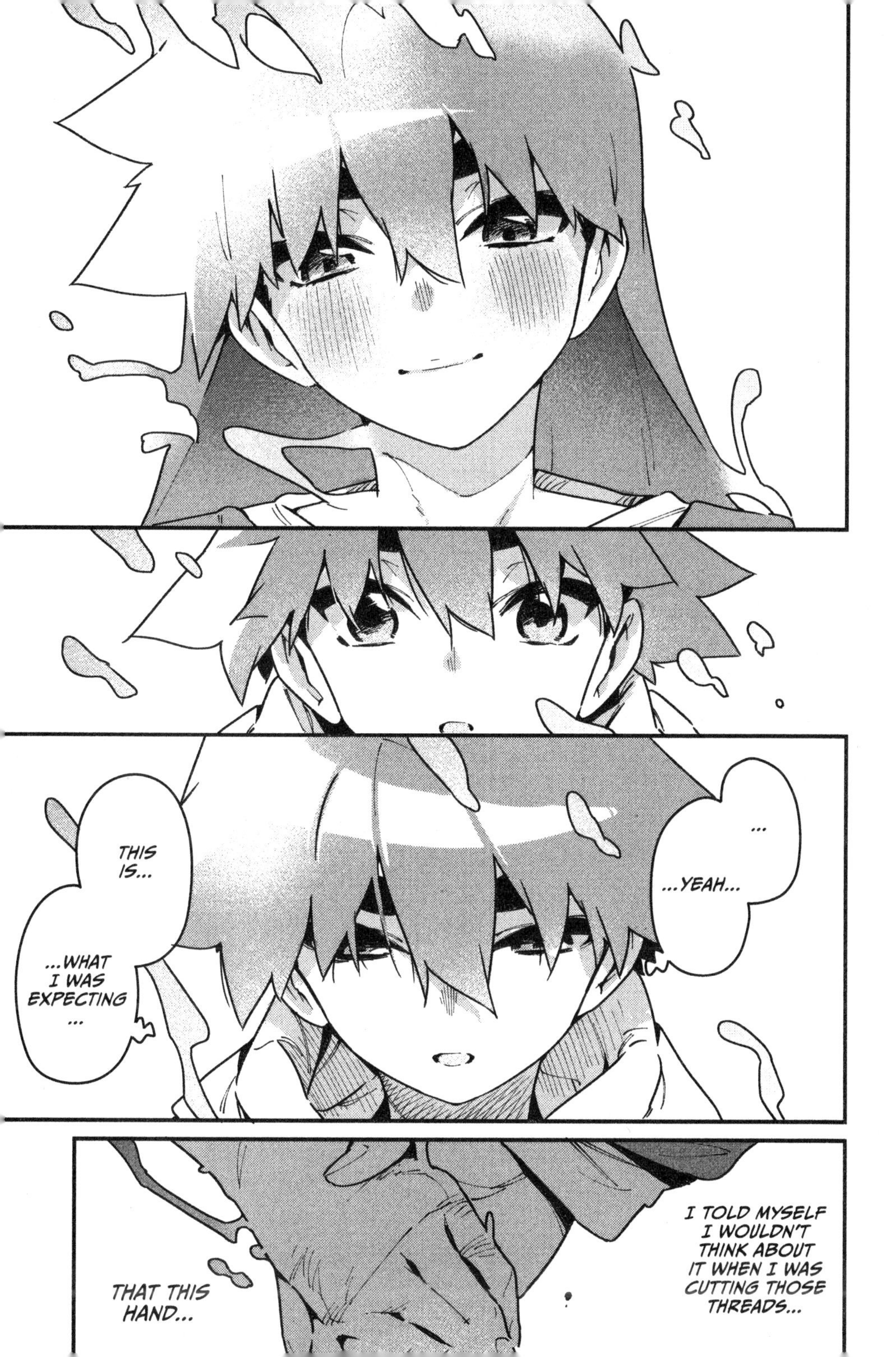
...
...YEAH...
THIS IS...
...WHAT I WAS EXPECTING ...
I TOLD MYSELF I WOULDN'T THINK ABOUT IT WHEN I WAS CUTTING THOSE THREADS...
THAT THIS HAND...

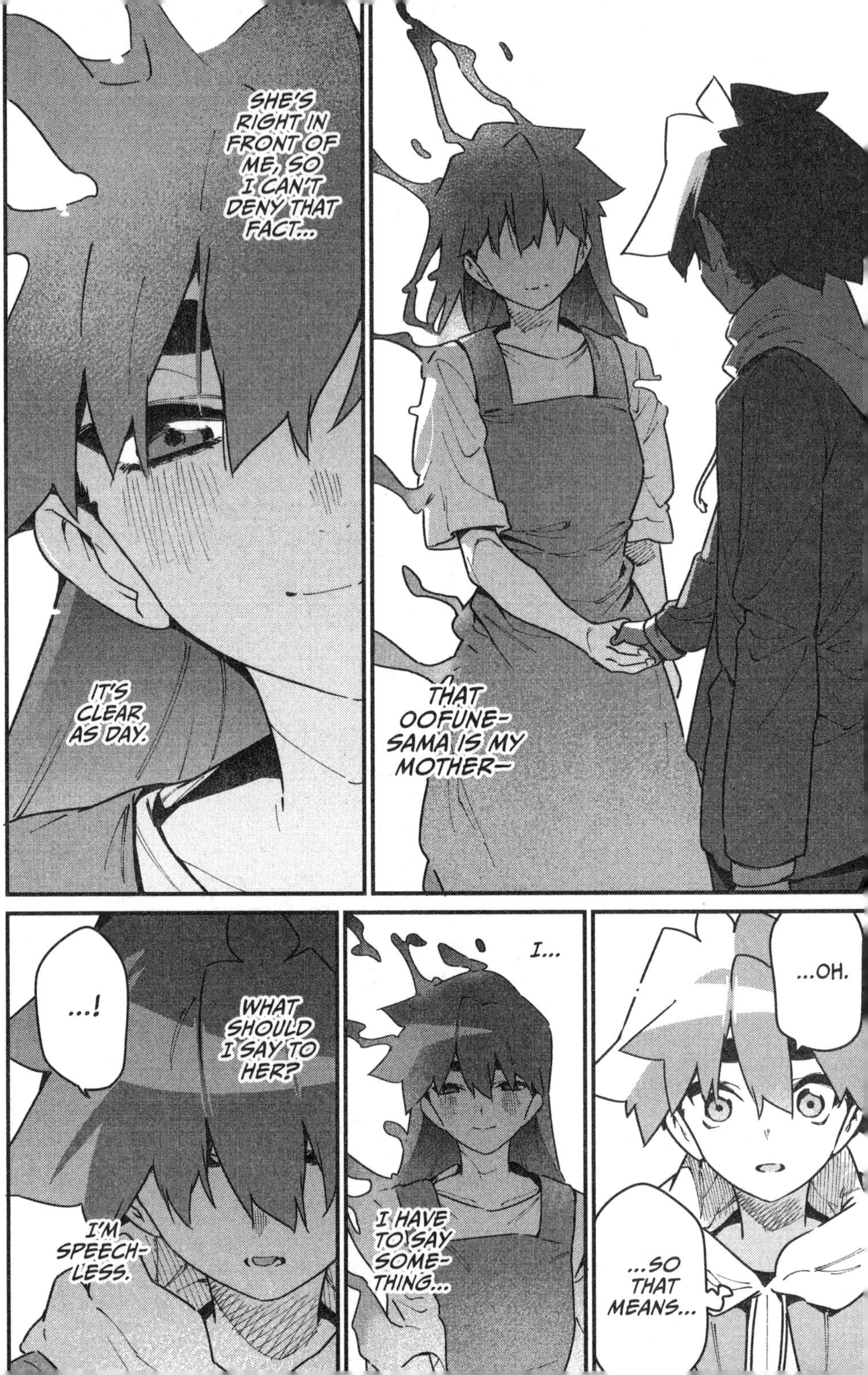
THAT OOFUNE-SAMA IS MY MOTHER—
SHE'S RIGHT IN FRONT OF ME, SO I CAN'T DENY THAT FACT...
IT'S CLEAR AS DAY.
...OH.
...SO THAT MEANS...
I...
I HAVE TO SAY SOMETHING...
...!
WHAT SHOULD I SAY TO HER?
I'M SPEECHLESS.

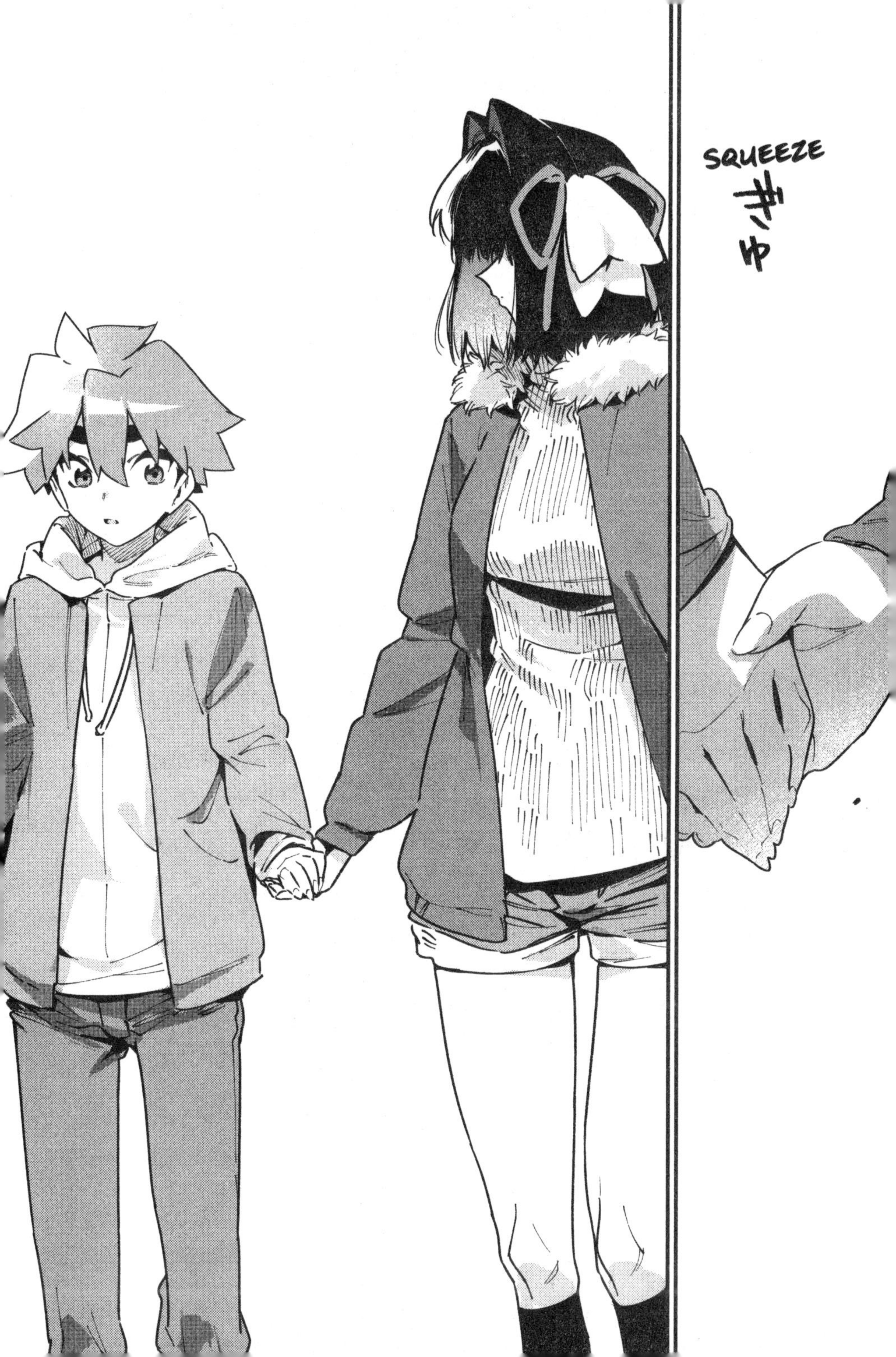
SQUEEZE
ぎゅ

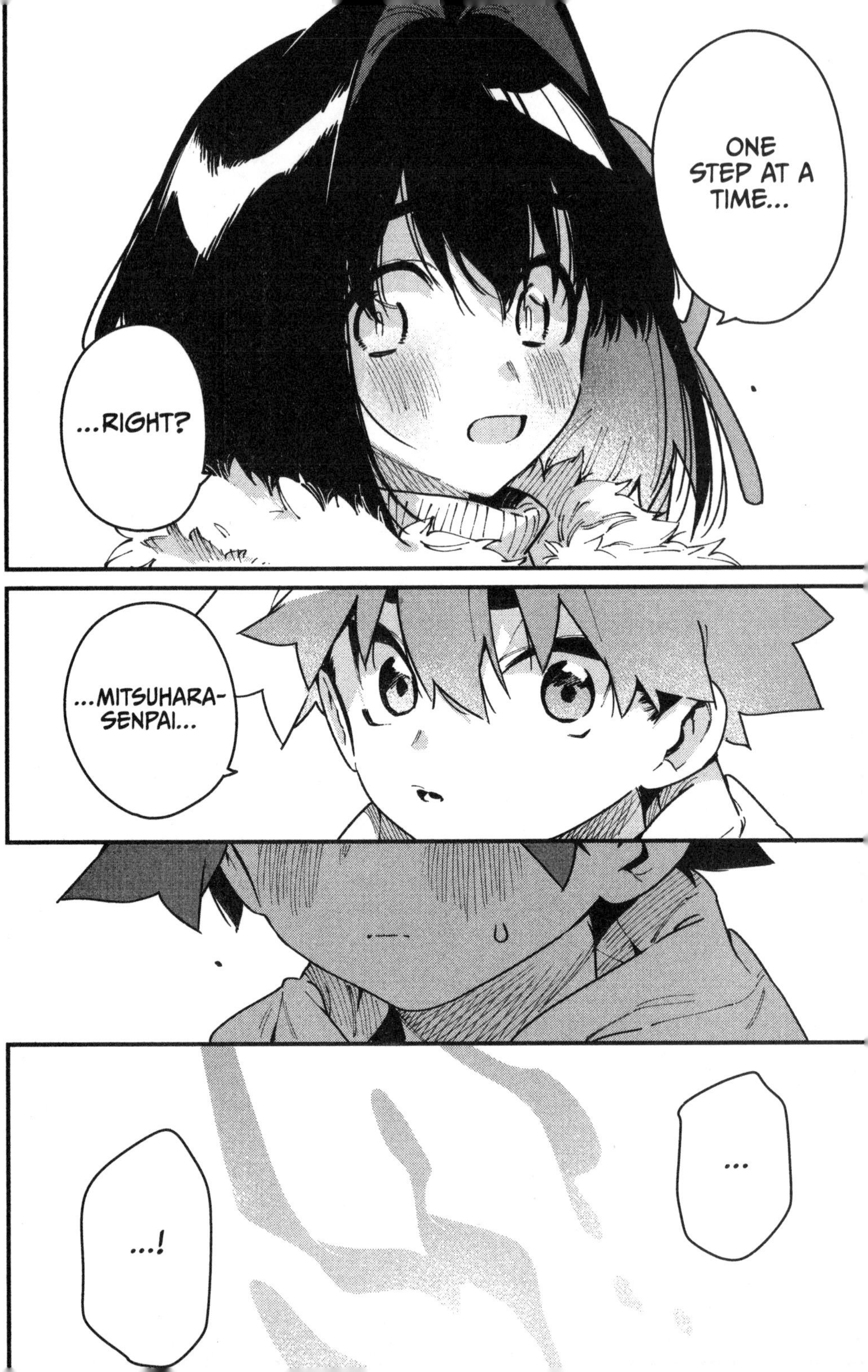
ONE STEP AT A TIME...
...RIGHT?
...MITSUHARA-SENPAI...
...
...!

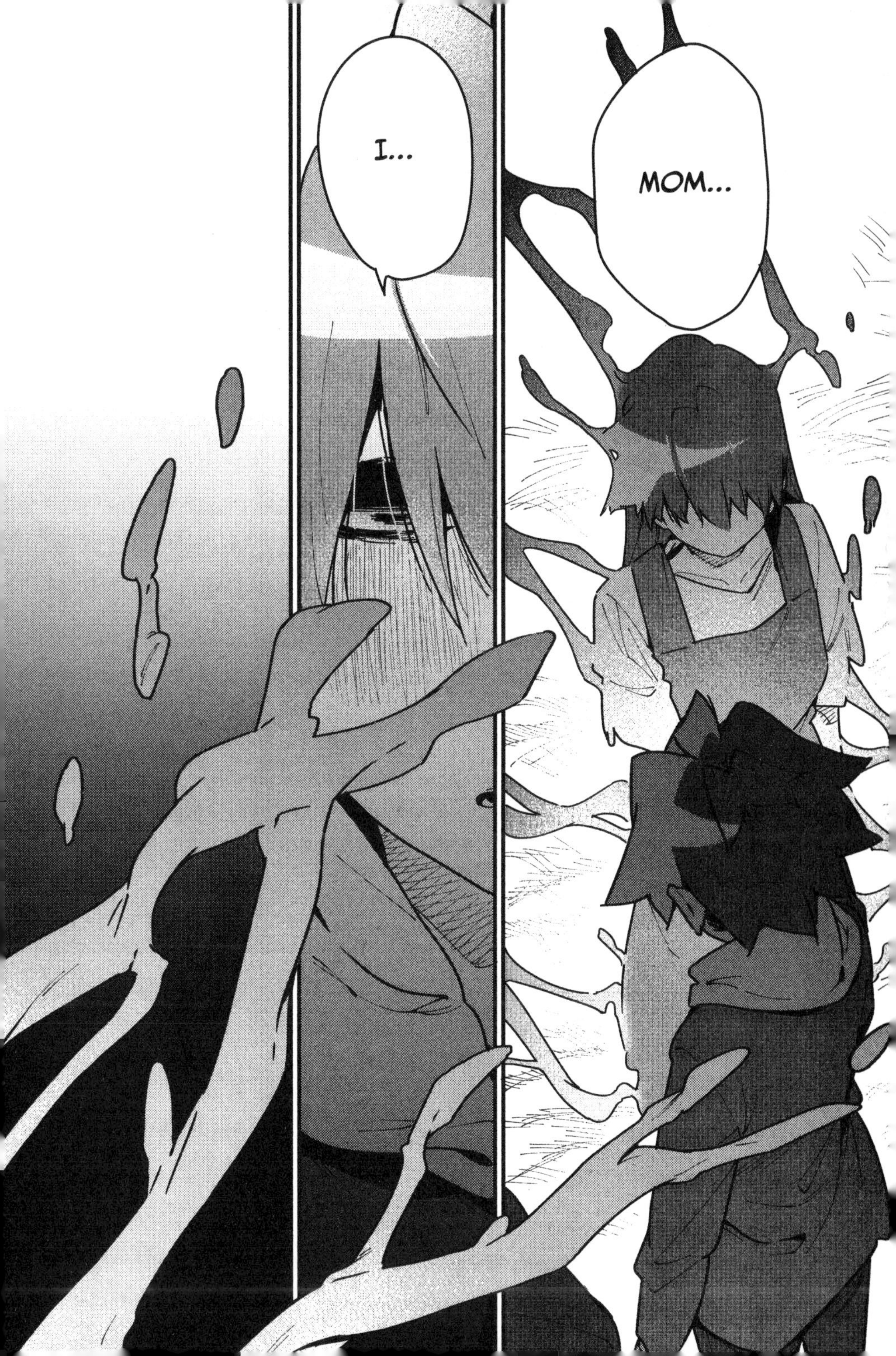
MOM...
I...

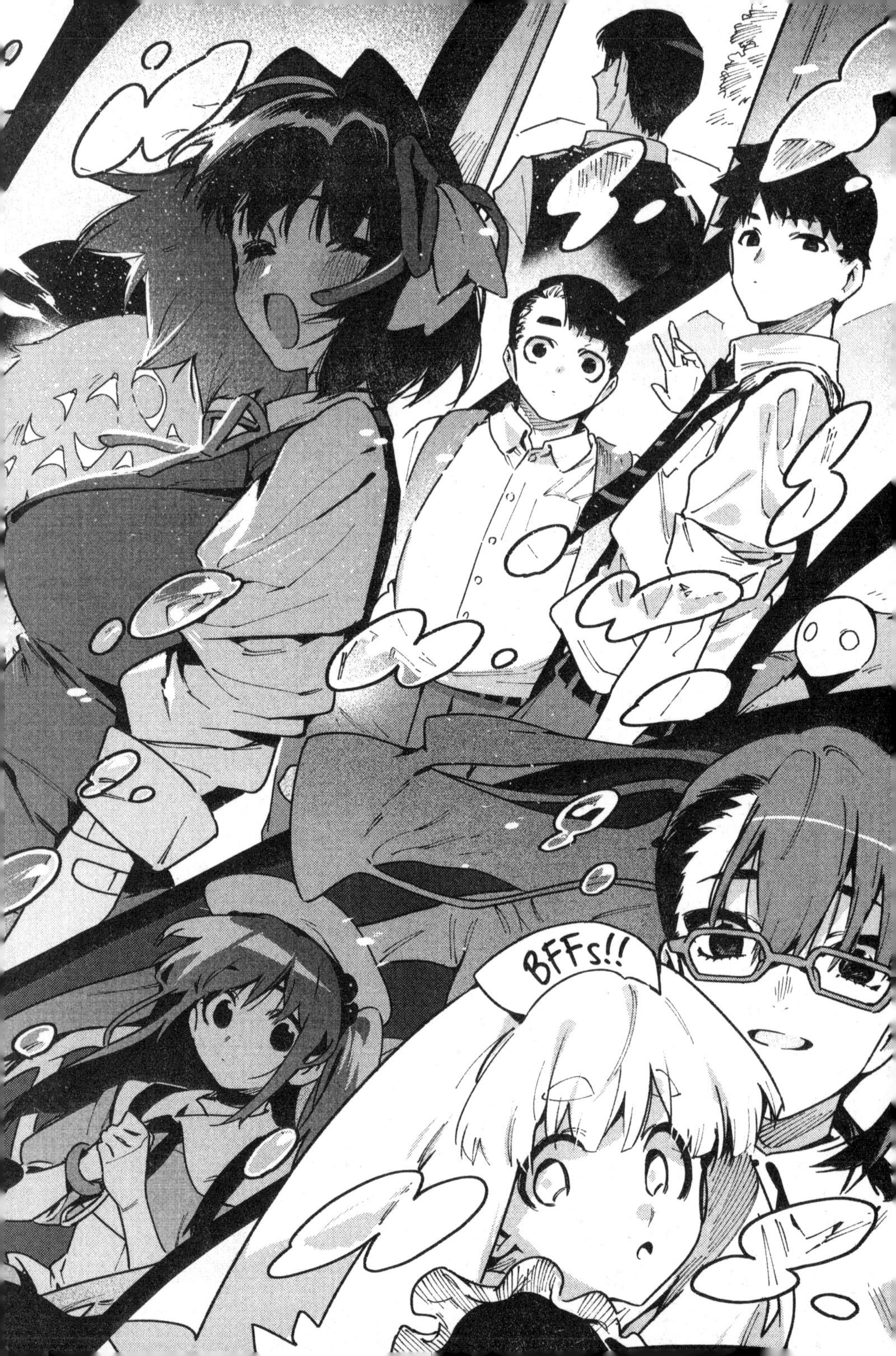
BFFs!!

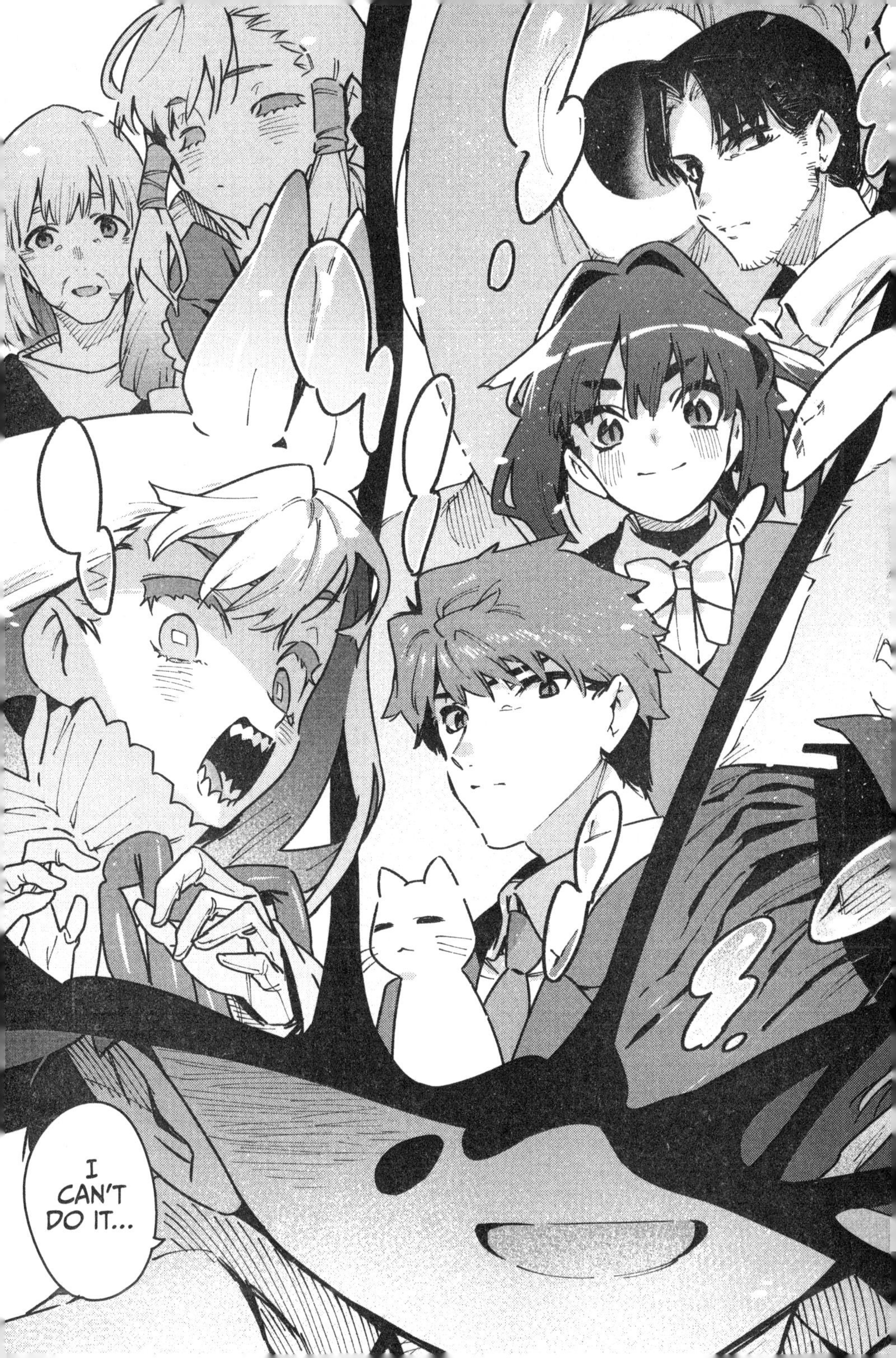
I CAN'T DO IT...

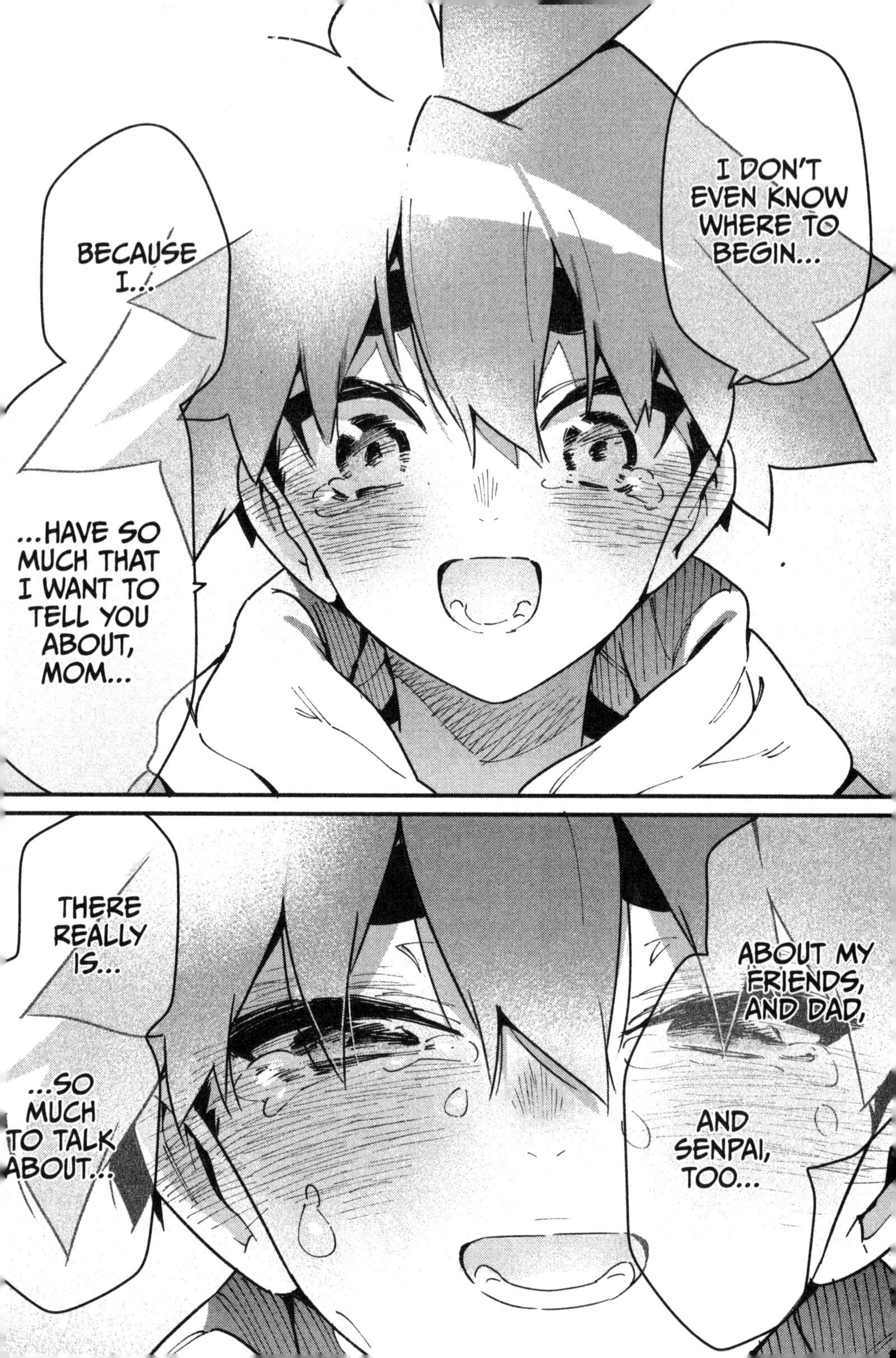
I DON'T EVEN KNOW WHERE TO BEGIN...
BECAUSE I...
...HAVE SO MUCH THAT I WANT TO TELL YOU ABOUT, MOM...
ABOUT MY FRIENDS, AND DAD,
AND SENPAI, TOO...
THERE REALLY IS...
...SO MUCH TO TALK ABOUT...

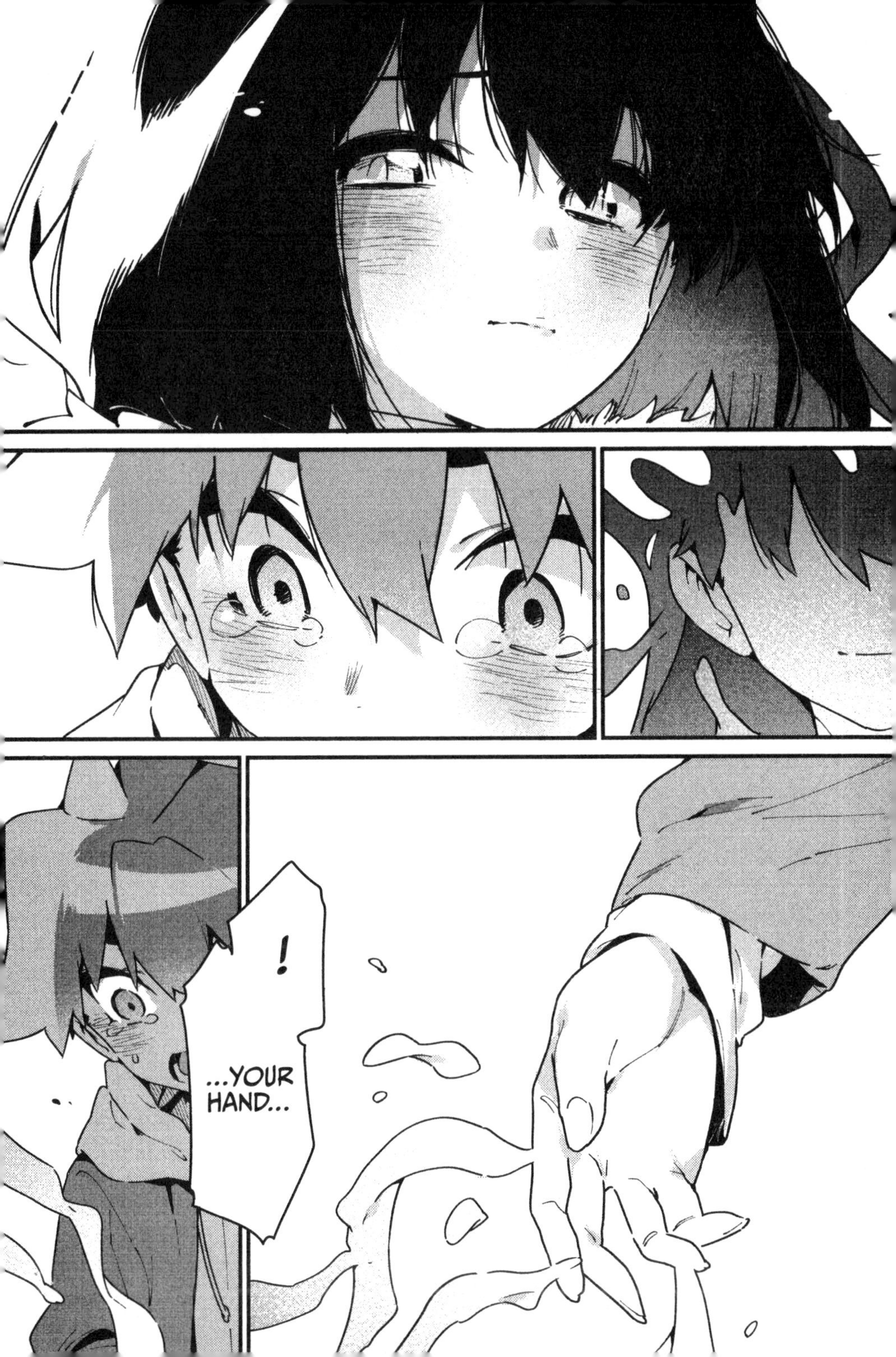
!
...YOUR HAND...

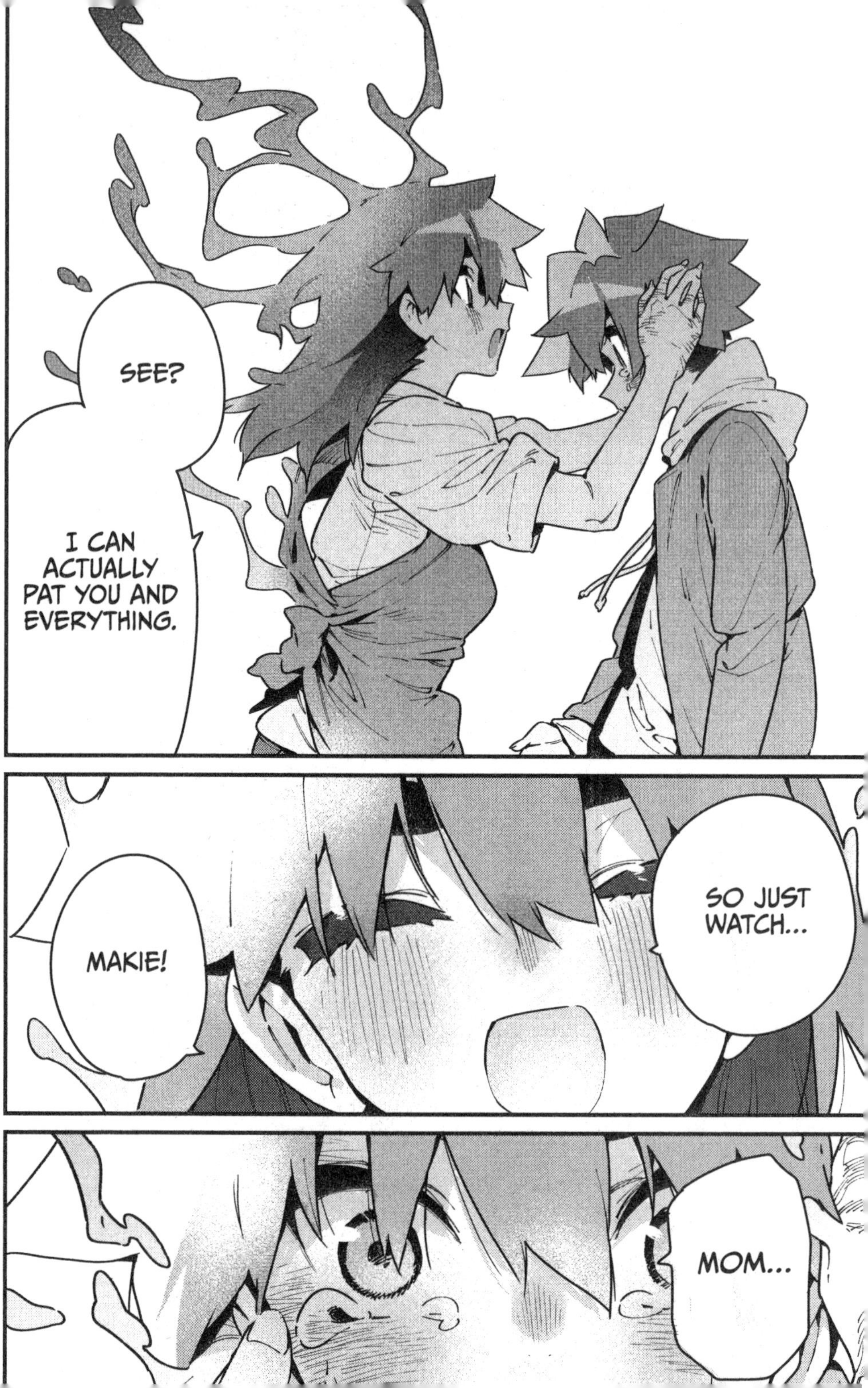
SEE?
I CAN ACTUALLY PAT YOU AND EVERYTHING.
SO JUST WATCH...
MAKIE!
MOM...

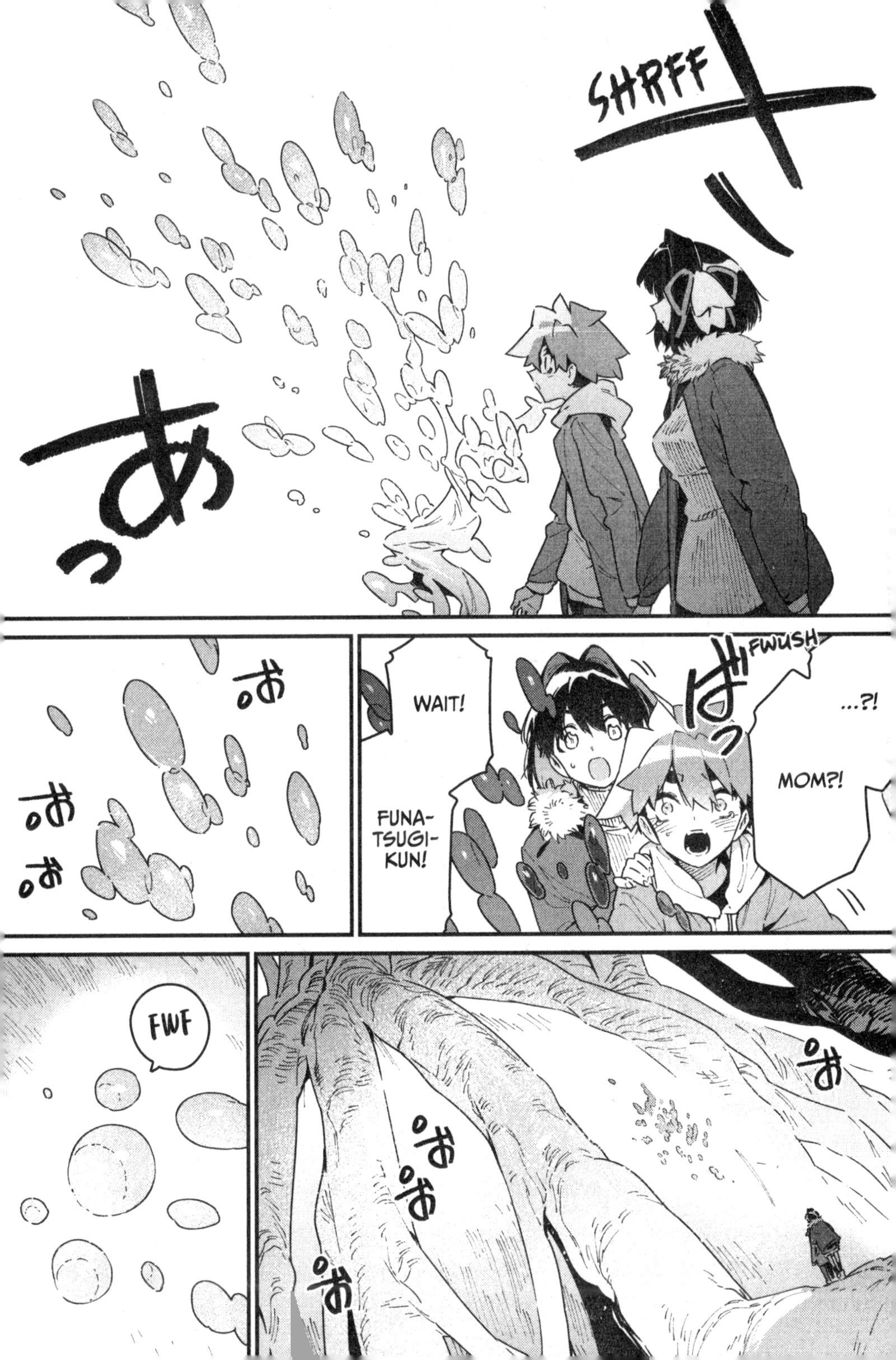
SHRFF
あっ
FWUSH
ばっ
...?!
WAIT!
MOM?!
FUNA-TSUGI-KUN!
FWF

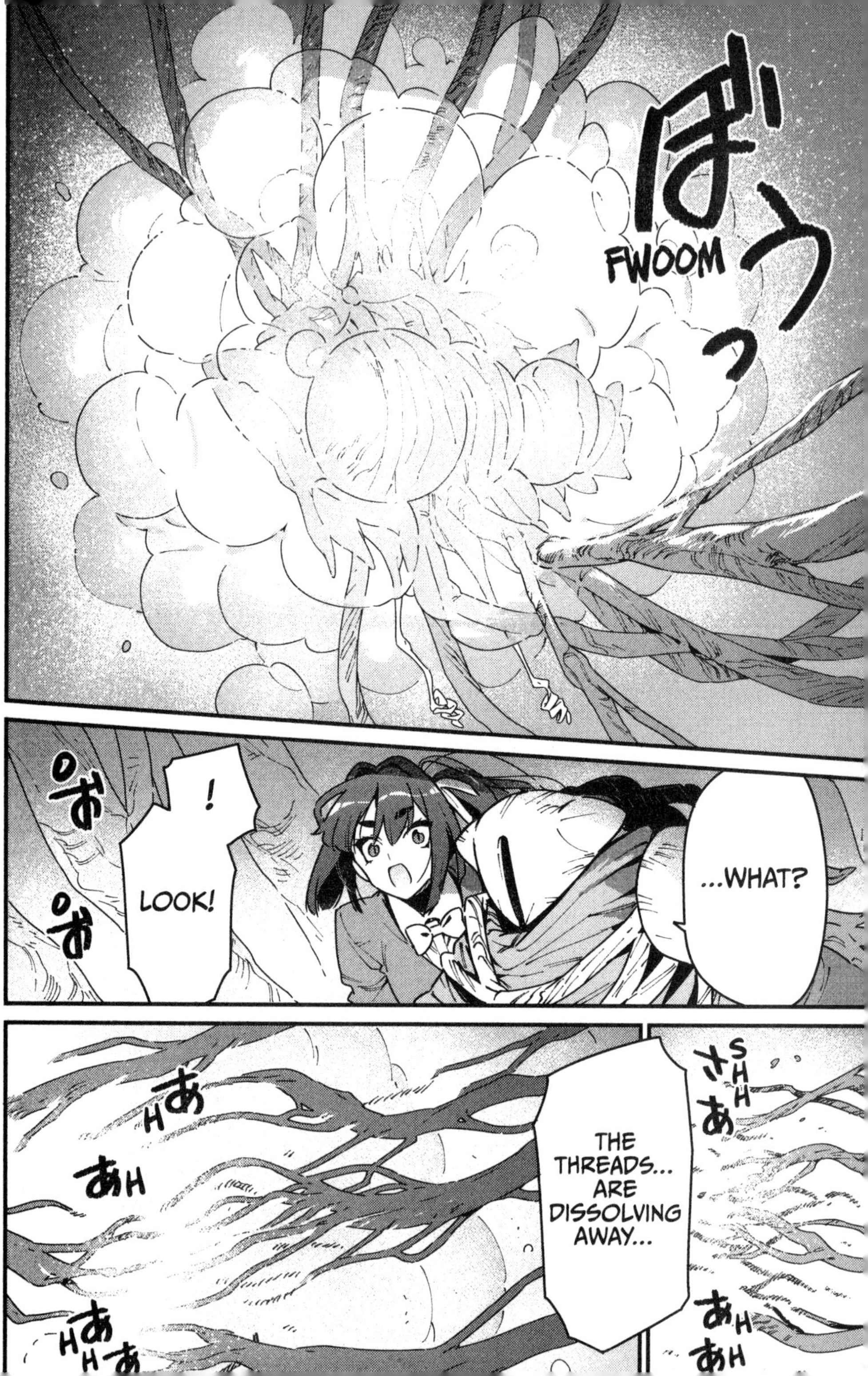
ぼうっ
FWOOM
...WHAT?
!
LOOK!
SHH
THE THREADS... ARE DISSOLVING AWAY...

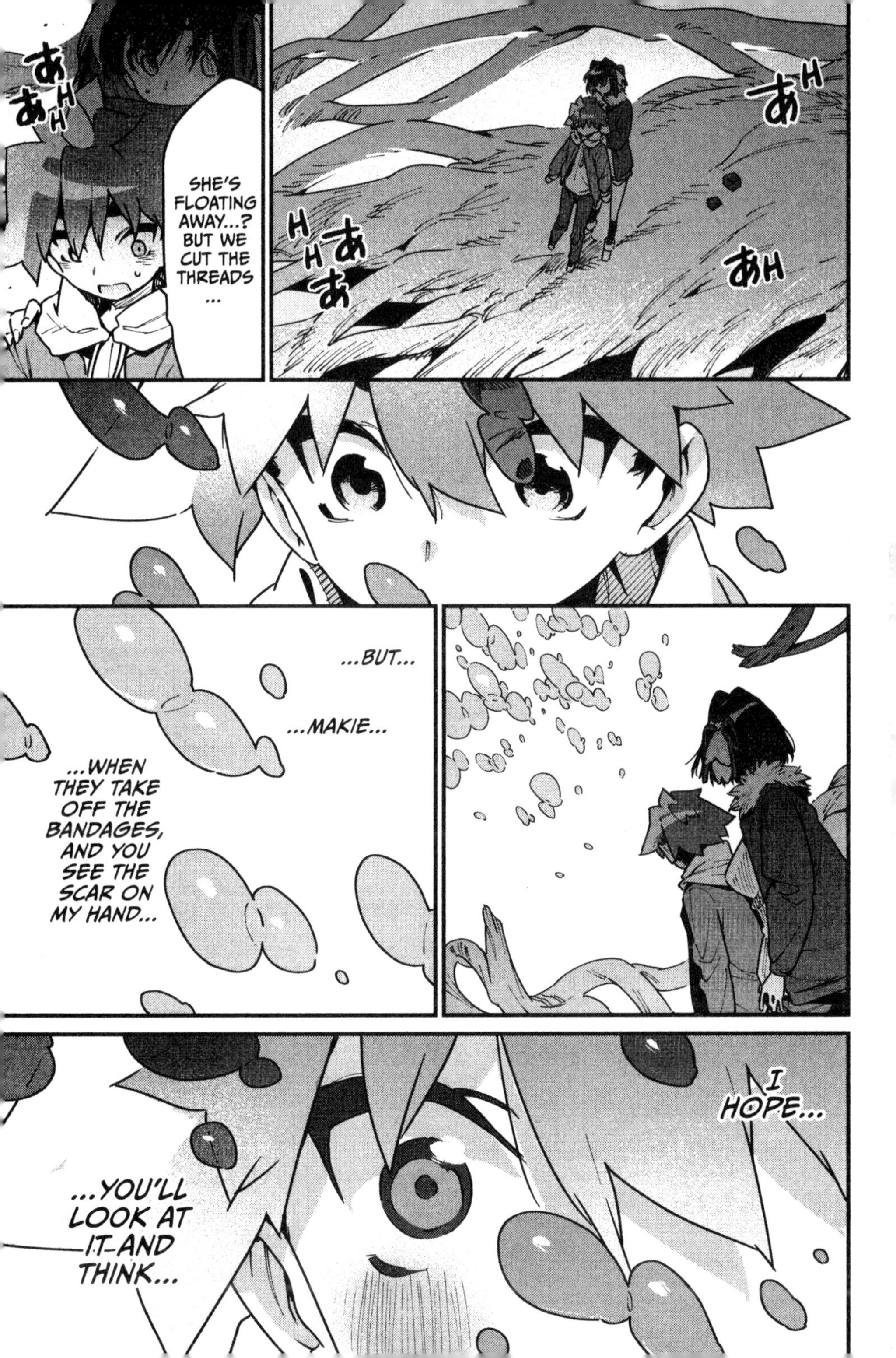

あH
あH
HHああ
ああHH
SHE'S FLOATING AWAY...? BUT WE CUT THE THREADS...
...BUT...
...MAKIE...
...WHEN THEY TAKE OFF THE BANDAGES, AND YOU SEE THE SCAR ON MY HAND...
I HOPE...
...YOU'LL LOOK AT IT AND THINK...

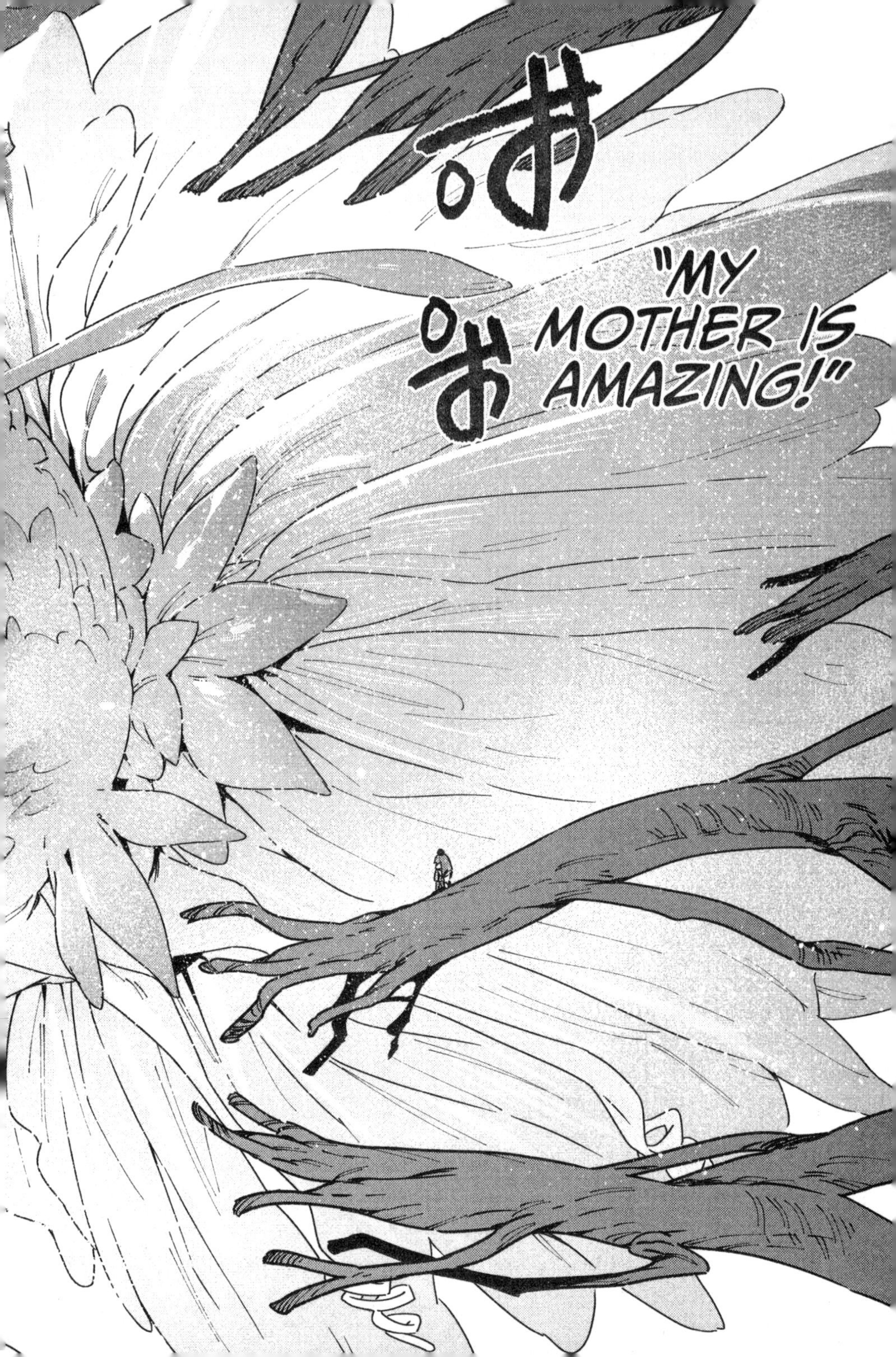
おお
"MY MOTHER IS AMAZING!"

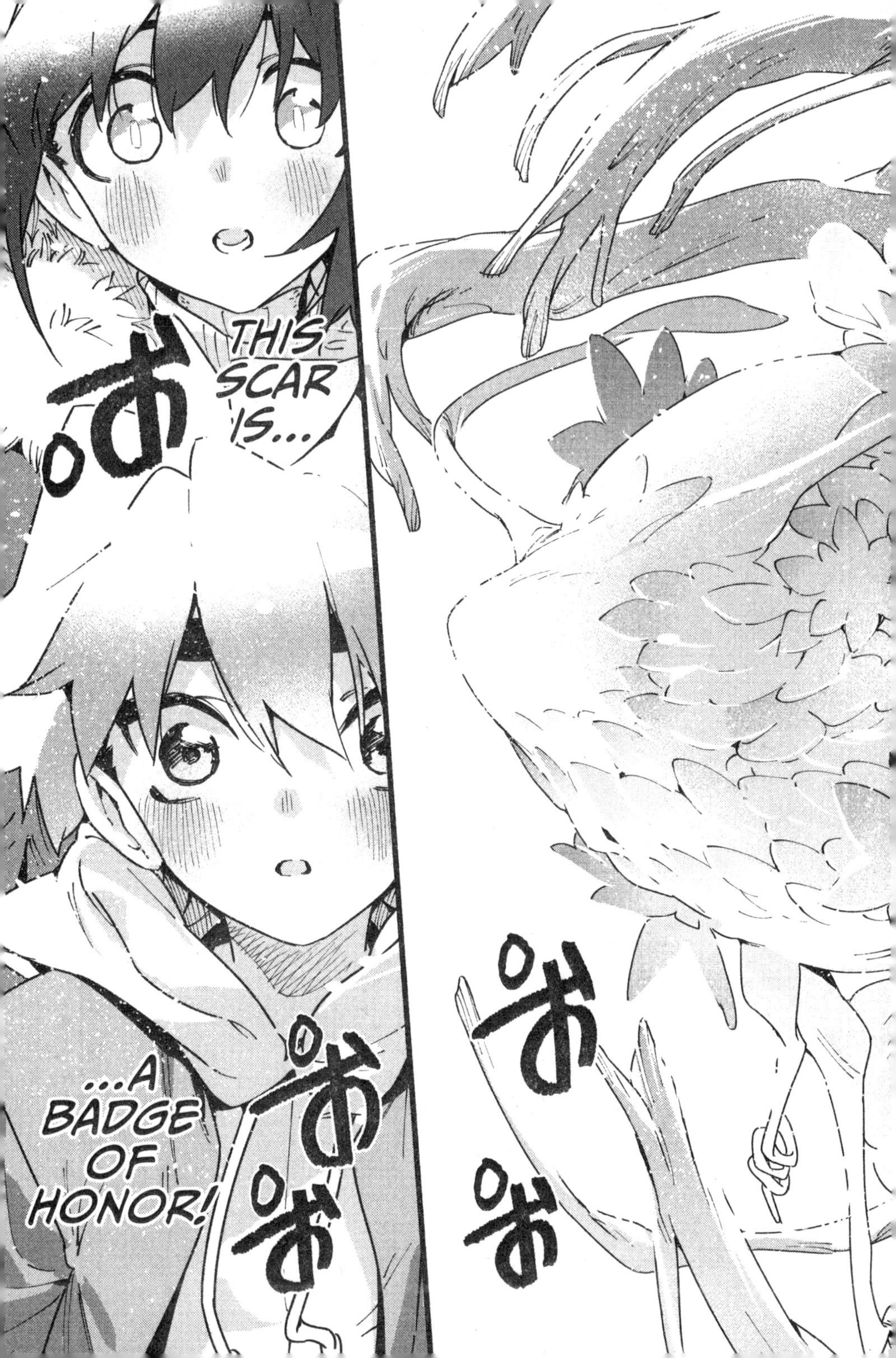
おお
おお
お
THIS SCAR IS...
...A BADGE OF HONOR!
おお

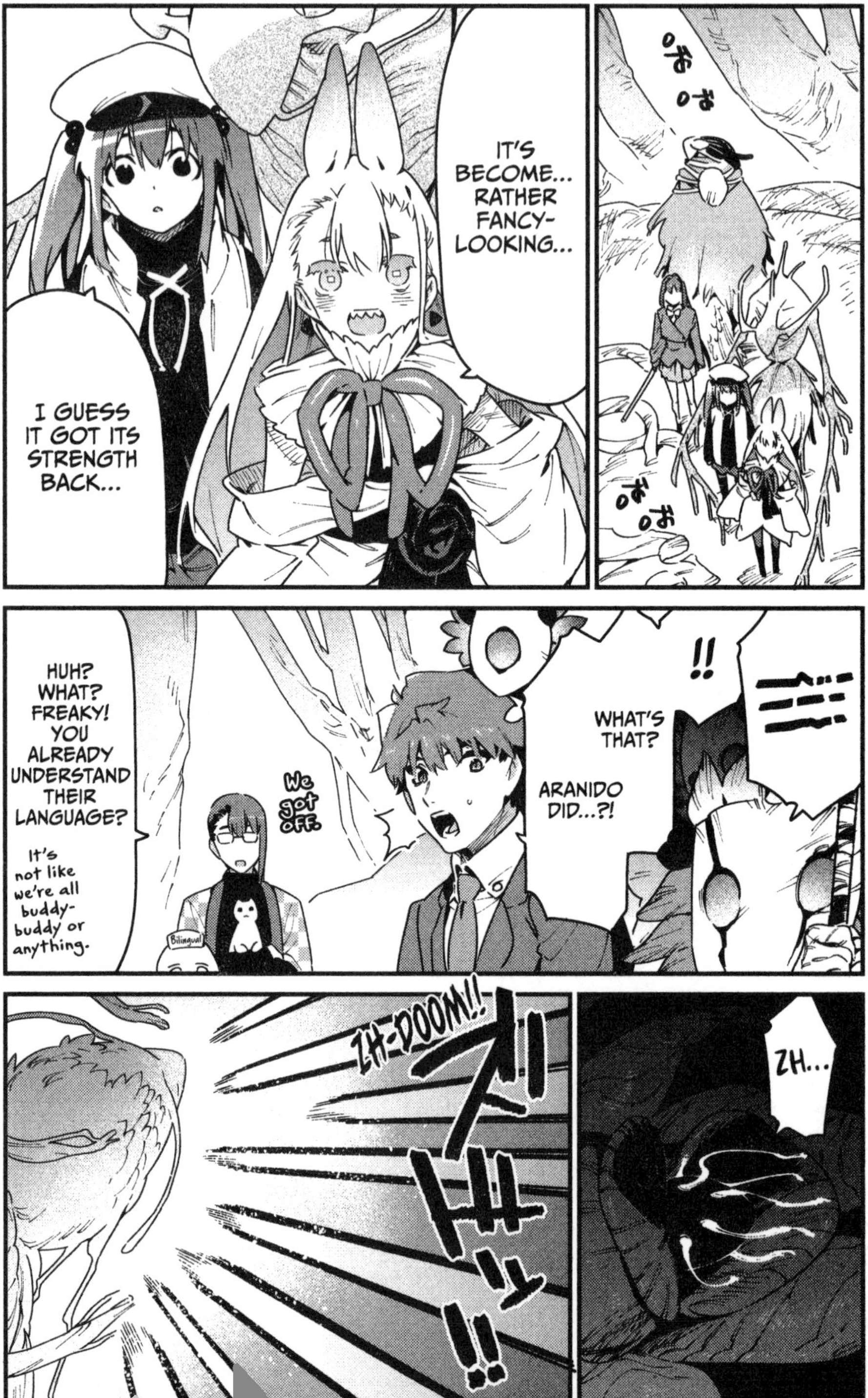
IT'S BECOME... RATHER FANCY-LOOKING...
I GUESS IT GOT ITS STRENGTH BACK...
!!
WHAT'S THAT?
ARANIDO DID...?!
We got off.
HUH? WHAT? FREAKY! YOU ALREADY UNDERSTAND THEIR LANGUAGE?
It's not like we're all buddy-buddy or anything.
Bilingual
ZH...
ZH-DOOM!!

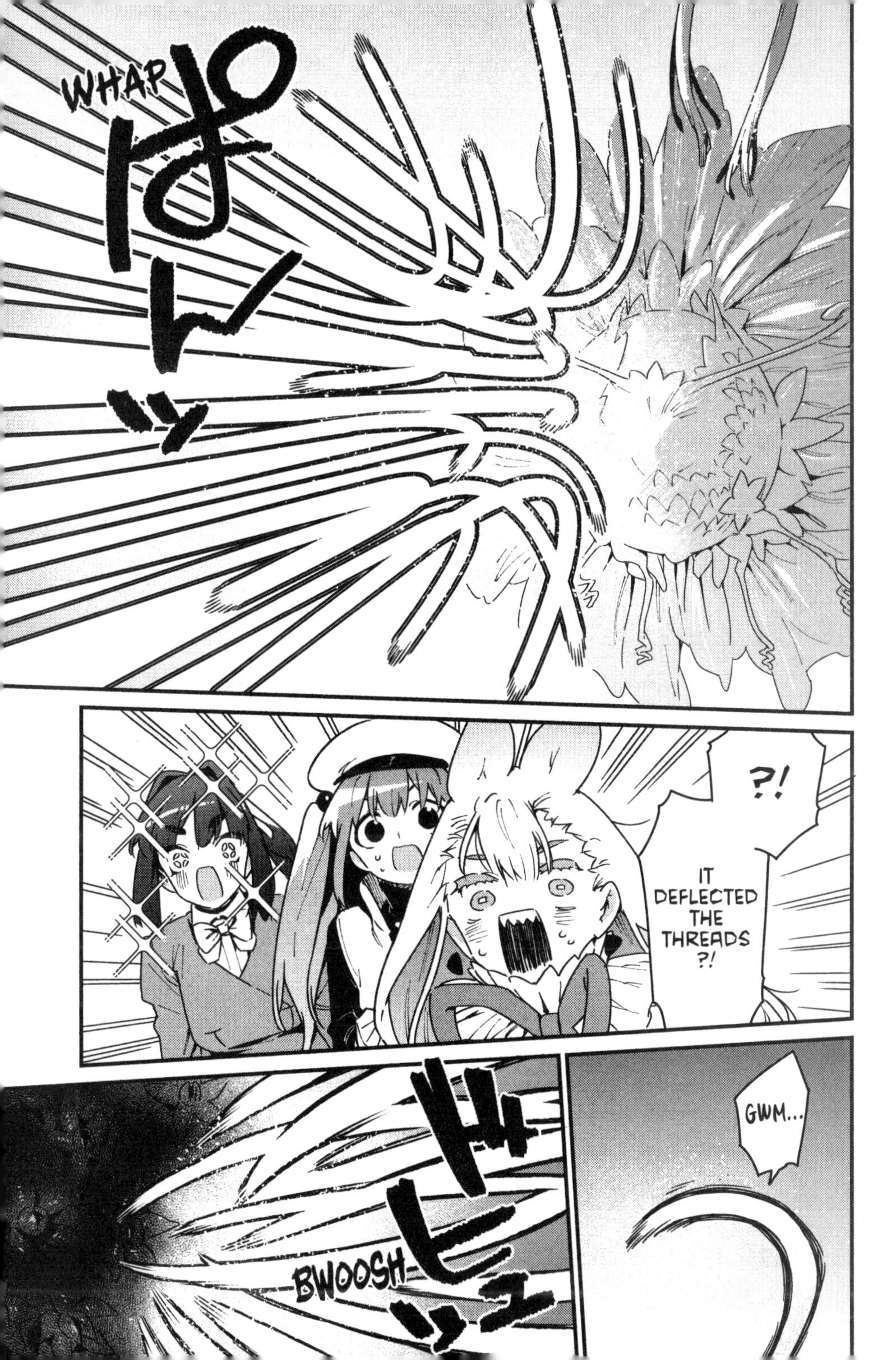
WHAP
ぱんッ
?!
IT DEFLECTED THE THREADS ?!
GWM...
ドヒュッ
BWOOSH

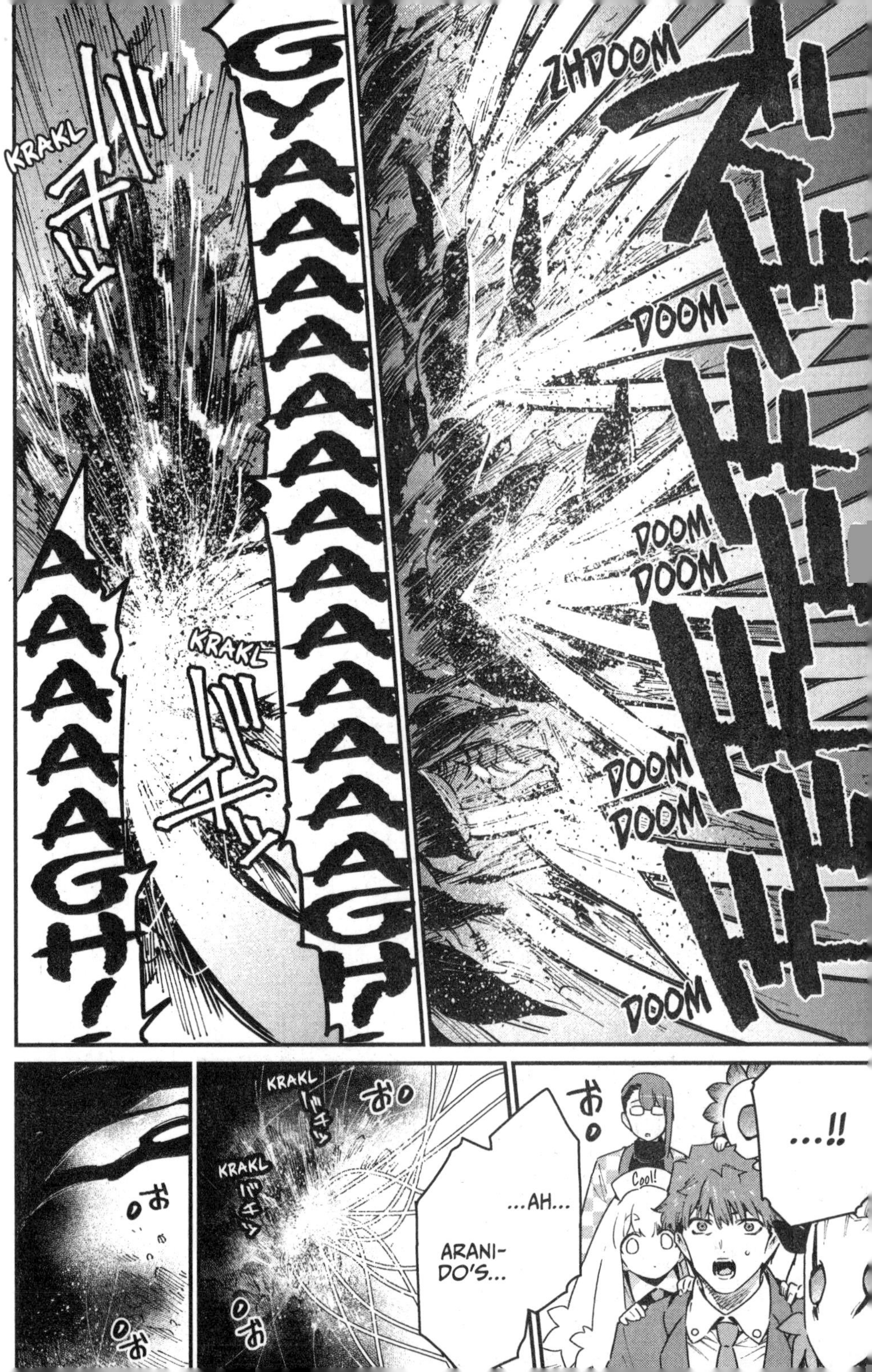
ZHDOOM
DOOM
DOOM DOOM
DOOM DOOM
DOOM
GYAAAAAAAAAAAAAAAGH?!
AAAAAAGH!!
KRAKL
KRAKL
…!!
お。
Cool!
…AH…
ARANI-DO'S…
おっ
KRAKL
KRAKL
おぉ
おっ
おぉ

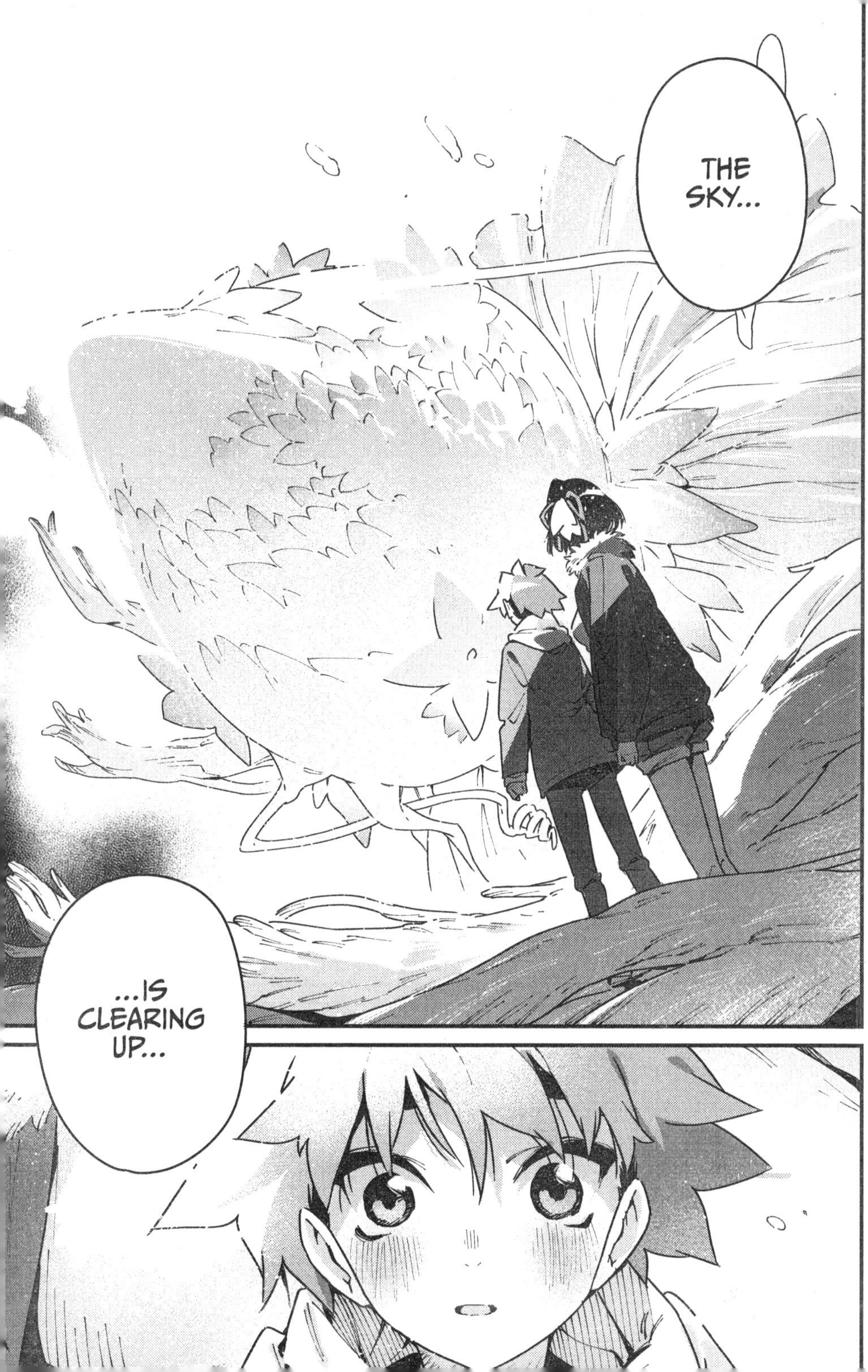
THE SKY...
...IS CLEARING UP...

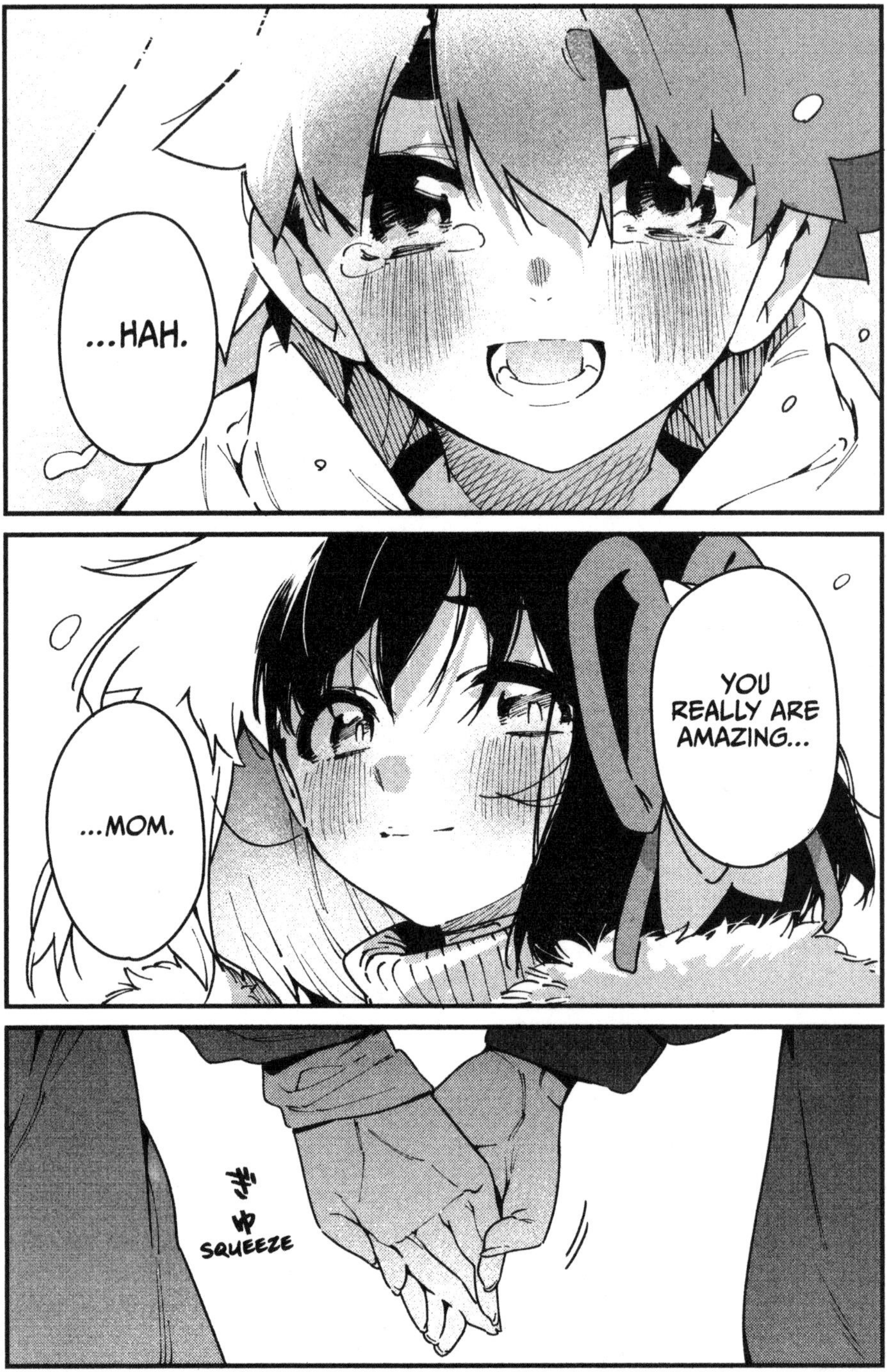
...HAH.
YOU REALLY ARE AMAZING...
...MOM.
ぎゅ
SQUEEZE

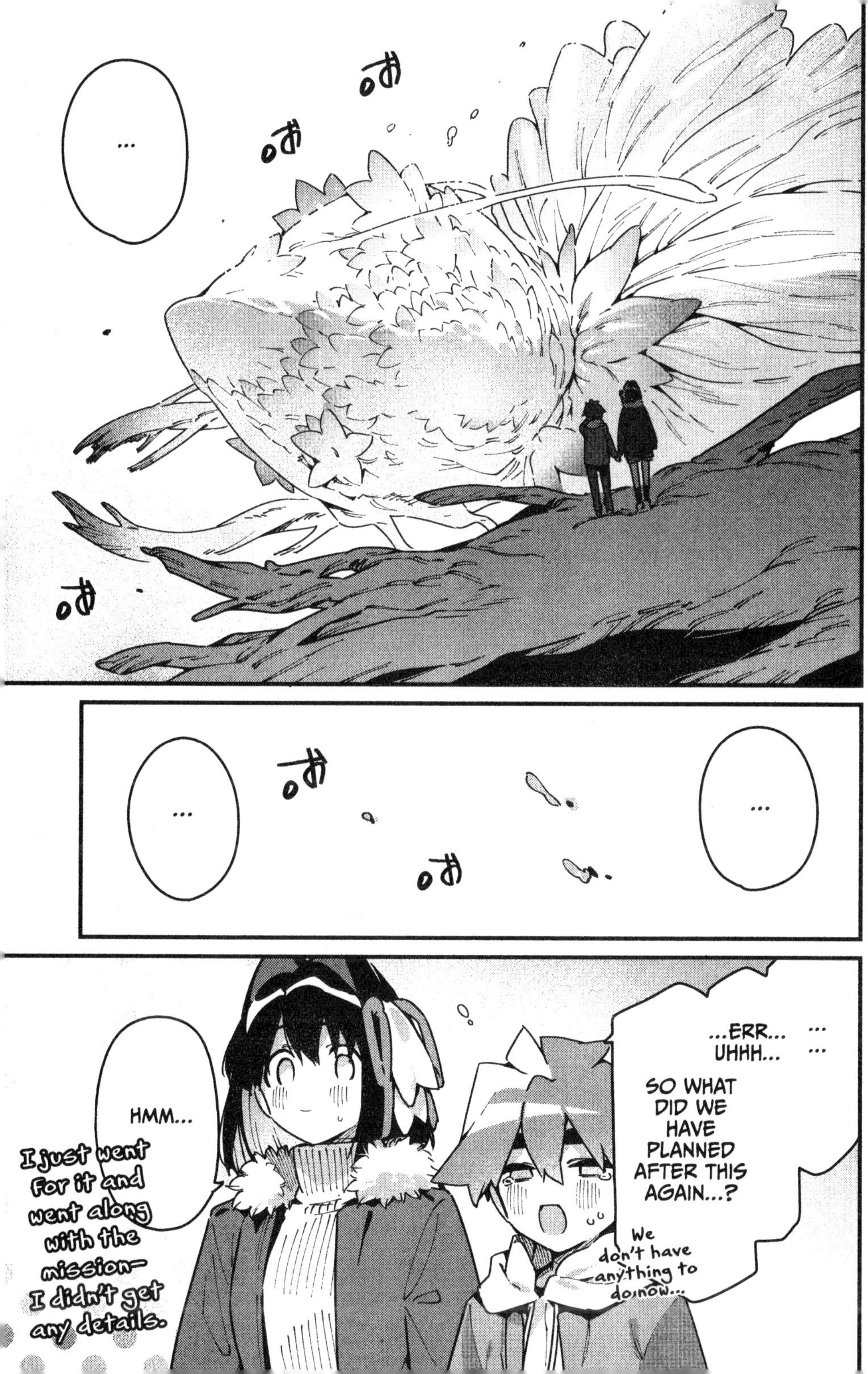
...
...
...
...ERR... ...
UHHH... ...
SO WHAT DID WE HAVE PLANNED AFTER THIS AGAIN...?
We don't have anything to do now...
HMM...
I just went for it and went along with the mission—I didn't get any details.

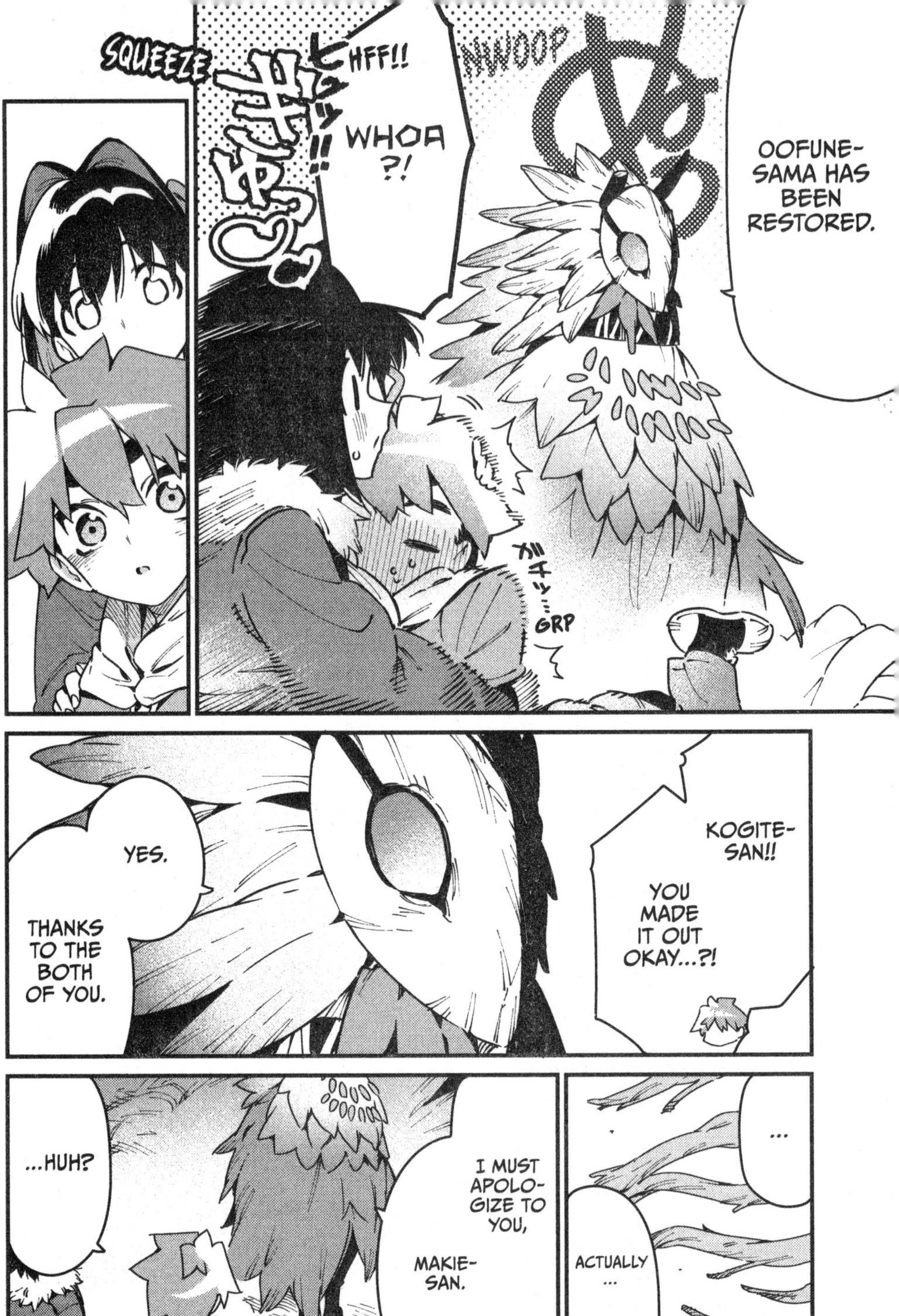
OOFUNE-SAMA HAS BEEN RESTORED.
NWOOP
WHOA?!
HFF!!
SQUEEZE
GRP
KOGITE-SAN!!
YOU MADE IT OUT OKAY...?!
YES.
THANKS TO THE BOTH OF YOU.
...
ACTUALLY ...
I MUST APOLOGIZE TO YOU,
MAKIE-SAN.
...HUH?

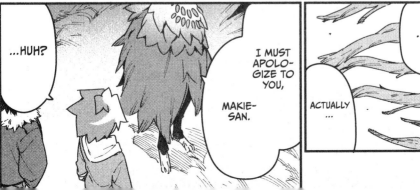

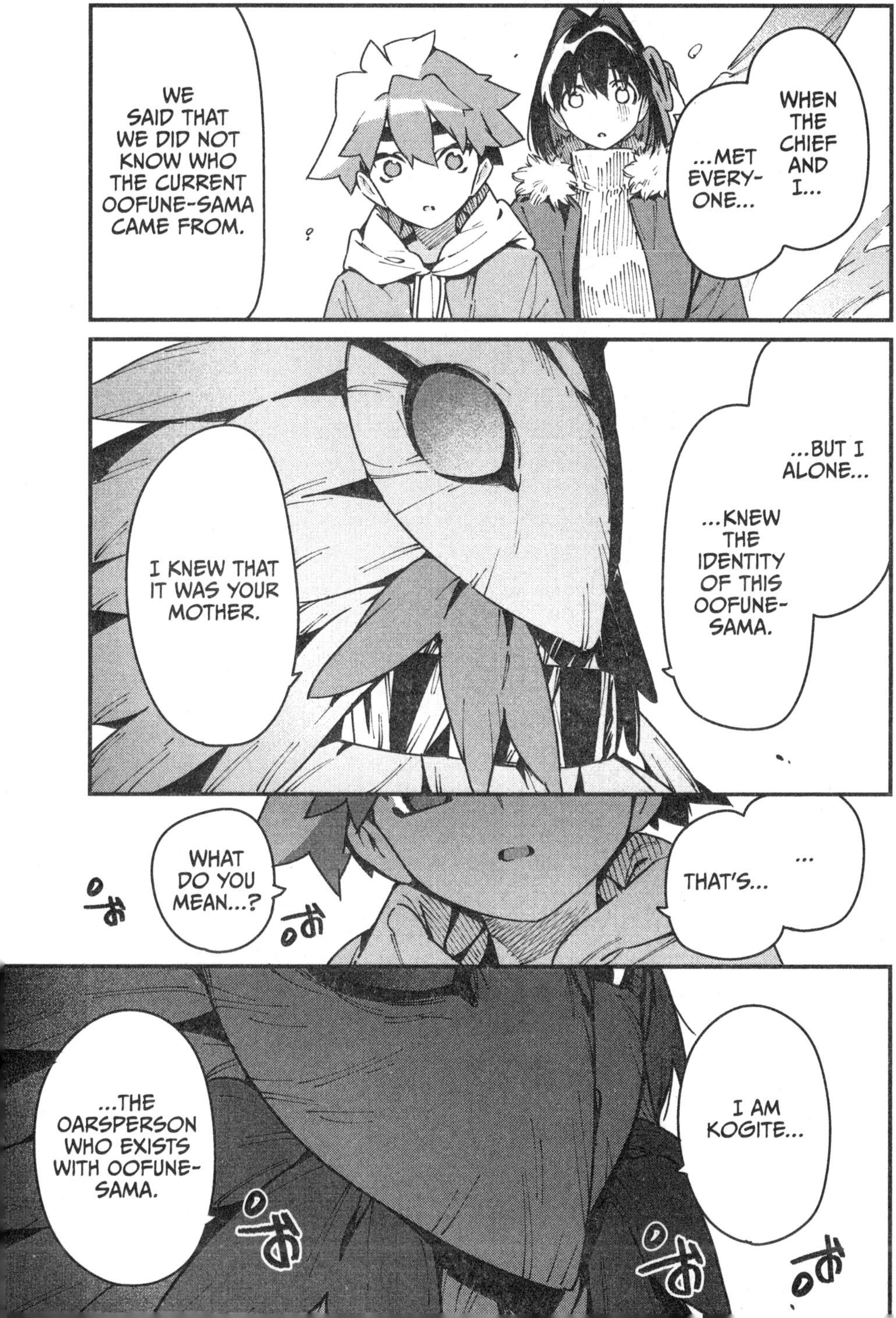
WHEN THE CHIEF AND I...
...MET EVERY-ONE...
WE SAID THAT WE DID NOT KNOW WHO THE CURRENT OOFUNE-SAMA CAME FROM.
...BUT I ALONE...
...KNEW THE IDENTITY OF THIS OOFUNE-SAMA.
I KNEW THAT IT WAS YOUR MOTHER.
... THAT'S...
WHAT DO YOU MEAN...?
I AM KOGITE...
...THE OARSPERSON WHO EXISTS WITH OOFUNE-SAMA.

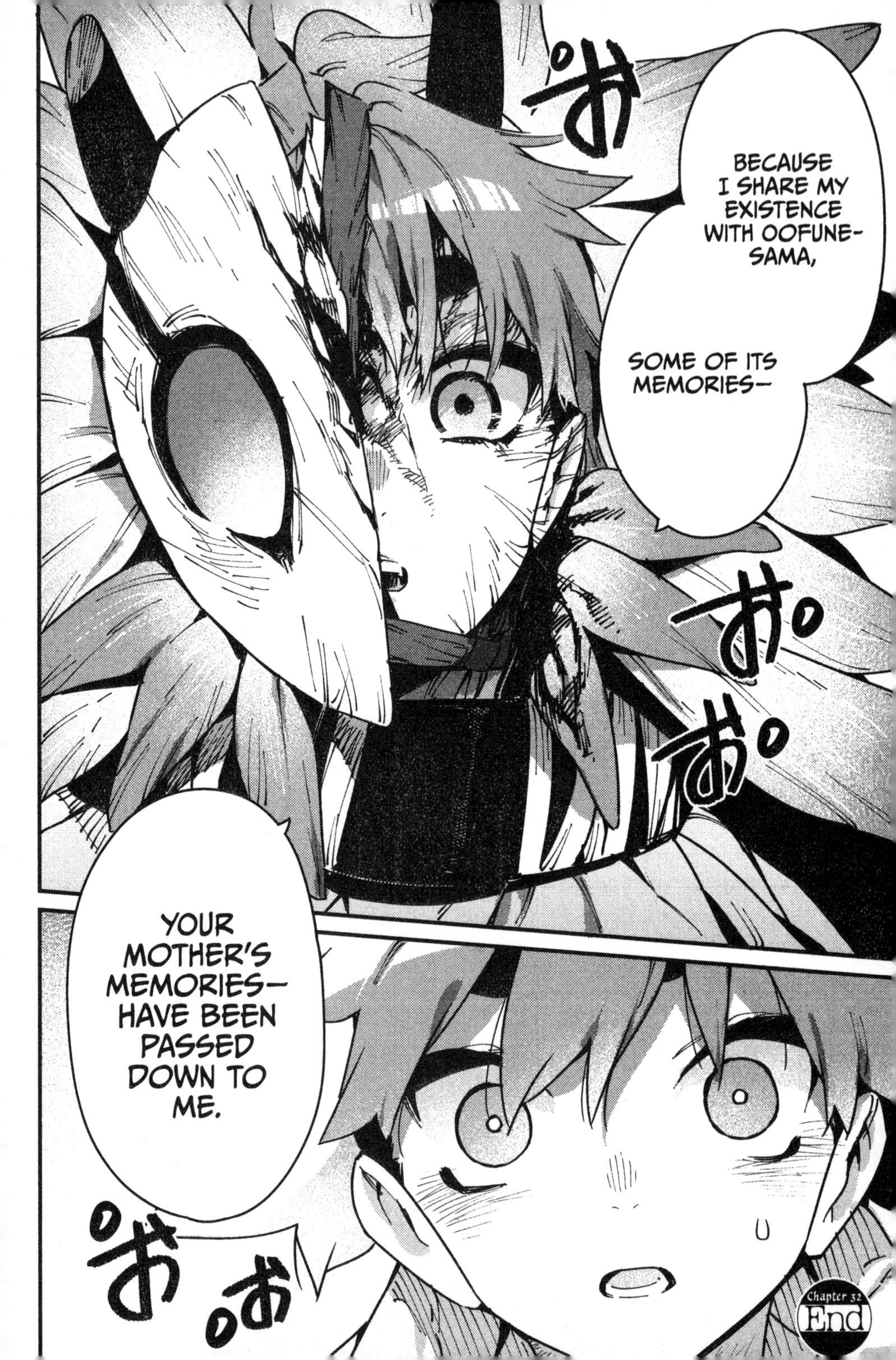
お
BECAUSE I SHARE MY EXISTENCE WITH OOFUNE-SAMA,
SOME OF ITS MEMORIES—
お
お
YOUR MOTHER'S MEMORIES—HAVE BEEN PASSED DOWN TO ME.
お
お
Chapter 32 End

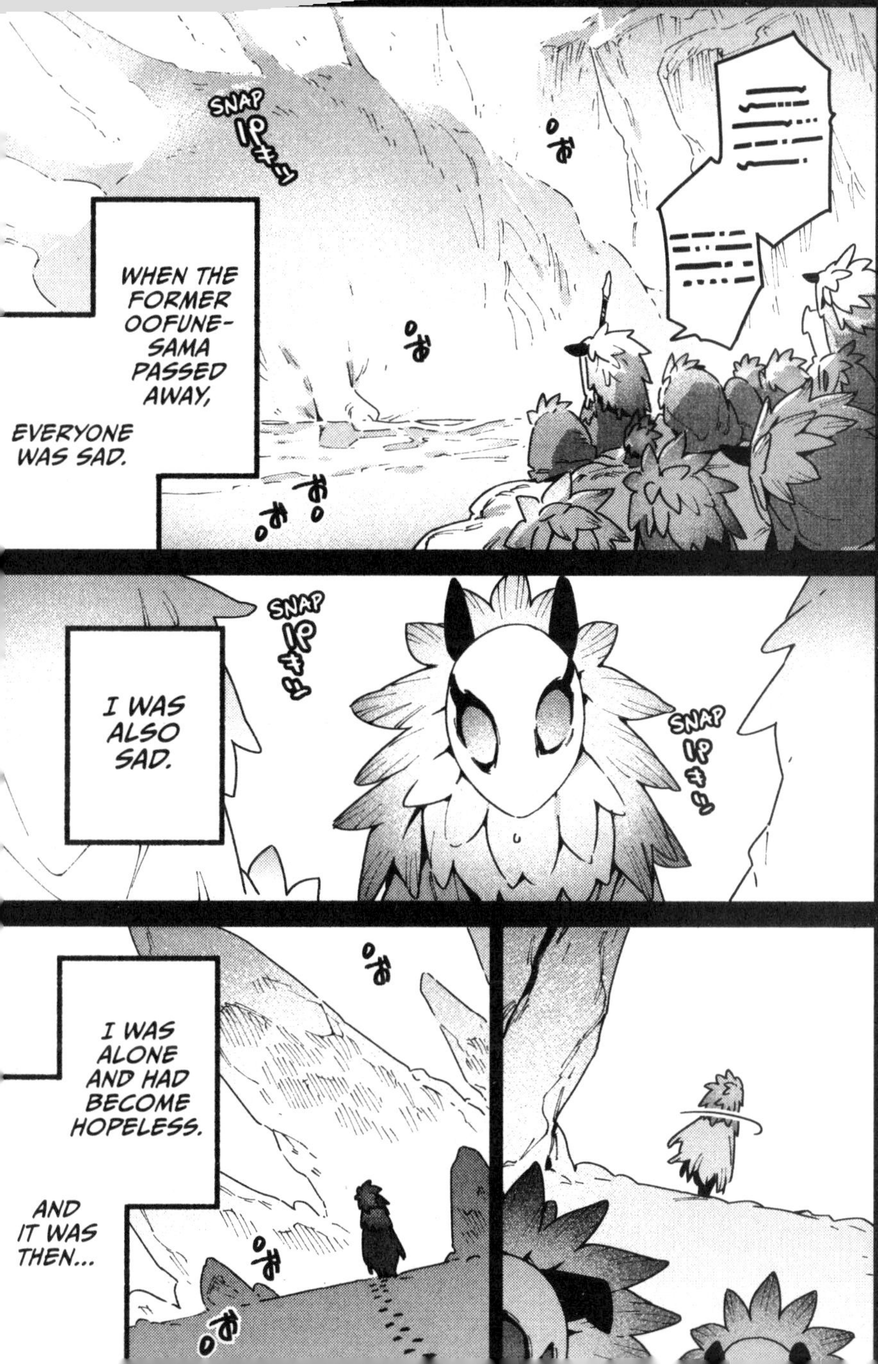

SNAP
WHEN THE FORMER OOFUNE-SAMA PASSED AWAY,
EVERYONE WAS SAD.
SNAP
SNAP
I WAS ALSO SAD.
I WAS ALONE AND HAD BECOME HOPELESS.
AND IT WAS THEN...

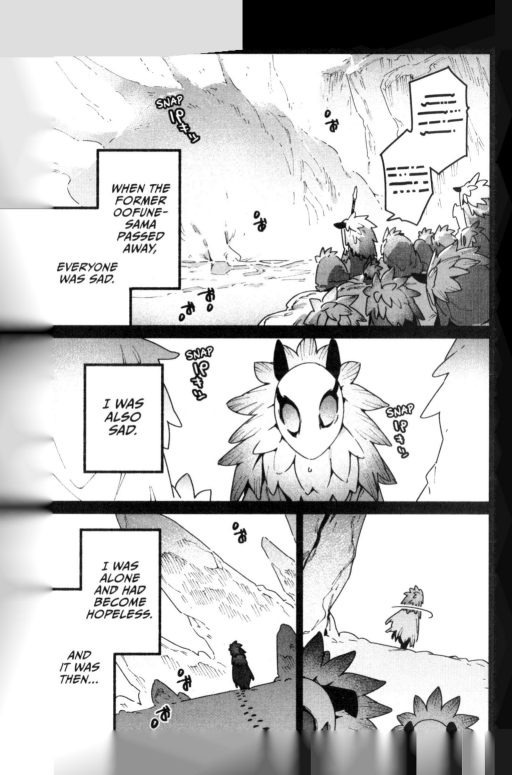

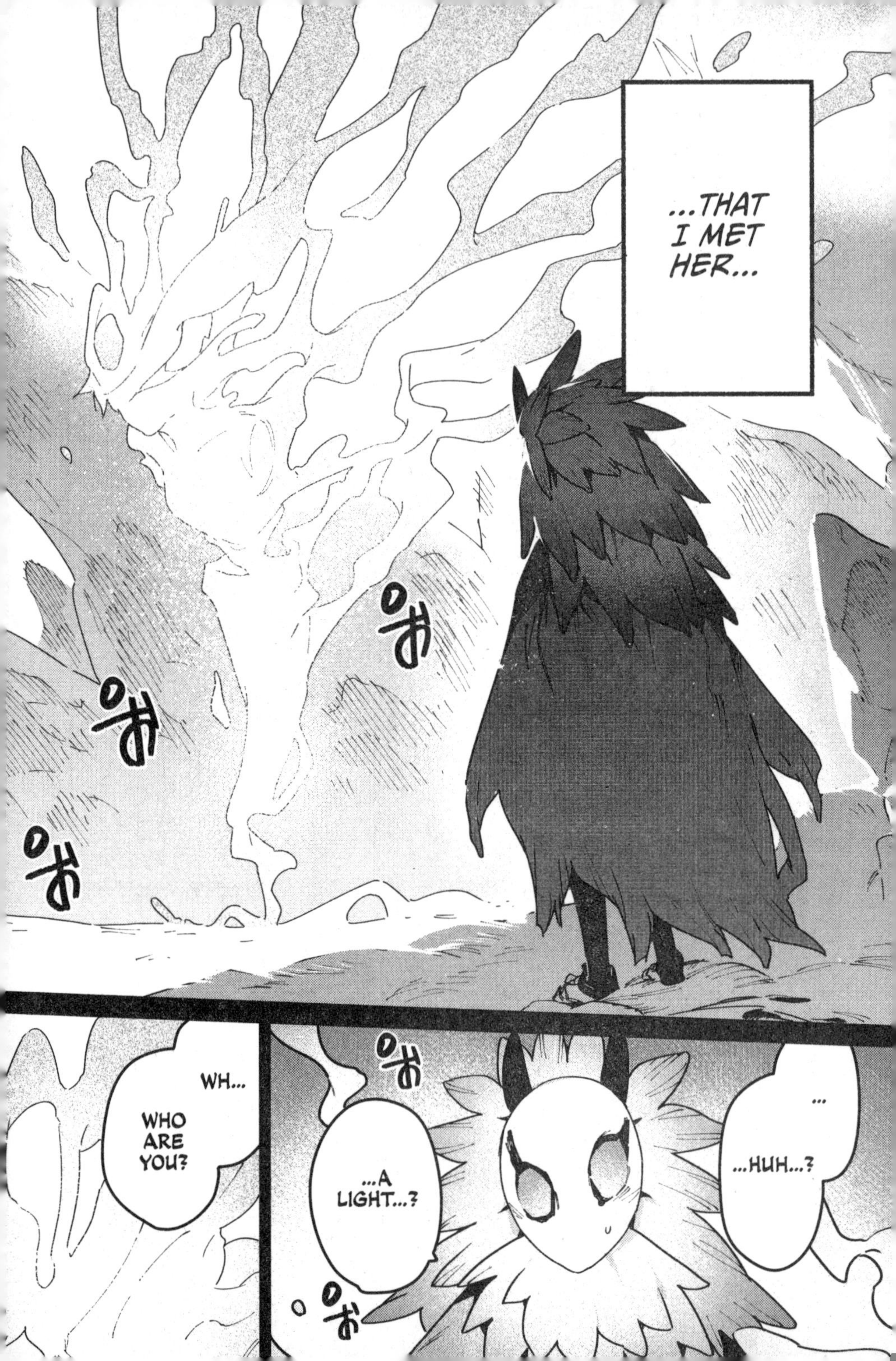
...THAT I MET HER...
...
...HUH...?
...A LIGHT...?
WH...
WHO ARE YOU?

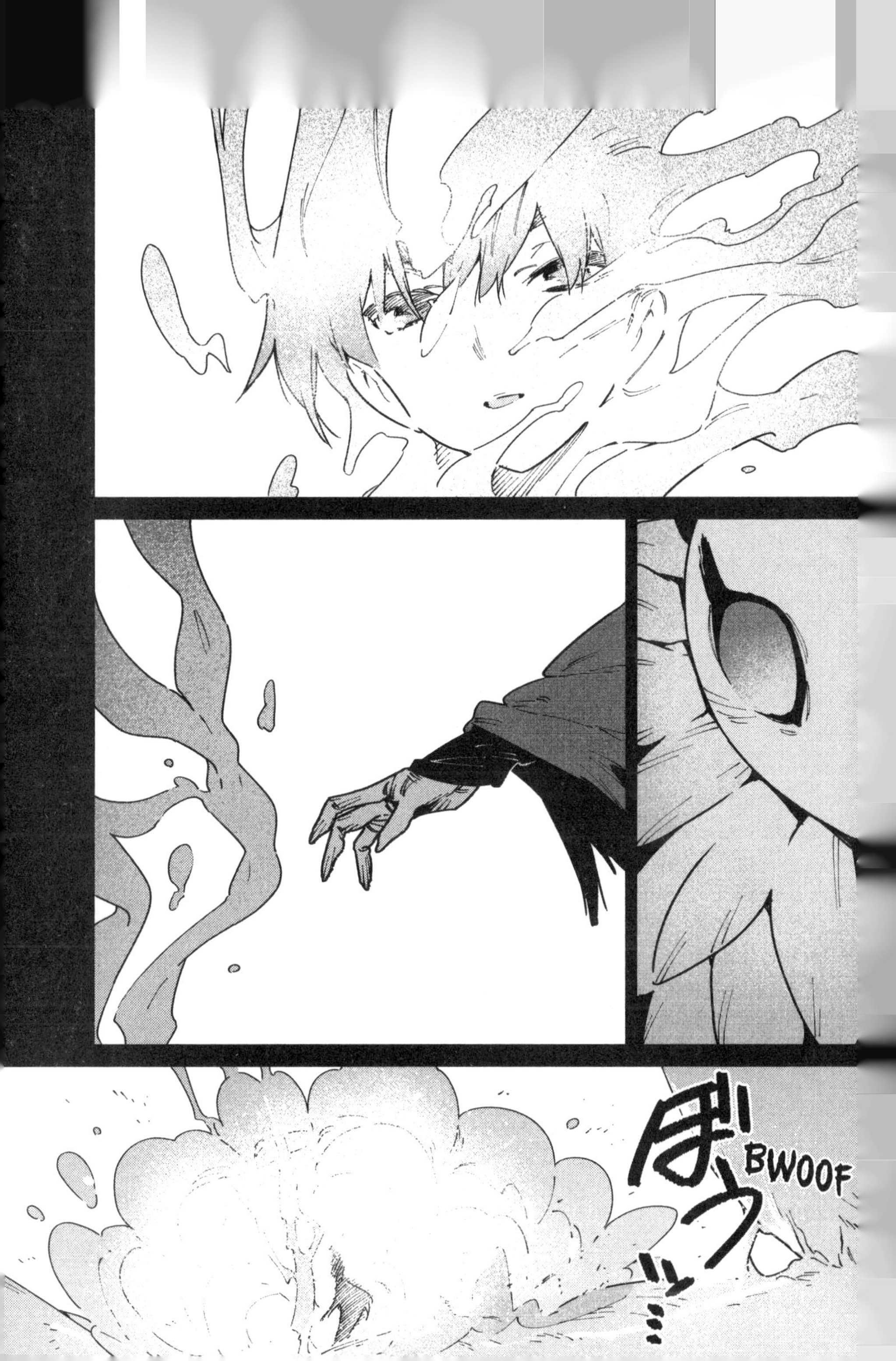
ぼうっ
BWOOF

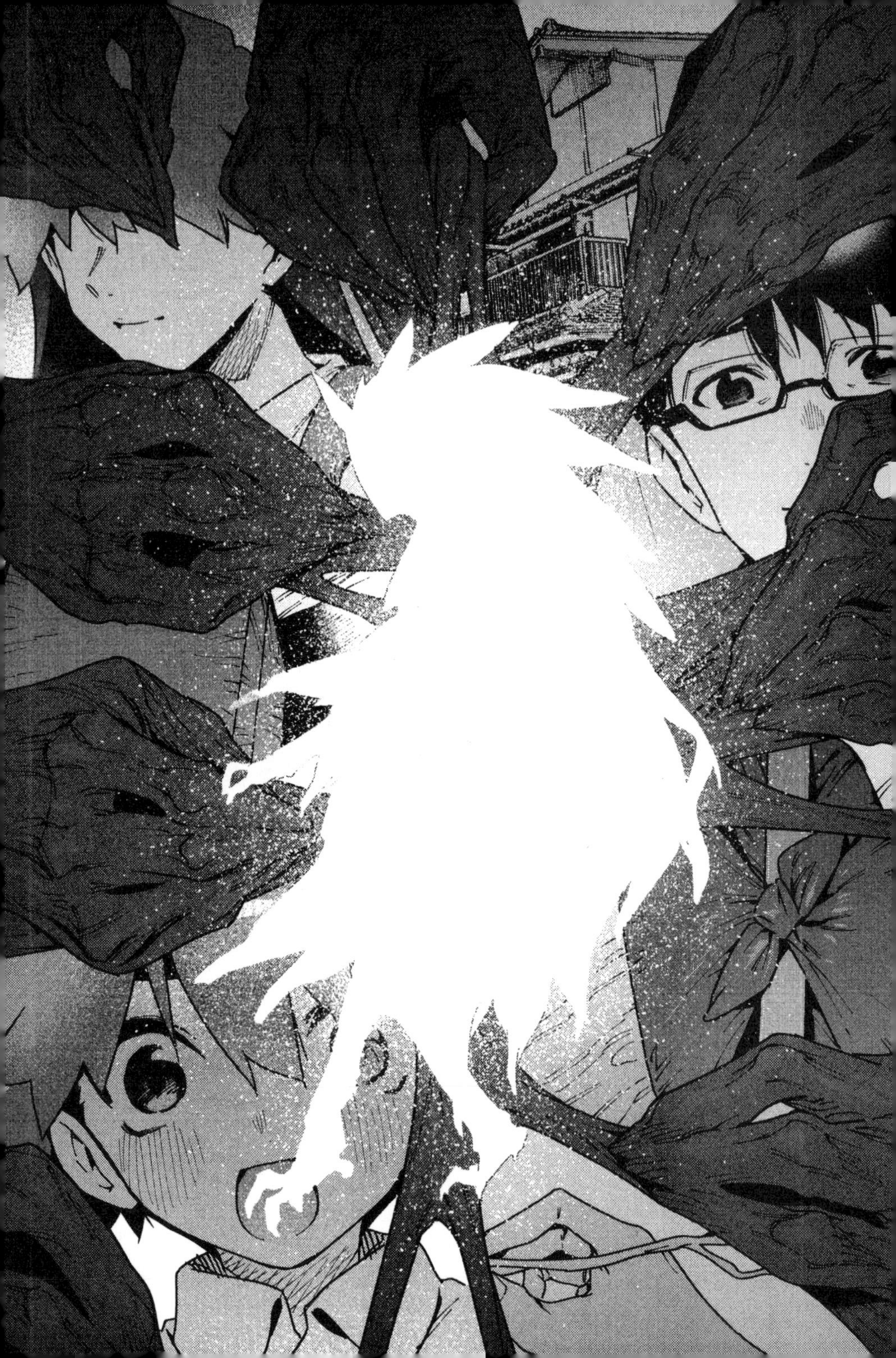

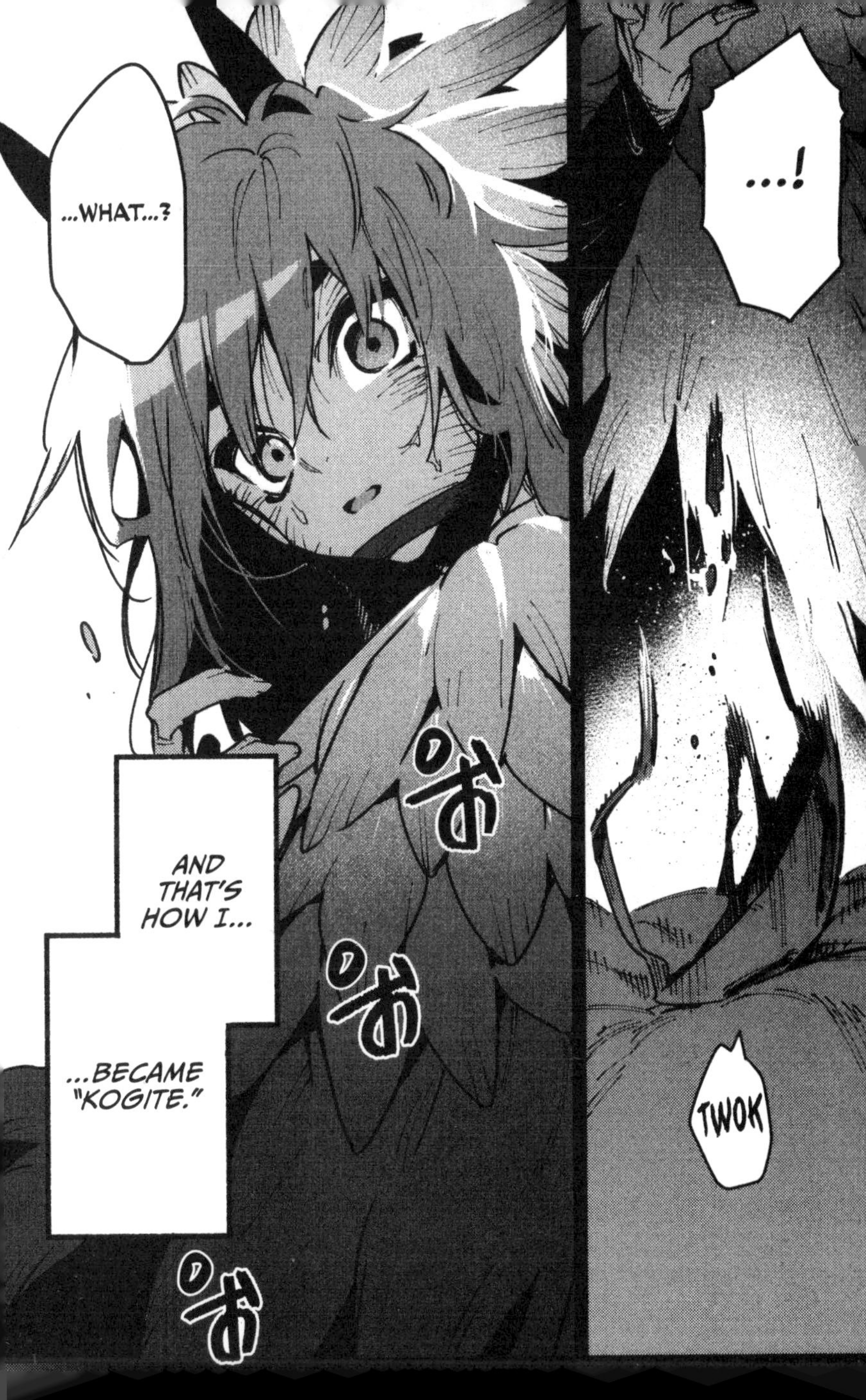
...!
TWOK
...WHAT...?
AND THAT'S HOW I...
...BECAME "KOGITE."

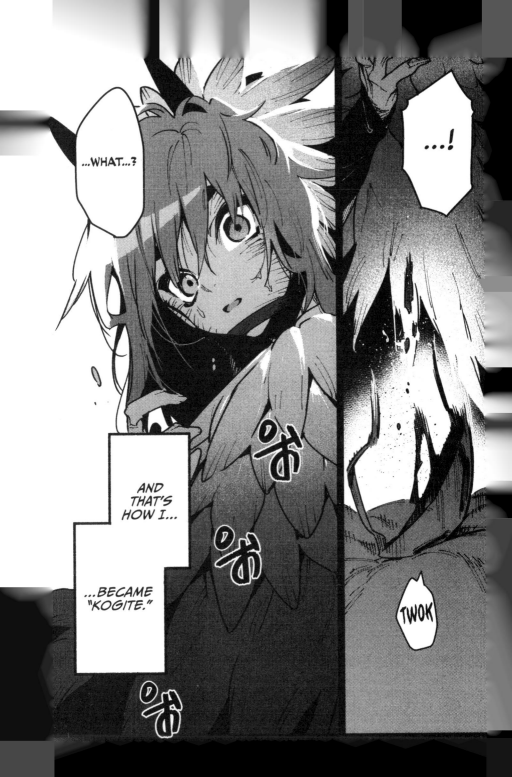

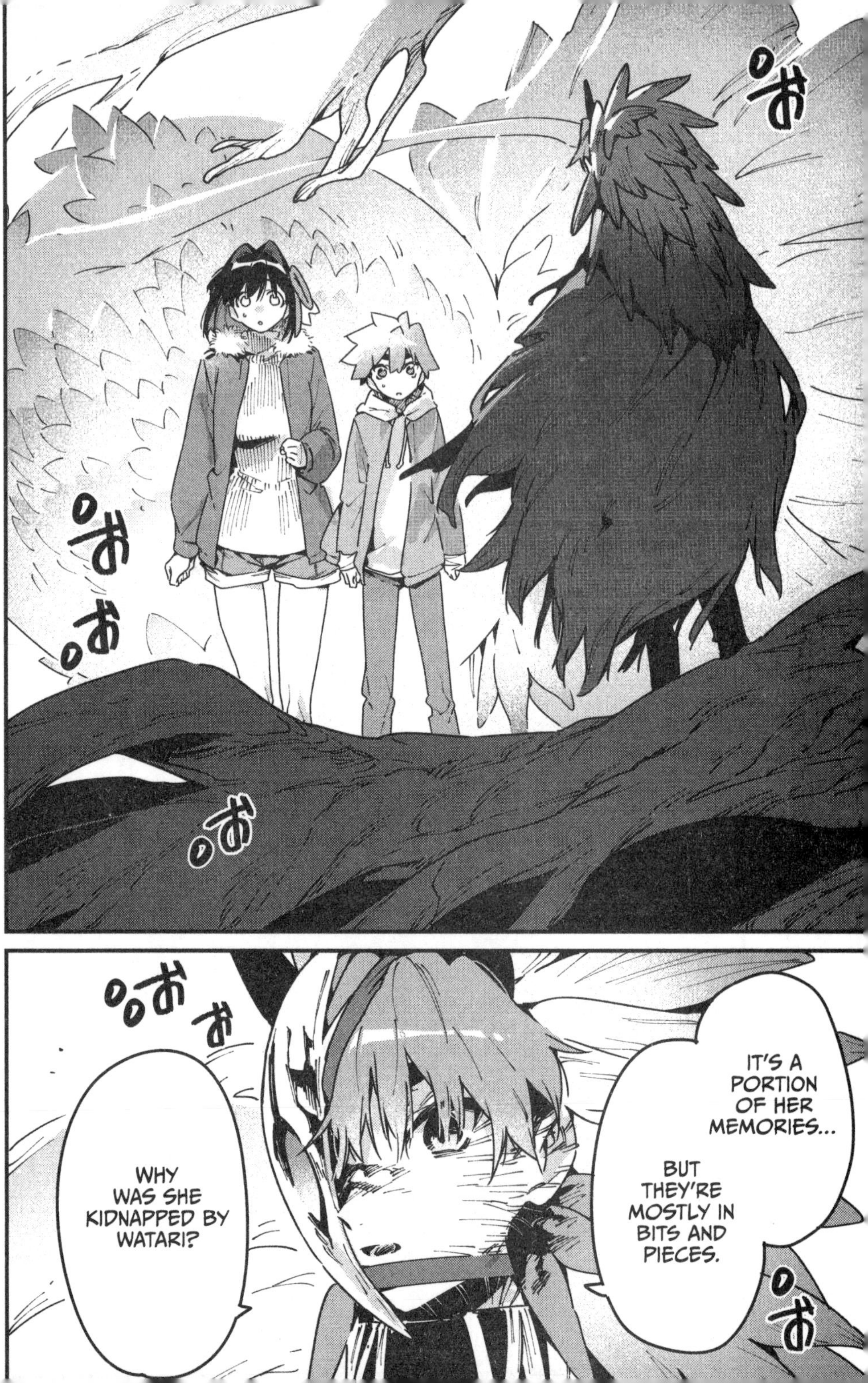
ぉお
ぉお
ぉお
ぉお
ぉお
ぉおぉ
IT'S A PORTION OF HER MEMORIES...
BUT THEY'RE MOSTLY IN BITS AND PIECES.
WHY WAS SHE KIDNAPPED BY WATARI?
ぉぉおぉ

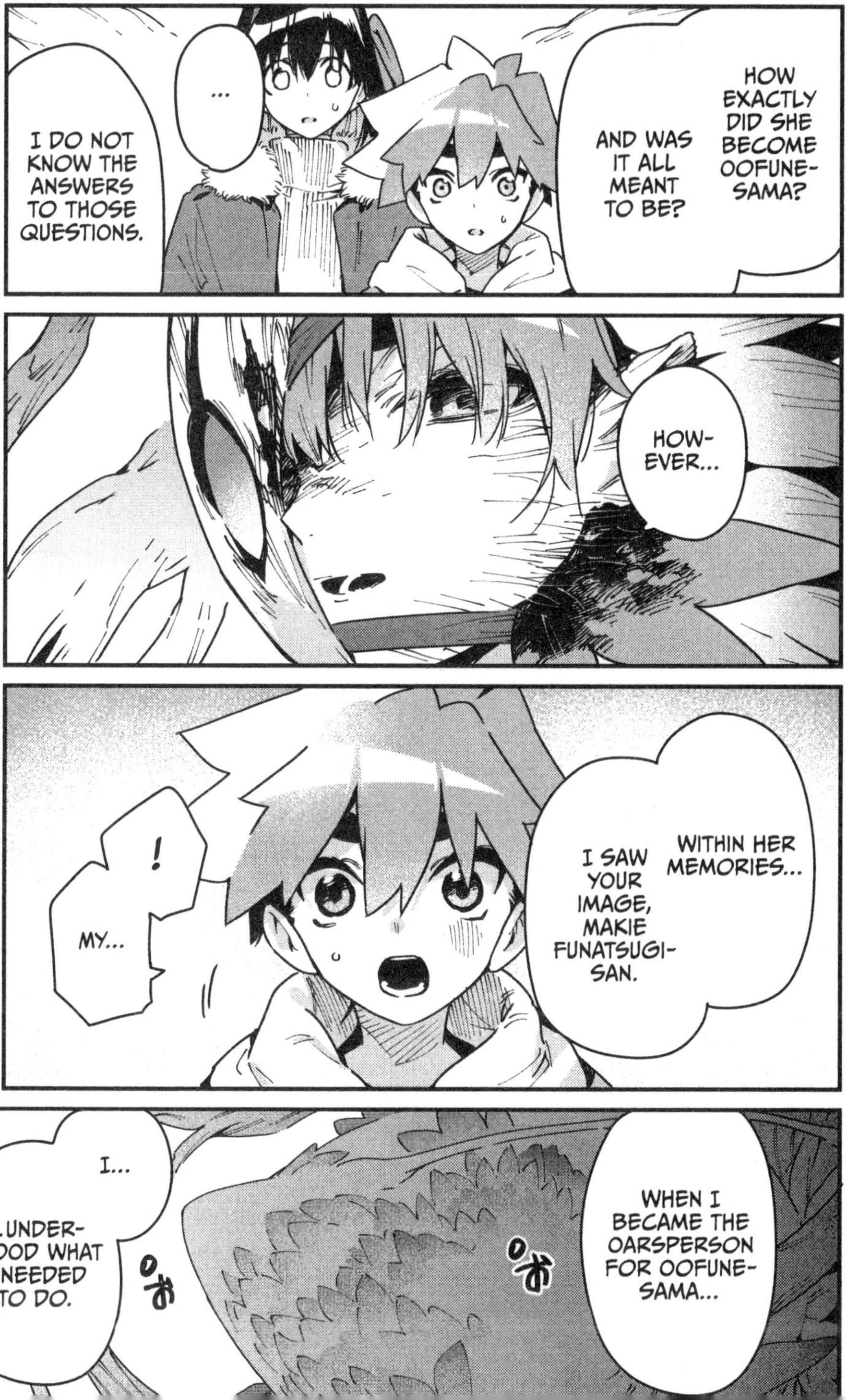
HOW EXACTLY DID SHE BECOME OOFUNE-SAMA?
AND WAS IT ALL MEANT TO BE?
...
I DO NOT KNOW THE ANSWERS TO THOSE QUESTIONS.
HOW-EVER...
WITHIN HER MEMORIES...
I SAW YOUR IMAGE, MAKIE FUNATSUGI-SAN.
!
MY...
WHEN I BECAME THE OARSPERSON FOR OOFUNE-SAMA...
I...
...UNDER-STOOD WHAT I NEEDED TO DO.

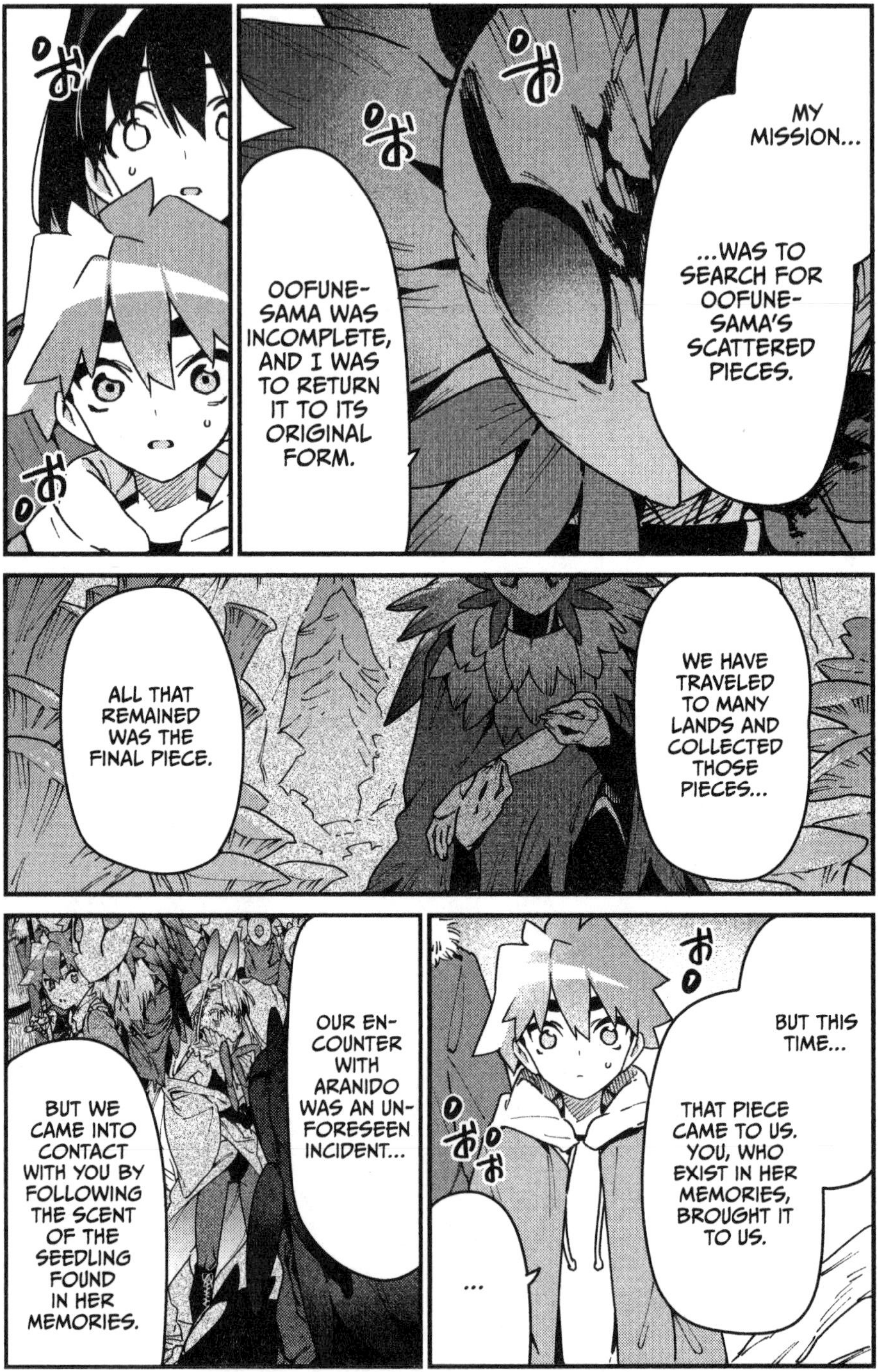
ぉ
ぉ
MY MISSION...
...WAS TO SEARCH FOR OOFUNE-SAMA'S SCATTERED PIECES.
OOFUNE-SAMA WAS INCOMPLETE, AND I WAS TO RETURN IT TO ITS ORIGINAL FORM.
ぉ
ぉ
WE HAVE TRAVELED TO MANY LANDS AND COLLECTED THOSE PIECES...
ALL THAT REMAINED WAS THE FINAL PIECE.
ぉ
BUT THIS TIME...
THAT PIECE CAME TO US. YOU, WHO EXIST IN HER MEMORIES, BROUGHT IT TO US.
ぉぉ
...
OUR EN-COUNTER WITH ARANIDO WAS AN UN-FORESEEN INCIDENT...
BUT WE CAME INTO CONTACT WITH YOU BY FOLLOWING THE SCENT OF THE SEEDLING FOUND IN HER MEMORIES.

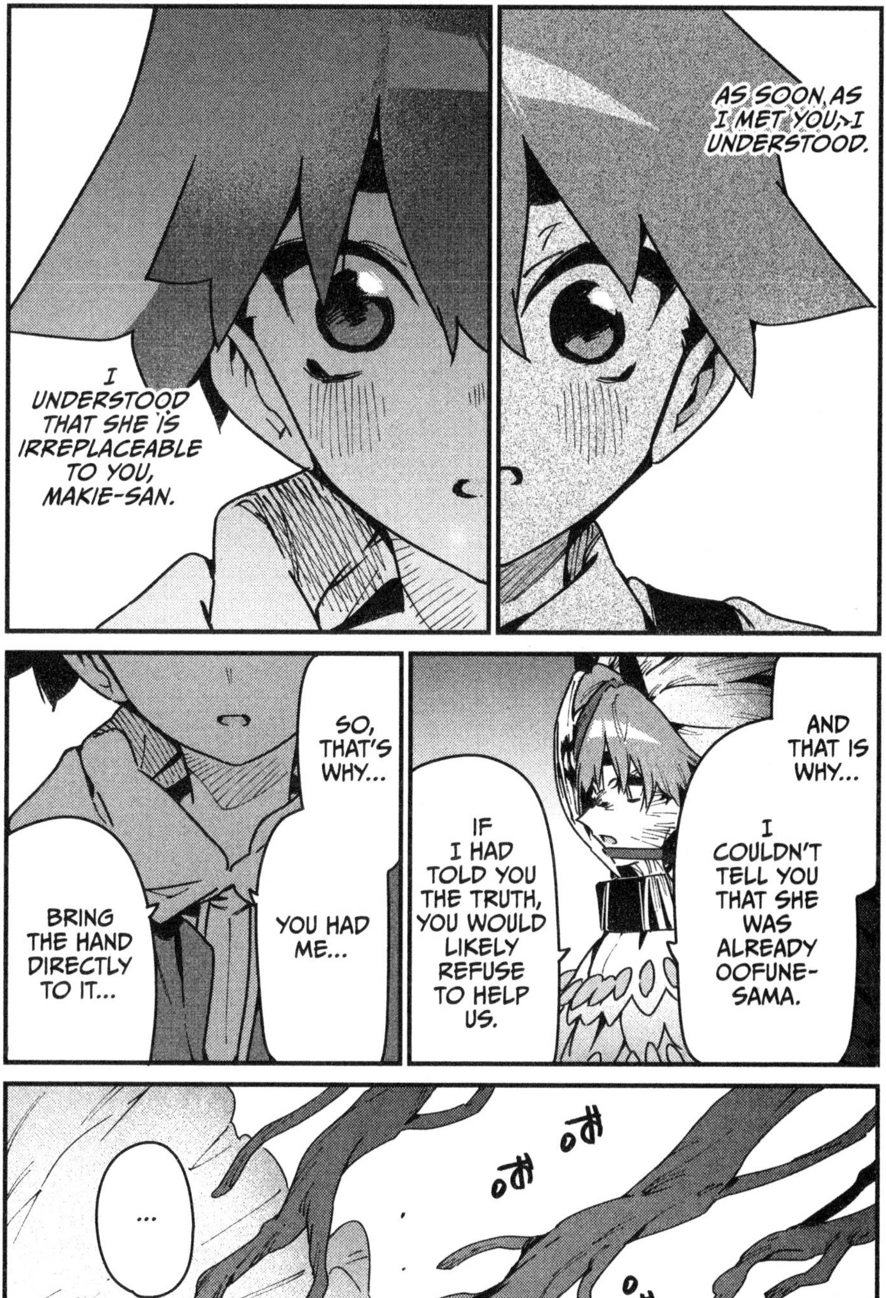
AS SOON AS I MET YOU, I UNDERSTOOD.
I UNDERSTOOD THAT SHE IS IRREPLACEABLE TO YOU, MAKIE-SAN.
AND THAT IS WHY...
I COULDN'T TELL YOU THAT SHE WAS ALREADY OOFUNE-SAMA.
IF I HAD TOLD YOU THE TRUTH, YOU WOULD LIKELY REFUSE TO HELP US.
SO, THAT'S WHY...
YOU HAD ME...
BRING THE HAND DIRECTLY TO IT...
お
お
お
...
お

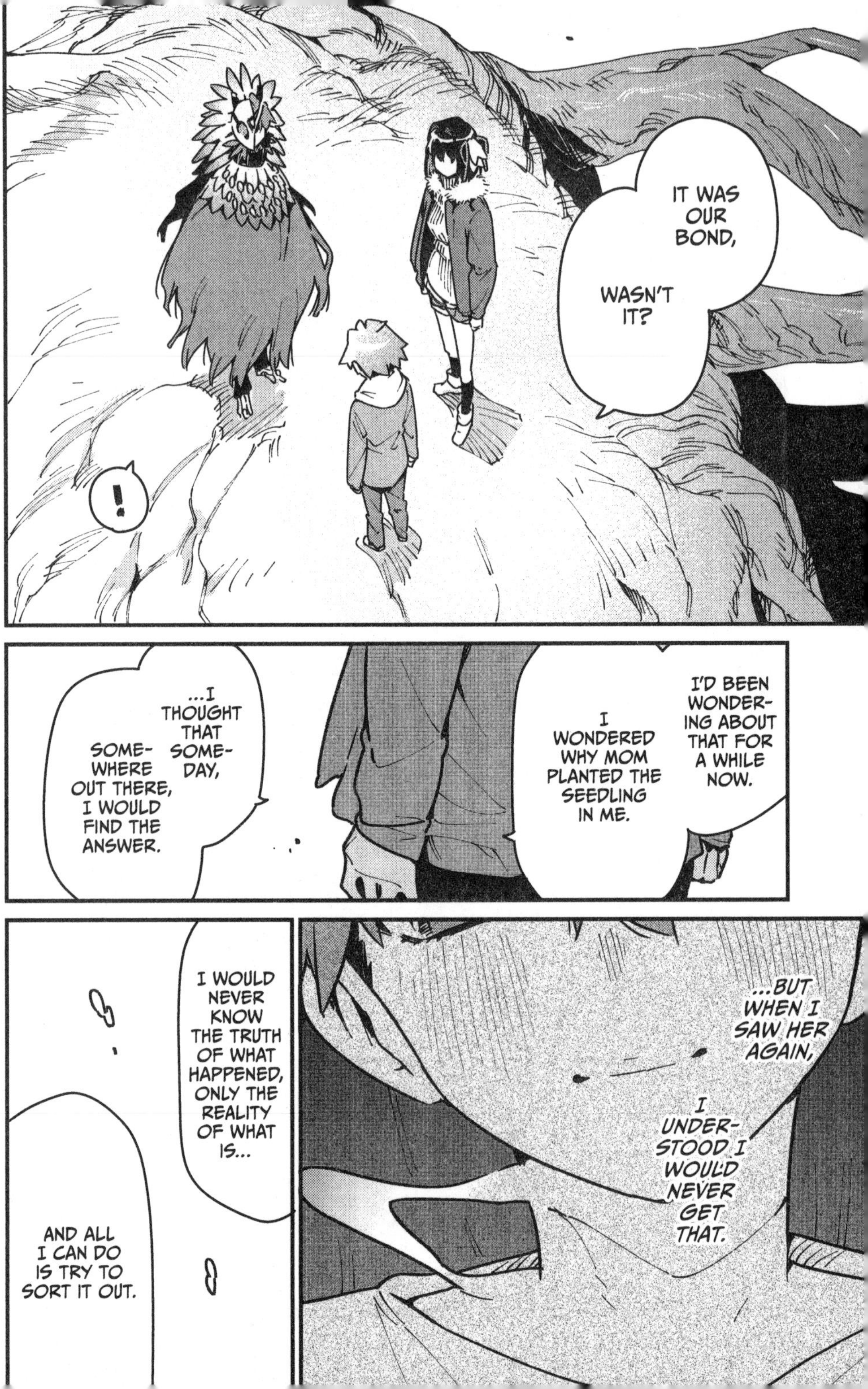
IT WAS OUR BOND,
WASN'T IT?
!
I'D BEEN WONDERING ABOUT THAT FOR A WHILE NOW.
I WONDERED WHY MOM PLANTED THE SEEDLING IN ME.
...I THOUGHT THAT SOMEDAY,
SOMEWHERE OUT THERE, I WOULD FIND THE ANSWER.
...BUT WHEN I SAW HER AGAIN,
I UNDERSTOOD I WOULD NEVER GET THAT.
I WOULD NEVER KNOW THE TRUTH OF WHAT HAPPENED, ONLY THE REALITY OF WHAT IS...
AND ALL I CAN DO IS TRY TO SORT IT OUT.

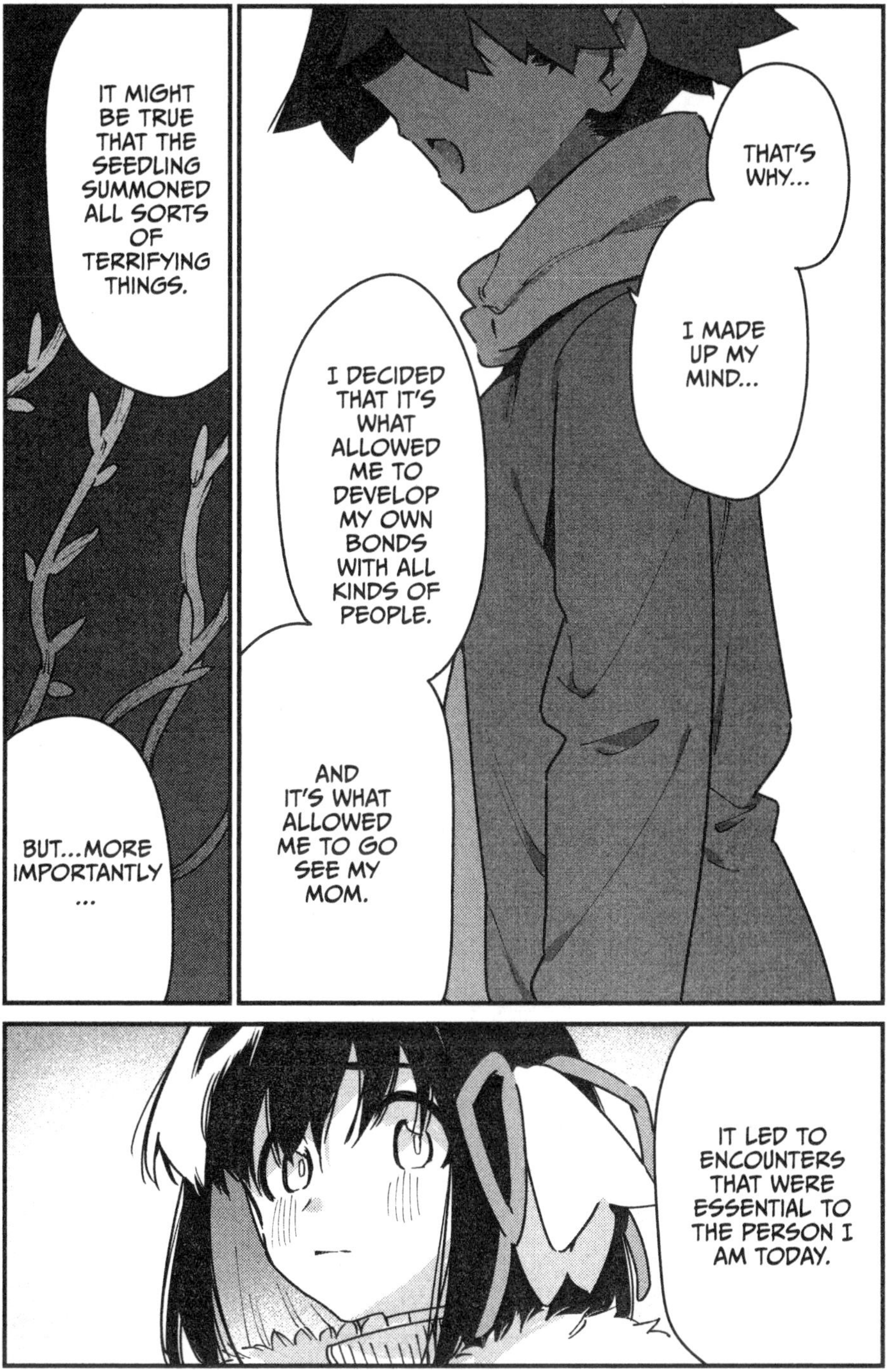
THAT'S WHY...
I MADE UP MY MIND...
I DECIDED THAT IT'S WHAT ALLOWED ME TO DEVELOP MY OWN BONDS WITH ALL KINDS OF PEOPLE.
AND IT'S WHAT ALLOWED ME TO GO SEE MY MOM.
IT MIGHT BE TRUE THAT THE SEEDLING SUMMONED ALL SORTS OF TERRIFYING THINGS.
BUT...MORE IMPORTANTLY...
IT LED TO ENCOUNTERS THAT WERE ESSENTIAL TO THE PERSON I AM TODAY.

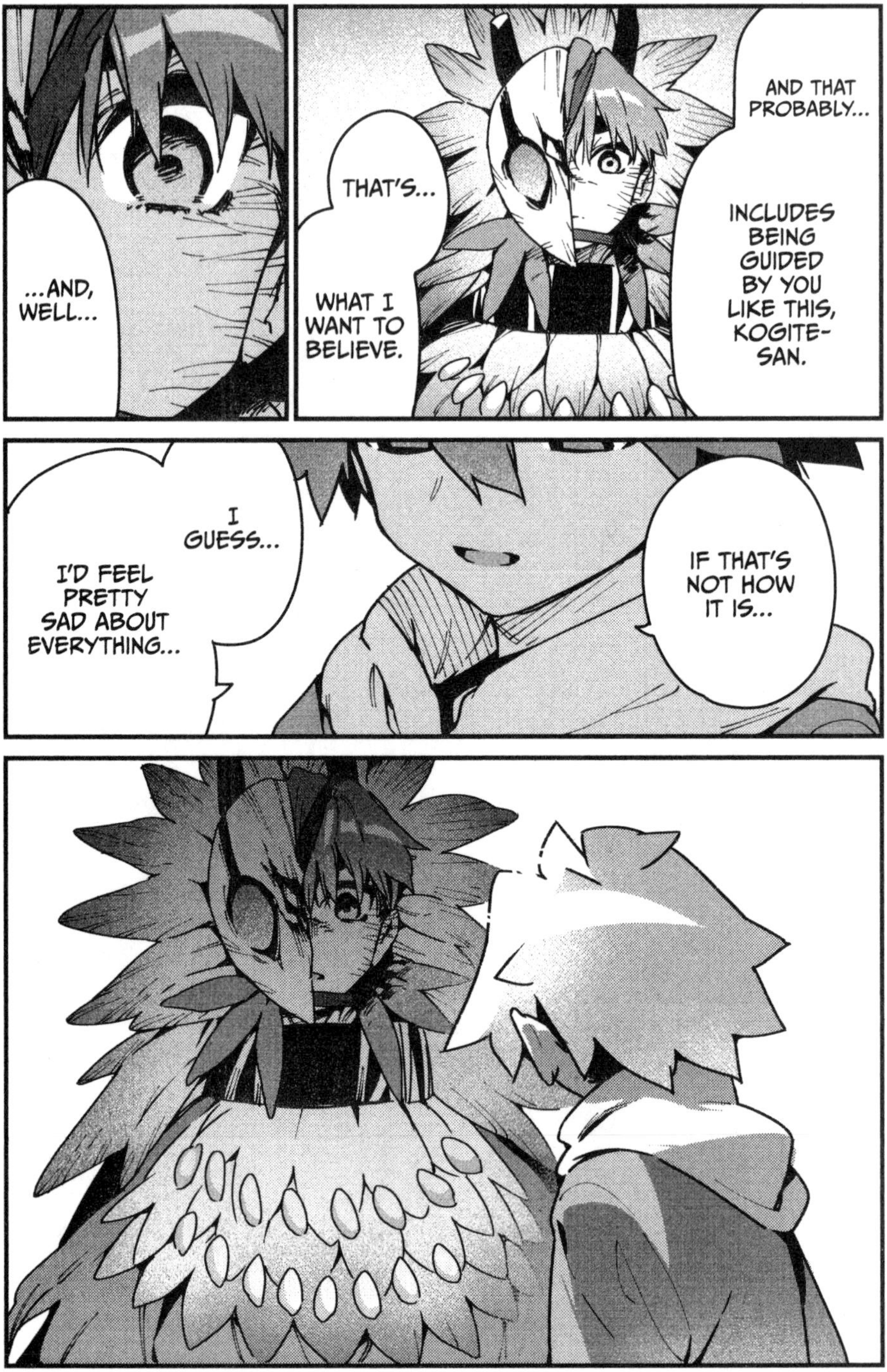
AND THAT PROBABLY...
INCLUDES BEING GUIDED BY YOU LIKE THIS, KOGITE-SAN.
THAT'S...
WHAT I WANT TO BELIEVE.
...AND, WELL...
IF THAT'S NOT HOW IT IS...
I GUESS...
I'D FEEL PRETTY SAD ABOUT EVERYTHING...

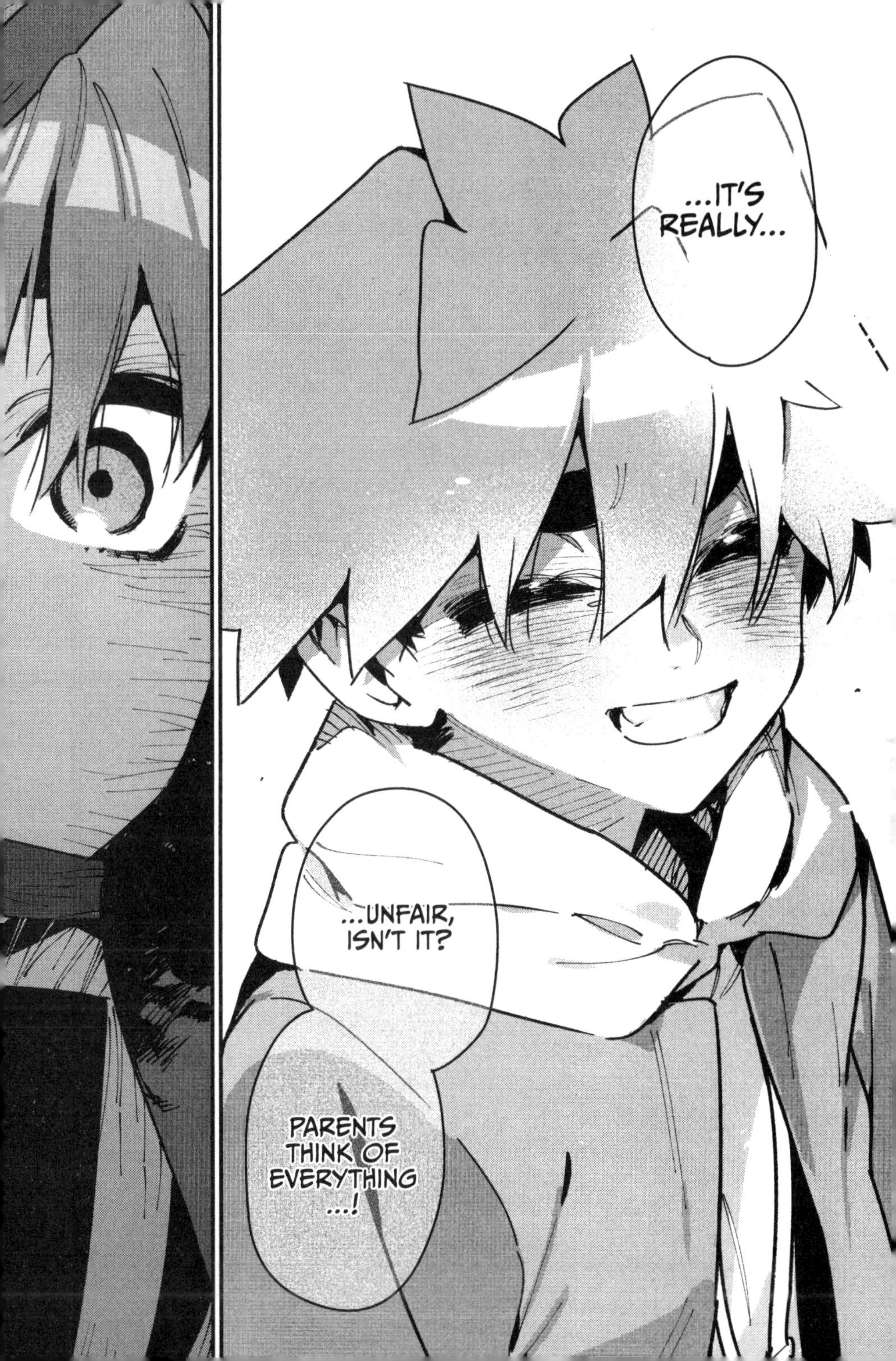
...IT'S REALLY...
...UNFAIR, ISN'T IT?
PARENTS THINK OF EVERYTHING ...!

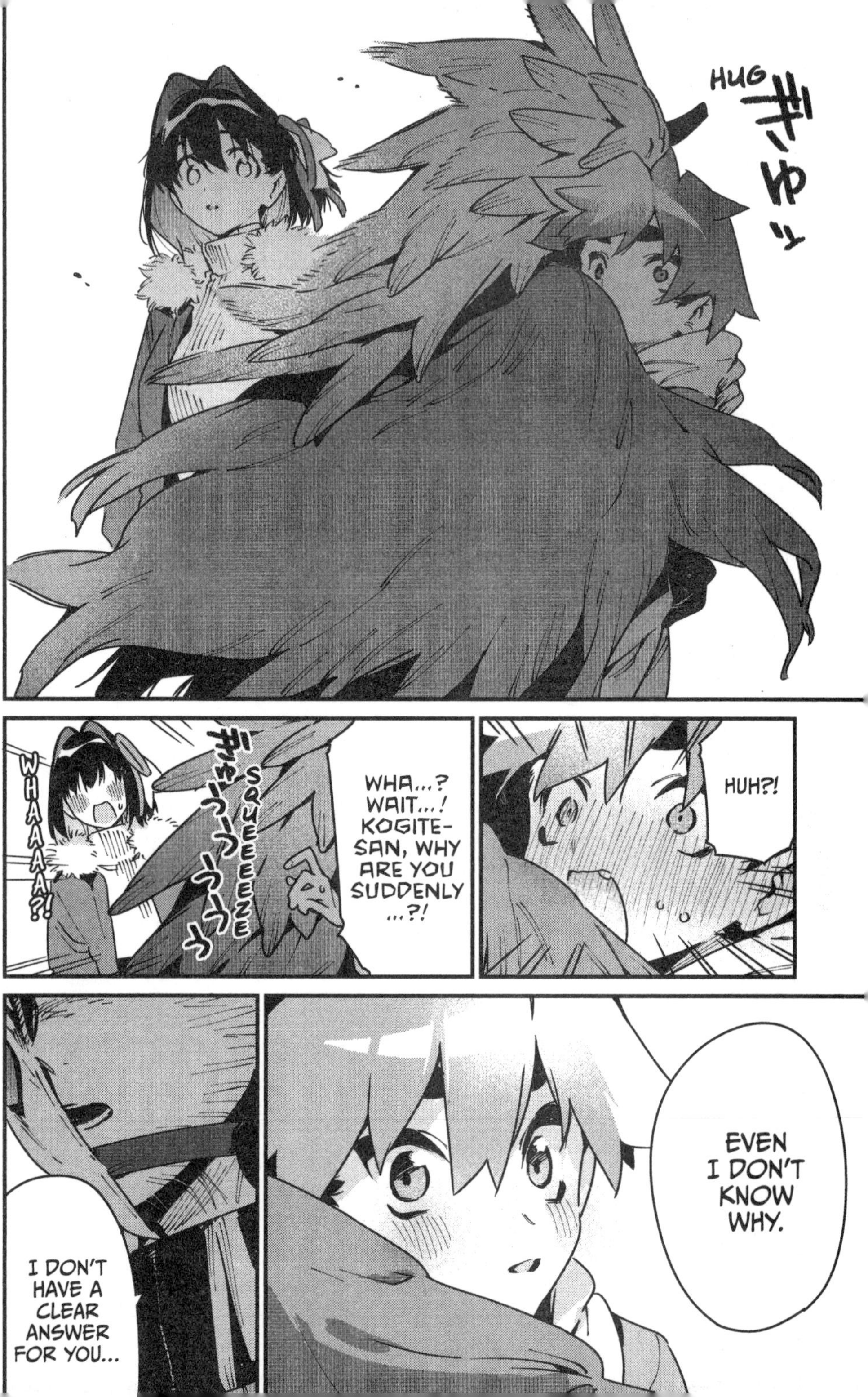
HUG
ぎゅっ
HUH?!
WHA...? WAIT...! KOGITE-SAN, WHY ARE YOU SUDDENLY ...?!
SQUEEEEZE
ぎゅうううううっ
WHAAAAA?!
EVEN I DON'T KNOW WHY.
I DON'T HAVE A CLEAR ANSWER FOR YOU...

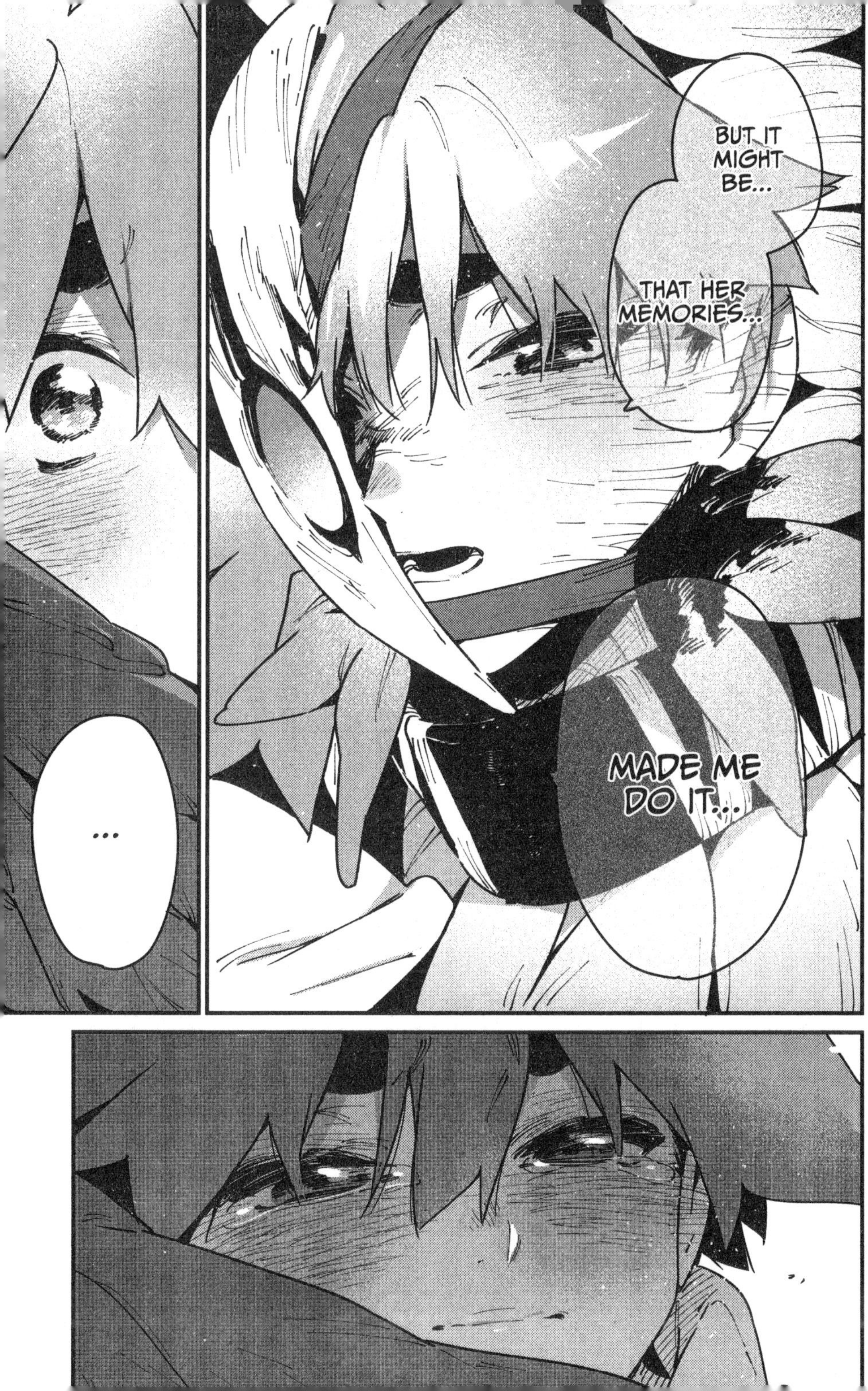
BUT IT MIGHT BE...
THAT HER MEMORIES...
MADE ME DO IT...
...

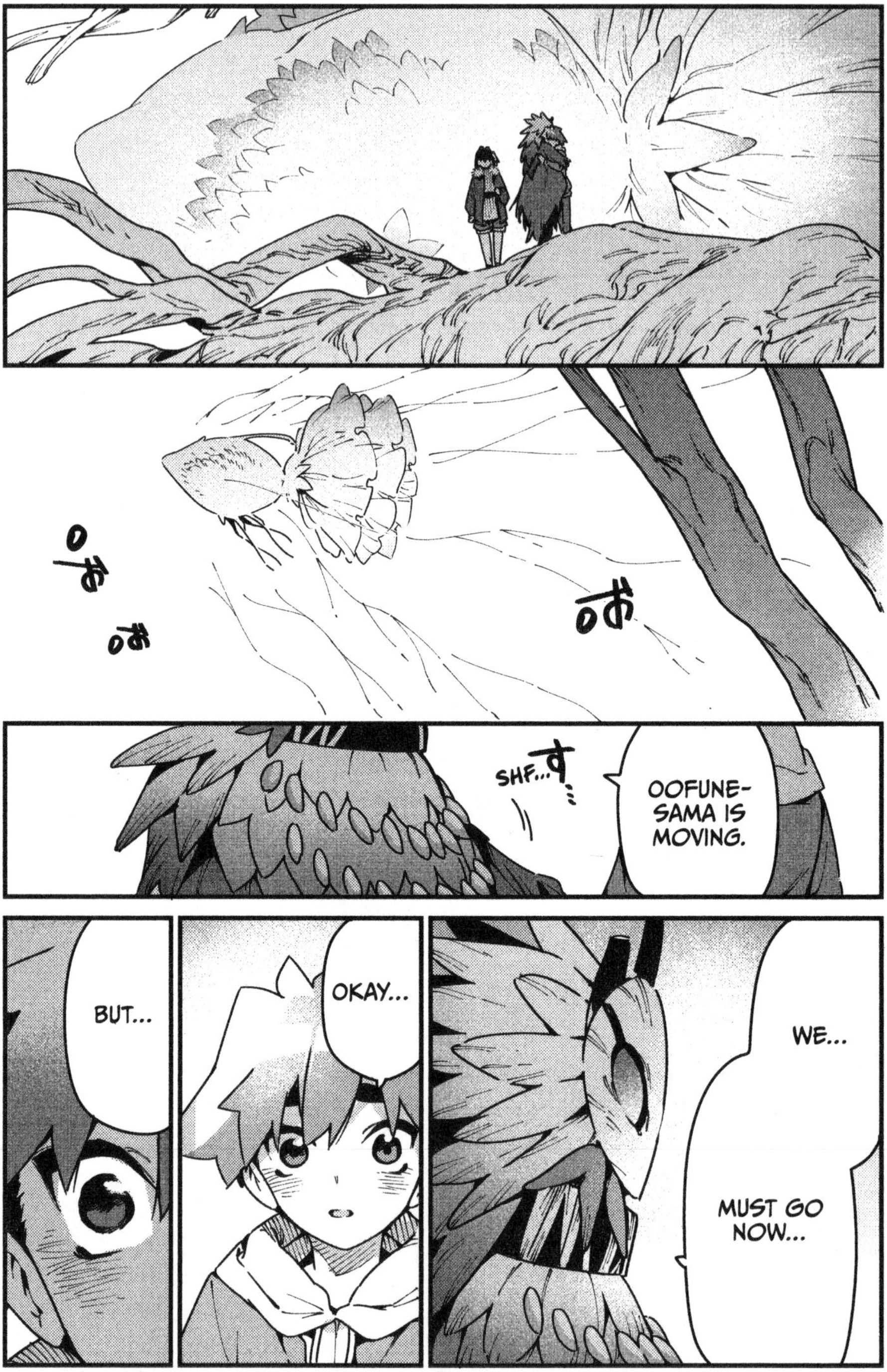

おお
おお
おお
OOFUNE-SAMA IS MOVING.
SHF...す...
WE...
MUST GO NOW...
OKAY...
BUT...

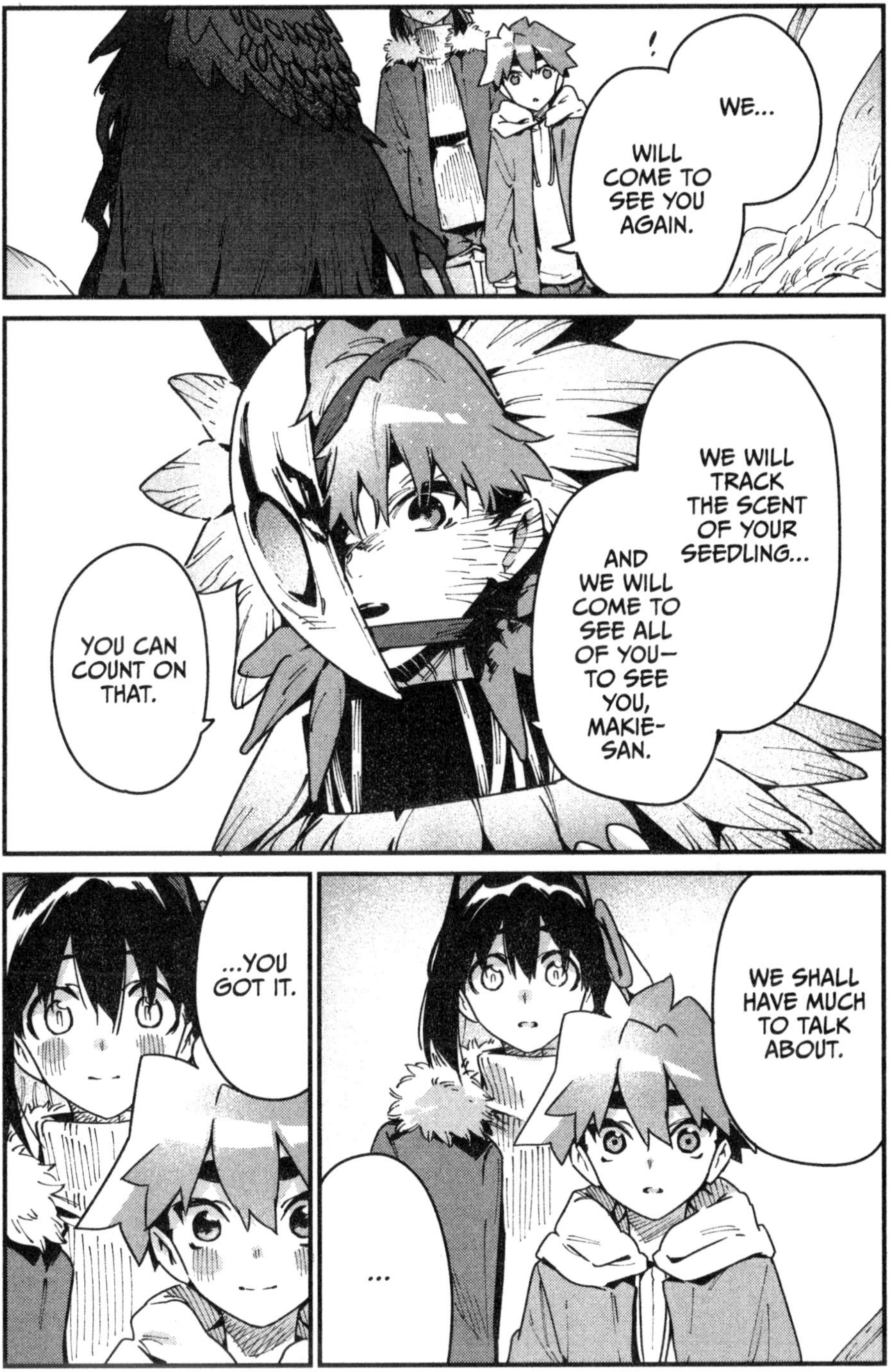
!
WE...
WILL COME TO SEE YOU AGAIN.
WE WILL TRACK THE SCENT OF YOUR SEEDLING...
AND WE WILL COME TO SEE ALL OF YOU— TO SEE YOU, MAKIE-SAN.
YOU CAN COUNT ON THAT.
WE SHALL HAVE MUCH TO TALK ABOUT.
...
...YOU GOT IT.

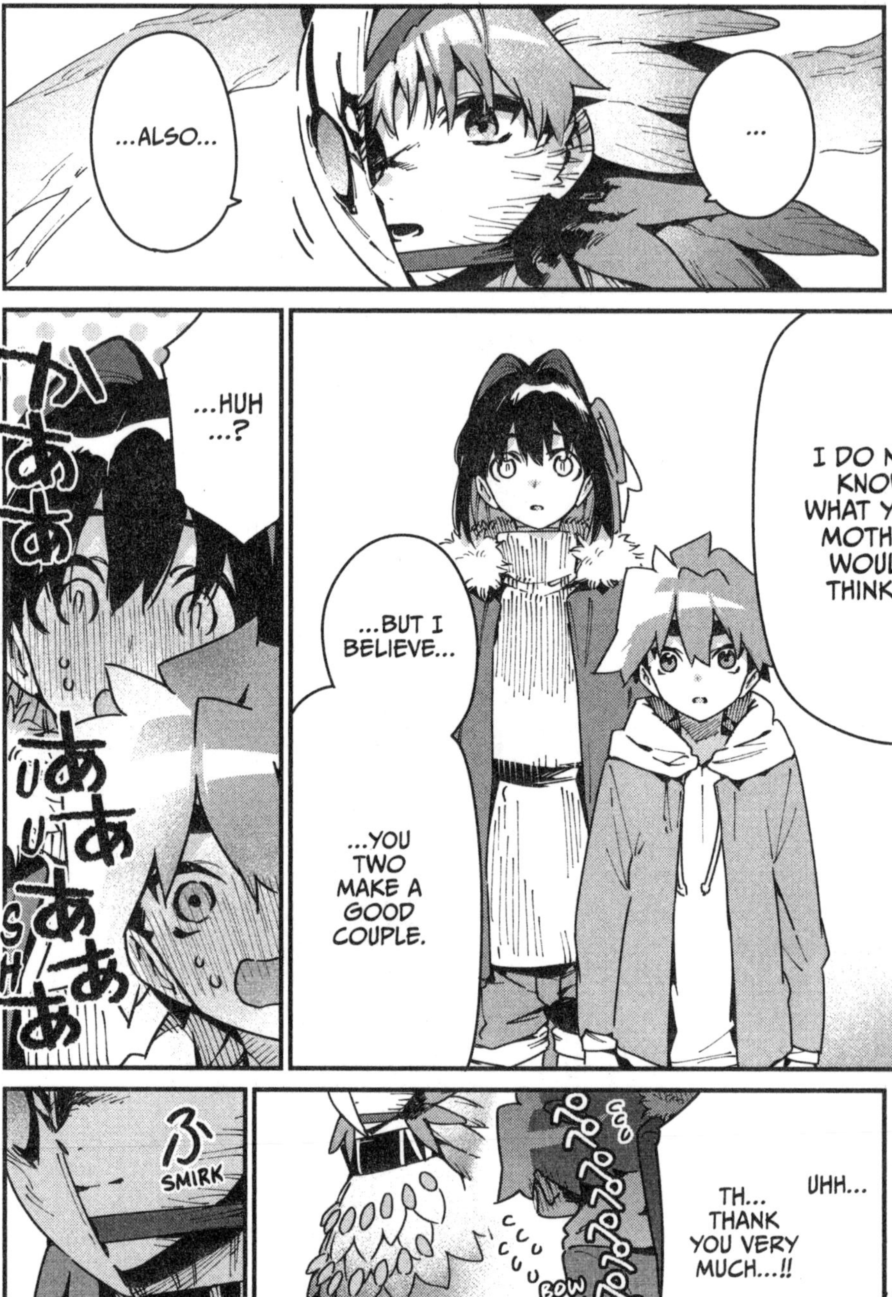
...
...ALSO...
I DO NOT KNOW WHAT YOUR MOTHER WOULD THINK...
...BUT I BELIEVE...
...YOU TWO MAKE A GOOD COUPLE.
...HUH ...?
かあああ
ああああ
BLUUUUSH
UHH...
TH... THANK YOU VERY MUCH...!!
BOW BOW BOW BOW
ふ
SMIRK

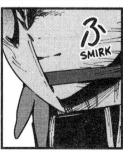

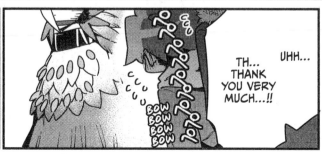

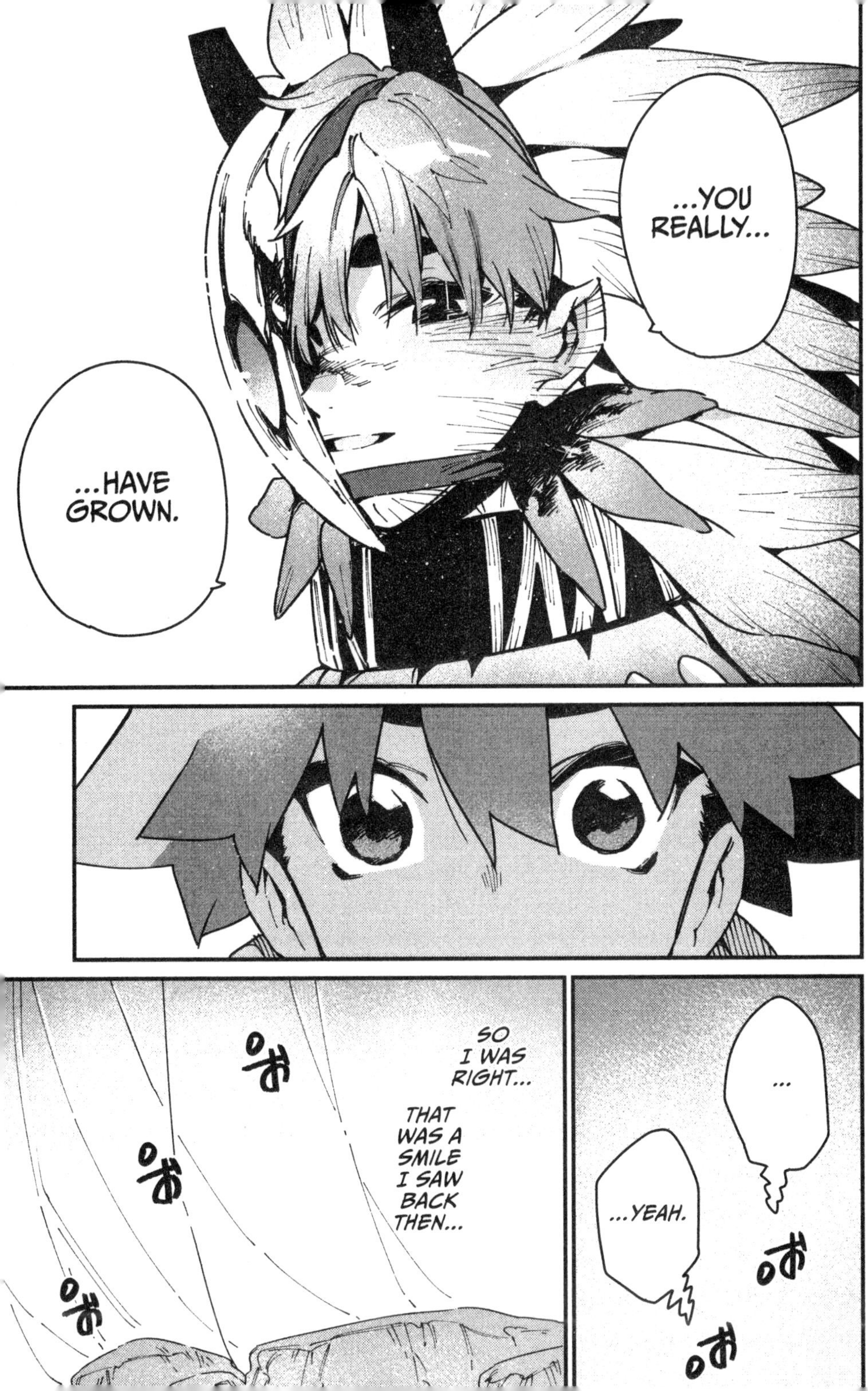
...YOU REALLY...
...HAVE GROWN.
...
...YEAH.
SO I WAS RIGHT...
THAT WAS A SMILE I SAW BACK THEN...

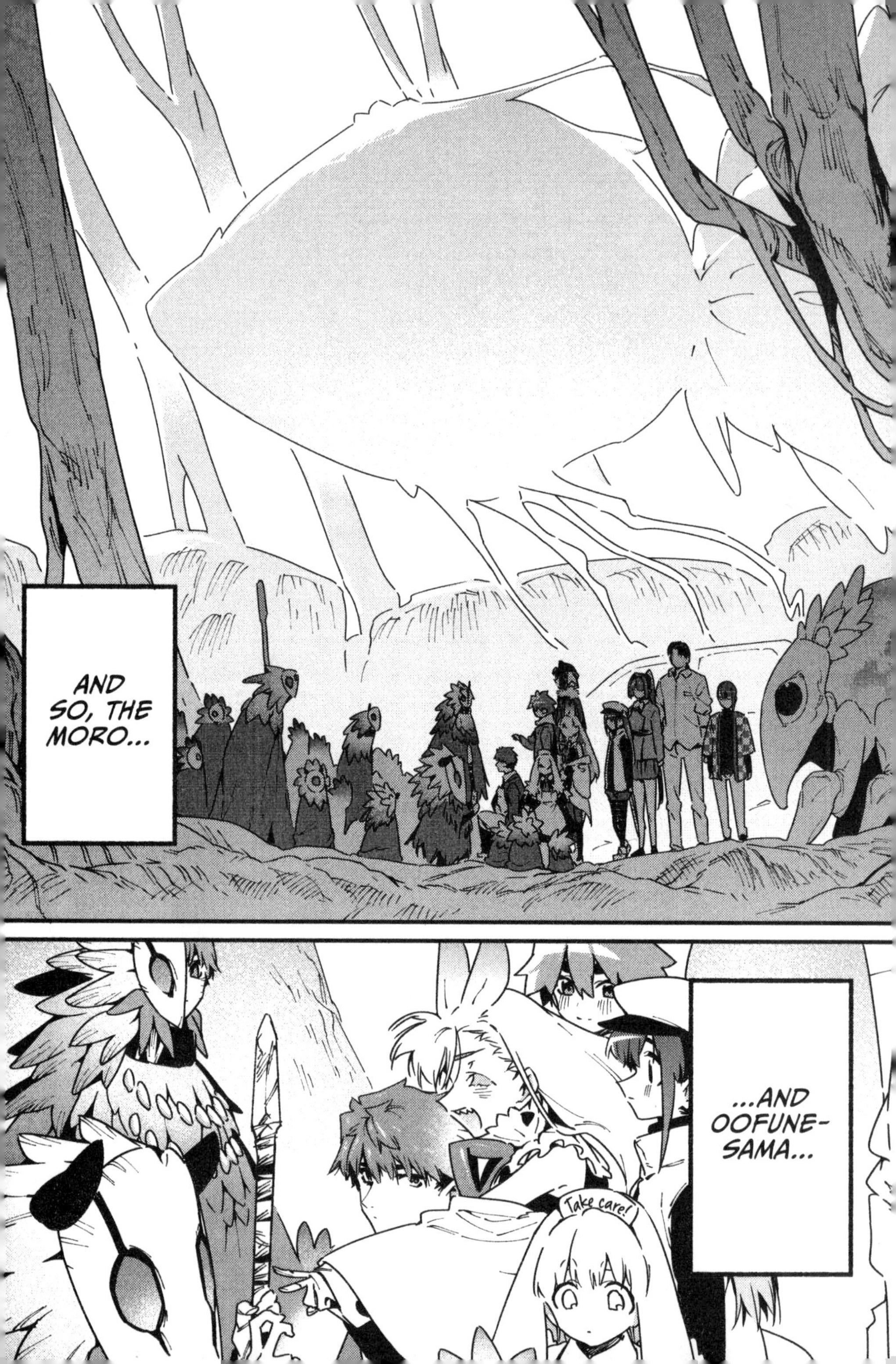
AND SO, THE MORO...
...AND OOFUNE-SAMA...
Take care!

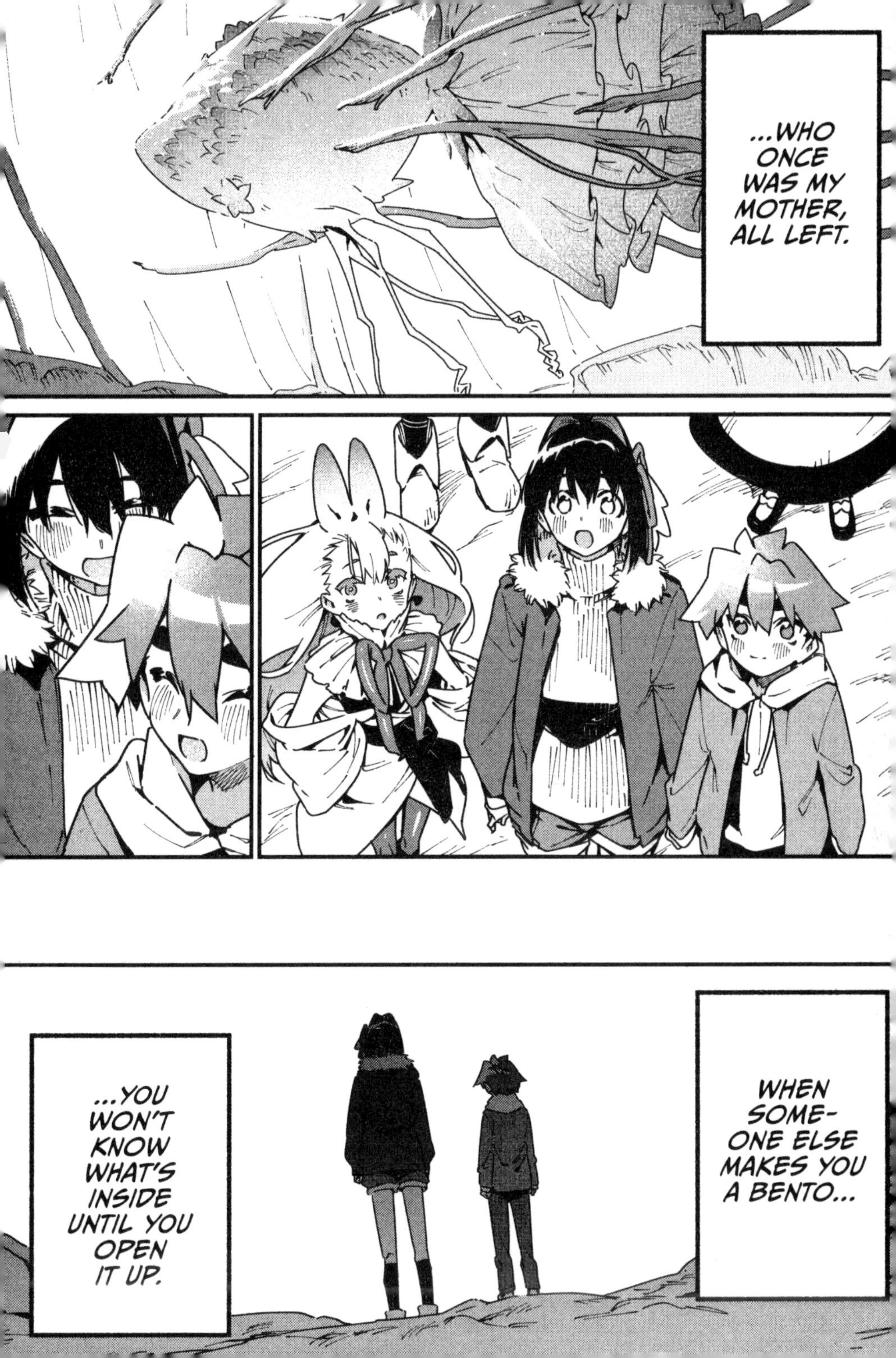
...WHO ONCE WAS MY MOTHER, ALL LEFT.
WHEN SOME-ONE ELSE MAKES YOU A BENTO...
...YOU WON'T KNOW WHAT'S INSIDE UNTIL YOU OPEN IT UP.

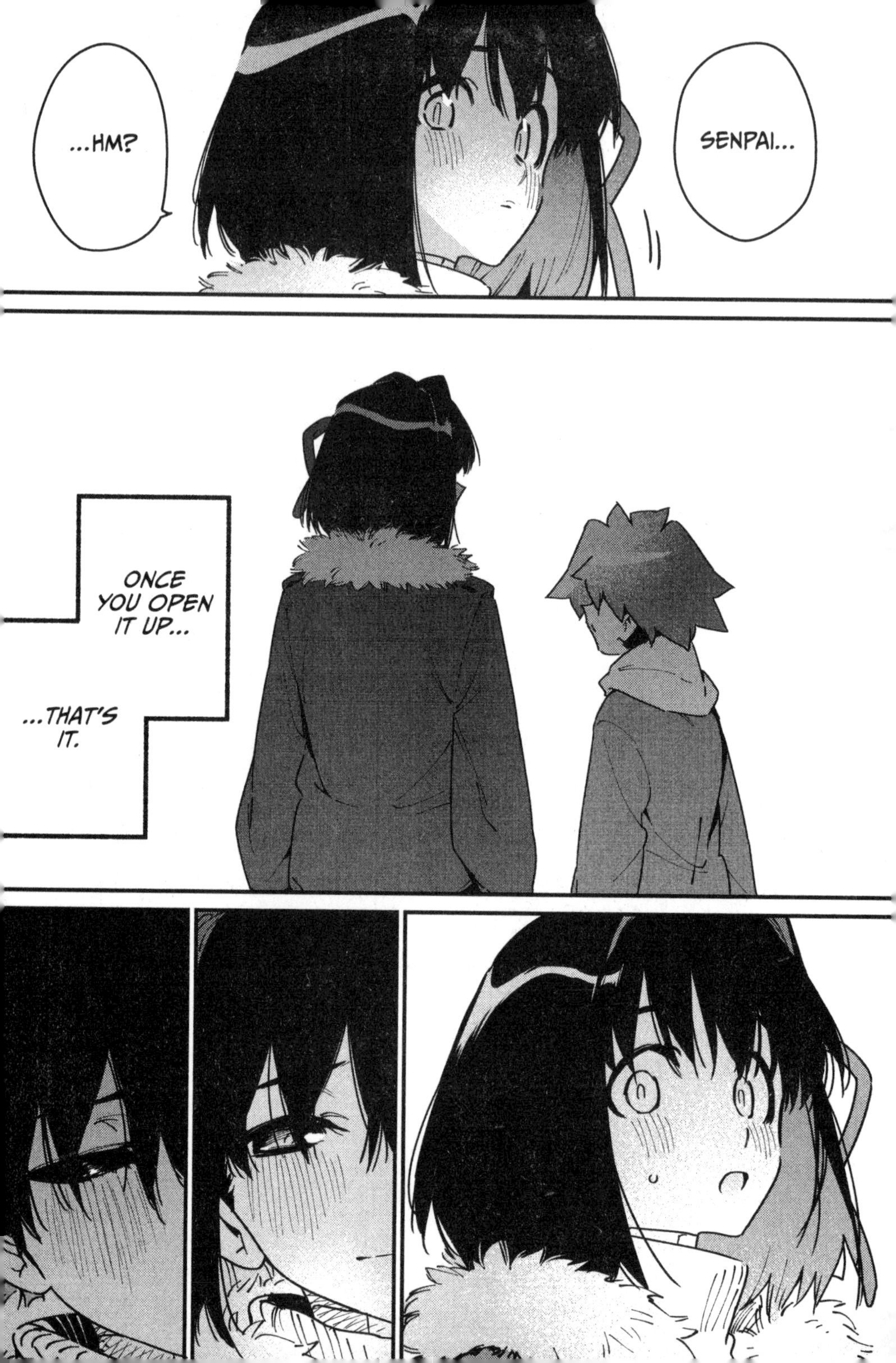
SENPAI...
...HM?
ONCE YOU OPEN IT UP...
...THAT'S IT.

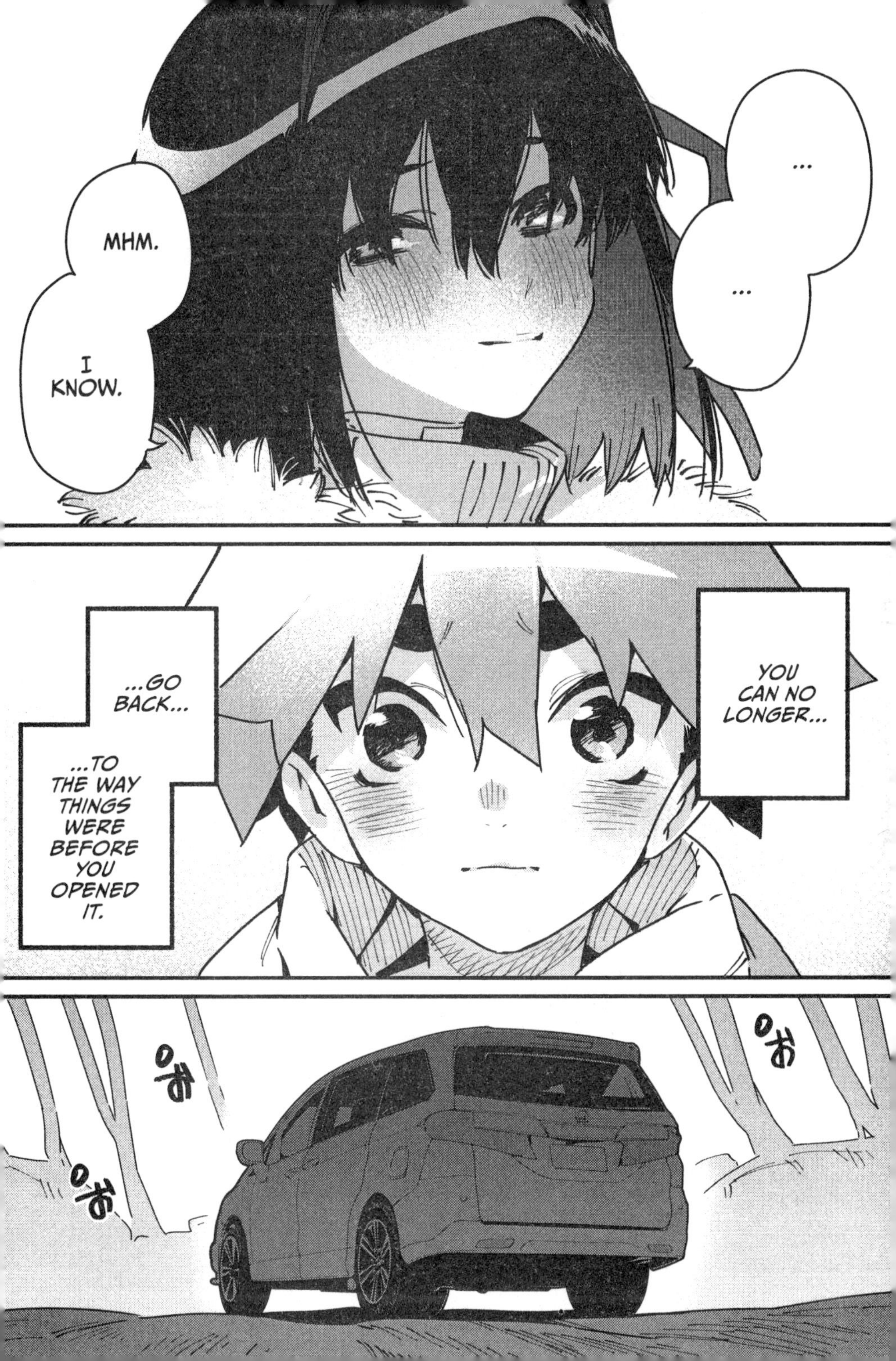
...
...
MHM.
I KNOW.
YOU CAN NO LONGER...
...GO BACK...
...TO THE WAY THINGS WERE BEFORE YOU OPENED IT.

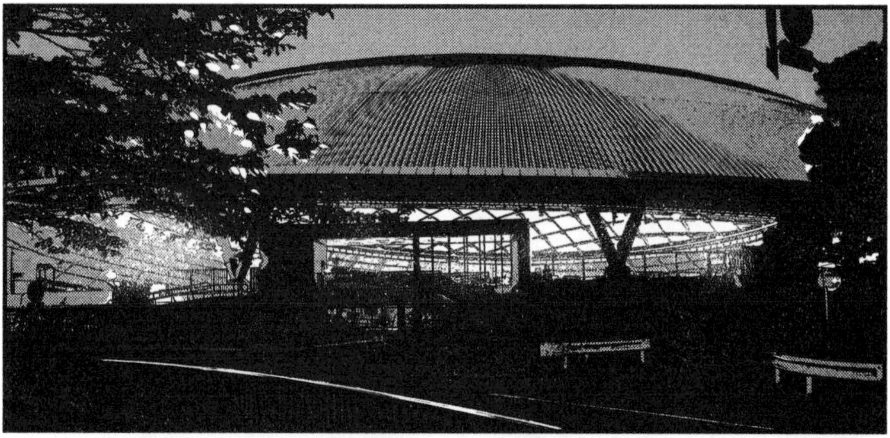
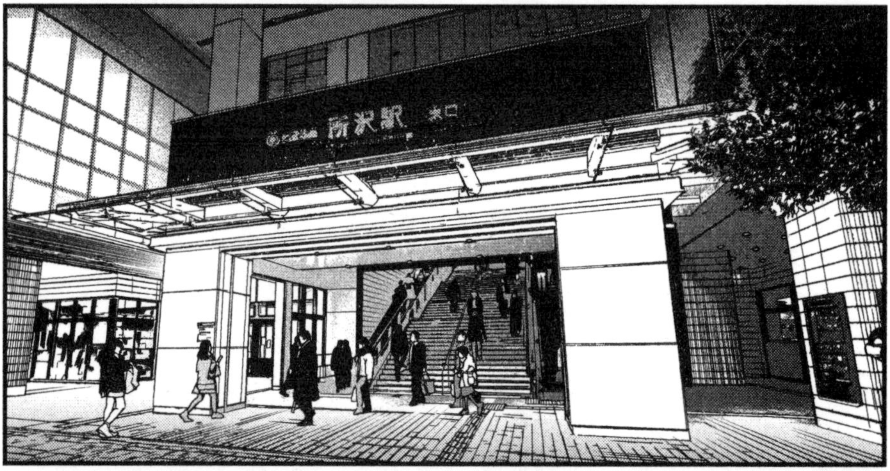
所沢駅
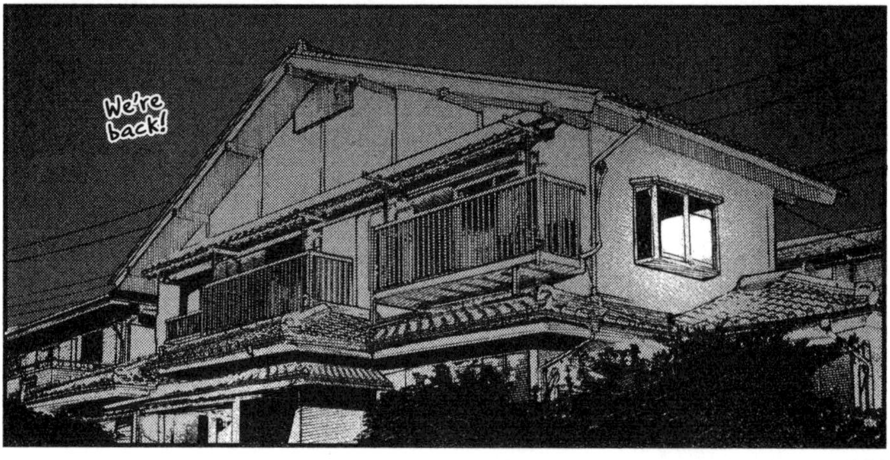
We're back!

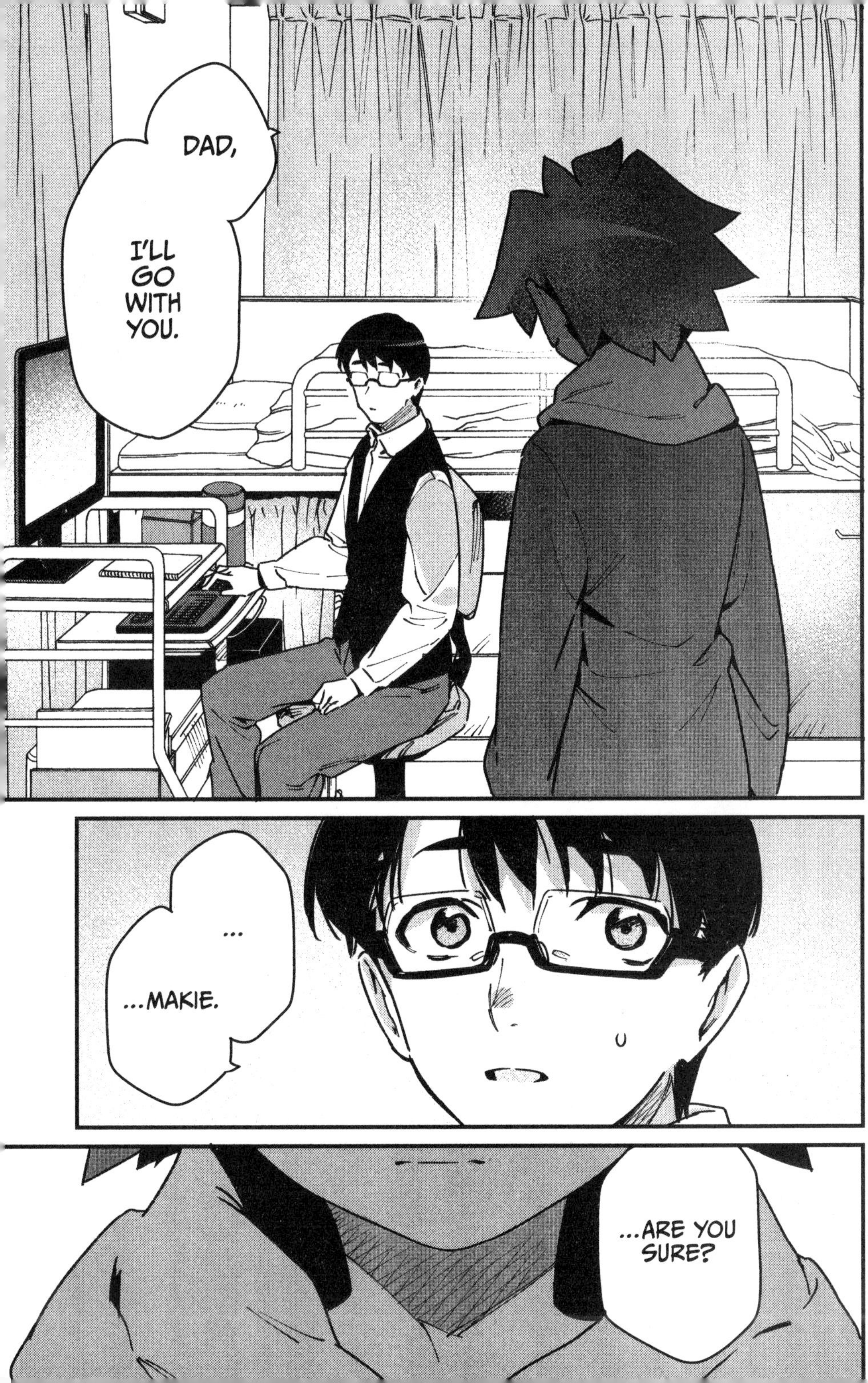
DAD,
I'LL GO WITH YOU.
...
...MAKIE.
...ARE YOU SURE?

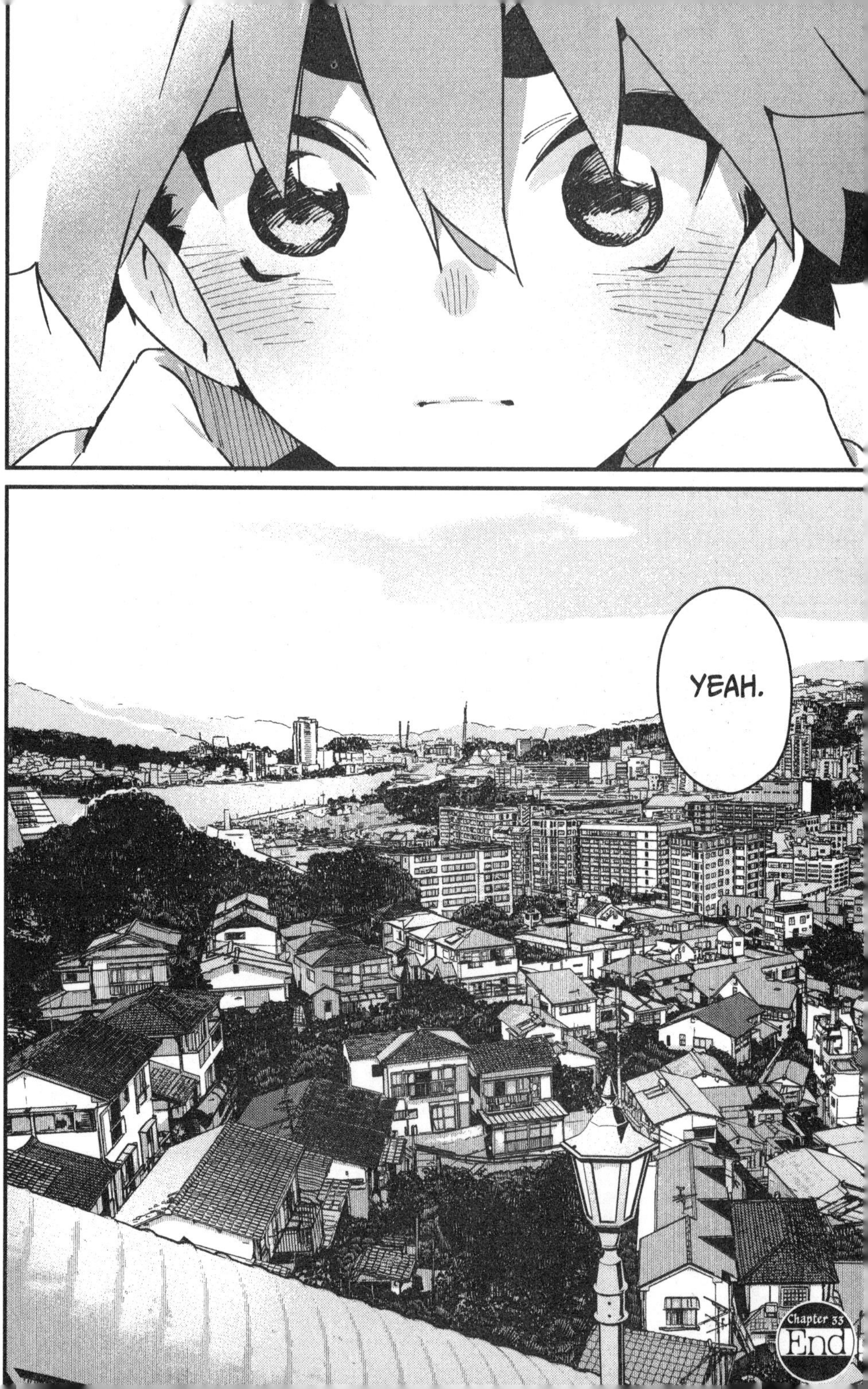
YEAH.
Chapter 33
End

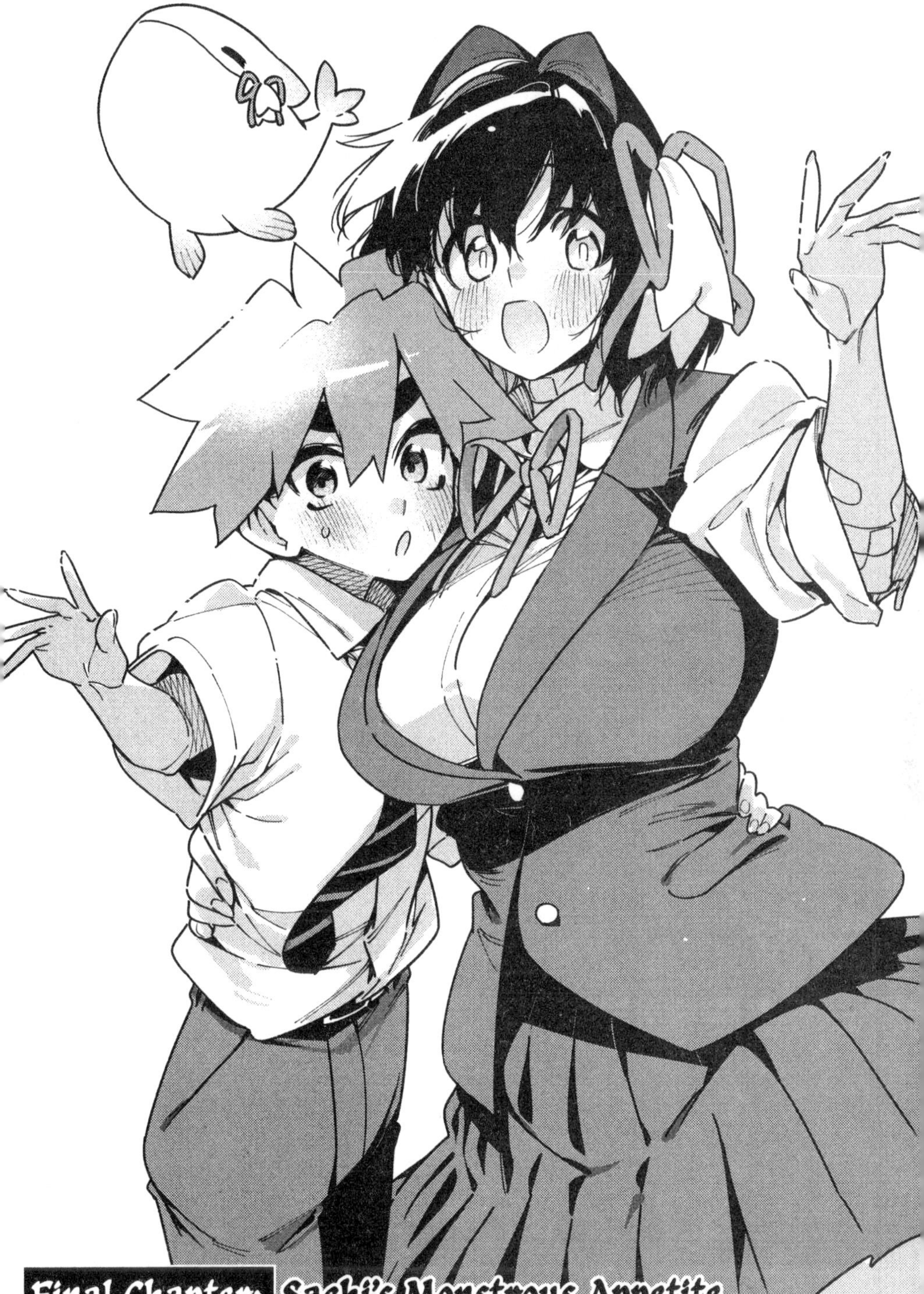

Final Chapter: Sachi's Monstrous Appetite

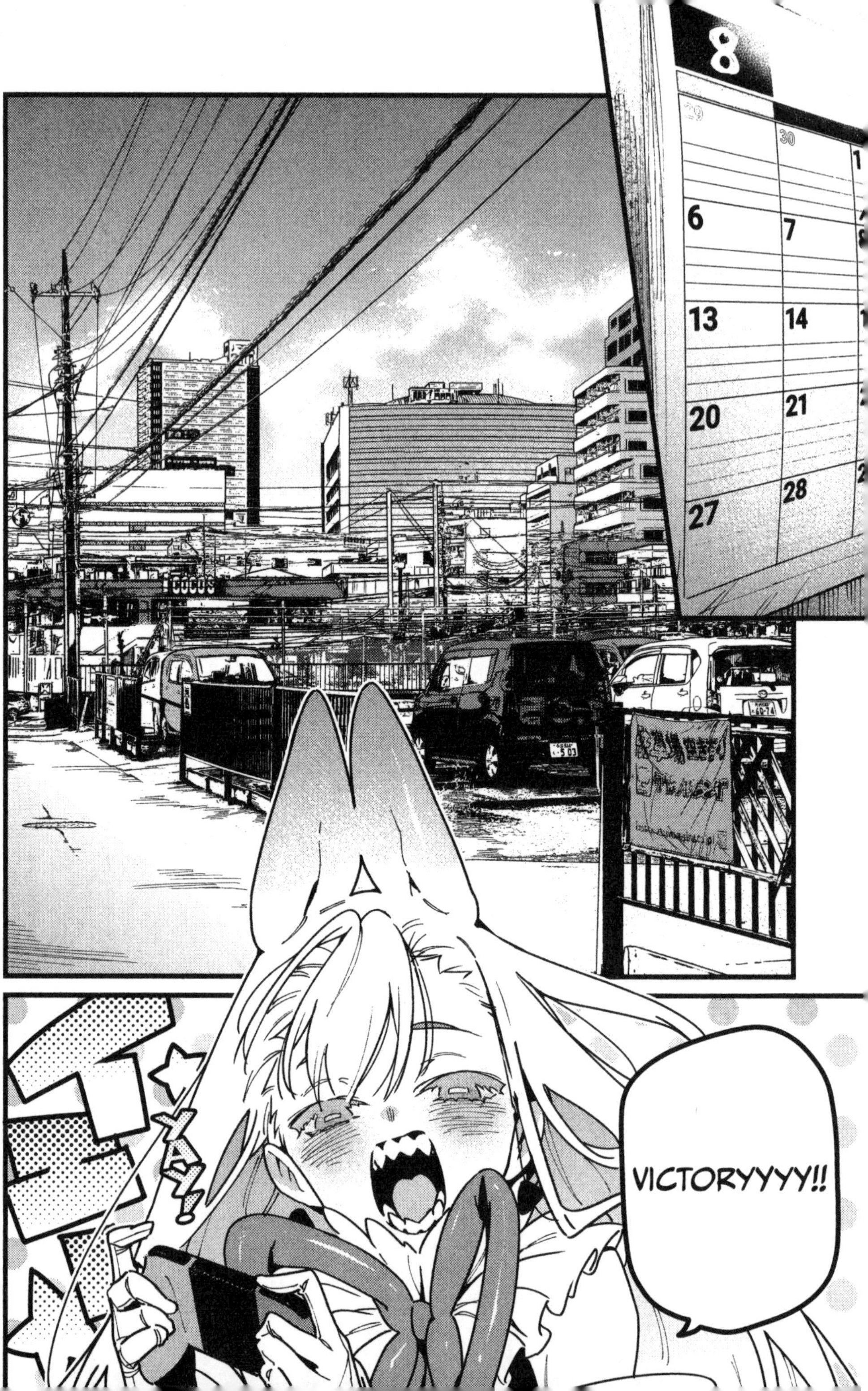
8
VICTORYYYY!!

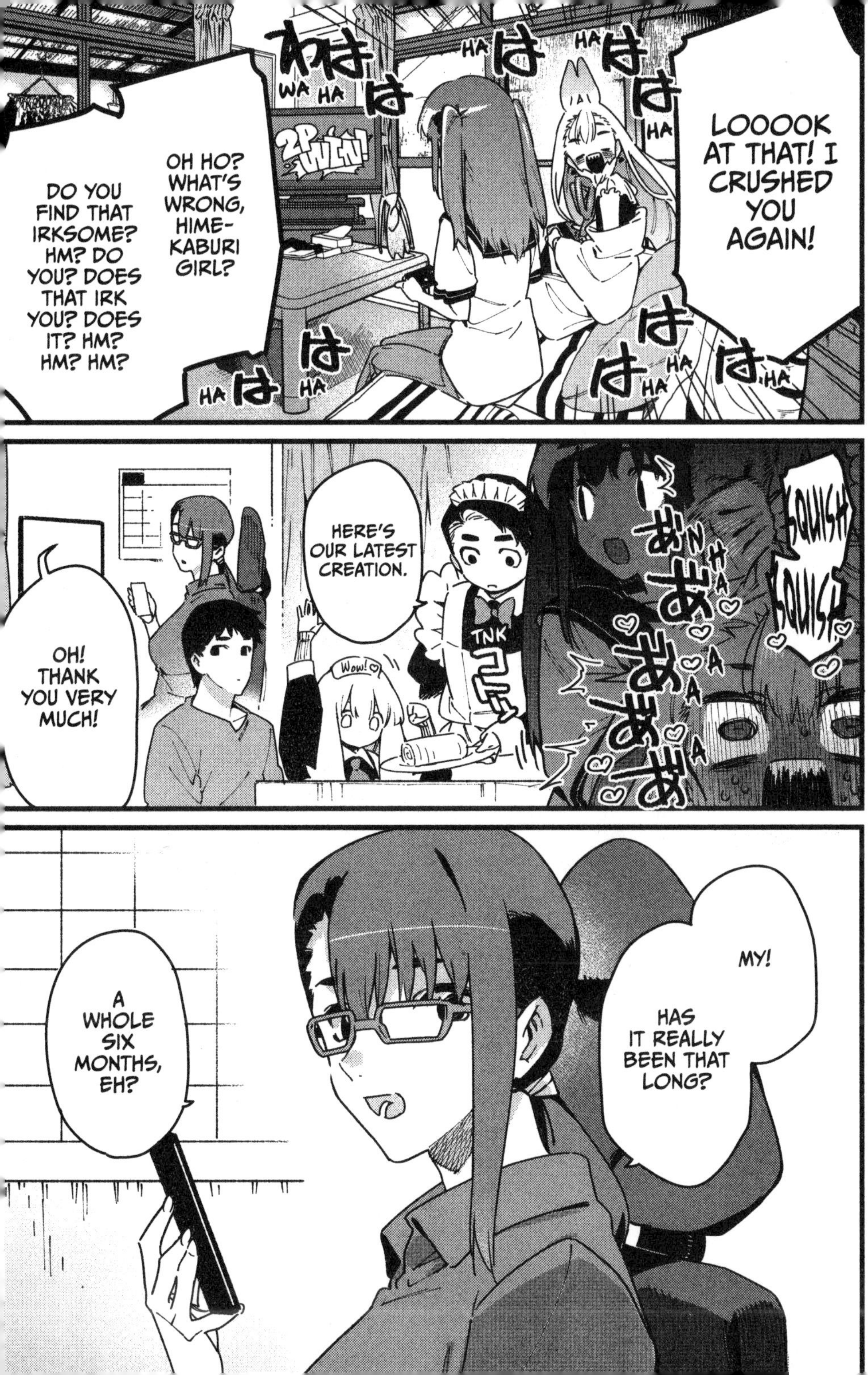
LOOOOK AT THAT! I CRUSHED YOU AGAIN!
わははははは
WA HA HA HA HA
2P WIN!
OH HO? WHAT'S WRONG, HIME-KABURI GIRL?
DO YOU FIND THAT IRKSOME? HM? DO YOU? DOES THAT IRK YOU? DOES IT? HM? HM? HM? HM?
ははははは
HA HA HA HA HA
SQUISH SQUISH
あんあああああ
N HA A A A A
HERE'S OUR LATEST CREATION.
TNK
Wow!
OH! THANK YOU VERY MUCH!
MY!
HAS IT REALLY BEEN THAT LONG?
A WHOLE SIX MONTHS, EH?

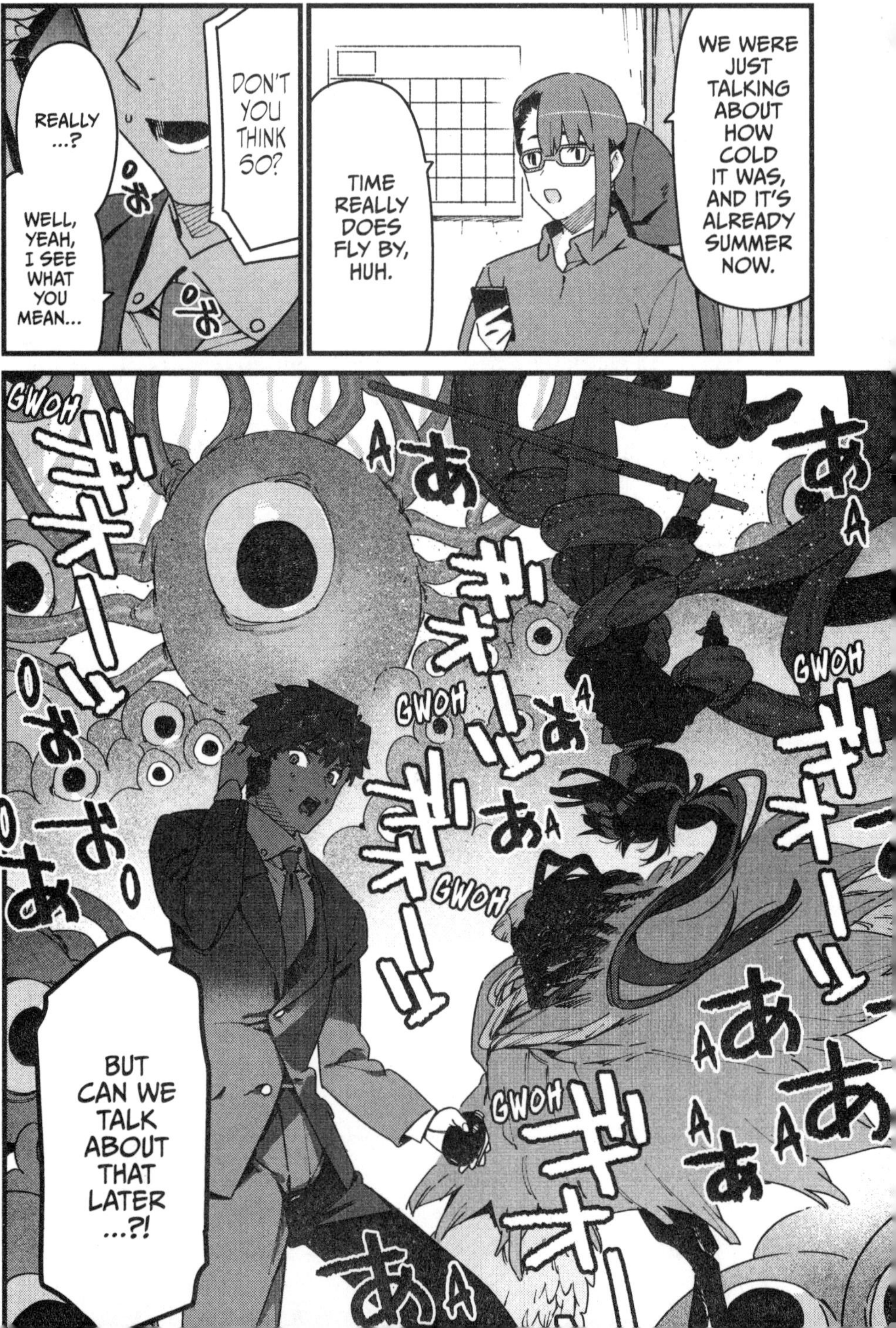
WE WERE JUST TALKING ABOUT HOW COLD IT WAS, AND IT'S ALREADY SUMMER NOW.
TIME REALLY DOES FLY BY, HUH.
DON'T YOU THINK SO?
REALLY ...?
WELL, YEAH, I SEE WHAT YOU MEAN...
GWOH
ギオーッ
A
あ
BUT CAN WE TALK ABOUT THAT LATER ...?!

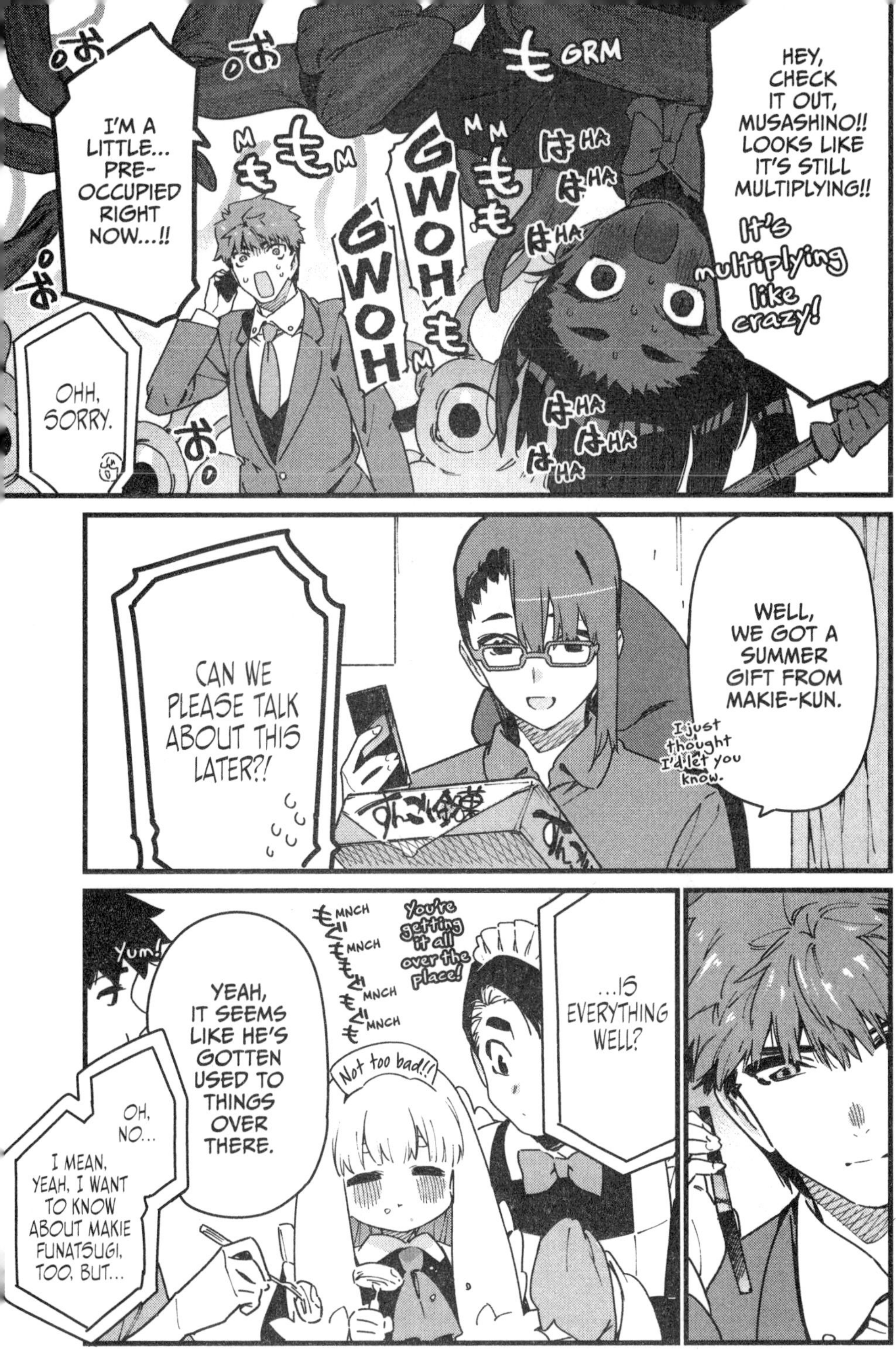
HEY, CHECK IT OUT, MUSASHINO!! LOOKS LIKE IT'S STILL MULTIPLYING!!
It's multiplying like crazy!
はHA はHA はHA
もGRM
MM もも
GWOH GWOH
M もも M
I'M A LITTLE... PRE-OCCUPIED RIGHT NOW...!!
はHA はHA はHA
OHH, SORRY.
WELL, WE GOT A SUMMER GIFT FROM MAKIE-KUN.
I just thought I'd let you know.
CAN WE PLEASE TALK ABOUT THIS LATER?!
...IS EVERYTHING WELL?
You're getting it all over the place!
MNCH MNCH MNCH MNCH
YEAH, IT SEEMS LIKE HE'S GOTTEN USED TO THINGS OVER THERE.
Not too bad!!
Yum!
OH, NO...
I MEAN, YEAH, I WANT TO KNOW ABOUT MAKIE FUNATSUGI, TOO, BUT...

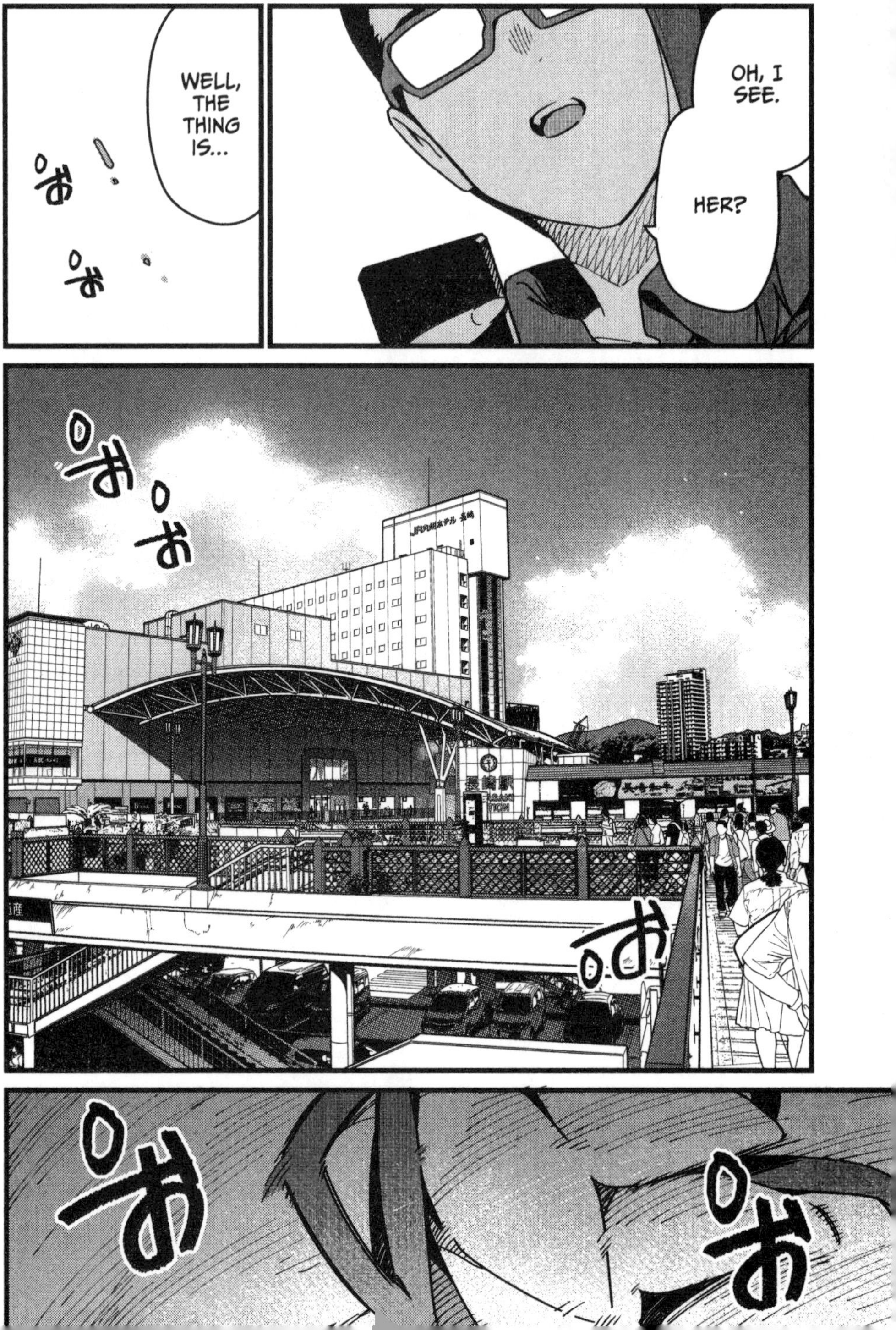
OH, I SEE.
HER?
WELL, THE THING IS...
ぉお
ぉお
ぉお
ぉお
長崎駅
ぉお
ぉお
ぉお

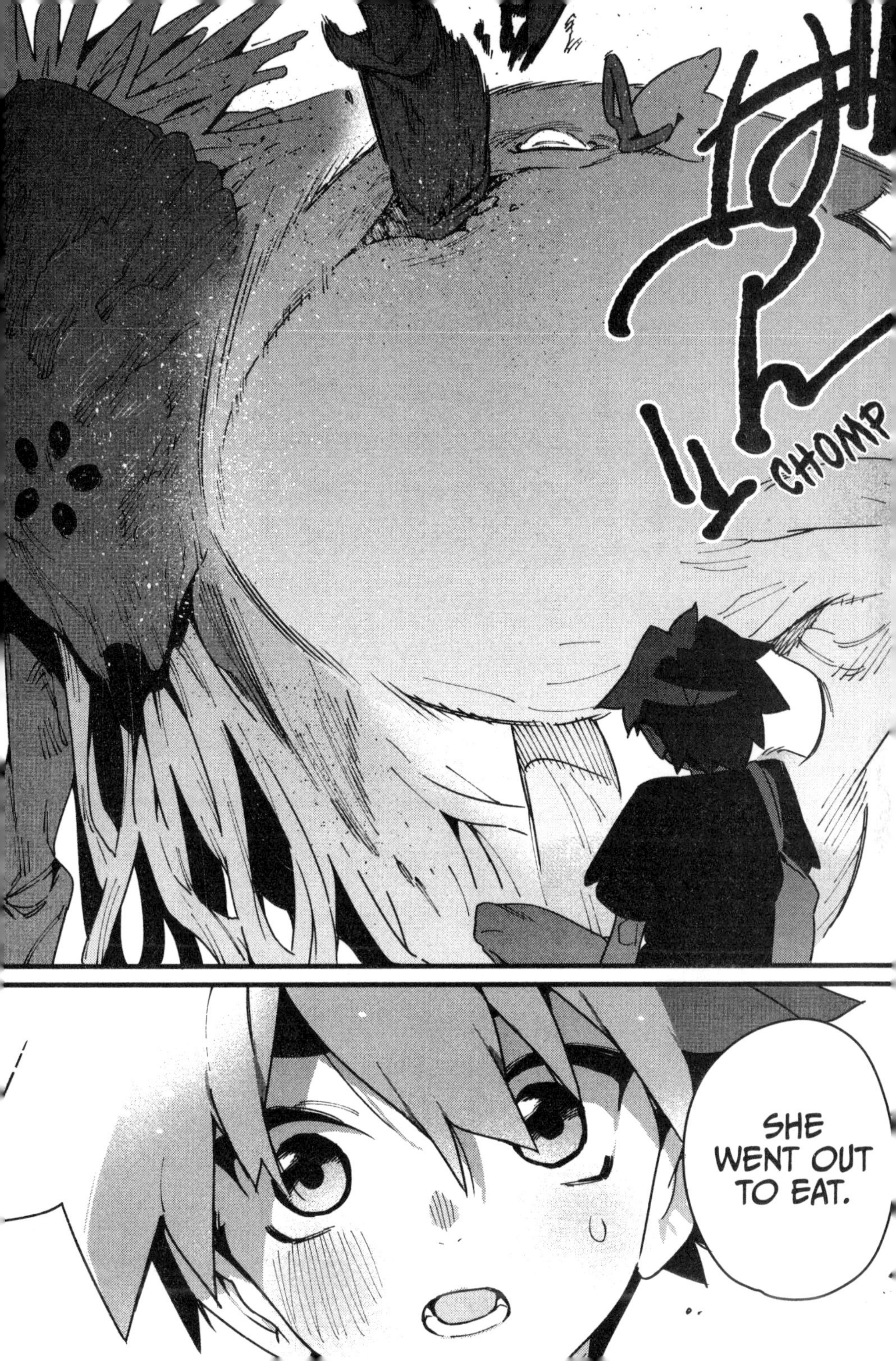
CHOMP
SHE WENT OUT TO EAT.

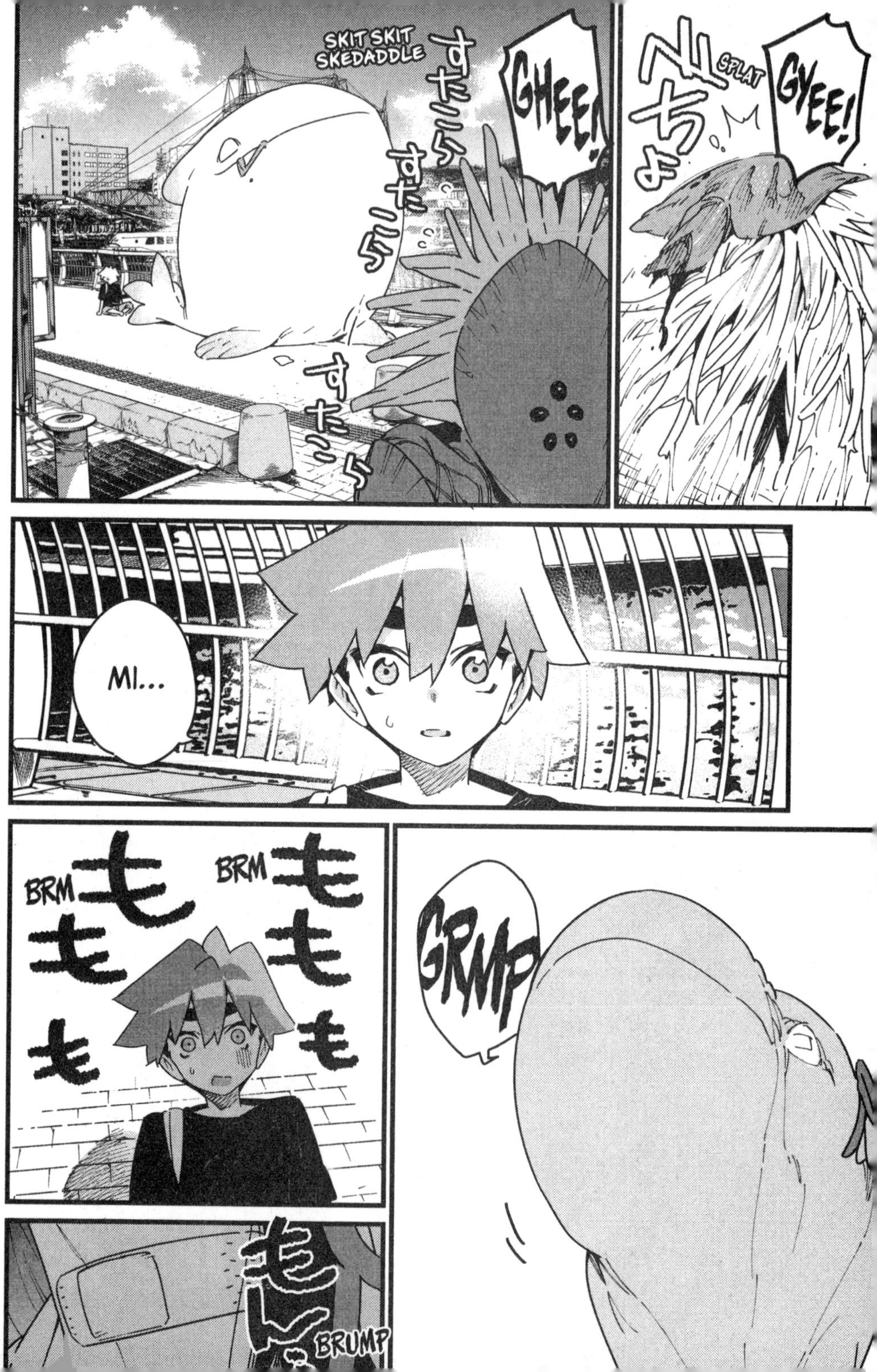
へちょ
SPLAT
GYEE!
GHEE!
すたこら すたこら すたこら
SKIT SKIT SKEDADDLE
MI...
GRMP
BRM BRM
BRUMP

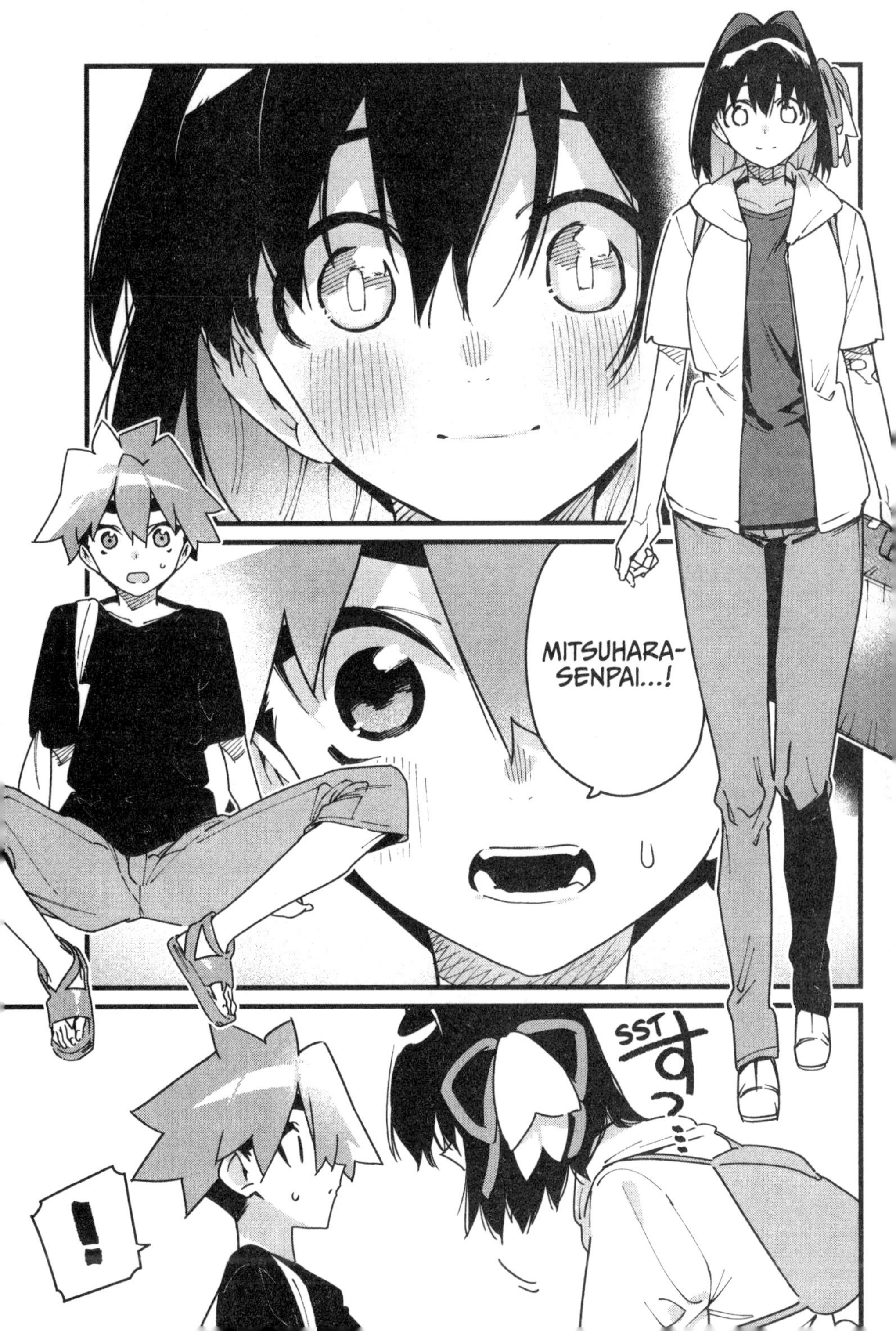
MITSUHARA-SENPAI...!
SST
すっ…
!

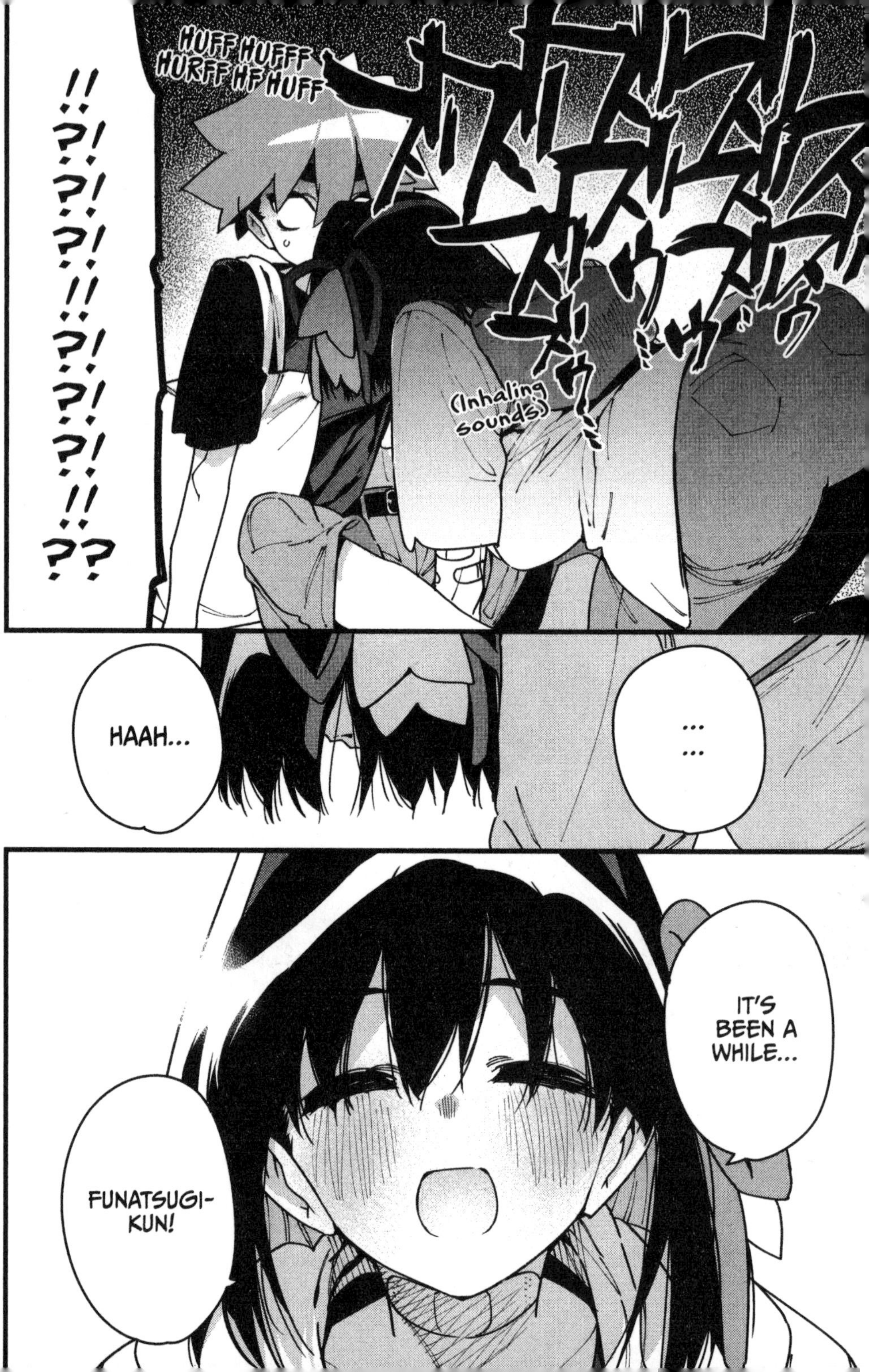
HUFF HUFFF
HURFF HF HUFF
(Inhaling sounds)
... ...
HAAH...
IT'S BEEN A WHILE...
FUNATSUGI-KUN!

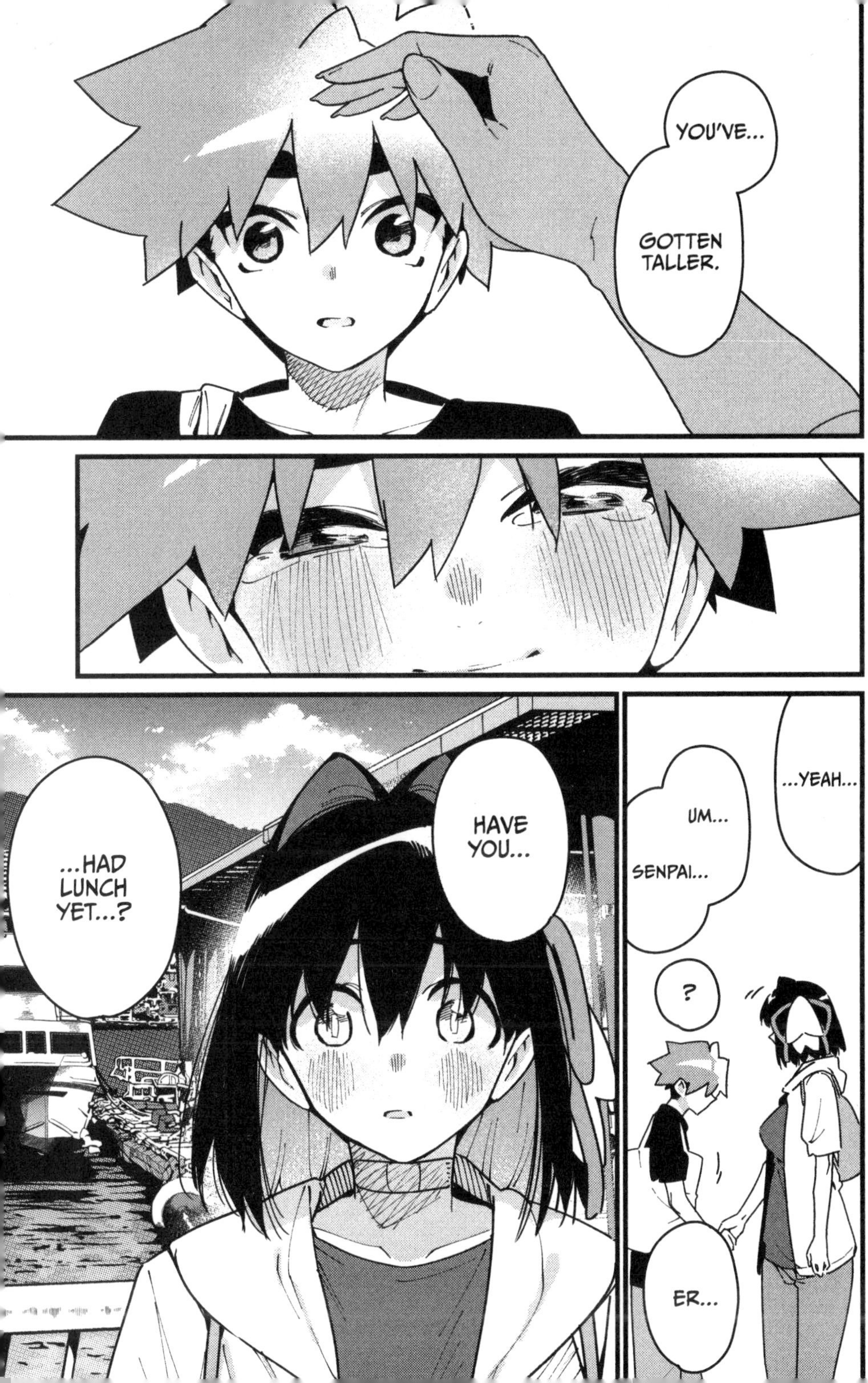
YOU'VE...
GOTTEN TALLER.
...YEAH...
UM... SENPAI...
?
ER...
HAVE YOU...
...HAD LUNCH YET...?

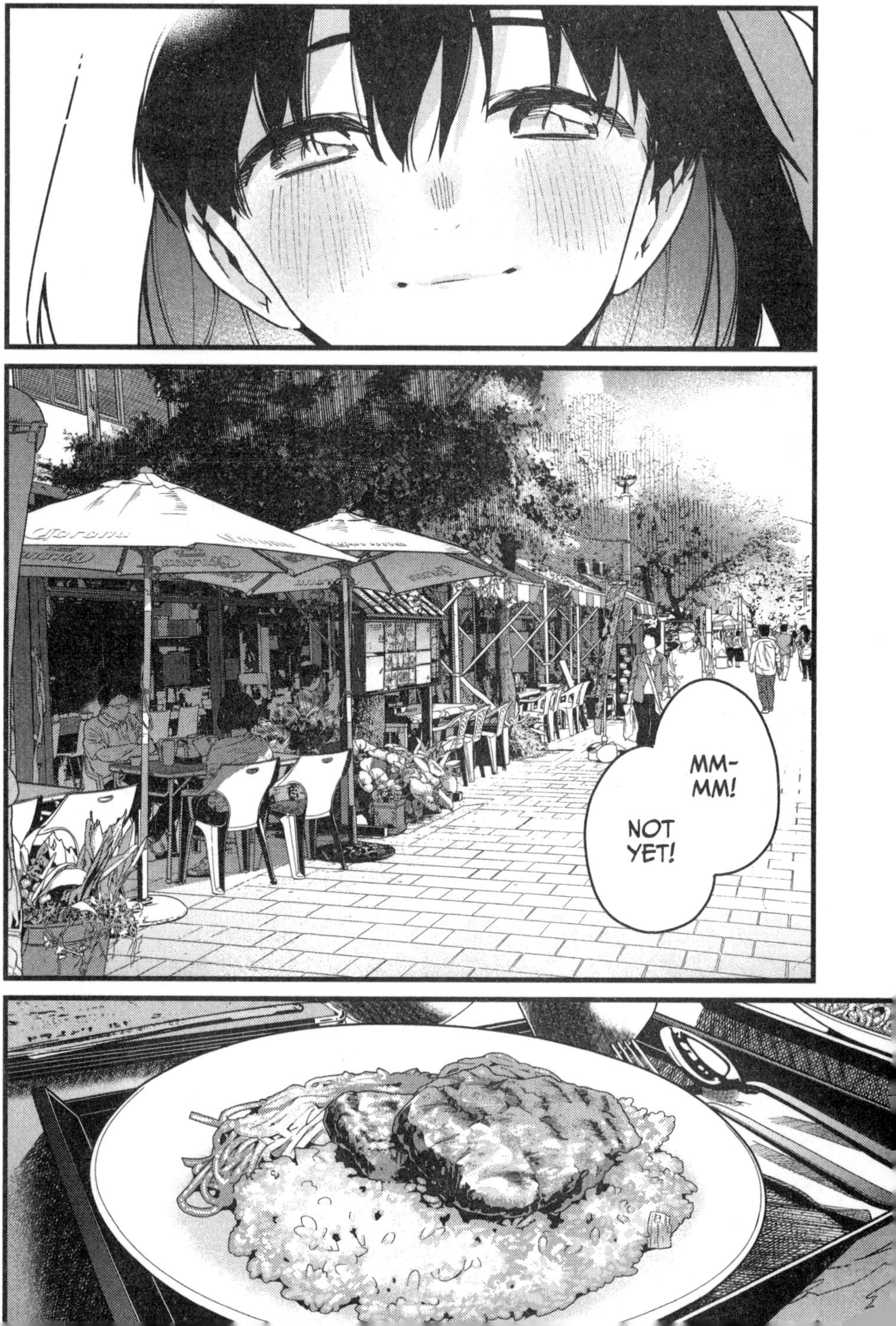
MM-
MM!
NOT
YET!

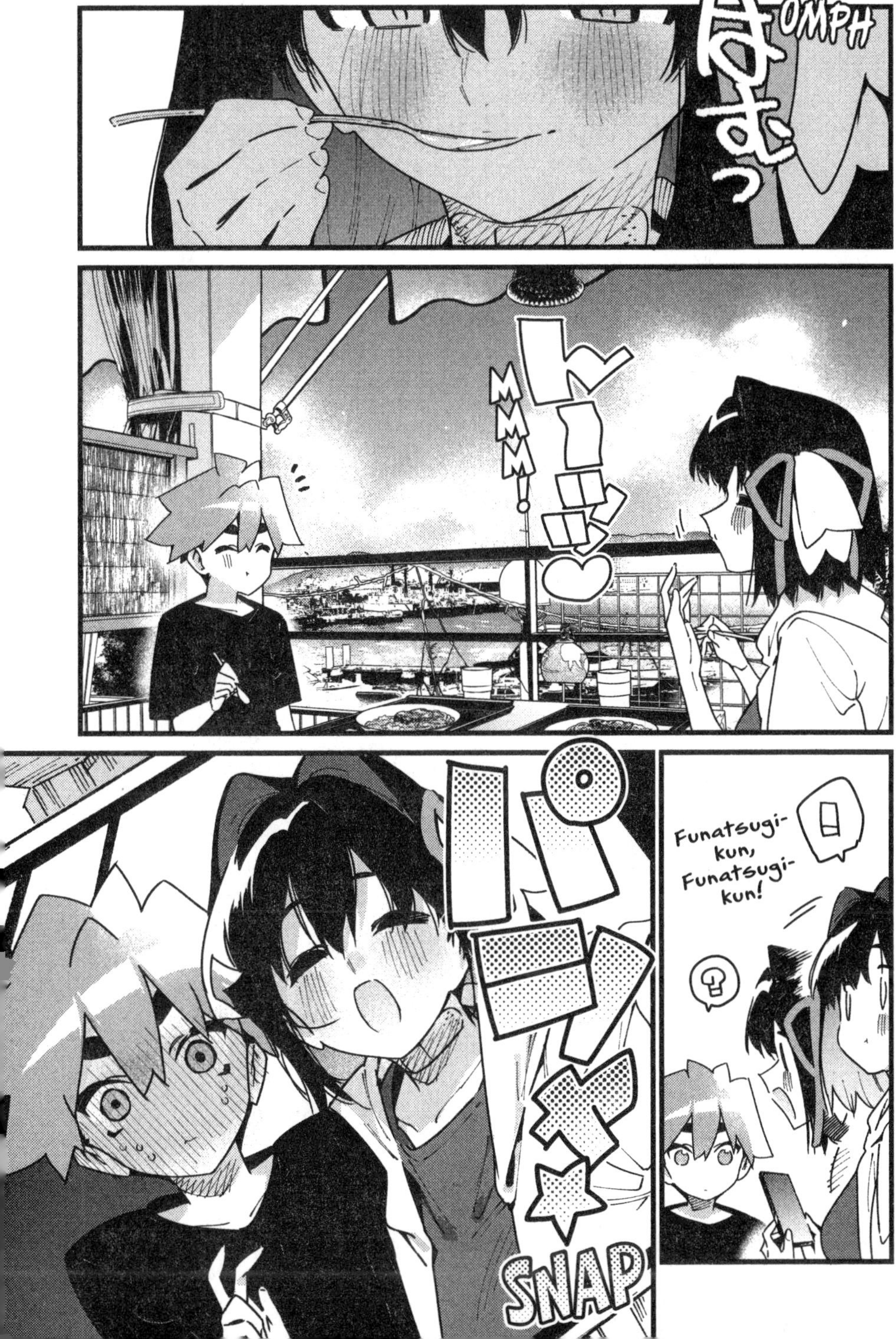
はむっ
OMPH
んーーっ♡
MMMM!
Funatsugi-kun, Funatsugi-kun!
パシャ
SNAP

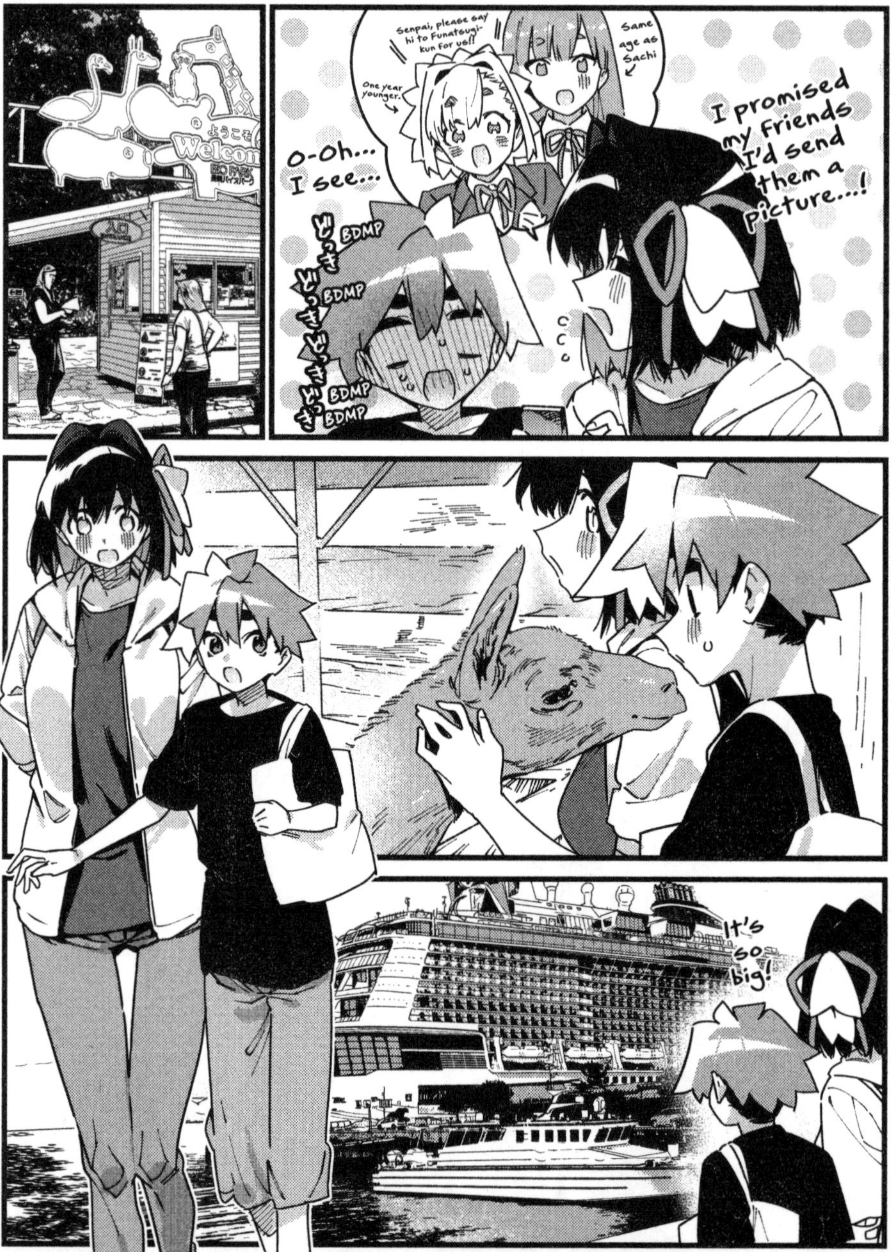
I promised my friends I'd send them a picture...!
Same age as Sachi
Senpai, please say hi to Funatsugi-kun for us!!
One year younger.
O-Oh... I see...
どっき BDMP
どっき BDMP
どっき
どっき BDMP
BDMP
ようこそ
Welcom
BIO PARK
It's so big!

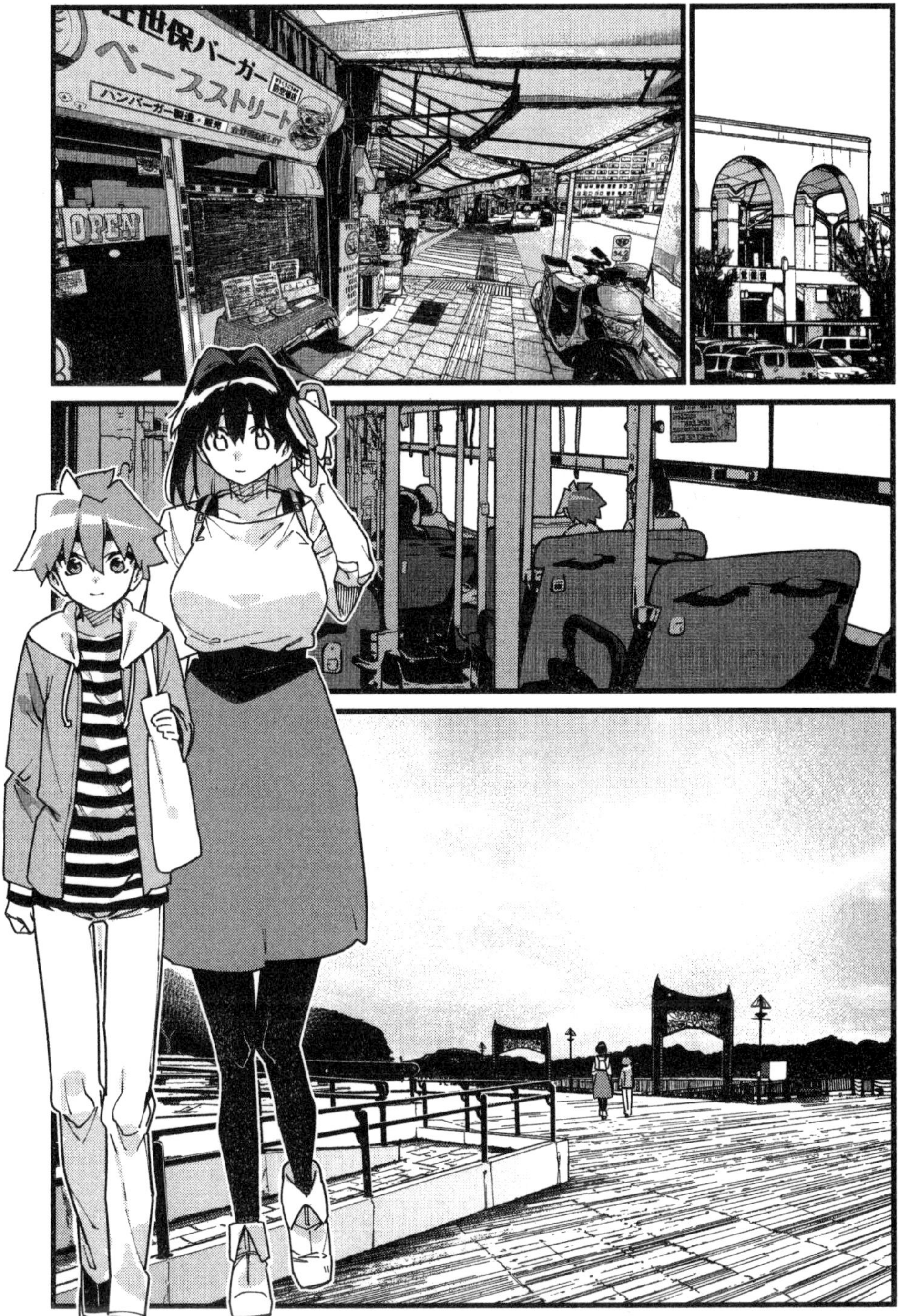
世保バーガー
ベースストリート
防空壕店
ハンバーガー製造・販売
OPEN

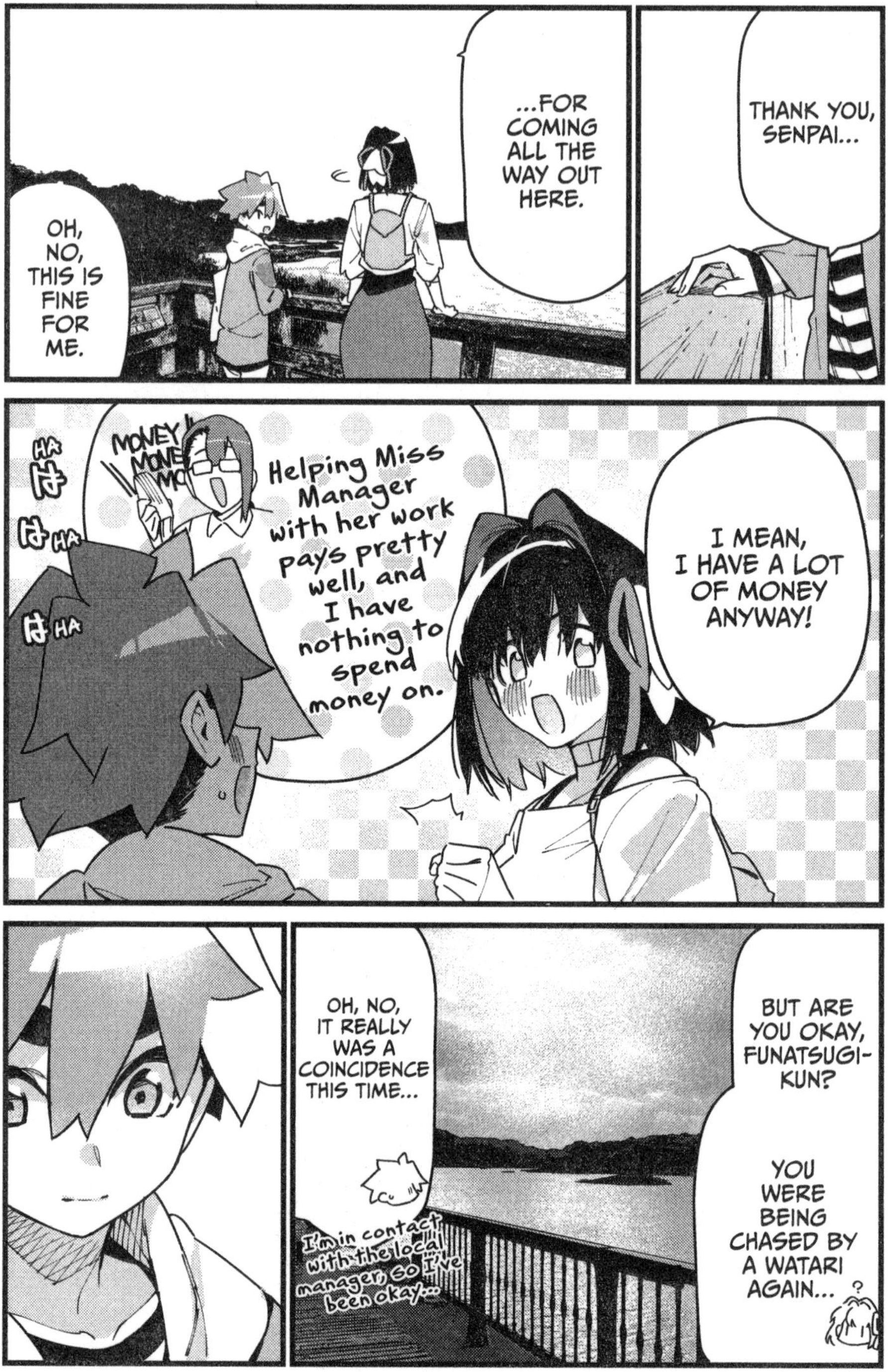
THANK YOU, SENPAI...
...FOR COMING ALL THE WAY OUT HERE.
OH, NO, THIS IS FINE FOR ME.
I MEAN, I HAVE A LOT OF MONEY ANYWAY!
Helping Miss Manager with her work pays pretty well, and I have nothing to spend money on.
MONEY
HA
HA
HA
BUT ARE YOU OKAY, FUNATSUGI-KUN?
YOU WERE BEING CHASED BY A WATARI AGAIN...
OH, NO, IT REALLY WAS A COINCIDENCE THIS TIME...
I'm in contact with the local manager, so I've been okay...

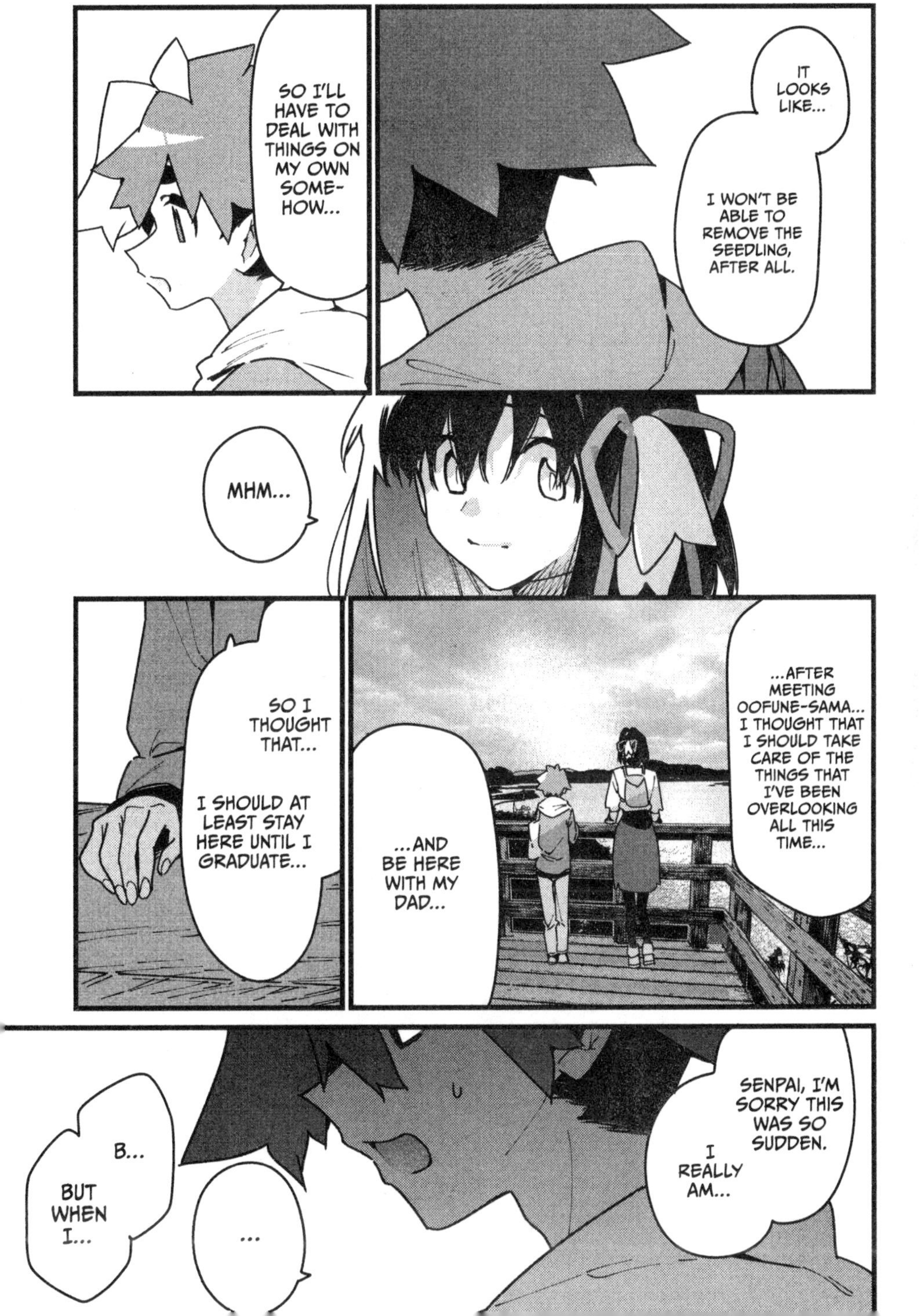
IT LOOKS LIKE...
I WON'T BE ABLE TO REMOVE THE SEEDLING, AFTER ALL.
SO I'LL HAVE TO DEAL WITH THINGS ON MY OWN SOME-HOW...
MHM...
...AFTER MEETING OOFUNE-SAMA... I THOUGHT THAT I SHOULD TAKE CARE OF THE THINGS THAT I'VE BEEN OVERLOOKING ALL THIS TIME...
...AND BE HERE WITH MY DAD...
SO I THOUGHT THAT...
I SHOULD AT LEAST STAY HERE UNTIL I GRADUATE...
SENPAI, I'M SORRY THIS WAS SO SUDDEN.
I REALLY AM...
...
B...
BUT WHEN I...

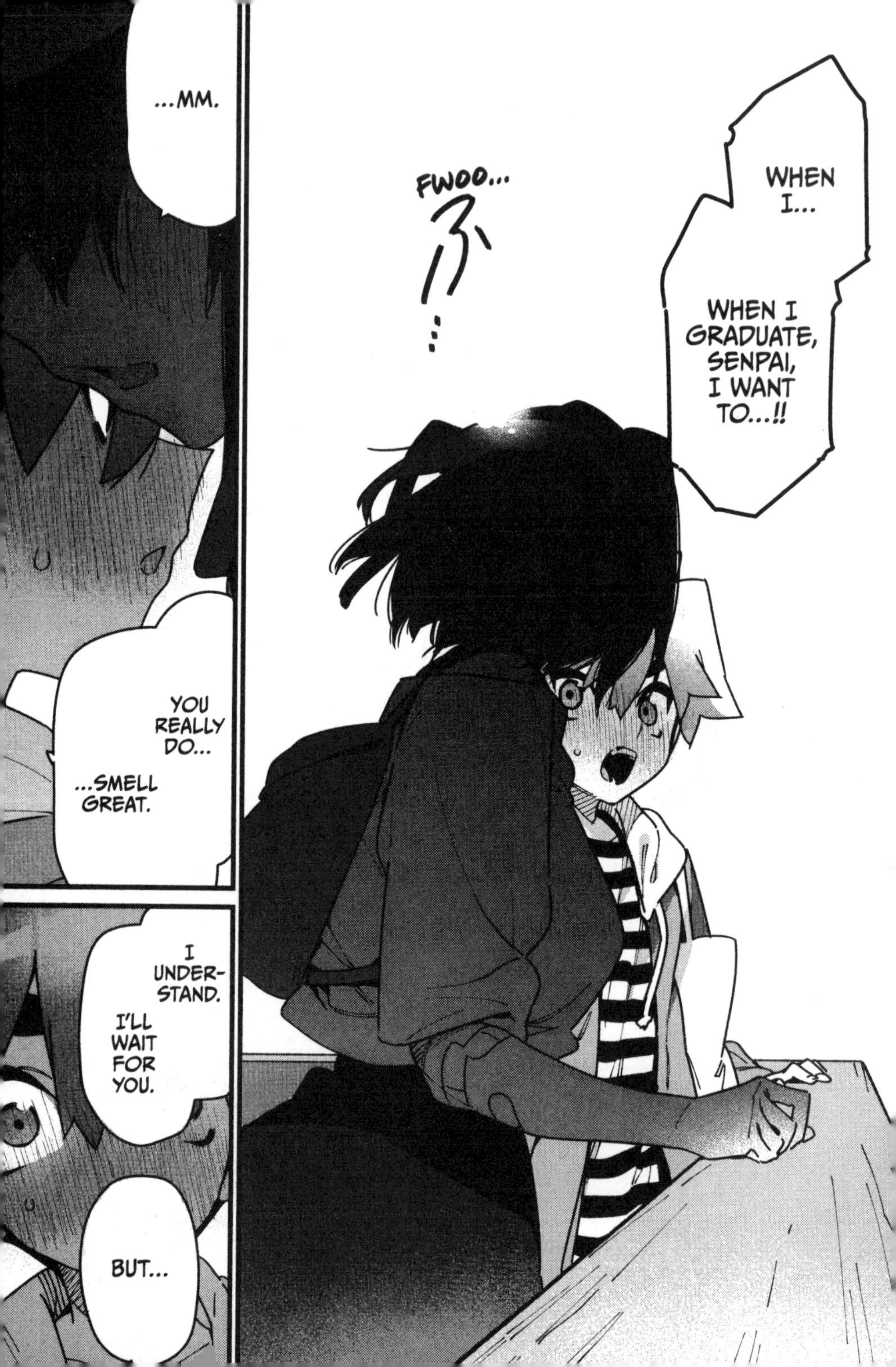
WHEN I...
WHEN I GRADUATE, SENPAI, I WANT TO...!!
FWOO...
...MM.
YOU REALLY DO...
...SMELL GREAT.
I UNDER-STAND.
I'LL WAIT FOR YOU.
BUT...

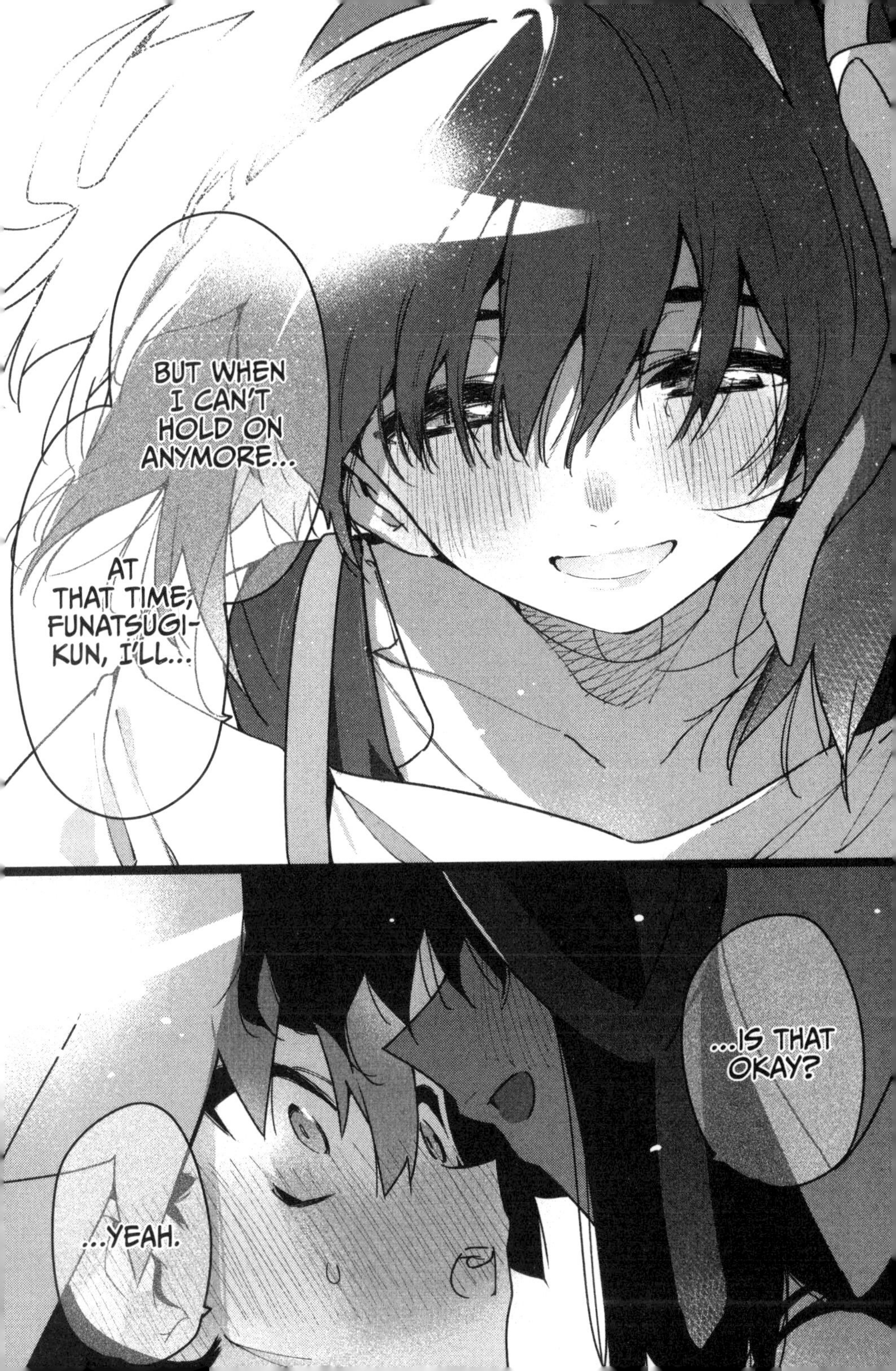
BUT WHEN I CAN'T HOLD ON ANYMORE...
AT THAT TIME, FUNATSUGI-KUN, I'LL...
...IS THAT OKAY?
...YEAH.

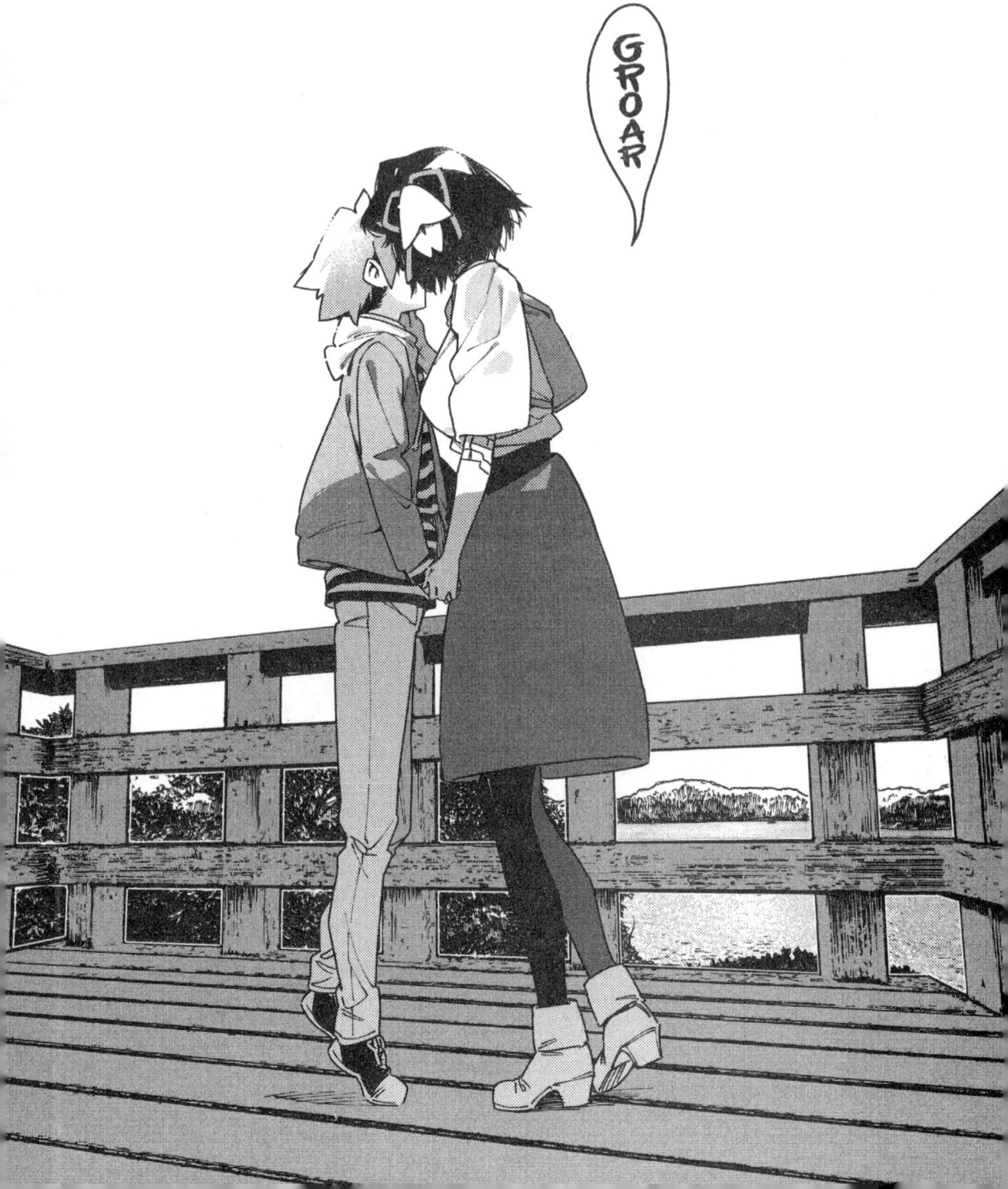
GROAR

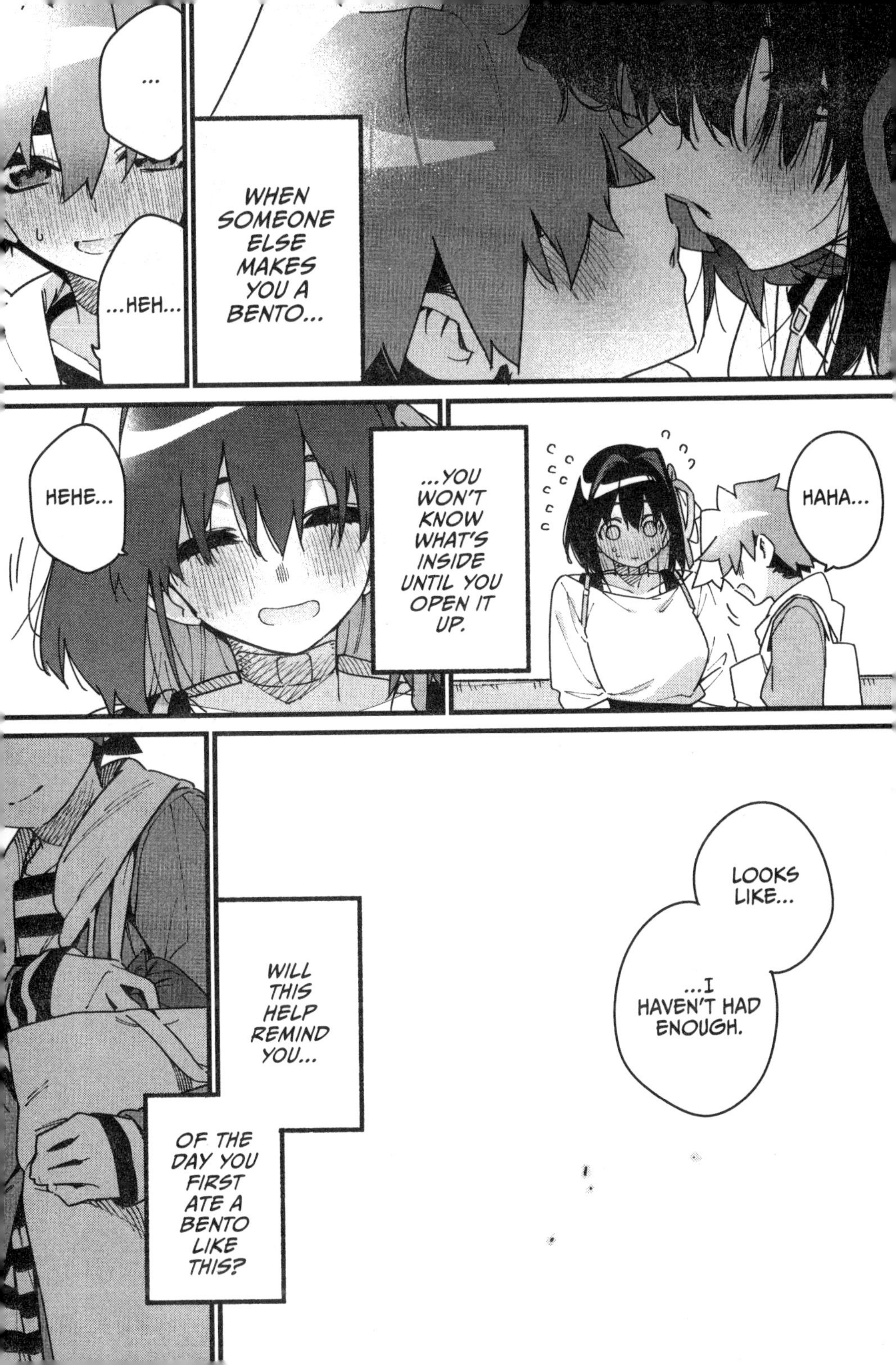
WHEN SOMEONE ELSE MAKES YOU A BENTO...
...
...HEH...
HAHA...
...YOU WON'T KNOW WHAT'S INSIDE UNTIL YOU OPEN IT UP.
HEHE...
LOOKS LIKE...
...I HAVEN'T HAD ENOUGH.
WILL THIS HELP REMIND YOU...
OF THE DAY YOU FIRST ATE A BENTO LIKE THIS?

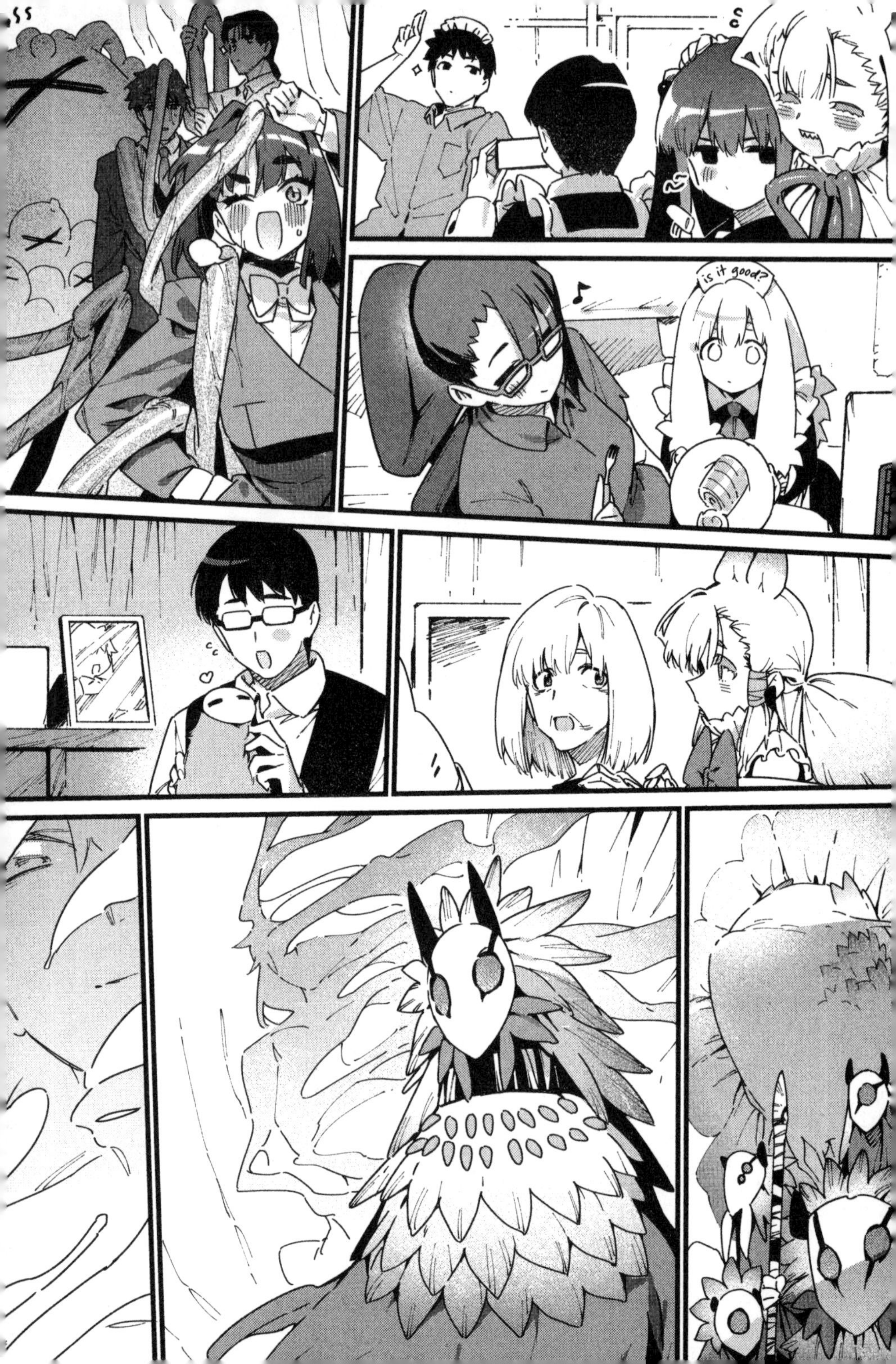
is it good?

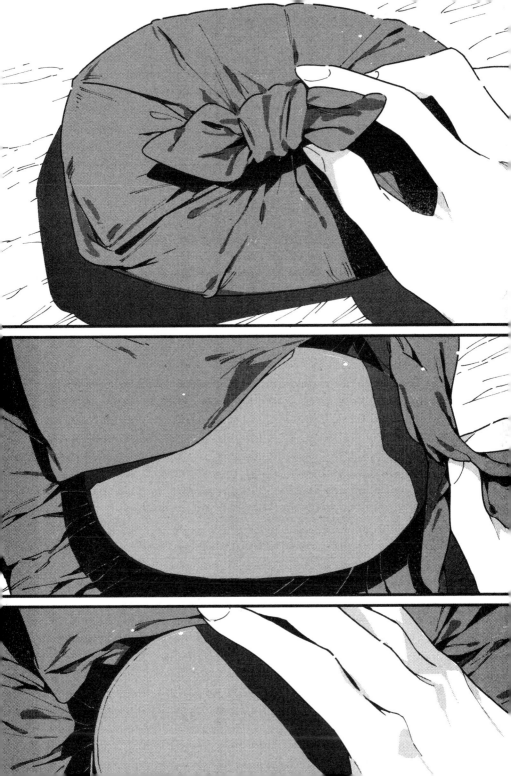

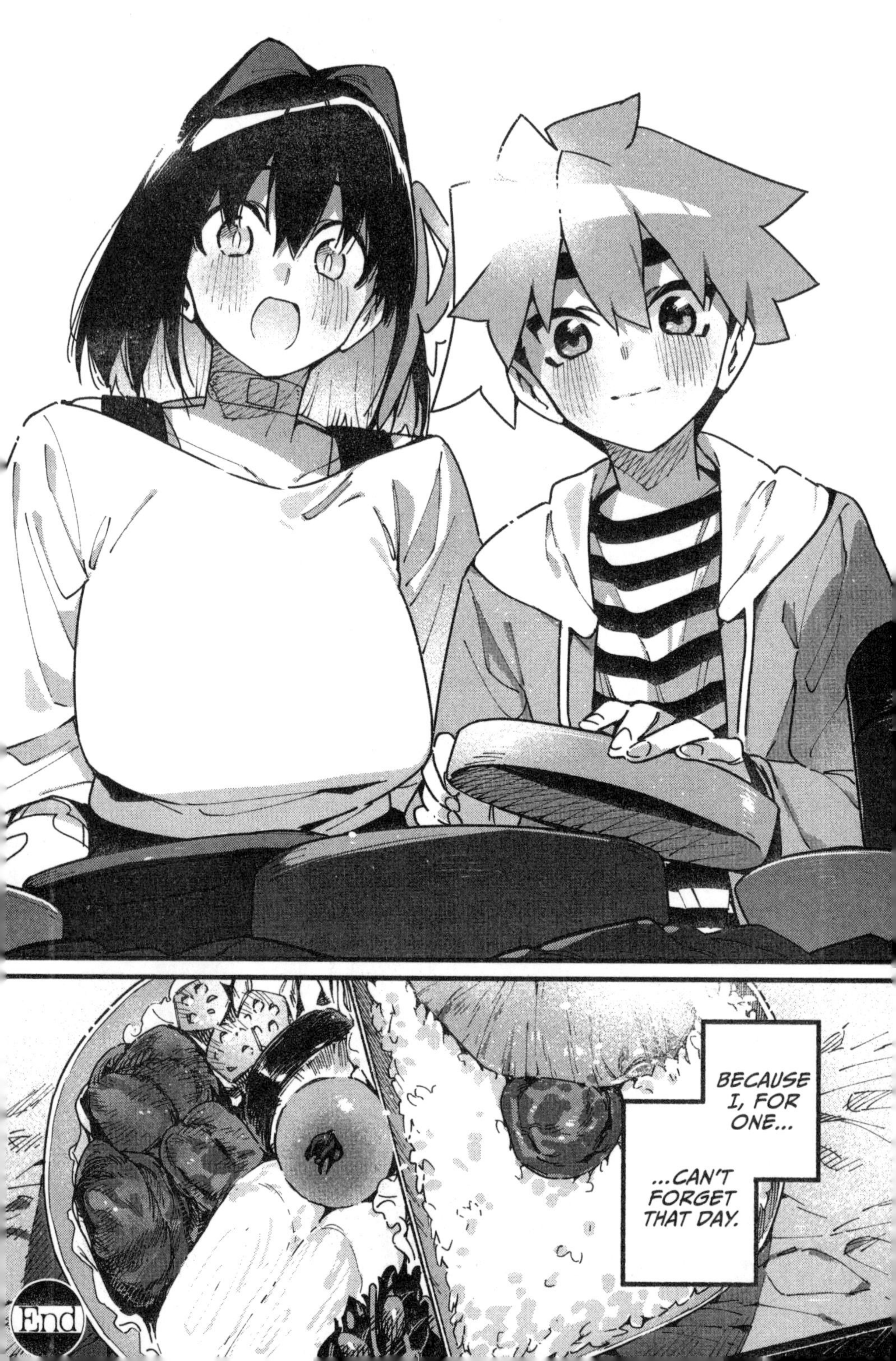
BECAUSE I, FOR ONE...
...CAN'T FORGET THAT DAY.
End

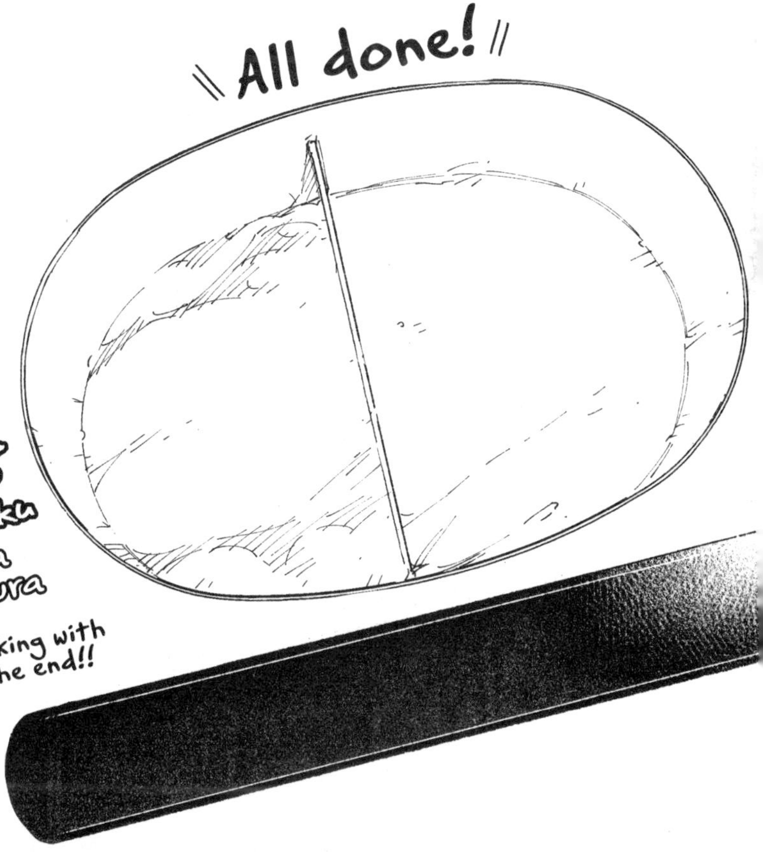
All done!
THANKS
moku×Moku
Hotaruika
Editor I-mura
Thank you for sticking with the series until the end!!
There's bonus content under the cover! Check it out!!

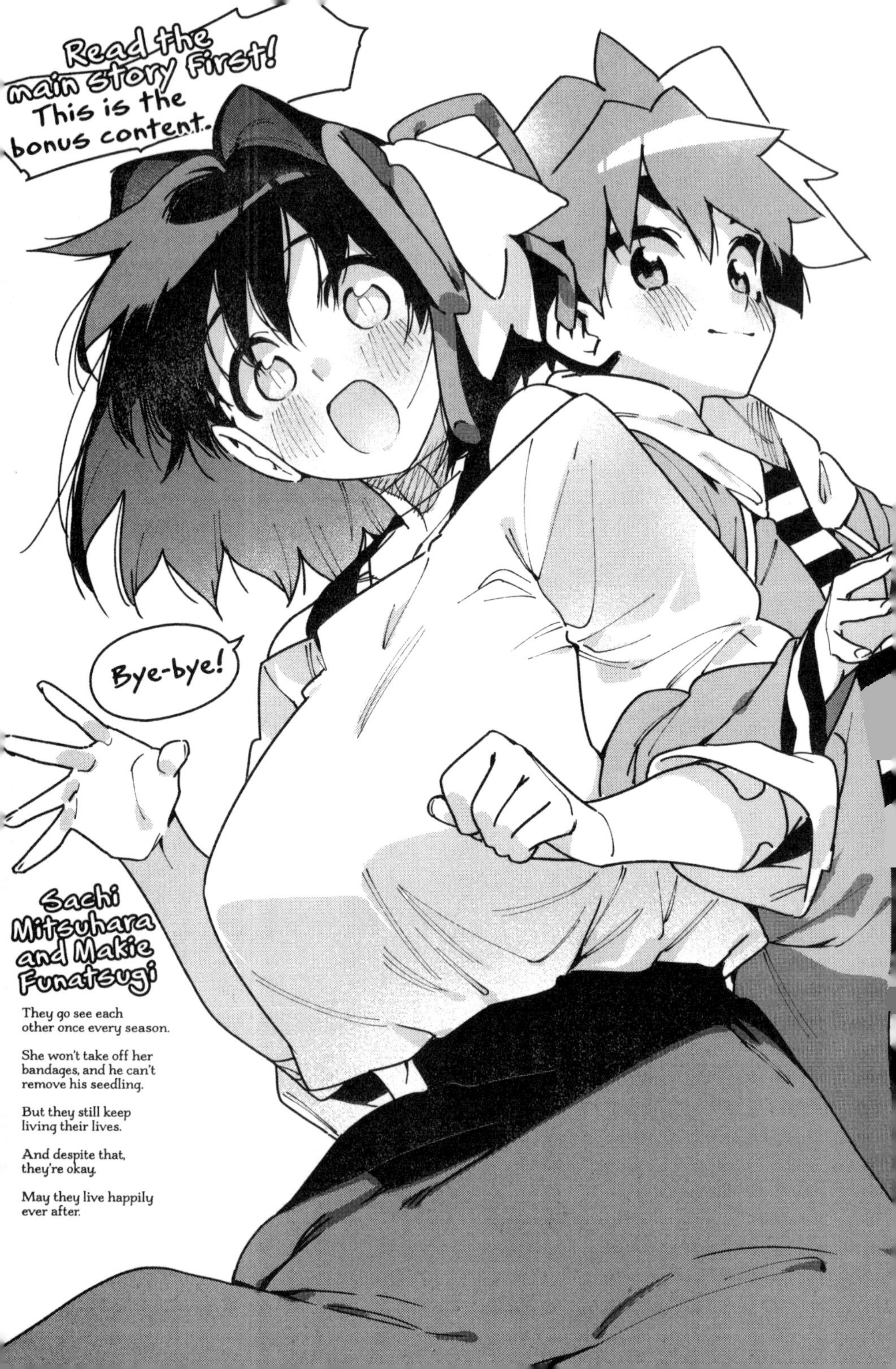
Read the main story first! This is the bonus content...
Bye-bye!
Sachi Mitsuhara and Makie Funatsugi

They go see each other once every season.

She won't take off her bandages, and he can't remove his seedling.

But they still keep living their lives.

And despite that, they're okay.

May they live happily ever after.

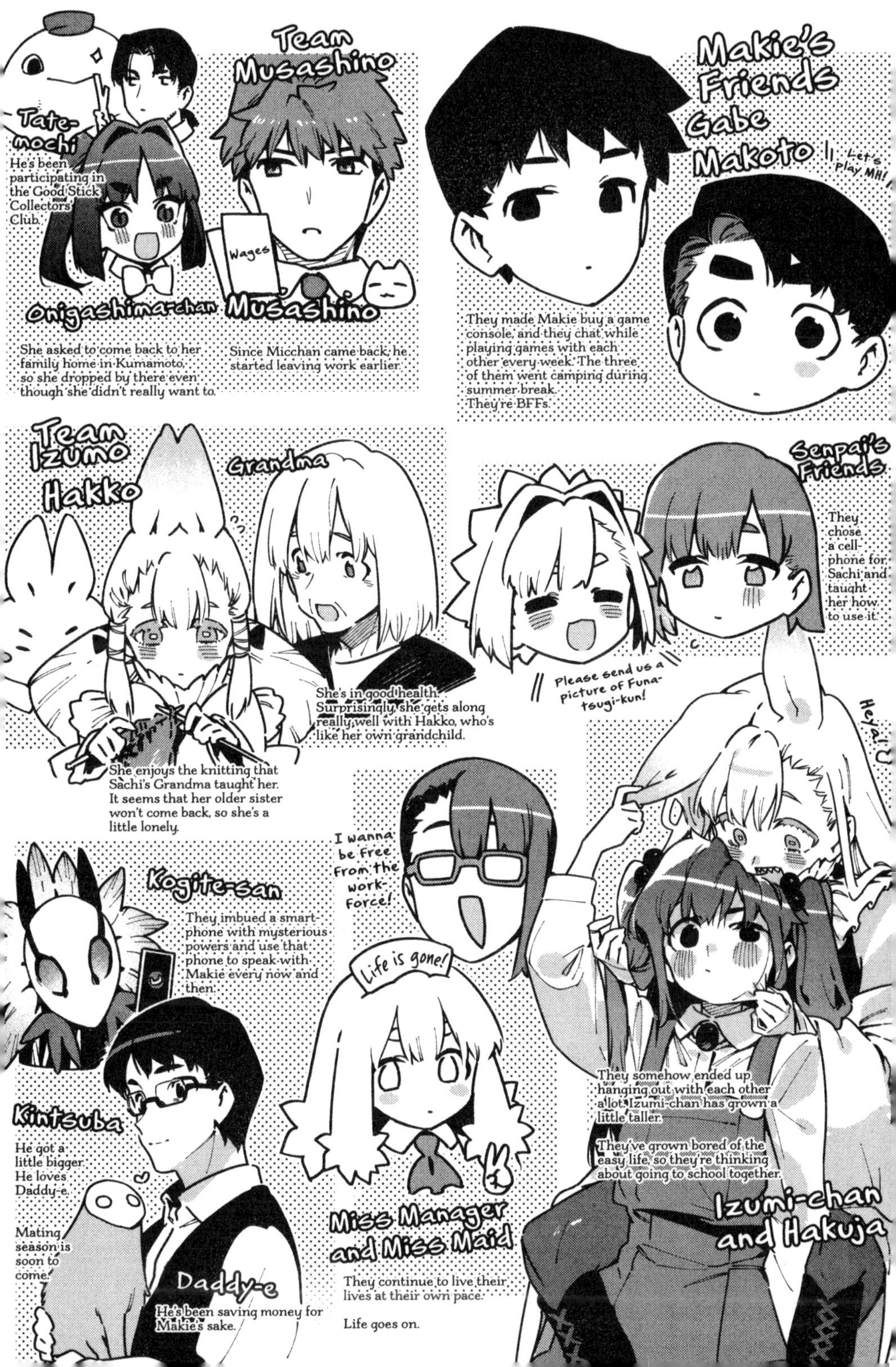

Makie's Friends
Gabe
Makoto
Let's play MH!
They made Makie buy a game console, and they chat while playing games with each other every week. The three of them went camping during summer break. They're BFFs.
Team Musashino
Tate-mochi
He's been participating in the Good Stick Collectors' Club.
Wages
Onigashima-chan
Musashino
She asked to come back to her family home in Kumamoto, so she dropped by there even though she didn't really want to.
Since Micchan came back, he started leaving work earlier.
Senpai's Friends
They chose a cell-phone for Sachi and taught her how to use it.
Please send us a picture of Funa-tsugi-kun!
Team Izumo
Hakko
Grandma
She's in good health. Surprisingly, she gets along really well with Hakko, who's like her own grandchild.
She enjoys the knitting that Sachi's Grandma taught her. It seems that her older sister won't come back, so she's a little lonely.
Heya!
They somehow ended up hanging out with each other a lot. Izumi-chan has grown a little taller.
They've grown bored of the easy life, so they're thinking about going to school together.
Izumi-chan and Hakuja
I wanna be free from the work-force!
Life is gone!
Miss Manager and Miss Maid
They continue to live their lives at their own pace.
Life goes on.
Kogite-san
They imbued a smart-phone with mysterious powers and use that phone to speak with Makie every now and then.
Kintsuba
He got a little bigger. He loves Daddy-e.
Mating season is soon to come.
Daddy-e
He's been saving money for Makie's sake.

Translation Notes

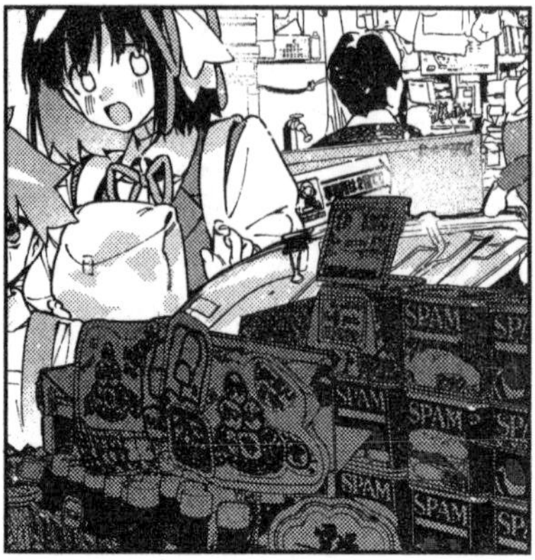

Okinawan Specialties, page 55

The scene displayed at the beginning of Chapter 28 features an array of specialty products from or associated with Okinawa. Some of the items included here are SPAM (which enjoys a similar popularity in Hawaii), *mozuku* (a seaweed native to Okinawa), Tulip-brand pork luncheon meat, gourmet "snow salt," and food/drink made from *shiikuwasha* (citrus depressa or Okinawa lime).

Oofune-sama, page 58

"Oofune" could be interpreted as "great boat" (usually pronounced "oo-bune"), and in Japanese, the character for "boat" is the same that is used for the "funa" in Makie Funatsugi. Also, this particular character is used to signify a smaller boat that might typically be rowed, which is why Kogite is "The Oarsperson."

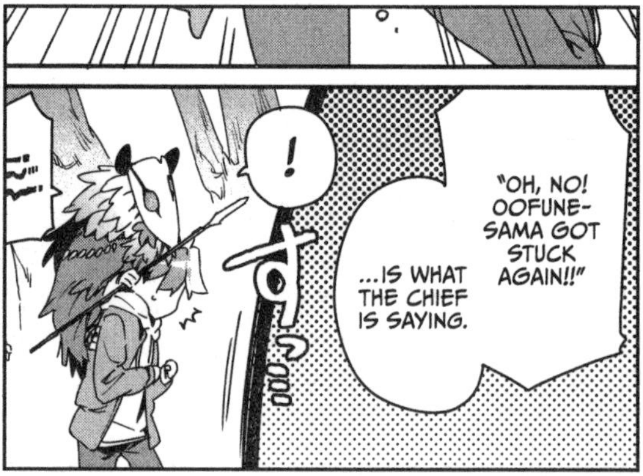
!
"OH, NO! OOFUNE-SAMA GOT STUCK AGAIN!!"
...IS WHAT THE CHIEF IS SAYING.

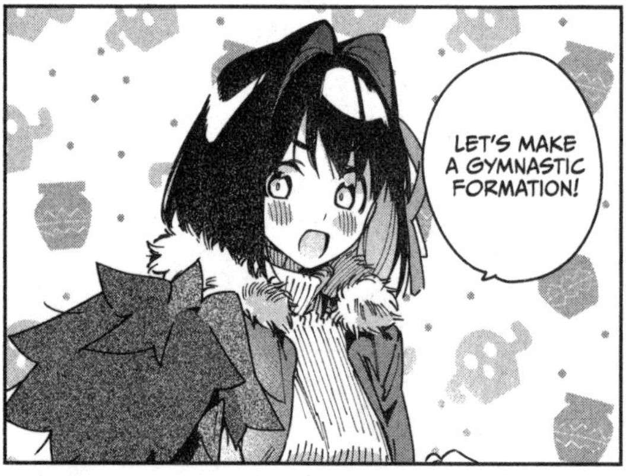
LET'S MAKE A GYMNASTIC FORMATION!

Gymnastic formation, page 71

Also known as group or mass gymnastics, gymnastic formation is a physical activity where different shapes and forms are expressed using only human bodies in collaboration with each other. One example of this would be the human pyramid. This activity is sometimes part of the Japanese physical education curriculum.

Summer gift, page 203

Gift giving is an important part of Japanese culture, and there are two major gift-giving seasons. One of those is at the end of the year (*seibo*), but the other is in the middle of the year (*chugen*). *Chugen* takes place between July and August. The "summer gift" that Miss Manager received from Makie is a *chugen* gift that he sent to her as an expression of his gratitude.

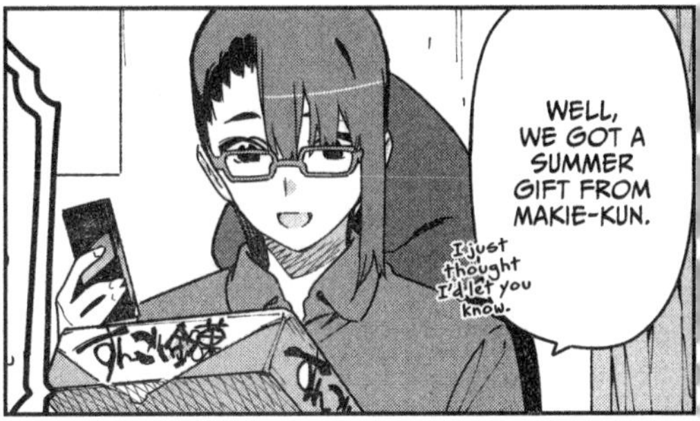
WELL, WE GOT A SUMMER GIFT FROM MAKIE-KUN.
I just thought I'd let you know.

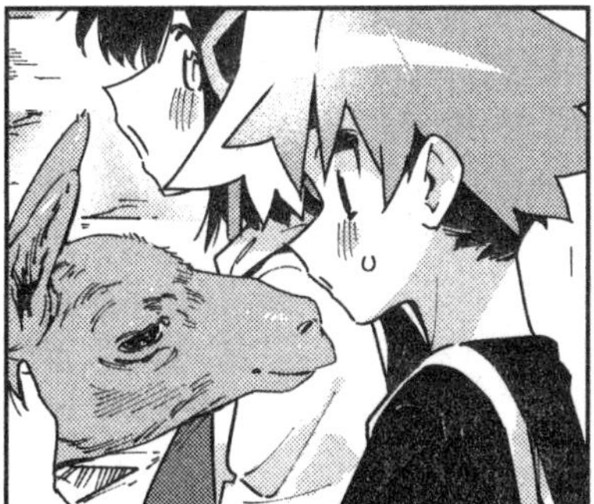

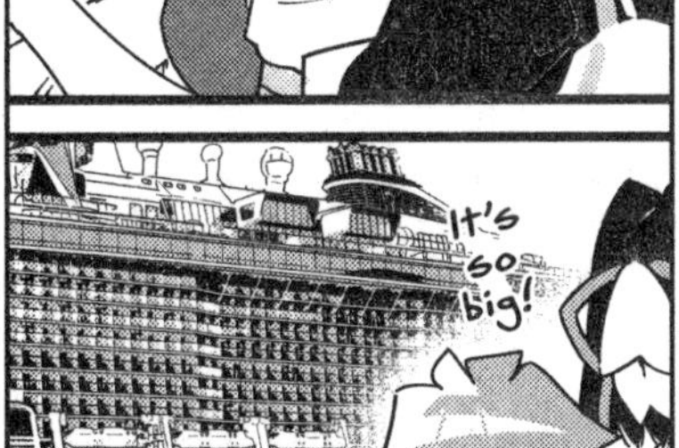
It's so big!

The sights of Nagasaki, pages 204, 212, 213

When Sachi visits Makie, they go on a tour of Nagasaki, one of the prefectures in the southernmost of Japan's four major islands (Kyushu). From Nagasaki Station, Makie and Sachi travel to a number of sights and attractions. One of those is Nagasaki BIO PARK, a novel type of zoo where the animals live naturally outside of cages. They also visit the city of Sasebo, which is famous for the Sasebo Burger and features a burger restaurant built in a former air-raid shelter.

Young characters and steampunk setting, like *Howl's Moving Castle* and *Battle Angel Alita*

Beyond the Clouds © 2018 Nicke / Ki-oon

A boy with a talent for machines and a mysterious girl whose wings he's fixed will take you beyond the clouds! In the tradition of the high-flying, resonant adventure stories of Studio Ghibli comes a gorgeous tale about the longing of young hearts for adventure and friendship!

Knight of the Ice ©Yayoi Ogawa/Kodansha Ltd.

Yayoi Ogawa

SKATING THRILLS AND ICY CHILLS WITH THIS NEW TINGLY ROMANCE SERIES!

A rom-com on ice, perfect for fans of *Princess Jellyfish* and *Wotakoi*. Kokoro is the talk of the figure-skating world, winning trophies and hearts. But little do they know... he's actually a huge nerd! From the beloved creator of *You're My Pet* (*Tramps Like Us*).

Chitose is a serious young woman, working for the health magazine *SASSO*. Or at least, she would be, if she wasn't constantly getting distracted by her childhood friend, international figure skating star Kokoro Kijinami! In the public eye and on the ice, Kokoro is a gallant, flawless knight, but behind his glittery costumes and breathtaking spins lies a secret: He's actually a hopelessly romantic otaku, who can only land his quad jumps when Chitose is on hand to recite a spell from his favorite magical girl anime!

KODANSHA COMICS

A SMART, NEW ROMANTIC COMEDY FOR FANS OF *SHORTCAKE CAKE* AND *TERRACE HOUSE!*

A romance manga starring high school girl Meeko, who learns to live on her own in a boarding house whose living room is home to the odd (but handsome) Matsunaga-san. She begins to adjust to her new life away from her parents, but Meeko soon learns that no matter how far away from home she is, she's still a young girl at heart — especially when she finds herself falling for Matsunaga-san.

PERFECT WORLD

Rie Aruga

A TOUCHING
NEW SERIES
ABOUT LOVE AND
COPING WITH
DISABILITY

An office party reunites Tsugumi with her high school crush Itsuki. He's realized his dream of becoming an architect, but along the way, he experienced a spinal injury that put him in a wheelchair. Now Tsugumi's rekindled feelings will butt up against prejudices she never considered — and Itsuki will have to decide if he's ready to let someone into his heart...

KC
KODANSHA
COMICS

The boys are back, in 400-page hardcovers that are as pretty and badass as they are!

Saiyuki

THE ORIGINAL SERIES

KAZUYA MINEKURA

KC KODANSHA COMICS

"AN EDGY COMIC LOOK AT AN ANCIENT CHINESE TALE." –YALSA

Genjo Sanzo is a Buddhist priest in the city of Togenkyo, which is being ravaged by yokai spirits that have fallen out of balance with the natural order. His superiors send him on a journey far to the west to discover why this is happening and how to stop it. His companions are three yokai with human souls. But this is no day trip — the four will encounter many discoveries and horrors on the way.

FEATURES NEW TRANSLATION, COLOR PAGES, AND BEAUTIFUL WRAPAROUND COVER ART!

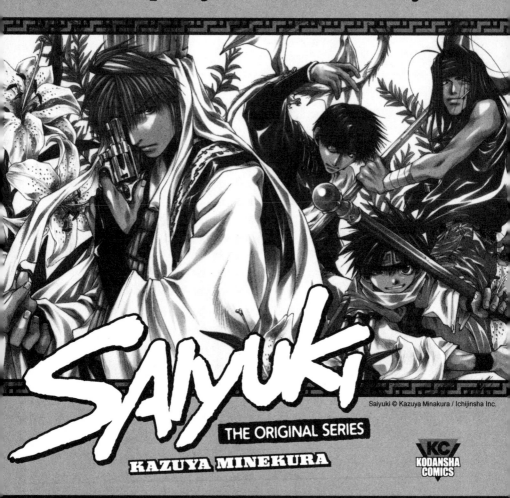

THE SWEET SCENT OF LOVE IS IN THE AIR! FOR FANS OF OFFBEAT ROMANCES LIKE *WOTAKOI*

Sweat and Soap © Kintetsu Yamada / Kodansha Ltd.

In an office romance, there's a fine line between sexy and awkward... and that line is where Asako — a woman who sweats copiously — meets Koutarou — a perfume developer who can't get enough of Asako's, er, scent. Don't miss a romcom manga like no other!

CUTE ANIMALS AND LIFE LESSONS, PERFECT FOR ASPIRING PET VETS OF ALL AGES!

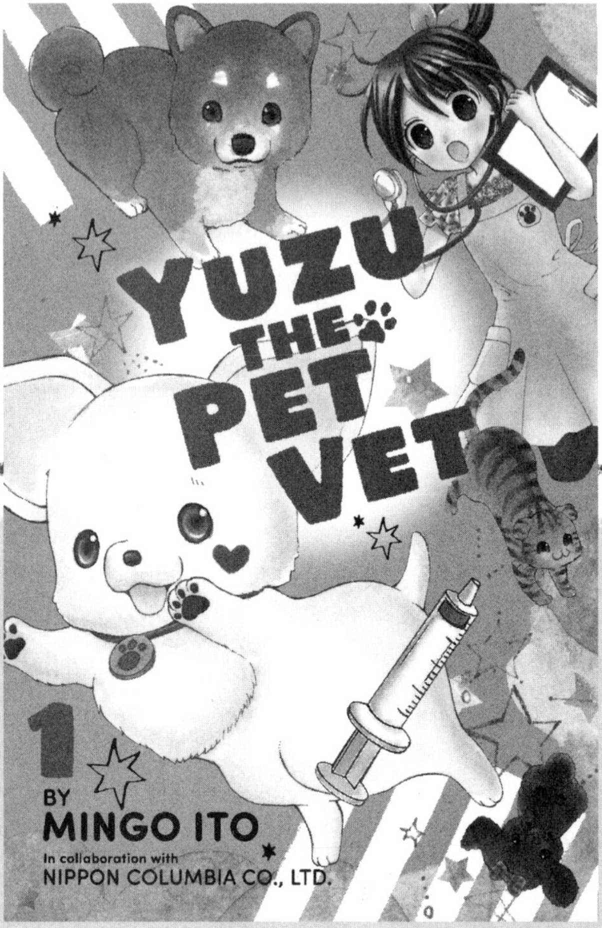
YUZU THE PET VET
1
BY
MINGO ITO
In collaboration with
NIPPON COLUMBIA CO., LTD.

For an 11-year-old, Yuzu has a lot on her plate. When her mom gets sick and has to be hospitalized, Yuzu goes to live with her uncle who runs the local veterinary clinic. Yuzu's always been scared of animals, but she tries to help out. Through all the tough moments in her life, Yuzu realizes that she can help make things all right with a little help from her animal pals, peers, and kind grown-ups.

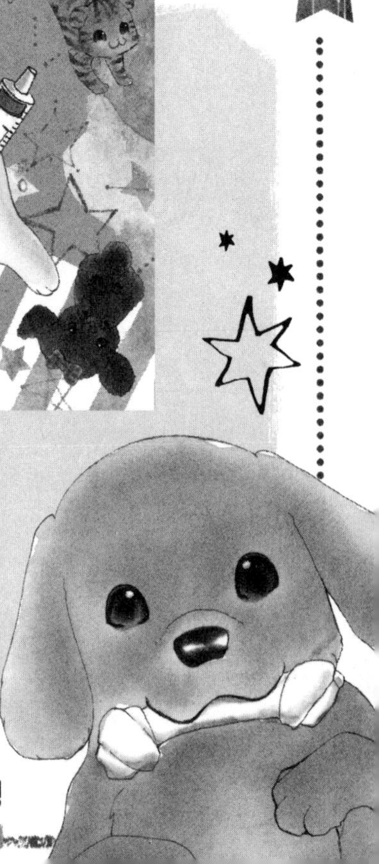

Every new patient is a furry friend in the making!

THE HIGH SCHOOL HAREM COMEDY WITH FIVE TIMES THE CUTE GIRLS!

"An entertaining romantic-comedy with a snarky edge to it." —Taykobon

Futaro Uesugi is a second-year in high school, scraping to get by and pay off his family's debt. The only thing he can do is study, so when Futaro receives a part-time job offer to tutor the five daughters of a wealthy businessman, he can't pass it up. Little does he know, these five beautiful sisters are quintuplets, but the only thing they have in common...is that they're all terrible at studying!

THE **QUINTESSENTIAL QUINTUPLETS**

negi haruba

ANIME OUT NOW!

Magus of the Library

Mitsu Izumi

MITSU IZUMI'S STUNNING ARTWORK BRINGS A FANTASTICAL LITERARY ADVENTURE TO LUSH, THRILLING LIFE!

Young Theo adores books, but the prejudice and hatred of his village keeps them ever out of his reach. Then one day, he chances to meet Sedona, a traveling librarian who works for the great library of Aftzaak, City of Books, and his life changes forever...

EDENS ZERO
エデンズゼロ

HIRO MASHIMA IS BACK! JOIN THE CREATOR OF *FAIRY TAIL* AS HE TAKES TO THE STARS FOR ANOTHER THRILLING SAGA!

EDENS ZERO © Hiro Mashima/Kodansha, Ltd.

A high-flying space adventure! All the steadfast friendship and wild fighting you've been waiting for...IN SPACE!

At Granbell Kingdom, an abandoned amusement park, Shiki has lived his entire life among machines. But one day, Rebecca and her cat companion Happy appear at the park's front gates. Little do these newcomers know that this is the first human contact Granbell has had in a hundred years! As Shiki stumbles his way into making new friends, his former neighbors stir at an opportunity for a robo-rebellion... And when his old homeland becomes too dangerous, Shiki must join Rebecca and Happy on their spaceship and escape into the boundless cosmos.

A Kodansha Comics Trade Paperback Original
Sachi's Monstrous Appetite 6 copyright © 2021 Chomoran
English translation copyright © 2021 Chomoran

All rights reserved.

Published in the United States by Kodansha Comics, an imprint of Kodansha USA Publishing, LLC, New York.

Publication rights for this English edition arranged through Kodansha Ltd., Tokyo.

First published in Japan in 2021 by Kodansha Ltd., Tokyo.

ISBN 978-1-64651-270-6

Original cover design by imagejack danyumi

Printed in the United States of America.

www.kodansha.us

1st Printing
Translation: Ajani Oloye
Lettering: Brandon Bovia
Editing: David Yoo
Kodansha Comics edition cover design by Adam Del Re

Publisher: Kiichiro Sugawara

Director of publishing services: Ben Applegate
Associate director, publishing operations: Stephen Pakula
Publishing services managing editorial: Madison Salters, Alanna Ruse
Production managers: Emi Lotto, Angela Zurlo
Logo and character art ©Kodansha USA Publishing, LLC